A Biblical Theology
of Missions

A Biblical Theology of Missions

George W. Peters

MOODY PUBLISHERS
CHICAGO

TO SUSAN
Mother of Maryann
Arnold   Eldon   LoisGrace
cheerful companion and faithful supporter
in life and work
this book is affectionately dedicated

© 1972 by
THE MOODY BIBLE INSTITUTE
OF CHICAGO

Paperback Edition, 1984

Library of Congress Catalog Card Number: 72-77952

ISBN: 978-0-8024-0706-1

We hope you enjoy this book from Moody Publishers. Our goal is to provide high-quality, thought-provoking books and products that connect truth to your real needs and challenges. For more information on other books and products written and produced from a biblical perspective, go to www.moodypublishers.com or write to:

Moody Publishers
820 N. LaSalle Boulevard
Chicago, IL 60610

29 30

Printed in the United States of America

CONTENTS

Chapter   Page

Foreword   7

Preface   9

Introduction   15

Part I — Biblical Foundation of Missions

1. Missionary Theology and Jesus Christ   35

2. Missionary Theology and the Nature of God   55

3. Missionary Theology and the Old Testament   83

4. Missionary Theology and the New Testament   131

Part II — Biblical Delineation of Missions

5. The Missionary Task   159

6. The Church and Missions   199

Part III — Biblical Instruments and Dynamics of Missions

7. The Instruments of Missions   245

8. The Dynamics of Missions   299

Summary and Conclusion   346

Notes   352

Bibliography   355

Selective Subject Index   364

Scripture Index   366

ACKNOWLEDGEMENTS

Parts of the following chapters are reprints, with adaptations, of articles by the author:

Chapter 5. The Missionary Task
  The Nature of the Missionary Task
    From "Missionary Responsibility: Changeless and Relative," *Evangelical Missions Quarterly* 1, no. 4, pp. 29-35.

Chapter 6. The Church and Missions
  The Church in Missions
    From "The Church in Missions," *Bibliotheca Sacra* 125 (1968): 45-55.
  The Missionary Society as the Sending Agency.
    From "The Missionary Society as the Sending Agency," *Bibliotheca Sacra* 125 (1968):116-22.

Chapter 7. The Instruments of Missions
  The Call of God and the Ministry of the Word
    From "The Call of God," *Bibliotheca Sacra* 120 (1963): 322-33.

Summary and Conclusion
    From "The Primacy of Missions," *Bibliotheca Sacra* 119 (1962): 335-41.

Foreword

THIS IS AN IMPORTANT BOOK. It touches on all of the issues fundamental to missions in our time. Probably no specifically missionary book has ever undertaken as profound and comprehensive a treatment of the subject as this one. Add to this the significant fact that the author is clearly identified with the conservative evangelical position. Unfortunately, serious and substantial missions literature is in short supply from those of us who share that commitment.

Many current books on missions which are influential and valuable are flawed by theological ambiguity and tentativity. On the other hand, strangely enough, much of what is written with impeccable theological precision lacks missionary passion. Dr. Peters has managed to get together and keep together a broad, biblical, theological affirmation with missions right at the heart of it. The distinctiveness of the book is the way in which it unifies and integrates the whole range of theological themes in and around the idea of missions.

The style and content of the book itself will engage the attention of many readers. The text is illustrated and supported with an immense amount of Scripture correlated in an impressive way. There are many evidences that the author has read widely and examined the important literature on missions. The format and organization of the book itself is ambitious and engaging. All of these things will be noted in the reading. The thing that could be missed is the way in which the man behind the book has woven so much of himself into the material he has written.

I can best serve those who happen to scan this page by underscoring the vital relationship of the "Personal Perspective" as presented in the Preface to the rest of the book. George Peters has succeeded in breathing something of his own spirit into these pages. His

7

sturdy, unequivocal, theological stance is evident on every page. The wealth of his wide-ranging contacts and experiences as a "citizen at home" in several cultural and linguistic worlds gives credence to his claims. The knowledge derived from his indefatigable and peripatetic missions study is reflected in many ways. The elements of his Mennonite heritage and those of his Dallas Theological Seminary loyalties show through at certain points and sometimes combine in interesting and helpful ways. There is here a view of missions that is authentically biblical and soundly theological, but it is also important to know that it is in the inimitable style of Professor George Peters.

As is characteristic of the author, this whole volume has an emphatic finality about it. However, it certainly does not represent the last word on all of these truths. In fact, the book is a kind of index to areas that invite and require the same kind of diligent scholarship that led to the preparation of this volume. It is to be hoped that Dr. Peters and others who share his missionary theology will persevere in the preparation of other publications on these great and urgent themes.

J. F. SHEPHERD
Education Secretary
Christian & Missionary Alliance

Preface

MISSIONARY THEOLOGY IN PERSONAL PERSPECTIVE

THIS PRESENTATION of *Biblical Theology of Missions* is the outgrowth of years of studies and teaching in theology and missions. It is my impression that the Bible is not a book about theology as such, but rather, a record of theology in mission — God in action in behalf of the salvation of mankind. I believe Georg F. Vicedom comes very near to biblical thinking when he says, "The Bible in its totality ascribes only one intention to God: to save mankind."[1]

It is understood throughout the Scriptures that the end result of such *Missio Dei* will be the glorification of the Father, Son and Holy Spirit. In the presentation of the subject I have taken Christ as the center and starting point. It is my conviction that the Bible must be interpreted Christocentrically, as Christ Himself interpreted the Scriptures to His disciples (Lk 24:25-27, 44-49). Christ is the center of revelation and also the key to its understanding.

I make no apology for accepting the Bible uncritically and authoritatively. The Bible is the basis and source of faith and not the result of faith. I am much concerned to bring everything under the judgment of the Word. Without hesitation I accept the inerrancy of the biblical record, the historicity of the foreword of the Bible — Genesis 1 — 11, the Mosaic authorship of the Pentateuch, and the historic, conservative and evangelical position of all the books of the Bible. I do not take such a position blindly, nor because I am not acquainted with the modern and higher criticism, the debate about the revelation and inspiration, and authenticity and integrity of the Book. For several years I listened carefully and studiously to the philosophical and critical approaches to the Bible. I found the theories wanting, for they presented themselves to me as neither revelational, historical nor rational. They lacked historical evidences and authorita-

9

tive criteria. They built neither my faith nor my life. They were subjective, uncritical speculations. They did not nurture missions' motivation or create missionary dynamic. The theories failed to captivate my heart or dynamize my volition. Thus I abide with the Bible as my guide, directive and authority.

I also want to say that I am well acquainted with the writings of modern councils and men. I have read and digested the reports of the great and historic councils sponsored by the International Missionary Council, and *The International Review of Missions* has been on my reading list for many years. Such recent books as edited by Gerald Anderson and the writings of Max Warren, Douglas Webster, John V. Taylor, Stephen Neill, Lesslie Newbigin, Johannes Blauw, Hendrik Kraemer, Wilhelm Andersen, R. K. Orchard, Daniel T. Niles and many others have not gone unnoticed.

If the thinking of these men is not reflected in my book it is because I have consciously and deliberately avoided all conflict. My book is not a polemic; it is an exposition of the missionary intent of God as I see it in the progressive unfolding of the Bible, regardless of what other men have said or are saying. I write neither to refute nor to correct but to expound, thus controversy has been avoided at all cost. It is my hope that this will contribute rather than subtract from the value of the writing.

I owe much to some of my professors who molded my thinking. I am grateful to Dr. David Strathy Dix, late principal of St. Andrew's College, Saskatoon, Saskatchewan, Canada, who introduced me more fully to the glory of the "kingdom of God" concept which spans the revelation of God in the Bible like a rainbow and overarches the chasm between time and eternity, earth and heaven, man and God; to the Reverend William Bestvater, who first made the Bible dear to me and introduced me to the principle of progressive revelation in the Bible and who opened my eyes to the glory of the church of Jesus Christ, to the total program and plan of God through the ages and future glory and mission of Israel; to the Reverend Abram Unruh who taught me many deeper truths of the Word and who unfolded the concept of *Heilsgeschichte* to me in a remarkable way. The concepts received contributed positively to the development of my missionary theology.

It is impossible to enumerate all men who made special contribution to my thinking through their writings. However, the *Theologie des Alten Testaments* by Edward Koenig of Bonn, and *Das Lebendige Wort* by Jakob Kroeker of Wernigerode am Harz, Germany (some 14 volumes on the Old Testament) have greatly enriched my understanding of the Old Testament. They taught me much of the religious significance of the books of the Old Testament in the religious literature of the world. I owe more to these writers than I am able to express.

In addition to the above, I must mention the writings of Dr. Robert E. Speer, whose books have done much in shaping my thinking in missions. Many thoughts of these men I have absorbed to the degree that they have become a part of my thinking. Consequently, I am not always aware when I use their thoughts and words.

USAGE OF MISSIONARY TERMS

The usage of certain words needs to be explained. Much is being said today of *mission* and *missions*. The reader will find both words used in these pages. They are not synonyms. *Mission,* in my usage, refers to the total biblical assignment of the church of Jesus Christ. It is a comprehensive term including the upward, inward and outward ministries of the church. It is the church as "sent" (a pilgrim, stranger, witness, prophet, servant, as salt, as light, etc.) in this world. This book does *not* delineate or describe the mission of the church.

Missions is a specialized term. By it I mean the sending forth of authorized persons beyond the borders of the New Testament church and her immediate gospel influence to proclaim the gospel of Jesus Christ in gospel-destitute areas, to win converts from other faiths or non-faiths to Jesus Christ, and to establish functioning, multiplying local congregations who will bear the fruit of Christianity in that community and to that country.

Similarly, the terms *evangelization, Christianization, socialization* and *civilization* need clarification. They do not express the same idea.

Evangelization refers to the initial phase of Christian ministry. It is the authoritative proclamation of the gospel of Jesus Christ as revealed in the Bible in relevant and intelligible terms, in a persuasive manner with the definite purpose of making Christian converts. It is a presentation-penetration-permeation-confrontation that not only elicits but demands a decision. It is preaching the gospel of Jesus Christ for a verdict. It is the effective presentation of the gospel for the conversion of the unbeliever or nonbeliever, making him a believer in Jesus Christ.

Christianization is organically related to evangelization and logically follows the latter. It is the indoctrination and enculturation of the believer in the gospel and Christian ethics. It is the transformation of the believer of Jesus Christ into a disciple of Christ. His whole life is to be permeated with the mind and principles of Christ in order to make him conformable to the image of Jesus Christ and an effective witness and useful servant of the Lord. He is to be made into a conscious, committed follower of the Master and is to commit his whole life to Christ and accept the lordship of Jesus Christ. In the full sense of the word, this will be a lifelong process.

Socialization is not a biblical term, but it expresses a biblical idea. While Christianization deals more with the conformity of the individual believer to Christ, socialization refers to the process by which the individual believer is led to conform to Christian ideals, standards, institutions, and a way of life as perceived by a group of believers, a church or a Christian institution. It is a molding process and, ideally, it is a postconversion process.

Civilization, a secular term which refers to the level of cultural development, is little used today in relation to Christian ministries. Insofar as it is used, it betrays a remnant from Albrecht Ritschl's idea of *Kultur-Christentum* which he practically identified with Western civilization.

Today it is freely admitted that no truly Christian civilization exists anywhere. The West is dying in secularism — the divorce of culture from God and religion — and the East is drowning in a pantheistic osmosis and religio-socio-cultural symbiosis — the total merging to the degree of identification of culture and religion.

I hope *Biblical Theology of Missions* will meet a need in mission thinking. Too long America has propagated missions on the basis of philanthropy, Christian duty and responsibility, gospel necessity and church expansion. These are not altogether unworthy motives but they are not the deepest motives nor do they generate the highest degree of spiritual dynamism. We need theological thinking in missions. What are the deepest foundations of missions? What are the most legitimate goals and means of missions? What is the nature of Christian missions? How is missions related to the church? Is missions an abiding or terminal phenomenon, What are the real dynamics of missions? What is the relation of the gospel to eschatology? Such are some of the basic questions which theology must answer. I hope that the reader will find answers to some of these questions through his studies in this volume.

Introduction

Christian missions makes sense only in the light of an existing abnormality or emergency and in the conviction that an answer to and remedy for such a malady is available. Therefore I address myself first of all to the malady or emergency which exists and which, from the historical and eternal perspective, demands action. The emergency is the fact of *sin* in the world which has overpowered and infected the human race and which threatens the very existence of mankind. There would be no need for Christian missions if sin were not a serious reality. Neither would the doctrine of soteriology make sense without the presence and awfulness of sin. Sin made salvation necessary and sin makes Christian missions necessary.

Numerous and well-written treatises on the doctrine of sin (hamartiology) are available, therefore it is not necessary to enter upon an exhaustive exegetical and historical exposition of this doctrine. Only some basic facts need to be emphasized.

THE FACT OF SIN

Sin is written in bold letters upon the pages of the Bible. Only four chapters are exempt from this evil. According to Genesis 1 — 2, sin was not a part of original human history. Neither is it found in Revelation 21 — 22. There is thus a brief pre-sin history (Gen 1 — 2) and a post-sin history (Rev 21 — 22). The rest of the Bible (Gen 3 — Rev 20) is a record of human sin and divine intervention, preparation, accomplishment and actualization of salvation.

The Bible does not spell out in unequivocal terms the origin of sin as such. But, it leaves no doubt that Satan is the supranatural agent by whom sin and evil enter into God's creation, man included. However, the Bible is unequivocal about certain facts of sin in relation to mankind:

15

Man is a uniquely created being.

Man is a peculiar being, apart from all other creation, a creature in the image of God, an intelligent, volitional, emotional personality, perfectly related to God and endowed with capacities and authorities which defy our present comprehension, definition and realization.

Man was created sinless and for a divinely designated purpose, mission and destiny.

Such is man according to Genesis 1 — 2. The realization of this ideal is recorded or forecast in Revelation 21 — 22.

THE ENTRANCE OF SIN INTO HUMAN HISTORY

Genesis 3 radically changes man in his being, divine relationship, history, mission and destiny. Sin in all its reality, satanic impact and consequences encounters man, and man consciously and deliberately sides with sin against God and the command of God. At the same time sin penetrates, permeates and overpowers man. Thus man becomes a *willful sinner,* entering into a state of rebellion against God and into a life of disobedience to the command of God. He also becomes an *enslaved sinner* who is guilty before God, defiled in his being, depraved in his personality constitution, separated from God, and destitute of divine purpose, mission and destiny. Man is lost, and life is rendered meaningless and empty. Man is at enmity with God. At the same time, man is fallen prey to the horribleness of death as a process and destiny. This is the tragic story of Genesis 3. History is but a duplication, multiplication, expansion and intensification of man's experience in that chapter.

THE NATURE AND EXTENT OF SIN

The Bible knows nothing of the superficial views of sin floating about today which are advocated by theologians who listen more to humanistic psychology and sociology than they listen to the Bible.

According to revelation, sin is sinful not only because of its inherent evil and awful consequences in time and eternity, in man and the universe, in the natural, social, moral and spiritual realms, but supremely because it is committed against God. God is the measure of all sin. Sin derives its seriousness from the character and being of God against whom it is committed. Here lies its gravity, its heinousness, its depth, its fatality.

Sin is not merely error, or weakness, or natural imperfection, or the absence of good. Sin is moral perversity, social evil, a false direction of mind, affection, relationship and life. It has moral and experiential existence, even though it has no separate, metaphysical existence. It is a living, dynamic principle of a degenerate spiritual life. "Sin is not an original law of the human will; for it is the striving, desiring and acting against God."[1] Sin is man confronting God in rational (or irrational) disbelief, in volitional disobedience, in brazen self-love, self-rule, self-redemption, self-worship. Therefore, rationalism and its present corollary of scientism, rebellion and religious philosophy and systems of worship have constituted man's supreme bulwark of self-defense against God.

John B. Champion depicts sin in realistic and vivid terms when he writes,

> Sin is preeminently a wrong to God. It is the terrible treason that tries to wrest the throne from Perfect Goodness and Illimitable Love. It is one long, incessant attempt to dethrone the Deity. The Apostle John well describes it as lawlessness, anarchy. It turns the heart into a dark chamber of treacherous plotting against the government of God. It is the ceaseless attempt to undermine the dominion of the Divine.
>
> One sin is incipient war with God and all good, a league with the devil and all evil, a potential hell replacing heaven. It is not merely assault upon the throne of God; it is the blow struck full at the face of the Father. Sin is the unsheathed sword and the straight thrust at the heart of God. It is the crucifixion of the good, the slaying of the Son-of-God-nature, the murder of life divine. Sin never rests till it has crowned innocence with thorns, and made its spear-thrust into the heart of unsullied righteousness.[2]

Certainly the diabolic nature of sin cannot be overstated. Indeed, the prince of fools is he who stands smiling at that which has destroyed his sanity, or continues to deny that which threatens him with destruction and leads to his eternal doom.

A word study of the scriptural designations of sin will substantiate all that has been said above about sin. I also refer the reader to such passages as Genesis 6:5; Jeremiah 17:9; Romans 1:18-32; 5:6, 8, 10; 6:21; 2 Corinthians 4:4; Ephesians 2:1-3.

The unity of the human race and the universality of sin are assumed and asserted in the Scriptures. The Bible in proposition, biography and history testifies to the universality and perpetuity of sin, and human history is its fullest exposition and most convincing demonstration (Ro 3:23; 5:12 ff.; 1:18 — 3:20).

The consequences of sin are stated in no uncertain terms. Sin is inherent evil and therefore disruptive, corruptive, defiling, degrading, and bears destruction and death in its very nature. In addition, it brings the wrath of God upon man and leads to eternal separation from God, which is the second death (Ac 28:27; Eph 2:2; 4:18; Mt 13:15; Ro 8:7; 5:12; 6:21; Lk 16:19-31; Rev 20:11-15).

THE REMEDY FOR SIN

However, man is still human. As such, he is left with the capacity and an awareness for the need of salvation, but not with the wisdom to design salvation nor with the power and capacity to procure or achieve it. In salvation, man is as dependent upon God as he was in his original creation. In himself, he is helpless and hopeless. The turning point and beam of light lie in the words "But God!"

In infinite wisdom God designed salvation; in infinite grace and at infinite cost God procured salvation in Christ Jesus, His only begotten Son; in infinite power God sent forth the Holy Spirit to actualize salvation in the individual and in history; in infinite compassion God instituted mission and missions — first through Israel and now through His church — in order that helpless and hopeless mankind might hear, know and believe the good news of the infinite salvation of God for mankind. This, too, is the story of Genesis 3 through Revelation 20.

Thus we have a parallelism in the sin-and-salvation portion of the Bible (Gen 3 — Rev 20). On the one hand this portion is the record of the fact and horribleness of sin operating in mankind and of man's sinfulness and depravity in consciously and volitionally yielding to sin. On the other hand this portion shows the grace, faithfulness, long-suffering and loving-kindness of God toward mankind in providing salvation, though the seriousness of the holiness and justice of God in judgment and sufferings inflicted is not absent.

The divine aspect in this parallelism is constituted in the provision of salvation in Christ Jesus and in the proclamation and actualization of the salvation of God provided for mankind. The first is exclusively divine intervention. The latter is committed to the church of Jesus Christ (relatively so, as we shall see later) indwelt and endowed by the Holy Spirit.

All this was made necessary because of the awfulness of sin as present evil and continued consequences in time and eternity.

MISSIONARY THEOLOGY AND BIBLICAL UNIVERSALITY

Before tracing the underlying universality of missionary intent in the Bible, the meaning of terms must be clarified.

THE MEANING OF UNIVERSALITY

I have chosen to use the term *universality* rather than *universalism*. This should help to avoid a common misunderstanding. The word *universalism* in itself is not a bad word. Its usage, however, has been greatly limited and distorted in much of recent literature. Because of this, Webster defines universalism as "the theological doctrine that all souls will eventually find salvation in the grace of God." This, of course, is but one definition which need not be necessarily normative.

In recent philosophical theology and interreligious dialogue the word has most often signified the recognition that God has revealed Himself in all human history and particularly in all living religions. This is thought of as revelational universalism. This position denies the Christian theological concept of *Heilsgeschichte* as recorded in the Old Testament in contrast to general or secular world history. Neither does this position admit an essential distinction between general and special revelation. Because of the presence of such revelation we are told that all religions witness to the same God and eventually lead to the same destination. It is believed that all religions offer salvation in God here and heaven hereafter.

It is readily admitted by liberal theologians and philosophical religionists that some religions have a fuller revelation and therefore offer a way more easily discernible. However, they contend that no religion is completely devoid of "the way." This type of universalism of revelation and salvation holds wide acceptance today and strongly bids for official approval and popular acceptance. It is undergirded by an ancient "Logos theology" and by the misapplication of certain Bible passages.

I have postponed dealing with the false concepts as expressed in the above types of universalism. They appear in chapter 7 on the gospel and missions. Here I merely state that the Bible constrains me categorically to reject both theories.

Because of such usages of the word *universalism,* I have avoided the word and chosen to use such words as *universality, comprehensiveness* and *inclusiveness, all-embracing intent* and similar descriptive words.

In the biblical sense, universality connotes that God's purpose is comprehensive rather than particularistic, including the total human race rather than being national or merely individual. It holds that God's promise and provision of salvation include all mankind and not just an "elect remnant." According to this usage, it teaches that God's provision of salvation is for all mankind and that His offer of salvation is sincerely made to every man. It is in this sense that I use the word *universality.* It is a convenient and technical term to express the missionary intent and provision of the Bible which addresses itself to the whole race, whether directly or indirectly — first through Israel and now through the church. Theologically we may make the following distinctions:

Ideal universality speaks of God's gracious provision of salvation in Christ for all men. It is implied in the fact that "God was in Christ, reconciling *the world* unto himself" (2 Co 5:19), that "Christ is the propitiation . . . for the sins of the *whole world*" (1 Jn 2:2), that "God sent not his Son into the world to condemn the world; but that *the world* through him might be saved" (Jn 3:17), that Christ is the Lamb of God who took away "the sin of *the world*" (Jn 1:29). God's provision is for all mankind. It is racial rather than particularistic.

Practical universality implies that it is the will of God that the gospel should be proclaimed universally, that all mankind and each individual should have the opportunity to hear the good news of redemption.

Ideal and practical universality constitute the basic thesis of this book and will be fully established. Both are emphatically expressed in the Great Commission.

Realized universality expresses the idea that all people have already been saved in Christ and therefore are assured of eternal salvation. It teaches that all people in history, in death or after death, will come to the knowledge and experience of salvation. It must be emphatically stated that such a theory is extrabiblical. In vain students will search the pages of Holy Writ to find any substantiation for such teaching. In fact, the Bible teaches in no uncertain terms that not all people will be saved. Unbelievers will perish from the presence of the Lord and will be condemned to eternal punishment (2 Th 1:8-10).

THE METHODOLOGY OF UNIVERSALITY

Universality must not be confused with *missions* as it is thought of at present. Missions literally means "sending." Universality, especially as presented in the Old Testament, does not necessarily imply sending. In fact, nowhere in the Old Testament was Israel "sent" to the nations. It was not commissioned to go to the nations to proclaim the revelational truth committed to God's people. Universality is a biblical principle expressing the purpose and provision of God. The actualization of this principle and purpose is a matter of methodology and of time. In regard to methodology, the Scriptures prescribe a twofold way — the *centrifugal* and the *centripetal*. It must be recognized that the Old Testament is wholly built around the latter method, whereas the New Testament enjoins the former method (see fig. 1).

The Old Testament upholds the centripetal method which may be thought of as sacred magnetism that draws to itself. Israel, by living a life in the presence and fear of the Lord, was to experience the fullness of the blessings of God. In this way they were to startle the nations to attention, arouse their inquiry, and draw them like a magnet to Jerusalem and to the Lord. Universality was to be actualized by drawing the people to the Lord rather than by sending out messengers with a message. The principle is illustrated in the queen of Sheba coming to Jerusalem to see and to hear. So also did the eunuch of Ethiopia come to Jerusalem in search for the truth.

It is in the light of this methodology, as well as in his narrow nationalism, that Jonah in his unwillingness to go to Nineveh must be judged. Also because of Old Testament methodology, the disciples found it difficult to understand their Master in His commission to go into all the world. According to the Old Testament, the world of nations is to come to Jerusalem. There the nations are to learn the way of the Lord and to worship. It will be remembered that the disciples were the last to leave Jerusalem during the early years of persecution and go farther and preach the gospel (Ac 8:1). No doubt they found it easy to preach on the day of Pentecost to the people who had come *to* Jerusalem. But why must they go *from* Jerusalem? It constituted a turnabout in methodology but not in principle and purpose.

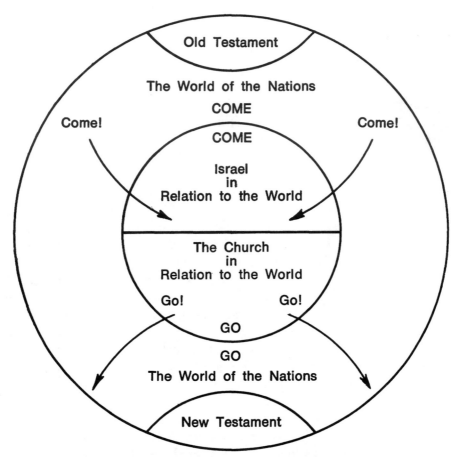

Fig. 1.   Missions in the Bible

THE ACTUALIZATION OF UNIVERSALITY

In regard to the time of the actualization of universality, caution must be exercised in the interpretation of the Old Testament. A careful study established the thesis that the Bible makes a fourfold presentation of universality which finds its culmination and full expression in the second coming of Christ.

First, there is a universality of revelation and actualization which relates to the total human race. This is recorded in Genesis 1 – 11, where God reveals Himself to and deals with the entire race. All nations share alike in the knowledge of God, for His approach is to all mankind. There is no special or mediating people. Shem is such only in prophecy.

Second, in the Old Testament there is a universality in which Israel becomes the mediator between God and the nations. This in no way interrupts the original comprehensive purpose and intent. Rather, it is God's method of mediating Himself to the world. God is still the God of mankind; He is the God of all nations. Israel, however, is to be the priesthood of God among the nations to mediate God's revelation, salvation and purpose. This inclusive intent is maintained throughout Old Testament history, as we shall see more fully in the coming pages. Never was there a time when the nations did not have access to God, although God mediated His revelation through Israel. It was the responsibility of the nations to inquire and to seek God. In the light of this principle, Paul's strong indictment of the nations in Romans 1:18-32 must be read. Instead, entering upon the search of truth, they rather suppressed the truth they possessed. Thus the nations as well as Israel failed in the Old Testament dispensation.

Third, because of failure on the part of Israel to be the light of the world and the salt of the earth to the degree of her enabling and the need of the world, God has temporarily set aside Israel as His chosen servant. He has called the church of Jesus Christ to be a chosen generation, a royal priesthood, a holy nation, a peculiar people, to show forth the praises of Him who hath called believers out of darkness into His marvelous light (1 Pe 2:9). The *function* of Israel has been transferred temporarily to the church of Jesus Christ which has become the witness, the priesthood, the servant, the light, the salt. Thus in the present dispensation the church is God's mediating agency not of salvation but of the message of God's salvation in Christ Jesus. She is under the solemn responsibility to make known the unsearchable riches of Christ among the nations. The gospel must be preached to every creature. Her calling is unique and specific, her equipment in and through the Holy Spirit adequate. There is no uncertainty about the purpose and program of God, and there ought to be no hesitancy in obedience, commitment and action.

Fourth, the Scriptures emphatically forecast a prophetic, Messianic universality of the gospel in the millennium when the comprehensive intent of God in Christ will be more fully realized and the knowledge of the Lord and His salvation will become universal (Hab

2:14; Ps 22:27; Is 11:9). The nation of Israel will be raised up by the
Lord and will turn to the Lord and become the "servant of Jehovah."
This national miracle, which is foretold in numerous passages in the
Old Testament, is most vividly presented by Isaiah in the second part
of his great prophecies (chaps. 40-66) under the image of a servant.
Ezekiel portrayed it in a symbolic manner in his last great chapters
under the visions of the dry bones being revived and the temple and
worship being restored to serve the nation and the nations (chaps.
37-48).

Having been restored nationally and spiritually, Israel will then
lead the nations to the knowledge of the Lord and the nations will
worship and serve the Lord (Zec 14:9, 16-19; Is 60 — 66). This will
be in contrast to the present age when God is calling to Himself a
people — the church — from among the nations of the world.

I realize that it is difficult for us to think in terms of national
conversions, but such are anticipated by the Scriptures. They will
surely come, and the cause of Christ will triumph in an unprecedented
manner.

Upon the new earth, either in the millennium or after the millennium, nations will be found surrounding New Jerusalem, walking in
the true light of the Lord, finding healing in the fruit of the tree of
life, serving the Lord and worshiping the triune God. The triumph of
the Lamb become racial.

God has a marvelous plan and program. History has purpose and
meaning. There is a *Heilsgeschichte Gottes* which cannot be frustrated nor can it be defeated. God is in it and He moves triumphantly
from stage to stage; in this all writers and seers of the Bible agree.
The Bible is a book of hope and triumph.

Many faithful and true servants of God do not see the latter point
this way. They spiritualize the numerous passages of the Old Testament and apply them to the New Testament. I cannot accept such
spiritualizations, no matter how well and how zealously preached and
defended. I see little difference in the application of a hermeneutical
principle which spiritualizes prophecy and which demythologizes history only insomuch that the one is positive and the other negative. It
seems to me that there is a close affinity of principle although not of
motive and intent. Yet, as the latter destroys the fact of history, the
former destroys the meaning of history. The one undermines the

historicity (*Geschichte*) of the Scriptures; the other undercuts the philosophy of the Scriptures. The Holy Spirit would preserve both.

Universality, thus, is a broad concept. It expresses the missionary program of God in the world of mankind, rooted in the racial purpose of God and the all-sufficient provision of salvation in Christ Jesus.

Missionary Theology as a Theological Discipline

The study of Christian missions has been for centuries a separate and distinct discipline not usually considered to be material for the theologian or for the pastor. In fact, most theologians and pastors passed by the courses in missions and ignored mission literature and matters of mission organization. The church, the pastor and the theologian often remained detached if not aloof from mission studies and mission movements. In most countries of Europe and England separate schools of missions functioned to train missionary candidates in missiology.

In the last decades an alignment of church and missions has come about, but the practical outworking of this is difficult to predict. The identification of church with mission may become as abnormal and detrimental to the cause as was the earlier divorce of church and missions. However this may develop, missions has been joined to ecclesiology, and mission studies have become a part of the departments of the church either in its practicum or in its history. Theoretically, this is a step forward.

I maintain, however, that this token alignment is inadequate from a biblical perspective. Allowing for a theoretical distinction between missionary theology and practicum, missionary theology must move up until it finds its place in theology itself. Ideally, it should be integrated with the very theology of the triune God.

In his little booklet, *Unchanging Missions — Biblical and Contemporary*, Douglas Webster opens his lecture series with these words: "We begin, then, where mission begins, with God."[3] Only such an approach does justice to the well-sustained claim of Georg F. Vicedom that mission is "Missio Dei."[4]

Only as mission has its source in and derives its nature and authority from the triune God can it truly generate lasting and enduring motivation and become really Christian, really meaningful. On any other level it remains humanism, no matter how "religionized" or "Christianized" such humanism may be.

The failure of Reformation Protestantism to generate the dynamic of missions and later to sustain this dynamic in its world outreach can be blamed principally on its incomplete and unbalanced theology. Protestant theology concerned itself almost exclusively with the "being" and "character" of God as manifested by His attributes. To this it added an extensive study of the "works" of God. These are two tremendously important aspects which are of fundamental consequence to all theology.

However, this only established the "otherness," greatness, majesty and glory of God and made all His works dependent upon Him. Strangely and silently this theology has bypassed the biblical concept of *the living God*, the God of purpose, the God of history, action and existential relationships, the God of here and now, the God who presently is working out His plan and program, the God who is an outgoing God, a God of mission. Thus theology has occupied itself more with the God of heaven and the God of creation than with the God of the eternal presence in salvation and missions. Such inadequacy naturally leads to a divorce of theology and missions.

A similar charge must be registered concerning the doctrine of Christology as taught in theology. It usually is presented in two sections: the *person* of Christ and the *work* of Christ. This is good. But is it complete? Is it doing justice to the biblical presentation of Christ? Did He not also have a plan and a program to accomplish that for which He came, lived and died? Was He not *sent* authoritatively and purposively by the Father? Are we not to proclaim the gospel and gather out the church "according to the eternal purpose which he [God] purposed in Jesus Christ our Lord" (Eph 3:11)? Is a study of His *work* complete without a study of His *purpose* for the historic effectuation of the work?

Well does W. O. Carver define missions as "the extensive realization of God's redemptive purpose in Christ Jesus by means of human messengers."[5] Are we doing justice to the doctrine of Christ without fully expounding the missionary purpose and program for which He came, lived and died? The missionary purpose and outreach of God are essential factors in the work of Christ, and their disassociation is unnatural. Its negative outworking is felt at home and around the world.

No less crucial is a truly biblical exposition of the Holy Spirit, the

Paraclete of the triune God in this world. His pre- and extra-Pentecostal and suprahuman movements and ministries within culture and society are little understood and expounded. While we debate such vital doctrines as the indwelling, sealing, baptism and empowering of the Holy Spirit, we practically ignore the broader and deeper ministry of the Holy Spirit who in wise providence is creating high-potential areas around the world where the gospel may triumph to the glory of God and the blessing of mankind. Theology is neglecting a most vital doctrine of the Bible and thereby is missing a most crucial opportunity to become what it ought to be — a missionary theology of dynamic proportions rather than simply an exposition of dogma or a defense of the faith. While the latter is necessary, the former is imperative.

Missions is the progressive objectification of the eternal and benevolent purpose of God which roots in His very being and character and which embraces all ages, races and generations.

Missions is the historic effectuation of God's salvation procured on behalf of all mankind in Christ Jesus because of His incarnation, death and resurrection. It offers forgiveness of sins and new life and dynamic to all who believe in Him as eternal Son of God and Saviour of mankind.

Missions is the practical realization of the Holy Spirit operating in this world on behalf of the eternal purpose of God and the actualization of salvation procured through Christ Jesus in the lives of countless individuals, families, tribes and people. Thus missions relates to the triune God.

Missionary theology is not an appendix to biblical theology; it belongs at its very core. No doctrine of God, Christ or the Holy Spirit has been expounded completely according to the Bible until it has established the triune God as the outgoing God of mission, the God of saving purpose and relationship to mankind who undertakes a program for the progressive realization of His purpose.

We agree with W. O. Carver when he says, "No thought of God is true to His revelation of Himself that does not rest on the fact that He 'so loved the world that He gave His only begotten Son' that by believing in Him "the world should be saved through Him.""[8]

It must be confessed that the evangelical and nonecumenical part of Christianity in America has concerned itself very little with a theology of missions. While the Bible has been believed and taught, missions has been related very little to theology and to the purpose of God through the ages. Thus our bookshelves are bare of literature on this subject. The closest we have come to it in America is a volume written by Harold Lindsell originally published under the title, *A Philosophy of Christian Missions*. More recently it has been reprinted as *An Evangelical Theology of Missions.*[7]

The 1966 Wheaton Congress on "The Church's Worldwide Mission" wrestled seriously with certain phases relating to the theology of missions, but failed to come to grips with the subject as such. It must be admitted that no formulated theology of missions exists from the evangelical, nonecumenical perspective. It is time to wake up, lest the foundations erode completely.

Such a dearth does not exist in the ecumenical world. Considerable material on the subject is included in the official reports of the International Missionary Council at the 1910 Edinburgh Conference on Missions. In more recent years numerous volumes have appeared on the subject. It must be stated that the result of these conferences and after sessions has been as much debate as it has been dialogue, as much interreligious compromise as Christian confrontation, as much evasion as formulation, as much confusion as illumination, as much hindrance as help. In part, human reason rather than revelation, aesthetics rather than truth, and religion rather than the Christ of God and of history dominated the sentiment of large segments of spokesmen. Thus relativism rather than absolutism gained preeminence. Well does Gerald H. Anderson state the present situation: "The major issues, despite a renewal of interest and discussion, have not been resolved. If anything they have become more crucial."[8]

Nevertheless, a tremendous volume of literature has poured off the ecumenical press. There is no lack of speculative material on theology and philosophy of mission. Much of it is of considerable value, much is of little profit, and much is definitely detrimental to the cause of Jesus Christ. Soundly biblical material is scarce and remains a challenge to the theologian in tune with the purpose and program of God.

MISSIONARY THEOLOGY AND THE CLAIMS OF CHRISTIANITY

Christianity claims to be the religion of *absolute fulfillment* and finality. In Christianity all the Old Testament promises and types find their completion, and all the religious needs and spiritual anticipation of mankind are fulfilled. Christ is the desire of all nations.

Christianity asserts absoluteness in religious *authority*, contending for total control over man's mind, his conscience, his conduct, and his relationships in all spheres of life. It is all-inclusive, all-regulative and totally normative. Such total jurisdiction is not merely legalistic but also existential. It is a matter of subjective moral persuasion, mental renewal and volitional redirection which generates spiritual appreciation, moral dynamic and joyous obedience. It is in the "heart" as well as in the "Book."

Christianity further claims *completeness and finality* as a revelation of God, His work and His purpose. It expects no modifications, additions, corrections or supplementations. Here God is truly and as fully, clearly, and absolutely revealed as He can be perceived by man or as He is needed by man to bring him perfect satisfaction, fulfillment, and existential realization of all human potentialities. It will never be superseded by another personality equal to the Jesus of Nazareth or by another religious revelation and system of equal worth and value.

Finally, Christianity claims *universality* in scope and rule. It promises to hold sole and universal sway over the inhabitants of all nations, judging and supplanting all other religious systems and philosophies. Its claims to inclusiveness and exclusiveness are startling, its optimistic view of ultimate and total triumphs most amazing. We are not surprised that such claims are a stumbling block to scientism, an obstacle to philosophical positivism, a rock of offense to secularism, and an irritation to agnosticism. They seem like a glowing example of religious imperialism to the devotees of non-Christian religious systems.

On the other hand, its optimism is charming, its missionary glow inspiring, its motivation in sacrificial service and life-outpouring heroism appealing. Christianity's history over the past nineteen centuries — especially the last century and a half — is assuring. Among the religions of the world, Christendom claims the greatest percentage of adherents, sponsors the greatest humanitarian institutions, supports the greatest missionary force in the world, and alone can claim true ecumenicity in the sense of being present in every nation. The phenomenon of Christianity is astounding and warrants investigation not only of its claims and appearance but of its very roots and foundations.

What is the justification of Christianity's claim? What are the

sources of its continuous and spontaneous drive in expansion? What
secrets account for the heroism of its adherents in sacrifice, suffering
and martyrdom? What are its ever replenishing, never exhausting resources for missionary expansion? What are the reasons for its optimism and hopeful anticipation of triumphant consummation?

These are justified questions in a world of pessimism, confusion
and despair. Do the hope and confidence of Christianity rest in its
genius of organization, its wealth of material resources, its skill of
technology? Or does its confident assurance spring from superior
idealism, and from its utter dependence upon the ultimate power of
the universe? Christians claim that the latter plays the decisive role.

Christianity claims superiority of idealogy and a unique and
extraordinary knowledge of the ultimate power of the universe whom
we call God. At the same time Christianity demands absolute surrender to and utter dependence upon God. Its truth, however, is not a
discovery of man. It is a gracious and miraculous disclosure — a
revelation of God Himself in *Heilsgeschichte* (the history of Israel in
particular), in propositional declarations and finally, completely and
perfectly in the person of His Son, Jesus of Nazareth, who was God
incarnated to reveal God fully, totally and finally to man. In Him,
God and man meet; God entered into union with man and at the
same time drew man to God in an unparalleled manner. Here mystery
and reality face man. Here miracle and history unite to speak to man.
The God-man informs us: "Believe me that I am in the Father, and
the Father in me: or else believe me for the very work's sake. He that
hath seen me hath seen the Father" (Jn 14:11, 9). Again, "No man has
ever seen God at any time; the only unique Son, the only-begotten
God, Who is in the bosom . . . of the Father, He has declared Him —
He has revealed Him, brought Him out where He can be seen; He has
interpreted Him, and He has made Him known" (Jn 1:18, Amplified).

In keeping with these claims, Paul declares that Christ is the
image, the exact likeness and representation of the invisible God (Col
1:15; 2 Co 4:4). The writer of Hebrews amplifies the thought: "He
[Christ as Son] is the sole expression of the glory of God, the Light
— being the irradiating of the divine — and He is the perfect imprint
and the very image of [God's] nature" (Heb 1:3, Greek NT).

Thus, while Christianity is God-centered, it is so only as God is
known in and through Jesus Christ. Therefore, it can be stated that

Christianity is Christocentric. Christianity is God-centered in orientation and purpose and Christ-centered in revelation and salvation. Christ in revelation and mediation becomes the foundation of Christian missions.

The above claims are made in the conviction that Christianity is truth revealed. Apologetics and Christian evidences have done a noble work in defending the rationale and historicity of Christianity and of the authenticity and integrity of the Bible. A study of comparative religions has sought to establish the supremacy and uniqueness of Christianity among the religions of the world. None of the disciplines, however, is able to produce evidences so conclusive that they cannot be challenged. In the end, a Christian takes his stand in faith upon revelation as it is recorded in the words of the Bible, substantiated by rational evidences, and verified in his own moral nature as the ultimate, absolute and final truth. His position, therefore, is neither purely objective nor merely subjective. It is objective-subjective.

Part I

BIBLICAL FOUNDATION
OF
MISSIONS

1

Missionary Theology and Jesus Christ

CHRISTIANITY is Christocentric. Christ, together with the Father and the Holy Spirit, is its object of faith and worship. Since He provides the supreme example and pattern of conduct, service, attitude and direction for life, a study of His life is illuminating and inspiring.

We concern ourselves here only with His relation to the world and to worldwide missions. What was Christ's attitude toward non-Jewish people? Does He relate His ministry to the world of nations? Was Christ a nationalist, particularist and provincialist, or was He a universalist? Was He an internationalist with a world mission? Were the benefits of His life and death designed for one people? Or was His ministry directed toward the nations of the world? Was Jesus in the days of His flesh conscious of His racial significance and of a universal mission? Did He have a universal horizon, a wider outlook than to restore Judaism?

Christianity would answer the last questions in the affirmative, seeing that present-day Christianity is substantially made up of peoples from the nations, so the universality of Christ is taken for granted. However, considerable debate has revolved around this point. Well does Dr. Samuel Zwemer summarize four historic views:

> The first is the extreme view of Hegel, Tolstoi and others that Jesus was anti-Semitic and conscious only of a universal mission! The exact opposite view is that Jesus was at heart a Jew and limited His horizon and message to the house of Israel. Reimarus, Strauss, Wellhausen, and Harnack are representatives of this other radical view and they have had many followers. A third school of critics says that Jesus was at first narrow and Jewish and that only toward

35

the end of His life did He become conscious of a world-mission (Keim, Hausrath, Bertholet, Bernard Weiss).

Against all of these radical views is the traditional one held by believing scholars, Roman Catholics, and Protestant — namely, that Jesus from the outset of His ministry had a view of humanity as a whole, but felt that He was sent especially to the lost sheep of the house of Israel, and that His earthly ministry was mainly to the people of Israel. Nevertheless, He taught His apostles by degrees that He was to be the Savior of all men and finally gave them their universal mission.[1]

Because His earthly ministry was mainly to His people, the question arises: Was such restriction a matter of principle or a matter of methodology?

THE PORTRAIT OF CHRIST

The four gospels present an authentic record of the life, words and work of Christ. But they are not written as a "life of Christ"; they are too brief and too sketchy for that purpose. Rather, they are four portraits of Christ or four presentations of the same Person from four points of view. Each of the evangelists portrays Christ accurately but according to his own purpose and intent, within his own frame of reference and design, without contradicting, destroying or minimizing his Coauthor's arrangements.

We admit that serious limitations and difficulties are encountered in an attempt to build a harmony of the gospels or a "life of Christ" upon the gospel records. However, a marvelous beauty appears when we synthesize the four portraits rather than harmonize the records. As we see Christ in His fullness and behold an ever enlarging view of Him as portrayed in the gospels, His missionary thrust and compassion become overwhelming. He shines forth as the ideal Missionary, the Apostle of God.

Assuming that Mark was the first to write his record, we note his historical-existential manner of presentation. Having been personally acquainted with Christ and having accompanied Peter on his journeys, Mark writes as a Christ-filled Jew. He introduces Christ as the Prophet of God and as the Servant of Jehovah. His whole portrait is that of the Prophet of God speaking forth the message of God and the Servant of Jehovah ever active, accomplishing the will and purpose of

God. Beautifully he summarizes it in a quote from the Master: "For even the Son of man came not to be ministered unto, but to minister, and to give his life a ransom for many" (10:45).

The urgency of such a ministry becomes emphatic in the constantly recurring words, "and," "immediately," and "straightway." The scope is expressed in the command to herald the gospel to all the creation (16:15-16). He is the Prophet whose message must be heralded in all the world (13:10).

Matthew principally accepts the portrait of Mark. However, he proceeds to enlarge it and add to it the royalty of Christ. The authoritative kingship of Christ becomes most prominent in Matthew. Fusing beautifully the various aspects of Christ's life, the writer proceeds to set the portrait of the royalty and kingship of Christ into the frame of Old Testament revelation to give it the full authority of the God of creation and history. He points out how Christ is the fulfillment of the visions and prophecies of Old Testament seers, the embodiment of anticipations and aspirations of mankind, and the reality behind all Old Testament typology. In Christ, spiritual reality has appeared and the shadows must flee. Beautifully, Matthew beholds the King to whom universal authority has been committed, issuing a command that all nations be discipled and united into a single body under the lordship of the triune God.

To the already enlarged portrait, Luke adds the priesthood and saviorhood of Christ which, though implicit in the previous presentation, had not been so fully amplified. Luke, no doubt, had first learned it from Paul; he had then experienced it in his life. Finally, diligent research led him to accept the fact and theology of it. This enlargement he then places into the framework of universal history which begins with Adam and which he sees as God's theater of activity without blurring the line between *Heilsgeschichte* (sacred story) as seen in Israel and general history as seen in the nations. The universal validity of the priesthood and saviorhood of Christ is evident from the genealogy which begins with Adam and culminates in the universal significance of the death and resurrection of Christ and the offer of repentance and remission of sins in the name of Christ among all nations as expressed in the commission of Christ.

The largest portrait is painted by John. In no way does he contradict the previous writers, nor does he erase or modify these portrayals. Though not explicitly stated, the reader "senses" that John appreciates all that has been said by the previous gospelers who are reflecting the views of the writers, numerous eyewitnesses, and the testimonies of Peter (Mark) and Paul (Luke). John, however, swings beyond and above them and lifts the curtain that we might see the position of Christ as the eternal Son of God, coequal and coeternal with the Father in His metaphysical and cosmic relationships. In the gospel of John, Christ is known as the *Logos*, the light which lighteth every man, the life, the Son. These concepts directly or metaphorically express unqualified deity.

In Christ, God directly relates Himself to this world spoken of as *kosmos*. Seventy-nine times John uses this concept and sets forth the various relationships of God to the *kosmos*. In the strongest possible terms, John presents the universalist activity of God. God is not a particularist in His interest, love and relationships; He has the world upon His heart and in His purpose.

We are informed that "God so loved the world, that he gave . . ." (3:16). "God sent not his Son into the world to condemn the world; but that the world through him might be saved" (3:17). We are told that Christ is "the Lamb of God, which taketh away [beareth] the sin of the world" (1:29); "the Saviour of the world" (4:42); "the bread of God is he which . . . giveth life unto the world" (6:33); "the light of the world" (8:12; 9:5; 12:46). The Holy Spirit is spoken of as the Comforter who will convict or "reprove the world" (16:8).

Whatever else the above passages may teach, the fact is firmly established by John that God is in benevolent contact with the world. In Christ Jesus there exists a redemptive relationship between heaven and the *kosmos*. The Holy Spirit is at present actively involved in this redemptive relationship. While this may be mysterious, it is nevertheless real. The Holy Spirit is convicting men everywhere (16:8), and He is drawing men from among all nations to Christ (12:32).

Thus we have an ever enlarging and deepening circle in the gospels. It is personal and cosmic. It is highly individual — "whosoever," and it is racial and includes all.

We are moving first into the historio-existential (Mark), next into the scriptural and revelational (Matthew), next into the universal history (Luke), and finally into the cosmic and metaphysical (John).

Time and eternity, heaven and earth are spanned in Christ, and God and man become reconciled.

We have the portraits of Christ as the Prophet of God and the Servant of Jehovah in Mark, as the Messiah of God and King of kings and Lord of lords in Matthew, as the Priest of God and Saviour of mankind in Luke, and as the Son of God in truth and reality who comes to bring life and immortality to man in John. Thus in Christ the fullness of God dwells bodily, a fullness adequate and available for all who believe.

The missionary movement and implications of such presentations are evident and overwhelming. Progressively but certainly Christ will triumph in all spheres of His relationship because He is indeed a missionary Christ — the Christ of all mankind and the Lord of the whole *kosmos*.

THE MAJOR THEOLOGICAL CONCEPTS OF CHRIST

The sense of the missionary thrust of Christ comes into clear focus as we consider His basic theological concepts and presuppositions. All of them are filled with missionary content and charged with missionary dynamic. They only awaited Pentecost to be discharged with full fervor and force. We summarize these basic theological concepts and presuppositions of Christ by pointing to His focal point of proclamation, central revelation, unique self-identification, supreme purpose, declaration as final Judge, and the Great Commission.

THE FOCAL POINT OF CHRIST'S PROCLAMATION — THE KINGDOM OF GOD

Mark summarizes the proclamation of Jesus Christ in these words: "Jesus came into Galilee, preaching the gospel of the kingdom of God, and saying, the time is fulfilled, and the kingdom of God is at hand: repent ye, and believe the gospel" (1:14-15).

Even a cursory survey of the gospels will soon convince the reader that the concept of the kingdom of God was most prominent in the teaching of Jesus and formed the focal point of His proclamation. He began with its preaching (Mk 1:14-15) and ended with a discourse on it (Ac 1:3). In between, numerous references point to it. Direct statements about it and parabolic interpretations of it characterized His preaching. Christ was, indeed, a Preacher of the kingdom of God (compare His more than sixty references to it in the gospel records).

The author is well acquainted with the literature that has either sought to identify and/or to differentiate between the designations of "kingdom of heaven" (in Matthew's gospel) and the "kingdom of God" as found in all four gospels and in the epistles. Since these technicalities do not enter into the present thesis, no pros and cons need be discussed.

We are interested in the meaning of the concept "kingdom of God" as it reflects either the particularism or universality of Christ. This concept is not altogether an Old Testament concept. In its full form it does not appear in the Old Testament. While its roots are there, its full blossoming forth is found only in the New Testament.

In the Old Testament we find the following facts: God is the King of Israel in a particular way; God is the King of all the nations in a general way; God is the King of all creation in a providential way.

To this the New Testament adds a new dimension: It is emphatic that God is the King of the inner man. It adds the inwardness, immediacy and actuality of the kingdom and kingship of God, making it personal, spiritual, moral and social. The kingdom of God is in you. God is the King of eternity and immortality, thus indicating the "otherness" and otherworldliness in value and nature of the kingdom and kingship of God. It lifts the concept of the kingdom out of space and time in origin and ultimate design and transplants it into the realm of the transhuman and transearthly in quality and duration.

The kingdom of God includes all of these aspects. It is individual, national, racial, cosmic. It is personal, spiritual, moral, social. It is worldly and timely. It is also transworldly, transhuman and eternal. It is history, yet it is ultimate. It is timely, yet it is eternal. It is qualitative, yet it is also spacial.

From the above it is evident that a simple definition of the kingdom of God is not sufficient. It is also well illustrated by the literature on the subject and the three basic hermeneutical systems of Scripture interpretation which have grown up around it: postmillennialism, premillennialism, and amillennialism.

It may be well to think of the kingdom of God in qualitative and quantitative terms. *Qualitatively* we may consider it as threefold:

a. The rule of God in the heart of man. The kingdom of God is within you. It is immediate and actual. As such it is moral, not nationalistic; it is spiritual, not materialistic; it is actual, not idealistic (that is, it is present and not totally futuristic).

b. The rule of God in the church. Neither God nor Christ is ever spoken of as the King of the church. Christ is the Lord of the church and this is but a Roman modification of the king or rulership concept. As Lord He is sovereign over His church. Thus Paul went about preaching the kingdom of God (Ac 14:22; 19:8; 20:25; 28:23, 31). In the epistles he uses the kingdom concept at least fourteen times. Certainly Paul did not feel that the church was not related to or a part of the kingdom of God. The content of his references, however, betrays that he thought of the kingdom more in moral and ethical terms than in terms of authority, royalty and rulership.

The fact remains, however, that Paul knew Christ as the Lord of the church. He is the Head of the church, and the church is His body (Eph 1:23; Ro 12:5; Col 1:18). To Christ belong all right, authority and rulership in the church. He bestows gifts and He dispatches His ambassadors. He is sovereign Lord of the church (Eph 4:7, 11; 2 Co 5:20).

c. The rule of God in the world. As such, though it is personal, it has strong social implications through the ministry of the individual Christian and the general impact of the gospel upon the conscience of society. The presence of the gospel in this world constitutes judgment, modification and enrichment of the order of society. It is strongly social in its general impact, regulating all relationships according to the will and purpose of God. As such, though it is local within the individual believer and the church of Jesus Christ, it is universal in the sense that the gospel is to be preached to all nations and that the church is to be constituted of believers from among all nations. As such, though it is present within the individual, within the Christian church, and within the providential government of God in this dispensation, its full manifestation is futuristic — first in the millennial reign of Christ upon the earth over all nations and, finally, in the consummation when the last enemy shall have been destroyed and the Son shall have subjugated all things, "then shall the Son also himself be subject unto him that put all things under him, that God may be all in all" (1 Co 15:28). It is immediate, progressive and cataclysmic.

Quantitatively the kingdom of God concept implies a realm, an objective reality. Repeatedly Christ admonishes man to "enter the kingdom of God," "receive the kingdom of God," "to give you the kingdom of God," "sit in the kingdom of God," "eat in the kingdom of God." Such expressions emphasize primarily realm and objective reality rather than a reign, though the latter is not excluded.

From this brief survey it is evident that there is nothing particularistic in the focal teaching of Christ. To the contrary, as God is not the God of the Jews only but of the nations also, so the kingdom of God is not the Jews' only, but also the nations'. The kingdom of God concept is definitely universalistic in designation and implication.

THE CENTRAL REVELATION OF CHRIST — THE FATHERHOOD OF GOD

Christ has unveiled for us the riches of heavenly truth. Indeed, he is the truth, for "grace and truth came by Jesus Christ." However, in the midst of all the splendor of revelation which came in and through Christ, the manifestation of the *Father* towers above all other truth. "The only begotten Son, which is in the bosom of the Father, he hath declared him," or as the New English Bible translates, "No one has ever seen God; but God's Son, he who is nearest to the Father's heart, he has made him known" (Jn 1:18).

The Fatherhood of God stands out in the teaching ministry of Christ and forms the core revelation of the message of the Son of God. This is evident even from the fact that the gospels record the frequent usage of the word by Christ: In Matthew, 44 times; in Mark, 5; in Luke, 16; in John, 109 — a total of 173 times.

The Father concept of God is not altogether new with Christ. God had been known as the "Father" of the nation of Israel (Deu 14: 1-2; 32:6; Ps 103:13; Pr 3:12; Is 9:6; Mal 2:10). He had also been spoken of as Father in relation to the King and the coming Messiah (2 Sa 7:14; Ps 2:7).

However, in contrast to the Old Testament Elohim and Jehovah idea, Christ made the Father concept the controlling image of God, thus advancing and completing the revelation of the God of the Bible and leading us to the deepest and most intimate God-man relationship. We have thus the following unfolding of God in the Bible:

a. The *Elohim-God* concept as the earliest revelation of God portraying principally God's relationship to man as Creator.

b. The *Jehovah-God* concept presenting God's covenant relationship to man and particularly to Israel.

c. The *Fatherhood-God* concept unveiling basically but not exclusively God's filial relationship to man.

Thus in the New Testament are men individually known as "children of God" and "sons of God" and only in the New Testament do men address God as "abba Father."

It is well to take note of this marvelous and completing result of progressive revelation of the concept of God, for it is a fact that the God concept remains the regulative concept of all revelation and relationships.

In the revelation of God as Father, our Lord distinguishes a threefold relation. He speaks of God as "my Father" and indicates His essential or metaphysical relationship to the Father. He was uniquely the Son of God, and God was uniquely His Father. He speaks to His disciples and followers of God as "your Father," thus establishing the filial relationship of God as Father. Finally, He speaks of God as "Father" or as "the Father," relating God as Father providentially to all mankind. Man as a creation of God is related to Him as Father.

Thus there is a fatherhood of God by creation which is universal to all mankind, a fatherhood of God by redemption which is particular to all believers, and a fatherhood of God by essence which is unique to the Son of God.

The first is providential and relates to time and space only, the second is filial and relates to time and eternity, the third is metaphysical and relates from eternity to eternity.

However, in no sense does the fatherhood relate God especially to the Jewish people. Thus in the central core of Christ's revelation, national particularism disappears and universality prevails. God is peculiarly the Father of all who believe, irrespective of nationality or race.

CHRIST IN HIS UNIQUE SELF-IDENTIFICATION — THE SON OF MAN

Though His human name was Jesus, His favorite designation was "Son of man." The gospels record eighty-four such references — in Matthew, 32; in Mark, 14; in Luke, 26; in John, 12. Dr. Wayland Hayd lists sixteen relationships in which the Master used this self-designation.[2]

The question for our studies is: What did Jesus mean to impress upon His hearers by using this self-designation?

Let us consider the title, "The Son of man." Five facts, all rooted in the Old Testament, stand out:

The reality of the humanity of Jesus. "Son of man" is a Hebraism which expresses the possession of true human nature. Jesus, by taking the name "Son of Man," signified His sharing in this lot at once with the low and with the high. He also expressed by it His community of feeling with men, His sharing in human affections and interests, His true experience of human life, His liability to temptation, His exposure like other men to hunger and thirst, suffering and death.

The ideal Man. Jesus Christ as the Son of man is the ideal Man in whom humanity finds its fulfillment, hope and pattern. He is "the son of . . . Adam, which was the son of God" (Lk 3:23-38). In direct fulfillment of Psalm 8:3-4, He is the true Son of man and not the son of any nation or race; He is the Man of universal relationships; the Son of man is His generic designation and title. In Him humanity is summed up, and the fullness of the race is made visible. He is the Head and Representative, not of the Jews only, but of all nations of mankind. This is a title by which Jesus de-Judaizes Himself and places Himself in such relation to the whole race of men that their enemies are His enemies, their sorrows His, their burdens His. He is bound up with their life and destiny. And as the race is so summed up and represented in Him, He is in St. Paul's language, the second Adam.

The Successor to the prophets. Jesus Christ as the Son of man is the true Successor to the prophets of Israel. Indeed, He is "the Prophet." In the prophecy of Ezekiel the phrase "Son of man" occurs with ninetyfold iteration. Jehovah constantly addresses the prophet by this term. The title becomes a designation for the man whom God addresses in a unique way and who represents God to the people.

The promised Messiah. Jesus Christ as the Son of man is the promised Messiah of Israel. In keeping with Psalm 80:17, Daniel 7:13-14 and intertestamental Jewish writings, the designation "Son of man" had become a technical word and title among the learned Jews for the Messiah they were expecting.

We need to note that in the three synoptic gospels the designation "Son of man" emphatically expresses the Messianic consciousness of Christ. The numerous passages roughly fall into three categories as follows:

Eschatalogical references

Matthew	Mark	Luke
16:27	8:38	9:26
24:30	13:26	21:27
26:64	14:62	22:69

Soteriological references

Matthew	Mark	Luke
17:9, 12, 22	8:31	9:22
20:18	9:9, 12, 31	9:44
26:24	10:45	22:22
26:45	14:21, 41	

References expressing Messianic authority and missions

Matthew	Mark	Luke
9:6	2:10	5:24
12:8	2:28	6:5
13:37	3:28-30	19:10
12:32		12:10

Yes, Jesus knew Himself as the Anointed of God, sent from God and by God to the people of God for the mission of God and in the authority of God.

Uniquely related to God and His reign. Jesus Christ as the Son of man is uniquely related to God and to the establishment of the reign of God. This is presented in Daniel 7:13-14. From the world vision of this passage, we note that Jesus Christ as the Son of Man not only identifies Himself with mankind, but He is the hope of Israel and the world, and the surety of the purpose of God. He Himself becomes the fulfillment of all Old Testament anticipations and promises.[3]

We note, however, that there is no narrow particularism attached to the title. It relates Christ to mankind. He is, indeed, the Saviour of the world.

CHRIST IN HIS FUNDAMENTAL PURPOSE —
HIS ATONING DEATH AND RESURRECTION

Did Christ come into the world to give mankind a perfect pattern of life? Did He live to declare to man the way of God? Did Christ come to manifest the Father by living and to unveil Him by teaching? To all these questions we must give an affirmative answer. Yes, Christ is our pattern; He is the way; He is the supreme, perfect and final image and manifestation of the Father. However, in all of these ministries He would only quantitatively distinguish Himself from the prophets of old. They, too, upheld ideals in the way of God and unveiled God in His person and purpose before man. As significant and marvelous as the contributions of Christ are in these areas, He is not absolutely unique in this field. This, therefore, neither fully explains nor justifies the great fact of incarnation. Neither does the New Testament make this central to His coming.

John the Baptist focuses the thrust of the New Testament when he points to Christ and declares, "Behold the Lamb of God, which taketh away the sin of the world." This is in keeping with the declared purpose of our Lord when He says, "For even the Son of man came not to be ministered unto, but to minister, and to give his life a ransom for many." Explicitly, he tells us that the good Shepherd lays down His life for the sheep (Jn 1:29; 10:11; Mk 10:45).

Here is the real purpose of the coming of Christ. Here is the heart of the incarnation. Christ Jesus came to deal effectively with sin, to become the atonement for sin, the liquidator of man's guilt, as well as the Conqueror and Annihilator of sin. That He did so is objectively evident in His resurrection and enthronement at the right hand of God the Father. Subjectively it is convincing in the experience of forgiveness of sin and deliverance from the power of sin of believers in Him who learn to appropriate His merits and power.

The vicarious death of Christ is difficult for the believer to deny. It is confirmed both in the message of the Bible and in personal experience. The question, however, remains: For whom did Christ die?

There has been a rift in Protestant evangelical theology. There have been advocates of limited atonement of the efficacy of the death of Christ. Others are teaching the inclusive atonement or the sufficiency of the death of Christ for all mankind. However, few if any have advocated the efficacy of the death of Christ for the Jewish people only. National particularism has never been attached to the atonement of Christ. We deal with the ideas of limited and unlimited atonement later. Here it suffices to note that, in the fundamental purpose of Christ, universality rather than national particularism breaks through. Christ purposed the salvation for all mankind.

CHRIST IN HIS POSTRESURRECTION COMMISSION

The prominence of the postresurrection commission is evident to every reader of the gospel records. The missionary thrust in it is quite pronounced. The phrases, "all nations," "all creation," "all the nations," "whosoever" and "the extremity of the earth" in the commission leave no room for particularism. Christ sent His apostles into all the world, commanding them to disciple all nations. Particularism has no place here.

CHRIST AND THE FINAL RECKONING

Paul said that God will judge the world righteously by one man, Christ (Ac 17:31). This is not Paul's speculative invention. Already Christ had said, "The Father judgeth no man, but hath committed all judgment unto the Son: that all men should honour the Son, even as they honour the Father" (Jn 5:22-23). And in a similar vein He said, "All authority is given unto me in heaven and in earth," which certainly includes universal judgment. Vividly our Lord set forth this truth in the scene of judgment when all nations shall be gathered before Him to be judged by Him and to receive their irrevocable verdict of reward or punishment (c.f. Mt 25:31-46 with Jn 5:24-29; 3:17-19). Clearly, the world is being judged and will be judged by the Son.

Again the missionary thrust rather than particularism shines through in the teaching of Christ.

CONCLUSION

Christ Jesus in His basic theological concepts and presuppositions undeniably sets forth the implicit universality of salvation and the gospel. All His major theological concepts — kingdom of God, fatherhood of God, Son of man, sin and salvation or redemption, the purpose of His life, His commission to disciple all nations and judge all nations — lift Him above His own nation, culture and religion, and place Him into race relationships and make Him the Redeemer of mankind and the world. Christ, indeed, has world significance — not because Christianity has made Him such, but because biblical Christianity incarnates Him.

It is well to remember again that these fundamental concepts are not merely theological concepts. First and foremost, they are vital, dynamic missionary ideas and ideals which Christ boldly proclaimed and deeply imbedded in the mind and conscience of His disciples. After Pentecost the Holy Spirit progressively unfolded the missionary dynamic of these ideas and fashioned the disciples into flaming, irresistible and unconquerable missionaries throughout the Roman Empire and beyond its borders. Thus the centrifugal force nurtured by the missionary ideas of Christ overcame the traditional centripetal force, and Christianity shattered the bonds of Jewish nationalism and particularism and became a true missionary movement in keeping with the racial promise of Genesis 3:15 and the idealism of the Old Testament.

THE EXPLICIT UNIVERSALITY OF CHRIST

Implicit universality is definitely substantiated by an explicit universality of Christ. We merely present an outline of this aspect as recorded in the gospels:

THE UNIVERSALITY OF CHRIST IN THE ANNOUNCEMENTS

1. By the angels — Luke 2:10-14, The joy shall be to all people, and peace shall come upon the earth and goodwill to mankind.

2. By Simeon — Luke 2:25-32, He is the Salvation of God which God has prepared before the face of all people, a light to lighten the nation and the glory of the people of Israel.

3. By John the Baptist — Luke 3:3-6; John 1:29. In his early preaching he announces that "all flesh shall see the salvation of God." And seeing Jesus coming to him, he points to Christ and proclaims Him as the "Lamb of God, which taketh away the sin of the world."

THE UNIVERSALITY OF CHRIST IN HIS MINISTRY

We refer to the following recorded incidents which relate Christ to persons outside of His own people:

John 4:1-42, the Samaritan woman and the Samaritans.

Matthew 15:21-28, the Syrophenician woman who obtained help for her demon-possessed daughter.

Matthew 8:5-13, the centurion of Capernaum whose servant was restored to him.

John 4:43-54, the courtier (nobleman) of Capernaum who effectively pleaded for the healing of his son who was at the point of death.

Mark 5:1-20, the Gadarene from whom Christ cast out a legion of demons.

Mark 7:31-37, the deaf man of Decapolis who was healed of his impediment.

Of special interest in this connection is the cleansing of the temple as recorded in John 2:13-17.

We need to remember that the temple consisted of a series of courts leading into the temple proper and to the holy place. The first court was designed for the nations, next was the court for the women, then came the court for the Israelites, and finally the inner court for the priests. Buying and selling were going on in the court of the Gentiles, depriving the people of the possibility of worship within the precincts of the temple. Yet, Mark tells what the temple was to be called: "My house shall be called of all nations the house of prayer" (11:17). Thus, by cleansing the court, Jesus provided a place for the worshiper from among the nations in keeping with the purpose of the temple. At the same time He clearly emphasized the divine order in the universal worship of the living God.

This interpretation seems to be substantiated by the quoted passage from Isaiah 56:7 (ASV) in which it is clearly stated, "My house shall be called a house of prayer for all peoples [all nations]." The indifference and callousness of Israel in relation to the religious plight of the nations, and her utter neglect and abandonment of any mission toward the nations of the world become consuming motives in the seeming violent reaction of Christ to religious ceremonialism and performances devoid of compassion for the spiritual well-being of others.

THE UNIVERSALITY OF CHRIST IN HIS TEACHING

We merely classify some leading synoptic passages which explicitly state universality and then we refer to a number of parables teaching the same truth in parabolic form.

Some explicit statements:

Matthew 5:13-16, "Ye are the salt of the earth. . . . Ye are the light of the world."

Matthew 6:10, "Thy will be done in earth."

Matthew 21:43, "The kingdom of God will be taken away from you [the Jews], and given to a nation."

Luke 13:29, 28 "And they shall come from the east, and from the west, and from the north, and from the south, and shall sit down in the kingdom of God . . . and you yourselves [the Jews] thrust out."

Mark 14:9, "Wheresoever this gospel shall be preached through-out the whole world. . . . "

Parabolic teaching:

Luke 10:29-37, the good Samaritan.

Luke 14:10-24, the great feast for which a universal invitation is extended.

Luke 15:11-24, the beautiful story of the unchanged gracious Father who deals kindly with the prodigal son (a picture of the world of the nations) as well as with the self-righteous elder son (a portrait of the Jewish nation), hoping that both will return to the house and to the Father to enjoy Him forever in blessed fellowship.

Matthew 13:36-43, the story of the wheat and the tares, with the field being neither the Jewish nation nor the Christian church, but the world.

Matthew 21:28-32, the parable of the husbandman and his two sons, which may represent the two worlds of mankind: the Jewish world and the world of the nations.

To the testimony of the synoptics we add the witness of John, where we find these marvelous statements:

Concerning the Father —

John 3:16, "God so loved the world . . . ."

John 3:17, "God sent . . . his Son . . . that the world through him might be saved."

John 3:19, "Light is come into the world."

Concerning the Son —

John 1:9, Christ is the light "which lighteth every man that cometh into the world."

John 1:29, Christ is "the Lamb of God, which taketh away the sin of the world."

John 4:42, He is "the Saviour of the world."

John 6:33, He is "the bread of God which . . . giveth life unto the world" (cf. v. 54).

John 8:12, Jesus said, "I am the light of the world" (cf. also 9:5; 12:46).

John 12:47, He came to save the world.

John 17:21, He prays for the unity of His people "that the world may believe that thou hast sent me."

Concerning the Spirit —

John 16:8, "when He is come, He will reprove [convict] the world."

Thus the world is the sphere of the operation of the Father, Son and Holy Spirit. Add to this the "cloud of witnesses," "whosoever," "any man" and "all men," and the evidence of universality is overwhelming.

With this cloud of witnesses it becomes difficult to question the fundamental thrust of the life, ministry, mind and doctrine of Christ. He is the Son of the race, the Representative and Champion of mankind, the Saviour of the world.

CHRIST'S METHOD

In spite of this implicit and explicit universality of Christ, there is an undeniable particularism in the ministry of Christ.

1. It is an obvious fact (at least according to the gospel records) that Christ conducted no extended mission to the Gentiles or on Gentile soil. His major ministry confined itself to Judea and Galilee.

2. He explicitly tells us that He was not sent but to the lost sheep of the house of Israel (Mt 15:24).

3. He specifically forbids His disciples to go beyond the confines of Israel, even as He had not been sent to the nations but to the lost sheep of Israel (Mt 10:5-6; 15:24; 10:5-6).

4. In several sayings of the gospels, Jesus speaks of the non-Jewish nations and individuals in a distinctly uncomplimentary, even disparaging, manner:

Their prayers are "vain repetitions" (Mt 6:7).

They are earthly minded and think in terms of eating, drinking, and clothing — that is, they are this-life minded (Mt 6:32).

An excommunicated brother is to be considered as a heathen man and publican — separated, unclean and unworthy (Mt 18:17).

The Syrophencian woman is compared to a dog in contrast to Israelites who are children (Mk 7:27; Mt 15:26). The diminuitive form of the translated "dog" does not eliminate the sting.

They are power-hungry and exercise authority with little wisdom and mercy (Mk 10:42).

These are facts recorded by the gospel writers, seemingly without sensing any discrepancy between the obvious universality and seeming particularism of Christ.

Have we a contradiction here? Is it one of the insoluble polarities of the Scriptures? How can the seeming paradox be resolved?

The conflict between seeming particularism and obvious universality in the life, ministry and teaching of Christ does resolve itself in the light of two considerations:

1. It must be realized that there is no real gospel message — good news — for the Gentiles before the cross and resurrection of Christ. In His cardinal and redemptive facts of incarnation — sin-bearing, death and resurrection — Christ identified Himself with mankind. In His life, culture, and earthly ministry He identified Himself with Israel as predicted in the Old Testament.

2. Concerning the life and ministry of Christ, it is well to distinguish on the one hand His sympathies, thinking, ideals, principles and plannings, and on the other hand His methodology of accomplishing His purposes. The former are unquestionably and obviously universal; the latter seems particularistic and is determined by the methodology of the Old Testament. It must be kept in mind that universality can be either centrifugal or centripetal. Centrifugal universality is in effect when a messenger of the gospel crosses frontiers and carries the good news to the people of no faith. Centripetal universality, often mistaken for particularism, operates like a magnetic force, drawing distant peoples to a central place, people or person. The latter is the methodology of the Old Testament, with Israel and the temple as the center designed to draw people to themselves and to the Lord.

In keeping with this principle, our Lord addresses Himself first to Israel in order to restore the Jews to their place, purpose and destiny. Israel was to have the opportunity to be made into a servant of the Lord in order to draw the world to the Lord and/or to be transformed from centripetalism into a centrifugal force through the dynamic of Pentecost.

It may at first seem that Christ failed in winning a hearing among His own people. Indeed, John tells us that "He came unto his own, but his own received him not" (Jn 1:11). Through its leadership the nation rejected Him and demanded His crucifixion.

However, we must not interpret this as total failure. A substantial remnant came out of the rejection. The apostles, including Paul, were all Jews; the first Christian church was a Jewish Christian church in the city of Jerusalem. Judea, Samaria and Galilee had large numbers of churches, and tens of thousands of Jews became believers (Ac 9:31; 21:20). The first missionaries to the nations were Jews — Philip to Samaria, Peter to Cornelius, some Hellenistic Jews from Cyprus and Cyrene to Antioch, and then, of course, Paul to the world.

Thus the Jews gave us the Bible, the gospel, the missionaries and the first churches. Let us always keep this in mind.

THE MIND OF CHRIST

Having established the missionary intent of Christ, we naturally ask: Where did Christ find His missionary idea? How was His mind molded into a missionary mind? Was it intuitive or scriptural? Did He learn it from the Old Testament? Was it special illumination?

It is a fact that Christ claimed to have come to fulfill the Old Testament. It was His Bible, His guide, and His stay. He used it richly; He preached it freely; He honored it humbly; He believed it firmly. The Old Testament was for Him the very Word of God written. While He was its heart and content and all Scripture pointed to Him, He was also its true Interpreter. Indeed, the Old Testament reveals Christ while He unveils it. He is both its content and interpretation. But it is also true that He found not only His major theological concepts here but also the scope of God's redemptive plan. The latter was universalistic and included the totality of mankind, not merely a nation. This is the thesis we need to establish, for it seems strange to make such a claim for the Old Testament. However, even the Old Testament does not fully disclose the secret of Christ's missionary mind and purpose.

It is evident to every reader of the gospel records that Christ lived in a unique God-consciousness and self-consciousness. He knew Himself to be the only begotten Son which is in the bosom of the Father. He walked and labored in the full consciousness of having been sent into the world, of having entered the earthly realm from a higher realm. He had come here on a very specific mission, a mission essential to the consummation of the eternal purpose of God. As a Member of the eternal Godhead, He shared in the counsels of eternity which find their ground in the nature and character of the eternal triune God.

Therefore, before we turn to a biblical survey to study the universalistic purpose of God which underlies the missionary thrust of the Bible, we need to consider briefly the nature and character of the God in whom the missionary purpose is grounded.

2

Missionary Theology and the Nature of God

"THE LAST COMMAND of Christ is not the deep and final ground of the Church's missionary duty," reasoned Robert E. Speer in his Duff Lectures of 1910:

> That duty is authoritatively stated in the words of the great commission, and it is of infinite consequence to have had it so stated by our Lord Himself. But if these particular words had never been spoken by Him, or if, having been spoken, they had not been preserved, the missionary duty of the Church would not be in the least affected. The supreme arguments for missions are not found in any specific words. It is in the very being and character of God that the deepest ground of the missionary enterprise is to be found. We cannot think of God except in terms which necessitate the missionary idea. Though words may reveal eternal missionary duties the grounds are in the very being and thought of God, in the character of Christianity, in the aim and purpose of the Christian Church, and in the nature of humanity, its unity and its need.[1]

Such theocentricity in missions is refreshing to read in the midst of present-day anthropo- cosmo- and ecclesio-centricity. Theocentric missions finds its source, dynamic and goal beyond time and space in eternity, though it does not bypass current history. Time, however, cannot originate, sustain or exhaust it.

Theocentricity in missions is well established by the apostle Paul. In the chapter in which he leads us deepest into the mystery of the eternal counsel of God as it relates to salvation, Paul thrice asserts that all is "to the praise of the glory of his grace . . . that we should be to the praise of his glory, who first trusted in Christ" (Eph 1:3-14).

In the same epistle the apostle says that the entire drama of salvation is but the unfolding of a plan in keeping with the eternal purpose of God which He purposed in Christ Jesus our Lord (Eph 3:11).

In three chapters of his epistle to the Romans, Paul argues for the great missionary program of God (chaps. 9 – 11). He concludes his majestic but difficult discourse on missions throughout the ages in these words: "O the depth of the riches both of the wisdom and knowledge of God! How unsearchable are his judgments, and his ways past finding out! For who hath known the mind of the Lord? Or who hath been his counsellor? Or who hath first given to him, and it shall be recompensed unto him again? For of him, and through him, and to him, are all things: to whom be glory for ever. Amen" (Ro 11:33-36).

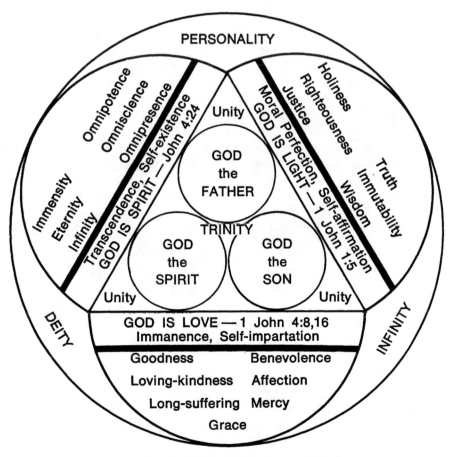

Fig. 2. The Biblical Doctrine of God

No less theocentric is the baptismal formula of our Lord. All baptism must be in the name of the Father, and of the Son, and of the Holy Spirit. No man, no church, no institution is involved in salvation. All originates and culminates in the triune God.

The theocentric emphasis may sound strange to the American ear tuned to pragmatism and to success reports from the mission fields. A rethinking of our missionary premises is therefore imperative. Not the welfare and glory of man, not the growth and expansion of the church, but the glory of God forms the highest goal of missions because the being and character of God are the deepest ground of missions "for of him, and through him, and to him, are all things: to whom be glory for ever."

In light of the above, let us inquire more closely into the God of missions as revealed in the Scriptures. Who is the God of the Bible, the God of missions? In a simple diagram (see fig. 2) I present some basic emphases of revelation of the God and Father of our Lord Jesus Christ, the God of creation, redemption and consummation.

While the definitive aspects of God's being — personality, deity, infinity, unity and trinity — have been much debated in speculative theology and religious philosophy, missionary theology is more interested in the qualitative aspects of the God of revelation — God as Spirit, God as light, and God as love (the Old Testament synonyms seem to be "the living God, the Holy One, the Lord of Hosts"). This is not the place to advance a detailed exposition of these meaningful characterizations. I merely point out a few missionary implications to establish the fact that the ultimate ground of missions rests in the very being of God.

GOD THE FATHER AS OUTGOING OR MISSIONARY

Our Lord declared at Jacob's well in Samaria that God is Spirit (Jn 4:24). Somewhat later John added through the revelation of the Holy Spirit that God is also light and love (1 Jn 1:5; 4:8, 16). Whatever else these deep and mysterious characterizations may indicate, they most certainly imply that God is an outgoing God. His inner nature is not bent upon self-containment. While the Bible asserts the "otherness" of God — the holy One — it teaches with equal emphasis that God is a God of relationships. He is the living God, not the impersonal Absolute of Aristotle or an isolated God of later Judaism.

Neither is He the neutral Brahma of Hinduism or the absentee god of Deism. He is the God and Father of our Lord Jesus Christ. He is the God of Abraham, the God of Isaac, the God of Jacob, the God of Moses, the God of Israel. He is our Father. "I am the LORD thy God, the Holy One of Israel, thy Saviour . . . the LORD, your redeemer, the Holy One . . . the creator of Israel, your King" (Is 43:3-15). Such passages can greatly be multiplied from the Old Testament as well as from the New.

God is not a God of isolation. He is not out there in outer space and silent, a spectator or neutral. He is not a withdrawn God. He may be hidden but He is not absent. He may be silent but He is not indifferent. He may not be overtly seen, but He is not uninvolved. The fact that God is Spirit, light and love eliminates the idea of the self-containment of God. He is the God of history — a God of relationships.

God is a Spirit (Jn 4:24). These weighty words were spoken by the eternal Son of God who came from the bosom of the Father to unveil God to man. No doubt these words were uttered for profoundly practical purposes and were designed to guide man in worship rather than to stimulate speculation. However, all true worship is grounded in God Himself. Thus the profoundly practical words became an unprecedented unveiling of God Himself.

The words that God is Spirit reveal Him as the absolute, underived and outgoing reality who has all the sources of existence within Himself. However, He is Spirit, He relates Himself, He seeks worshipers. He accepts worship offered in spirit and truth or in reality and honesty.

As Spirit He is not restricted by a body and confined by physical limitations. He is Spirit and, therefore, transcends all limitations. Immensity, infinity, omnipotence, omnipresence and omniscience cannot fully describe Him. He is the boundless and outgoing one. He is the God of missions.

God is light, the Bible declares (1 Jn 1:5). This metaphor is full of meaning, especially as it relates to the outgoing of God and consequently as it relates to missions.

The description "God is light" suggests that God is unapproachable, infinite, unchangeable, perfectly holy, perfectly open, perfectly inviolable, perfectly true. He is the source of all light, life, goodness, safety and joy as well as the power of transfiguration for all things. As light, He is, however, also consuming fire or severe judgment.

The positive and missionary message that is conveyed to us by the metaphor becomes evident when we keep in mind that light is diffusive, penetrating, searching, spreading itself over all space, and entering into every nook and corner. It covers the entire earth. Light is quickening and enlivening. Light makes life and action possible. It is a source of relief and gladness to those who walk in its bright and joyous rays.

Because God is light, darkness cannot hide Him; neither can it restrain Him. Indeed, He is the enemy of all darkness and evil. It is the very nature of light to banish darkness. No luminary shines unto itself; rather, it radiates its power upon the paths of others. Through its rays it relates itself to others in an unselfish and beneficial manner, illuminating all who avail themselves of it. God as light penetrates the world ("I am the light of the world," Jn 8:12) to overcome all darkness ("the light shineth in darkness," Jn 1:5), to destroy the works of the wicked one (1 Jn 3:8), and to enlighten every man who comes into the world (Jn 1:9).

The dogmatic and majestic statement that God is light bears directly and significantly upon the plan and work of redemption and consequently upon missionary theology. It implies that it is the nature of God to illumine darkened man, to shine upon his path, which most certainly leads to destruction. As man turns to the light in repentance and faith, He imparts Himself without limit and with beneficial design in order to quicken, enliven, cleanse and glorify man. The fact that God is light imparts hope and suggests that He will make some kind of provision for the salvation of fallen and darkened man in accordance with His own purpose and commensurate with His own nature. He is the outshining God; He is the God of missions.

God is love (1 Jn 4:8, 16). That fact is written into history and into the Bible. The words "God is love" are of unique significance, forming a most majestic description of the qualitative nature of God and standing unparalleled in all religious literature of the world. In vain we search for this fact in the sacred writings of the sages. The fact that God is love is disclosed only in the Bible.

Divine love is that impelling and dynamic quality in which God moves out of Himself and in which He relates Himself in all His beneficence and sufficiency to His creation. His love motivates Him eternally to communicate and to impart Himself to the object of His relationship.

Edgar Young Mullins defines love in the following words:

> [Love is] the self-imparting quality in the divine nature which leads God to seek the highest good and the most complete possession of His creatures. Love in its highest form is a relation between intelligent, moral and free beings. God's love to man seeks to awaken a responsive love of man to God. In its final form love between God and man will mean their complete and unrestrained selfgiving to each other, and the complete possession of each by the other.[2]

The Bible makes much of the fact that God is love. It is not my intention to enter into the breadth of the tremendous subject. It is sufficient that we note the following aspects:

1. Love is an outgoing, dynamic relationship. God *so loved* the world; God commendeth His love toward us. Paul describes God as the one "who loved me."

2. Love is a sacrificial, active relationship. "God so loved the world, that he gave his only begotten Son." "Hereby perceive we the love of God, because he laid down his life for us." " . . . who loved me, and gave himself for me." "God commendeth his love toward us, in that, while we were yet sinners, Christ died for us."

3. Love is a comprehensive relationship. "God so loved the world." "For God sent not his Son into the world to condemn the world; but that the world through him might be saved."

4. Love is a manifold relationship. It manifests itself according to the character, conditions and needs of its object (see chart on "The Biblical Doctrine of God" for manifestations of the love of God).

Summary: Looking back over the qualitative statements concerning the being of God — Spirit, light, love — the missionary implications are obvious. God is an outgoing God who, because He is light and love, wills the benevolence of mankind and ever seeks to impart Himself to man.

GOD THE SON AS OUTGOING OR MISSIONARY

I have already spoken of the missionary theology of our Lord

Jesus Christ. Such a theology was more than theory; it was more than
the living out of a commission. It was more than something He had
acquired from studies of the Scriptures or the needs of men. It was
not an imposition or acquisition; it was the outflow of His innermost
being. The Son shares with the Father all qualitative aspects of Deity.
He, too, is "light and love." While on the one hand He was *sent* by
the Father, it is equally true on the other hand that He *came* voluntarily into the world. Plainly He tells us: "The Son of man *came* not
to be ministered unto, but to minister, and to give his life a ransom
for many" (Mk 10:45). He further testifies that He did so voluntarily:
"Therefore doth my Father love me, because I lay down my life, that
I might take it again. No man taketh it from me, but *I lay it down of
myself*. I have power to lay it down, and I have power to take it
again. This commandment have I received of my Father" (Jn 10:17-
18).

Similarly Paul views Christ's coming as a voluntary act when he
writes, "Ye know the grace of our Lord Jesus Christ, that, though he
was rich, yet for your sakes he became poor, that ye through his
poverty might be rich" (2 Co 8:9). He "who, being in the form of
God, thought it not robbery to be equal with God; but made himself
of no reputation [emptied Himself], and took upon him the form of
a servant, and was made in the likeness of men: and being found in
fashion as a man, he humbled himself, and became obedient unto
death, even the death of the cross" (Phil 2:6-8).

With the Father, the Son shared the counsel, the will and purpose
of redemption. His very name "Jesus" implies that He is a Saviour.
His sevenfold "I am" identifies Him unmistakably with the Jehovah of
the Old Testament, the Redeemer of Israel. Salvation flows from His
person as well as from His office and work. His saviorhood is fully
and perfectly manifested and consummated in the incarnation-cross-
resurrection event.

The Centrality of the Incarnation-Cross-Resurrection Event

"According to the New Testament, the coming of Christ, his dying
and rising and ascension, is the decisive moment in God's plan of
salvation," writes Bishop Lesslie Newbigin.[3]

The incarnation-cross-resurrection event is crucial to the interpretation of history. It is focal in biblical revelation. Here the Old and

New Testaments merge and divide. This event is central to the divine history of salvation (*Heilsgeschichte*). Here promise exchanges for fulfillment — shadow gives way to reality — sin is judged — forgiveness is offered. Here wrath is propitiated, grace is enthroned, death is defeated, and life and immortality come to light.

At this point Satan received his mortal wound so that the final, complete and glorious victory of righteousness is assured. At this event the kingdom of darkness received its deathblow and the kingdom of His dear Son its triumph. The incarnation-cross-resurrection event is the cosmic divide that separates darkness from light, the temporal from the eternal, the carnal from the spiritual, death from immortality, perdition from life, condemnation from presence, and hell from heaven.

The incarnation-cross-resurrection event is the fountain and foundation of the salvation of God, the only hope for mankind. It is the pinnacle of Christ's self-giving love for mankind.

It is a spectacle to the world, a stumbling block to the Jews, foolishness to the Greeks, a rock of offense to the disobedient, and a mystery to the angels. It is the manifestation of the holiness and righteousness of God in relation to sin, and the language of the love of God in relation to the guilt and lostness of the sinner.

In the incarnation-cross-resurrection event, holiness, righteousness and love blend in beautiful harmony for the glory of God and the welfare of man, bringing about salvation and making propitiation, reconciliation, redemption, restoration and glorification divine realities and assuring their eventual realization.

Salvation is a reality because God willed it. He designed it and procured it. He actualizes it because He is the eternally outgoing God of missions.

Salvation began with God's uninvited visit with Adam and Eve in the Garden of Eden. There the protevangelium was announced (Gen 3:15). From here it blossomed forth until it concretized on Calvary's cross. Thus God miraculously, dramatically and savingly entered history in Christ Jesus. God sent forth His Son, made of a woman, made under law. Christ Jesus, the second Person of the triune God, became the great Apostle of God, the Prophet, Priest and King. He was, indeed, the sent one and the coming one.

The deity-humanity mystery is a great mystery; nevertheless, it is a blessed reality. In the incarnation, eternity invaded time and space, and Deity became humanity. God was in Christ. Thus the actualization of eternal salvation became a momentous event in time and space.

It is not my intention to enter into a full-length presentation of the salvation of God. However, I want to emphasize certain principles which underlie the biblical view of salvation. They formulate a philosophy of salvation and constitute the unifying substructure of the biblical doctrine of salvation. *As such, they demonstrate convincingly the missionary character of Christianity and put the cross-resurrection event at the heart of all missionary endeavor.* At the same time they demonstrate to all that the incarnation-cross-resurrection event is God's crucial missionary act.

THE INCARNATION-CROSS-RESURRECTION EVENT AND SALVATION

According to the eternal purpose of God, Jesus Christ entered history, was born of the virgin Mary, took on true humanity, and as the true God-man became the Saviour of mankind. According to the Scriptures, He was made sin for us who knew no sin, was made of God unto us wisdom, and righteousness, and sanctification, and redemption. In obedience "He emptied himself . . . and became obedient unto death, even the death of the cross." His sinless, perfect life, vicarious death, victorious bodily resurrection and glorious exaltation at the right hand of God procured salvation for all mankind. Thus stands the eternal salvation of God in Christ, having been neither foreseen nor sought by man. It is of God alone as it is also in Christ and by the Holy Spirit alone. Our glorying must be in God and not in man.

The salvation of God is rooted in eternity and actualized in time. Eternity with its spiritual glory, fullness and blessings is invading time and humanity. Salvation for man is here now. God in Christ Jesus and through the Holy Spirit enters human life. He is entering me. Salvation is not merely an objective reality to be wondered at, a theological dictum to be debated about, a philosophical theory to be speculated about — not even merely a marvelous subject to be preached about. It is a divine reality entering the human being to transform his fundamental disposition, cleanse him from sin and unrighteousness, redeem him from bondage and corruption, impart to him the nature of God, recreate in him the image of Christ, make him a child of God, a member of the household of God, and qualify him through the gift of the Holy Spirit to live a life of true discipleship in the midst of a world almost destitute of the consciousness of God and eternity.

Without apology I confess that I find no difficulty in the Pauline principle that all is of grace and grace is for all, that grace has bound us up in Christ, that grace is moral in nature and purpose and transforming in experience and effect. We thus lay down the following basic principles:

Salvation is essentially divine in origin.
Salvation is essentially Christocentric.
Salvation is essentially cross-resurrection related.
Salvation is essentially of grace.
Salvation is essentially an organic unit.
Salvation is essentially moral in content and purpose.
Salvation is essentially by faith.
Salvation is intentionally universal.
Salvation is potentially cosmic.

SALVATION IS ESSENTIALLY DIVINE IN ORIGIN

The Bible is most explicit in demonstration and doctrine that salvation originates with God, and finds its source and initiative in God. Thus God entered into the Garden of Eden without having been invited or requested after man had deprived himself of divine fellowship and depraved himself by yielding to the solicitations of Satan to enter the path of sin and estrangement from God. God took the initiative. Salvation and renewal of fellowship originated with Him.

We see the same principle operating in the life and history of Abraham and later in Israel in her redemption from Egypt. The initiative lay with God. Salvation originated in the heart and counsel of God and was realized by the mighty arm of God.

The principle is uniquely demonstrated by the coming of Christ into this world. No invitation was extended to heaven to send a redeemer. In fact, John tells us that "He was in the world, and the world was made through him, yet the world knew him not. He came to his own home, and his own people received him not" (Jn 1:10-11, RSV). To the contrary, we read that "God so loved the world, that he gave his only begotten Son" (Jn 3:16). Again, "But God shows his love for us in that while we were yet sinners Christ died for us" (Ro 5:8, RSV). Such New Testament statements could be greatly multiplied.

In the Old Testament, God *is* known as the "God of salvation." Humanism is an extrabiblical philosophy which finds no place in revelation. The declarations are numerous and specific and the demonstrations are convincing that the salvation of man originates with God and never with man. Thus all honor goes to God. He is the God of our salvation.

SALVATION IS ESSENTIALLY CHRISTOCENTRIC

Christocentricity is more than a principle of Bible interpretation. It is just as certainly related to the experience of salvation. Salvation is not a detached gift of God in some gracious and miraculous way bestowed upon man. Salvation is Christ, and to experience salvation is to experience Christ. Salvation is person-centered. It is Christ-identification. It is not the experience of *something*, but rather, the experience of *Someone*. The Bible does not teach that Christ *has* salvation and dispenses it like a benevolent master giving gifts to his servants who obey him. Christ *is* our salvation and gives Himself to us as our salvation. Salvation is not a bundle of costly gifts which the Lord distributes freely and from which we select whatever we like or find. It is rather the experience of a Person in whom all the fullness of the Godhead dwells. Thus in Christ I am becoming the recipient of the fullness of God. *He* is our life; *He* is our strength; *He* is our peace; *He* is our joy; *He* is our wisdom, righteousness, sanctification and redemption. Jesus Christ Himself is the content of our salvation. All that He is became mine the moment I received Him in simple faith. "But as many as received him, to them gave he power to become the sons of God." And again: "He that hath the Son hath life; and he that hath not the Son of God hath not life." "He that spared not his own Son, but delivered him up for us all, how shall he not with him also freely give us all things?" (Jn 1:12; 1 Jn 5:12; Ro 8:32).

Christianity is not primarily a philosophy of religion, a way of life, or a set of beliefs and practices. It is a Person, and the experience of salvation is the experience of the person of our Lord and Saviour Jesus Christ — not a gift *from* Him, or a part *of* Him. He can neither be divided in Himself nor separated from His salvation.

The realization of this central truth of Christianity is most significant to sound biblical doctrine and to a true Christian life. It will save us from erroneous teaching. It will make our lives Christ-related,

Christ-identified, Christ-dependent, Christ-centered, Christ-honoring. He will become all and in all in our experience and in our lives.

The mystery of the doctrine of our identification with Christ by faith that leads to experience has been sadly neglected in Christendom. The result is an anemic Christianity that has neither life, holiness nor purpose.

SALVATION IS ESSENTIALLY CROSS-RESURRECTION RELATED

Having emphasized the Christocentricity of biblical salvation, we find ourselves compelled to direct our thoughts to a specific event in the life and ministry of Christ. Modern theology since the days of Friedrich D. E. Schleiermacher (1768-1843) has made much of Christocentricity. However, to a large extent, current theological thinking has misplaced the accent. The Bible places the cross and resurrection of Christ in the very center of its Christocentricity at no expense to the life and teaching of Christ. The earnest Bible student does not find it difficult to see the cross-resurrection centeredness of salvation. In eternity's ages the cross was a reality in the counsel of God (1 Pe 1:20; Rev 13:8; Eph 1:4; 3:11) and constituted the basis of all of God's dealings with sinful man (Ro 3:25). This must be kept firmly in mind if a basis of absolute justice and unity is to be seen in the salvation of God. The Old Testament's forecast of the cross was at the same time the shadow of an eternal reality in the counsel of God. Calvary was the historical actualization of that which had taken place in the counsel of God before the ages began. Thus the cross, never the law or the animal sacrifices, was the real foundation of man's salvation in the old economy as well as in the new dispensation.

The cross-resurrection centrality is well established in the Scriptures by the multitude of sacrifices and the numerous prophecies in the Old Testament. The description of the cross-resurrection event in the four gospels is another evidence of this fact. It has been stated that "if all the three and a half years of His public ministry had been written out as fully as the last three days, we would have a Life of Christ of some 8,400 pages. Manifestly, the death and resurrection of our Lord were esteemed of supreme importance by the Holy Spirit." Again, "Torrey claims that the death of Christ is mentioned directly in the New Testament more than 175 times."

Christ no doubt considered the cross as central in His ministry and as the supreme purpose of His incarnation (Mk 10:45). Paul made it the subject of his preaching and glorying. The saints on the eternal shores deem it a worthy theme for their united praises. The Lamb remains the focus upon the new earth and in the new heaven. No one of the New Testament writers neglects to uphold it, with the exception of James, whose practical exhortations are built upon it (Ja 5:7-11).

Such, then, is the centrality of the cross-resurrection event in revelational history and salvation history. It remains forever the heart of the Christian gospel.

The cross is God's starting point, the foundation of all his dealings with man in guilt and sin. To disassociate Christ from the cross results in religious idealism or in a Christ cult. To disassociate the cross from the person of Christ results in dead orthodoxy and lifeless religion. It is in the Christ who lived, died and rose again that God relates Himself savingly to mankind. The cross precedes all of God's dealings with man. This we must keep firmly in mind. Every aspect of salvation, including that of election, must be related to the cross-resurrection event. Salvation is essentially cross-resurrection related.

SALVATION IS ESSENTIALLY ALL OF GRACE

Salvation is all of grace. The Bible has no illusions about the sinfulness of man, his natural and total depravity, and his darkened, enslaved and alienated condition; it firmly holds to the doctrine of original sin and guilt and the lostness of man. The Bible ascribes all honor and glory to the God of all mercy who purposed salvation, to the Lamb that was slain to procure salvation, and to the Holy Spirit who graciously operates upon the hearts of men to apply salvation and to lead man into a conscious appropriation and realization of salvation. The Bible sets itself drastically against all humanism and synergism and firmly upholds the doctrine of the sovereign grace of God in Christ Jesus. Humbly and gladly we confess that salvation from start to finish is of God, that it is a gracious gift of God, and that all glory must go to God. "For by grace are ye saved through faith; and that not of yourselves: it is the gift of God: not of works, lest any man should boast" (Eph 2:8-9).

SALVATION IS ESSENTIALLY AN ORGANIC UNIT

Since Christ is the source as well as content of man's salvation, the experience of salvation is essentially an organic unit and potentially bestows Christ in His fullness upon the believer. In Christ we have election, calling, wisdom, righteousness, sanctification and redemption. Only for logical and theological reasons and purposes can a distinction be made in the various aspects and designations of the salvation experience such as conversion, regeneration, justification, adoption, union with Christ and such other designations of the initial experience of salvation as we may adopt. In reality and actual experience, however, they can neither be separated nor chronologically tabulated. They are one great miraculous experience constituting the individual a child of God.

The compound Christian experience which constitutes the believer a child of God can be compared to a wheel. A wheel is a unit, yet it is constituted out of a central hub, a number of spokes, and rim. The hub may be made to represent the experience itself; the spokes may be compared to the various implications of the experience — conversion, regeneration, justification, adoption, union with Christ, etc. It is evident that when the hub begins to turn, all spokes turn at the same time. There is neither logical nor chronological priority in the moving of the spokes, so there is neither logical nor chronological order in the various aspects of the Christian experience. It is futile to argue that the legal precedes the vital or vice versa.

The initial salvation experience and all of salvation from start to finish are essentially an organic unit. Sanctification, separation, preservation, discipleship and glorification also are potentially bestowed in Christ upon the believer in the acceptance of Christ. As time progresses these essential qualities are progressively manifested. Christ cannot be divided or received in stages although the subjective, experiential and conscious appropriation by faith of the Christ in us may — and, in most individuals, does — take place by degrees in time. This is growth in grace, growth in Christ, true Christian progress, the realization of our potential salvation. This is what Peter expounds when he writes: "And beside this, giving all diligence, add [supplement, develop] to your faith virtue; and to virtue knowledge; and to knowledge temperance; and to temperance patience; and to patience godliness; and to godliness brotherly kindness; and to brotherly kindness charity" (2 Pe 1:5-7).

For study purposes and in keeping with experience we may subdivide the essential organic unit into three major stages and consider salvation in the following order, keeping in mind, however, that each subdivision is but a unit in the larger whole:

Salvation in the counsel of God:
 the biblical doctrine of election
Salvation as the initial bestowment:
 the biblical doctrine of calling, conversion, regeneration, justification, union with Christ, adoption
Salvation as progressive life:
 the biblical doctrine of sanctification, separation, preservation, discipleship, glorification

Essentially all these blessings are found in Christ. Potentially they have been bestowed upon every believer the moment he received Christ. In order that they become real in life, however, they must be recognized as divine realities and consciously appropriated by faith. Thus, while the *bestowment* was complete in Him, the *realization* by faith is progressive and continuous through life. To grasp this biblical view of salvation will aid greatly in our ministry to "make disciples."

SALVATION IS ESSENTIALLY MORAL IN CONTENT AND PURPOSE

The marvelous grace of God is not merely free grace but, like Christ Himself, it is *divine, moral* grace. It is the *grace of God* partaking in holiness and love as God is light and love. It is moral in nature as well as in its approach to man. It neither forces itself upon man nor exists without moral content and purpose.

Without extensively entering into the various theological and philosophical implications of the doctrine of election and predestination, I prefer to hold to a moderate position — that the source of all salvation is in God, yet that God deals with man as a responsible and moral agent, causing and enabling him to voluntarily respond to the grace of God and thus consciously, voluntarily and responsibly experience the salvation of God.

The grace of God thus received by faith enlightens man's mind, redirects man's will, transforms and revitalizes man's moral nature, imparts the nature of God and eternal life, and gives him a moral purpose — the purpose of God. Man becomes identified with Christ not merely for the rescue of his soul but also in the purpose of God, which purpose is summarily expressed by Paul, urging that we might "be conformed to the image of his Son, that he might be the firstborn among many brethren" (Ro 8:29). This of course implies true Christian discipleship and a life according to the missionary purpose of God.

SALVATION IS ESSENTIALLY BY FAITH

The Bible is a book of faith — faith which is the human response to the grace of God. By faith we understand and experience the salvation of God.

The significance of the biblical doctrine of faith is difficult to overstate. Fundamental and consistent throughout the Bible, its footprints can be discovered on every page of the divine record. Faith, the distinctive mark of all great Bible characters, begins where divine grace begins to manifest itself to man. In Christian experience it is the response of the human soul to God's gracious manifestations and operations. Basic to all faith is God's gracious relationship to man, making Himself known, "for whoever would draw near to God must believe that he exists and that he rewards those who [diligently] seek him" (Heb 11:6, RSV).

It must be emphasized that faith is more than belief, mental assent or mere conformity to certain dogmas. Faith is not the work of the human will, a creation of the human mind, or a result of human experience. It is a dynamic, all-inclusive personal response to the grace of God revealed in Christ Jesus and made possible by the gracious application of the dynamic, living Word of God by the Holy Spirit. In the words of Paul, "Faith cometh by hearing, and hearing by the word of God" (Ro 10:17).

Faith, the subjective aspect of man's relationship to God, divides all of mankind in two distinct classes — the believers and unbelievers. This may seem oversimplified, yet it is the distinction within and division of mankind on the deepest level. The believers in Christ Jesus are savingly related to God, and the unbelievers are not so related. Thus the unbelievers are still on the path that leads deeper and deeper in the way of separation from God. The end of the latter path is eternal separation from the presence of God.

Faith, according to the Bible, is not merely a mental attitude.

It is a relationship between a subject and an object. Saving faith is always a relationship between man and the God-man, Jesus Christ, who in the incarnation-death-resurrection event procured salvation for mankind. Faith is never blind, unrelated to a mere attitude. It is the anchor of the soul that anchors in the Son of God.

SALVATION IS POTENTIALLY UNIVERSAL

Pointing to Christ, John exclaimed, "Behold the Lamb of God, which beareth the sin of the world" (Jn 1:29, ASV marg.). Three terms here are of tremendous significance: *beareth, sin, Lamb of God.* They point to the sufficiency, efficiency and scope of the sacrifice on Calvary.

Beareth. John tells us that Christ *bears* the sin of total mankind. No theological speculations must be permitted to cloud this perspective and to narrow that scope. Christ took upon Himself the sin of the world. No doubt this was in direct fulfillment of the great pronouncement of God in the protevangelium to the human race in Genesis 3:15. Not since then had a direct promise of a world sacrifice been made. Thus, only as Christ became the Lamb of God to bear the sin of the entire race could Genesis 3:15 be fulfilled.

Paul was led by the Spirit of God to write words of similar import when he said, "God was in Christ, reconciling the world unto himself" (2 Co 5:19). Similarly, John emphasized, "We have an advocate with the Father, Jesus Christ the righteous: and he is the propitiation for our sins: and not for our's only, but also for the sins of the whole world" (1 Jn 2:1-2). The writer to the Hebrews emphasized the same fact when he wrote "that He [Christ] by the grace of God should taste death for every man" (2:9). Indeed, "the LORD hath laid on him the iniquity of us all" (Is 53:6). Therefore, Paul declares, "For this is good and acceptable in the sight of God our Saviour; who will have all men to be saved, and come unto the knowledge of the truth" (1 Ti 2:3-4). In plain words the New Testament teaches that Christ died for all men. In Christ, God has provided a potential salvation for all mankind and for every man. The scope of the atoning death of Christ is clear and emphatic: Christ died for the ungodly — without exception (Ro 5:6).

Sin. There is, however, a second and most profound emphasis in John 1:29. Christ, the Lamb of God, bears the *sin* of the world. It is noteworthy that the word "sin" is in the singular. Christ did not only atone for the guilt of *sins;* He dealt effectively with *sin,* the root and the principle of sin. Thus, He who knew no sin was made sin for us. The sinless one was made sin for mankind. Here is more than mere mathematical substitution. We shall never fully fathom the depth of this passage. It leads us into the mystery of Christ's identification and encounter not only with the cumulative sins of mankind in their guilt and filth but with the sin-death principle itself. In order to do this effectively and triumphantly, Christ had to identify with sin itself and enter the very chamber of death in order to defeat death. Thus He destroyed the works of the devil (1 Jn 3:8). Through death He destroyed "him that had the power of death, that is, the devil" (Heb 2:14). Only so could He become the Saviour from sin, fear and death.

The sin-death principle is one. It constitutes a unit which pervades all of mankind, binding the human race together in a common bondage and guilt. Thus we are all sinners. Because of this, death passed upon all men, for all have sinned. This is the depressing reality. The good news, however, is that Christ's counteroffensive in death overcame the sin-death principle and set mankind potentially free. "Therefore as by the offence of one judgment came upon all men to condemnation; even so by the righteousness of one the free gift came upon all men unto justification of life" (Ro 5:18). Thus potentially the guilt is liquidated, the filth is cleansed away, the power is broken, the sin-death principle is destroyed, and Satan himself is defeated.

Lamb of God. Turning back to John 1:29, we note a third emphasis. John speaks of Christ as the Lamb of God. A sacrificial Lamb is provided by God Himself in the person of the Son of God. This is a fact of tremendous consequence. Divine salvation is not provided according to need that can be measured, for sin is not the measure of redemption. Instead, divine salvation is commensurate with the sacrifice provided. A divine and infinite sacrifice procures a divine and infinite salvation, infinite in terms of quality and duration but also infinite in terms of potential as far as man and the universe are concerned (cf. Ro 8:19-21; Col 1:9, 20; Rev 21:22). The height and depth, the breadth and length of divine salvation can be measured by divine measures alone. Thus we are granted a salvation "according to his riches in glory."

This fact alone establishes the total sufficiency of the salvation of

God for all of mankind and for all ages. Thus it is known as an "eternal redemption" (Heb 9:12) providing an "eternal inheritance" (9:15). The sacrifice of the Lamb of God is as *sufficient* as the sin of Adam was *efficient* in infecting and affecting all of mankind. This is the argument of Paul in Romans 5:12-21. His "much more" is significant, and his "grace did much more abound" is conclusive. Therefore his argument is succinctly stated in conclusion: "Therefore as by the offence of one judgment came upon all men unto condemnation; even so by the righteousness of one the free gift came upon all men unto justification of life" (Ro 5:18).

The greatness of the sacrifice, however, also assures its finality. This is the strong and scriptural polemic of the book of Hebrews. The "once for all" in this book is conclusive. Never again will another sacrifice be necessary; neither will another sacrifice be accepted. The finality is absolute in terms of time and space (cf. Heb 7:27; 9:12, 26-28; 10: 2, 10).

An eternal salvation has been provided with sufficient potential to save all that is salvable on divinely ordained terms. The salvation available is commensuate with Him who provided it for mankind. (I am well acquainted with the theory of limited atonement, and I reply to it in chap. 7 on the gospel of God.)

SALVATION IS POTENTIALLY COSMIC

That creation is not in a redeemed state is evident from the fact that any good which is to come from it must be evoked by man's hard toil. It is further evident from the "natural evil" which this cosmos experiences. We are all familiar with the devastations resulting from such upheavals as earthquakes, floods, typhoons, tornadoes, volcanic eruptions, and other phenomena. The earth is filled with countless fossils buried in the processes of such disruptions. Again, we note the preying propensity in the animal world and the destructions wrought by insect invasions. Nature seems to be against itself and against man.

We naturally ask why. Whence this natural evil in a world that was "good" when it came from the hand of the Creator? Is the natural evil the result of incompleted evolution which this universe experiences on the way to maturity, or is it the result of sin and thus a curse which has come upon nature in the course of history?

The Bible is specific in relating all evil to sin. Without entering into a discussion of the "gap theory," which Genesis 1:2 may be implying, Genesis 3 makes it emphatic that man's fall also involved the "fall of the earth." The curse upon man extends to the earth he inhabits.

This becomes a basic premise throughout the entire Bible. It is in the light of this awful consequence of sin that Isaiah anticipates "new heavens and a new earth" (Is 65:17). Our Lord speaks of the "regeneration" when the Son of man shall sit on the throne of His glory (Mt 19:28).

Romans 8 is a classic presentation of this matter. Paul, by inspiration of the Holy Spirit, gives a spiritual interpretation of the natural evil in this cosmos with its woes and hopes. He teaches that creation is subjected to vanity by losing its original glory, goal and purpose; that such subjection has not occurred because of some inherent flaw in creation but because of an act of God; that creation today is in a state of imperfection and incompletion, and because of this it is groaning and travailing in eruptions and convulsions; that creation is waiting hopefully for the manifestation of the sons of God to experience its liberty and salvation.

In a beatific vision John saw the completion of these anticipations and set them forth in Revelation 21 — 22. Here are the new heaven, the new earth, the New Jerusalem, paradise restored.

However, at the center of this restored cosmos is the Lamb. As such, Christ is mentioned no less than seven times in these two chapters (21:9, 14, 22, 23, 27; 22:1, 3), or a total of twenty-eight times in the book as the one who makes all things new. This in itself tells us that the eventual cosmic renewal is intimately related to the Lamb of God who bears the sin of the cosmos. It tells us that salvation is at least coextensive with creation. The dictum stands confirmed that salvation is commensurate with Him who procures it. This is definitely the meaning of Colossians 1:20. Paul is granted here a view of cosmic salvation which includes the reconciliation of the total creation. A similar thought is expressed by the same apostle in Ephesians 1:10. In the latter passage Paul sees not so much creation's salvation as its consummation.

A grave fallacy is often read into these majestic passages announcing cosmic salvation. It is asserted that such comprehensive salvation must include Satan, his angelic followers, and eventually all mankind.

Such, however, is not the teaching of the prophets or of the apostles. They see Satan, his angelic cohorts, and his unbelieving followers perishing in the lake of fire burning from eternity with brimstone (Rev 19:20; 20:10, 15), away from the presence of God (2 Th 1:8-9).

The fact of the cosmic dimensions of salvation, however, is clear. Eventually salvation will be victorious and its triumph complete. The Word assures us that the time will come when the words will become reality as He says, "Behold, I make all things new" (Rev 21:5) and "when he [Christ] shall have delivered up the kingdom to God, even the Father; when he shall have put down all rule and all authority and power. And when all things shall be subdued unto him, then shall the Son also himself be subject unto him that put all things under him, that God may be all in all" (1 Co 15:24, 28). Only thus is the salvation of God commensuate with Him who procured it and who assured it!

The basic structure and philosophy of salvation reveal the outgoing nature of the triune God and the missionary intent of the cross-resurrection event. There is nothing humanistic or particularistic about it. Neither are there limitations imposed upon it which would make it impossible for all to participate in it. Salvation reveals the triune God outgoing in judgment upon sin and in redemption of mankind. It is God in benevolent operation and utmost sacrifice motivated by pure love in behalf of His creation. It manifests the nature of God in its deepest levels. Indeed, God is the God of salvation as well as the God of creation. Salvation is *of* Him because He is what He is. It is the eternal "I am" in operation for mankind. Because He is the "I am," He sent His only begotten Son that the world through Him might be saved. This is the language of salvation.

GOD, THE HOLY SPIRIT AS OUTGOING OR MISSIONARY

The Holy Spirit is the presence of God in the world. He is God outgoing as a Member of the Trinity. Sharing with the Father and the Son the qualitative aspects of personality, deity and infinity, He, too, is "light and love." Yet seldom is the doctrine of the Holy Spirit directly related to world missions, although this seems to be the major thrust of the Spirit's operation according to the Scriptures. The great book by Harry Boer, *Pentecost and Missions,* is therefore not only welcome but much needed. It brings some balance into the subject, though the book is almost totally disregarded by theologians today.

The two main *redemptive* outgoings of the Godhead are the incarnation of our Lord Jesus Christ and Pentecost, the descending of the Holy Spirit.

There are, however, a pre-Pentecost ministry and an extra-Pentecost ministry of the Holy Spirit. The pre-Pentecost ministry is fully exposed in the Old Testament and in the gospels, while the extra-Pentecost ministry particularly relates to world missions. We may speak of it as the general or universal ministry of the Holy Spirit, keeping in mind that the Holy Spirit is the presence of God and is omnipresent. As such He is operative in the world of mankind.

We must therefore distinguish not only between pre-Pentecost and post-Pentecost but also between the general cosmic and humanitarian ministries of the Holy Spirit and the soteriological ministries. The general ministries are immediate and are due to the omnipresence of the Holy Spirit as God who is light and love and therefore outgoing. The soteriological ministries are mediate, Word-related, and are experienced through the communication and acceptance of the gospel of God.

The failure to make this distinction underlies the present-day confusion between sacred and secular or *Heilsgeschichte* and world history. It is also the main reason for the present mixup of revelational-soteriological religion as recorded in the Bible and the ethnic-cultural religions of the world. The latter are a combination of formulations of man's search for rationality and reality, intuitive insights, expressions of religious needs and aspirations, and at the same time the making of a cloak of escapism from guilt and future judgment which man's conscience demands.

It is therefore imperative that we distinguish between the general humanitarian operations of the Holy Spirit which are worldwide and the unique soteriological functions of the Holy Spirit which are limited and operative through the communication and acceptance of the gospel of God. The former are sovereign and immediate and are often thought of as the providential dealings of God. They concern themselves principally with the general welfare of mankind and the preservation of man in a salvable condition. Thus they are of utmost significance.

In this section we consider only the general humanitarian ministries of the Holy Spirit as they directly relate to world missions. The soteriological operations are studied later.

THE HOLY SPIRIT IN HIS WORLD OPERATIONS

In the fourfold portrait of the Lord Jesus Christ offered by the four gospels, John presents a picture of the cosmic Christ. We have seen Christ in His cosmic relations which, of course, include all of mankind. In cosmic, as in divine relationships, we are not able to draw clear and precise lines, for they escape our limited vision and darkened understanding. However, the cosmic aspects are strongly present in this gospel.

John also presents to us a fourfold operation in the world which can be experienced only in the realm of the Holy Spirit. Four specific expressions are recorded in the gospel of John: 1:9; 6:45; 12:32; 16:7-8. These are four universalistic passages which are more overlooked than expounded, with the exception of the last one. No doubt they speak of verities which can be understood only in the sweep of the entire Scriptures. They present to us the positive approach of God in prevenient grace to mankind preserving man in a salvable condition.

The plight of man in his fallen condition is pathetic. His maimed, paralyzed, blighted, darkened, blinded, enslaved, fearing, dreading, hating, fleeing, scheming, and plotting condition and attitude make man the most miserable and the most dangerous of all creatures. This is why only man devises schemes of crime and conducts an underground mafia; this is why only man lives in class and racial strife and hatred; this is why only man becomes an alcoholic with all the miseries that follow; this is why only man produces dope fiends and drug addicts; this is why only man commits the most cruel and premeditated crimes; this is why only man operates a war machine to the horror of all intelligence and the woe of all mankind. Paul amplifies this list in Romans 1:18-32.

It cannot be said that mankind desires these conditions and phenomena. Though man is mystified and horrified by them, he presses on unchanged, as though driven by some uncontrollable force into an unknown and disastrous destiny. Man is a creation of God in rebellion against his Maker, fallen into the abyss of sin and destruction.

At times it seems that man could not sink much lower. Such

conclusion, however, is the result of a shallow view of sin in its utter wickedness. Society could be incalculably worse.

Present-day evil is but an outflow of the mutilated, defaced, marred, distorted, misdirected, defiled and captivated image of God in man. Yes, even after the fall, man still is man; he is neither a beast nor a demon. He is man — not ideal man or as man should be — but still human and still created in the image of God.

It is my conviction that the fall, though horrible in its historical and eternal consequences, was a disappointment for Satan. It had not accomplished all that the fall was intended to accomplish. Man had remained man and, as such, a salvable creature. The depth of the fall had not reached the core of the human being. It did not obliterate the image of God.

Often "total depravity" has been presented as though it included the total destruction of the image of God. Such an interpretation, however, is not scriptural. Total depravity affects man's total being, including his reason, and perverts all his thoughts and ways, including his religion. But the fall did not totally obliterate the image of God in man, for man would then have ceased to be man. Had this actually taken place, man would be beyond all hope, help and salvation. It is the "remnants" of the image of God in man after the fall which are our hope, from the human point of view.

Man left the presence of God estranged but with an awareness of God. This is manifesting itself in man's flight from and search for God. Man left Eden with a deep sense of sin, guilt and defilement, a sense which has become an abiding awareness of "wrongness" and guilt manifesting itself in fear and dread. Man left the garden with death and decay operating in him, yet with a promise of salvation which aroused a yearning that has never left him. This is his reach upward. Man, who left his erstwhile abode with the judgment of God upon him, is aware of a judgment to come. In consequence he devises systems of philosophy to justify himself or a religious cloak to cover himself. *Der Mensch im Widerspruch* (man in conflict and contradiction) is a terrible, yet hopeful, reality.

All these elements are living issues in the human soul and are traceable in all religions. They refuse systemalization and pacification. They are spontaneous, sporadic and spasmodic. They are realities in the life of mankind.

Thus man was not a totally destitute, blackened and dead (in the completed sense of the word rather than a present process) being when he left the presence of God. There was total depravity but not total destitution and deprivation.

It is my impression from the total sweep of the Scriptures that in the "conflict of the ages" Satan is not interested in merely heaping sin upon sin and thus making sin abound against grace. He is not concerned only in seeing his kingdom triumph over the kingdom of "His dear Son." He is primarily absorbed in bringing about an inner disruption in man which would push man over the brink of salvability. He aims at destroying in man the last vestiges of his God-awareness and sin-awareness, his salvation yearning, and his dread in life, darkness, and death which relates to judgment. This is the supreme aspiration of Satan. Toward this end he marshals all his tactics, for here is his supreme mission.

It must not be imagined that the so-called dark sins and deep moral degradation are man's major enemies and Satan's major tactics. His subtle attacks through human philosophy, art and religion are much more powerful and much more successful ways of misdirecting and captivating man. In a careful analysis of the present-day dangers of man, D. R. Davies speaks of "the sin of our age." His second chapter in the book *The Sin of Our Age* is an analysis of "The Root Sin of Western Civilization." Effectively he traces the course of Western philosophy from Renaissance and concludes:

> Here, then, is the radical sin of Western civilization. It is the great sin, the titanic, Promethean sin. It is the sin of believing and behaving as though man were an end in himself; as though humanity existed in its own right and for the sole purpose of its own glory and power. Here is the spring from which have risen the horrors that have descended upon our hapless civilization. The precious right and sanctities which are always imperilled in a world of sinful men and women are perishing in the hands of an omnipotent humanity. "They that forget God shall go down into destruction," says a biblical text. The twentieth century offers a bloodstained commentary on it. From this evil root — the deification of man — have issued three terrible consequences: (1) the effectual abolition of otherworldliness — the imprisonment of man in mere time and space; (2) the dissolution of spirit and the domina-

tion of matter; (3) the degradation of man, the transformation of the individual into mass man. These three evils, which are the necessary consequences of making man the center of life and thought, in their combined and total effect are threatening mankind with an unprecedented peril — which is nothing less than the de-humanizing of humanity.[4]

Should Satan actually succeed in his demonic pursuit, man would be something else than human and man would reach the stage of unsavableness. Satan's victory in the second round would be complete. Will he succeed? He would have more than a fair chance were it not for the gracious world operation of the Holy Spirit. In the final end it is a match between the Holy Spirit who operates as the divine Paraclete in keeping with the original and creative purpose of God, and Satan who seeks to thwart and destroy that purpose.

A closer study of the four passages in John's gospel referred to above and the existential condition of man as he left the presence of God and the Garden of Eden will soon show the relationship of the fatal attempts of Satan and the gracious operations of the Holy Spirit according to the passages from John's gospel.

It is not my intention to exegete the four passages in detail. I am familiar with the difficulties and the differences of opinions and convictions that have been advanced as to their meaning. I am interested in the factual rather than the theological and speculative.

From John 1:9, I deduce that the triune God does not permit man to lapse into total blackness and darkness, nor does He allow the God-awareness to be erased completely from the soul of man; from John 16:7-8, I learn that infinite and prevenient grace does not allow mankind to sink to a level where the sin- and guilt-awareness would become totally extinct or diminished to the extent that it could not be revived again; from John 12:32, I gather that the Lord in grace and mercy does not permit mankind to deceive itself to the degree that salvation yearning either becomes completely satisfied by false religious practices or the soul of man becomes so degraded that salvation yearning cannot be rekindled by the preaching of the gospel of Jesus Christ; from John 6:45, I conclude that man remains in a searching condition and mood because there is a universal though hidden teaching going on of which man is not even aware.

We have here a duplication of the Genesis 1:2 experience. Man has fallen into an abyss of chaos, darkness and void, hopeless and total-ly helpless in himself. But the Spirit of God is brooding over the soul of man.

The hope of man to remain in a salvable condition rests in two facts: first, in the inability of the historic fall to destroy the image of God in man; second, in the gracious, prevenient and universal opera-tion of the Holy Spirit to frustrate the attempts and onslaughts of Satan who seeks to obliterate all traces of the God-awareness and sin-aware-ness, of man's yearning for salvation and searching for reality.

It must be stated that this aspect of the operation of the Holy Spirit is totally sovereign and independent of all human agencies and means. These operations do not in themselves lead to the salvation experience. They are prevenient and preservative.

This ministry of the Holy Spirit in the world, however, uniquely relates to missions. The Holy Spirit not only preserves the world as a mission field; He also creates high-potential seasons and responsive people. In fact, it is the intensification of the general operations of the Holy Spirit along the lines indicated above that are always evident in high-potential areas. Indeed, high potentiality is mainly the result of the Holy Spirit's intensification of the gracious operations in the realm of the religious nature of man. Cultural factors may greatly enhance and/or collaborate in this matter; but without a special impe-tus of the Holy Spirit, no cultural conditions and movements could ever bring about times and people of high-conversion potential. It was the gracious ministry of the Holy Spirit who brought about the "fullness of times" into which the Son of God came and into which he sent His own apostles.

CONCLUSION

From the above study we may conclude that the triune God in His very being as Spirit, light and love is an outgoing God, a mission-ary God, ever sending Himself in benevolent relations to mankind, ever searching in love to bestow Himself in blessings upon mankind, and ever spending Himself in great sacrifice to make man's salvation possible. Father, Son and Holy Spirit are cooperating and coordinat-ing to bring man back from his sinful wandering and blundering, and restore man to his pristine state, purpose, destiny and glory. Our God is, indeed, the God of our salvation.

Our knowledge of God, of course, comes to us by way of revelation as deposited in the Bible. We turn therefore to the historic unfolding of God in *Heilsgeschichte* to learn more of His person, work and purpose.

3

Missionary Theology and the Old Testament

The Revelation of God to All Mankind

Jesus Christ constantly related Himself, His message and His mission to the Old Testament. He did not contradict or destroy but modified, enriched, expanded, and in many ways transformed and glorified the Old Testament.

He claimed to be the fulfillment of the Old Testament. In Him the old economy culminated and came to a glorious conclusion. Thus He did not set at nought the old order by abolishing it, but superseded it by fulfilling it.

Because of this fact, we inquire: Did He also find the substantiation of the missionary thrust in the Old Testament? This is a most important question because of erroneous interpretations of the Old Testament in relation to missions. Too often the Old Testament has been interpreted in narrow nationalistic terms or from a legalistic point of view. Seldom is the Old Testament seen as a marvelous thrust of God into the world for saving purposes. We turn, therefore, to a survey of Old Testament revelation, considering first the missionary intent of Genesis 1 – 11, a portion which uniquely belongs to all mankind. It is here that the protevangelium is first announced, and it is the protevangelium in its universalistic intent which becomes the leitmotif throughout the Old Testament until it culminates in the incarnation-death-resurrection event many centuries later.

The Protevangelium

The Bible is a beautifully unified book. Its major concepts are constant. Its basic theology, purpose and message are one magnificent and progressive unfolding from the seedbed of Genesis to their full blossoming in Christ and the New Testament — and this in spite of the fact that we have in the Bible three great block-sections of revelation.

I accept the Genesis record as historical and firmly hold to the fact that the revelation of Genesis 1 — 11 came to the entire human race, even though its writing was accomplished much later by Moses. From Genesis 12 and the rest of the Old Testament, God reveals Himself uniquely to and through Israel, although the design of this revelation was for the world. The New Testament comes to and through the church of Jesus Christ, the apostles being its direct recipients. Thus we have three great block-sections of revelation: racial, national and ecclesiological.

We turn our attention first to the first eleven chapters of Genesis. I investigate the content of revelation of this section more fully later; here I am interested mainly in the fact of the universality and missionary intent of the Old Testament.

Genesis 1 and 2 record the creation of Adam and Eve and thus the human race. The creation of Adam is seminal. Adam is more than an individual; he is more than a legal representative of the human race. He is the creation and incarnation of the entire human race, being its organic as well as legal head. This most certainly is the philosophy underlying the whole Bible as it is related to man, sin and salvation. This is also the argument of Paul in Romans 5, both as it relates to universal sinfulness, guilt and death in and through Adam, and the justification unto life of all in and through Christ. Adam, indeed, is the seminal head of the entire race.

Because of this organic unity of the race in Adam, the whole race fell into sin, guilt, moral pollution, separation from God and social disintegration.

> The sum total of all natural men forms an enormous racially articulated organism, and each individual through his mere birth, is inescapably a member thereof. He is in Adam (1 Cor. 15:22). Humanity is not simply a numerical total of many distinct individual persons, but one single colossal "body" which, according to its origin and nature, in a myriad manifold and differentiated branches, sets forth its first father, Adam. This involves the all-inclusiveness of the fall and the universality of sin (Rom. 5:12; 3:10-12, 23), with the necessity of the new birth of each individual (John 3:3), and

the incarnation of Christ as the Savior and Redeemer (Rom. 5: 12-21).[1]

GENESIS 3:15

Because of this solemn fact, the first promise of a coming Redeemer is of tremendous significance. This promise was given to *the entire human race*. Genesis 3:15, the protevangelium, the morning star in the midst of the darkest night of mankind, is a promise of universal significance. Here biblical universality was born as hope was announced to all mankind. This promise holds as much hope for China, India, the Negro or the American Indian as it holds for Israel or present-day Europe. Its racial scope must not be overlooked, for only as Christ becomes the Saviour of the total human race is Genesis 3:15 really fulfilled.

Genesis 3:15 upholds at least six facts:

1. Salvation is God-wrought; thus it is certain and full of grace. God is its source, Originator, Initiator and Procurer. Salvation is of God. He is mankind's only hope. This refutes humanism, the self-redemption of man, and the principle of inevitable progress, especially as it relates to the religious development of mankind.

2. Salvation will destroy Satan, the enemy. Thus evil is not a permanent scourge of mankind and this world. God and good will eventually triumph. This refutes the theory of dualism and also the cyclical theory of history and experience as it underlies most Oriental religions.

3. Salvation will affect mankind as a whole; it is broader than only the individual or a nation. This refutes the theory of narrow particularism in election and atonement. Salvation will reach the nations and eventually the race. This must not be interpreted to mean that all men will eventually be saved, for the Bible does not justify such a hope and claim. The fact, however, is that when God's program will be completed, there will be a reversal in the count; while numerous individuals will be lost, the race as such will be saved.

4. Salvation will come through a Mediator who in an organic way is related to mankind. He is of the seed of the woman. This passage is the only place in the Bible where the term "seed of the woman" is used. Thus the Redeemer will be true man, as Christ indeed was. He was real man although not *mere* man.

5. Salvation is bound up with the suffering of the Redeemer; the enemy shall bruise His heel.

6. Salvation will be experienced within history as the fall is a part of history. It is as real as the fall is real and as present as the fall is present. Salvation, therefore, as upheld in the Old Testament (Gen 3:15), includes mankind in promise, provision, purpose and potential.

Therefore, man left paradise not only with a sorrowful remembrance and painful sense of guilt, but also with a hopeful yearning and assured anticipation which he carried with him into the world outside of paradise. Ever since then man has lived in conflict or contradiction *(Widerspruch)*. On the one hand he is full of remorse, guilt and self-condemnation, while on the other hand he yearns, strives, hopes and anticipates. Hope and fear, anticipation and despair, love and hate mingle and confuse. Man is a bundle of complexes.

The universality of the protevangelium is basic to Old Testament revelation. It is the soteriological leitmotif (dominant, unifying, all-inclusive thrust and intent) and hermeneutical principle governing Old Testament interpretation. It cannot be revoked or modified, for it rests on the unconditional "I will" of the eternal God in whom there is no variableness. It becomes the guiding star throughout history and prophecy of the Old Testament until it finds its fulfillment in Christ, the seed of the woman.

The leitmotif gives coherence to the Bible, integrates it into a progressive structure, gives it direction and purpose as a whole, and clarifies the meaning of each individual section and part. Only as the leitmotif is grasped clearly and applied consistently does the Old Testament yield its rich and true fruitage to the reader.

It may well be that the kingdom of God concept forms the foundational concept which unifies the Bible. I believe that the kingdom was, is and remains the content and goal of the purpose of God. The thesis of this book, however, is a study not of the content and goal but of the thrust of the purpose of God — God in historical movement realizing His purpose. The fundamental concept and the fundamental thrust constitute a unit, though differently expressed. The one is the way; the other is the goal. Both find their origin and consummation in God.

NOACHIAN COVENANT

This universality is continued in the Noachian covenant and in Noah's pronouncement upon his own sons. We cannot overemphasize the fact that God entered into a covenant with "Noah *and his sons*" (Gen 9:1, 8-9). It is not merely Noah alone, or Noah and Shem. It definitely included Japheth and Ham also. That the word "sons" is used three times in the plural must not be overlooked, for it is an emphasis of tremendous significance. Universality is written into the covenant.

Because of this, the covenant of God with Noah and his sons definitely concerns all nations. There is no tribe or people that was not included in the covenant of God with Noah.

Neither does the later pronouncement of Noah upon his sons affect the basic universalistic intent as it relates to salvation. While there will be differences in social and cultural developments and in the granting of divine revelation and mediatorial position, the soteriological universality remains unaffected. A careful exegesis of the text will bear this out, and so does the listing of the people in Genesis 10.

The record of God's dealings with the total race concludes with the tragedy of the confusion of tongues, the breakup of the unity of mankind, and the dispersion and dismissal from the presence of God. One fact, however, remains unchanged. The basic soteriological universality of the intent of God and of the gospel message initiated by God Himself stands unrevoked and unmodified. God is still the God of mankind and the only hope of salvation. It is well to keep in mind that Genesis 1 – 11 is the preface to the entire Bible and the foundation upon which the rest of revelation is built.

The universalistic intent of God's redemption is thus unfolded in the earliest revelation of God and gives unity, direction, authority and meaning to the basic missionary thrust of the *Heilsgeschichte* and revelation which follow. God is the God of the race, and mission is God's outgoing to the race in salvation.

THE NATIONAL RELIGION OF ISRAEL

REVELATIONAL RELIGION AND ETHNICAL RELIGIONS

Religion is a universal phenomenon. No people has been found living without religion, and it is generally agreed that it constitutes the unifying and a most dynamic factor in the cultures of most peoples. Only in the West have men sought to divest themselves of religion.

Among the more primitive people, religion is little differentiated and all of life is sacred. It is woven into the total warp and woof of life. The principle of continuum prevails. Differentiation is mingled with pantheism in the living religions of Asia.

In order to gain the proper perspective of Old Testament revelational religion we need to set it into the framework of general religious history. From the standpoint of natural history, the religion of the Old Testament is only one religion among many. Only as we behold the total unfolding of the religions in the world can the message of the Old Testament be properly understood, evaluated and appreciated.

While unique qualitatively, Old Testament religion is not unique in structure, institutions, nomenclature, psychology or phenomena. Outwardly it relates itself to life and culture as religion in general does. Structurally and institutionally it appears as a part of the history of world religions. It has its temple, priests and sacrifices. Qualitatively, however, it is a distinct religion because it is a uniquely revealed religion. Old Testament religion does not find its roots, content and nurture in culture, psychology or human faith; neither is it dominated or determined by them. Its content comes from above and outside of man, while the continuing content of the ethnic religions comes from within man. The former is supernatural revelation; the latter are the unfolding of the religious consciousness of man based on intuitive insight, tradition, speculation and mystical experience.

Among all religions, Old Testament revelational religion constitutes the exclusive mission of God in the world in at least four ways:

1. It is a divine movement, expressing disapproval of ethnically developed, humanly devised religions and heathen practices of the world. It is designed to preserve the world from utter moral and religious decay and from a total spiritual blackout. It is God's continued witness in the world (Ac 14:17).

2. It is a divinely inspired ethical monotheism preserving man from utter lostness in polytheism, idolatry and spiritism. Ethical monotheism alone can give meaning to the universe, history, and particularly to the cross, as well as depth to the gospel of grace.

3. It is the creation of God to sustain the divinely inspired hope in the promised Redeemer (Gen 3:15) who would save mankind from

the predicament of sin and destruction and restore his original glory, purpose and meaning.

4. It is the calling unto God of a selective minority instrument for the purpose of making an effective missionary thrust into mankind with the intent of blessings and salvation to all mankind.

Thus the creation of a national religion introduced a particularism in methodology but not in design and purpose. God's universal purpose of salvation is constant throughout the entire Bible, and a change in methodology does not change His goal.

THE DESIGN OF THE NATIONAL RELIGION

Genesis 12 introduces a new epoch in the history of salvation — a history which is particularistic *in method* but universalistic in promise, design and effect. This needs to be seen clearly and grasped firmly, or else the God of the Old Testament Himself becomes a particularist. This could never be. As a particularist He would cease to be *Elohim*, the God of creation and the God of the nations.

The mission and history of Israel have been variously interpreted, both from the natural and supernatural, national and racial, specific and general, religious and cultural points of view. The call and task of Israel as they begin in Abraham are subject to much misunderstanding and even criticism. Unless they are seen in the light of the total development of the religious history of the world, their significance is not grasped, much less appreciated.

It is my thesis that Paul presents in Romans 1:18-32 a theological interpretation of the religious history of the nations as it took place after the dispersion of the people from Babylon and as recorded in Genesis 11:1-9. Thus the world was sinking rapidly into idolatry, sensuality and mental depravity. Therefore religion, morality and philosophy came under the judgment of God, and God gave up the nations (Ro 1:24, 26, 28). God punished sin with sin, lifting the divine restraints and permitting the nations to go their own ways and design their own cultures and religions. We do not know for how many centuries the process of degeneration was permitted to go on. We lack a full chronology, but the span of time is not significant for our purpose. Romans 1, however, implies that a time of general and deep religious darkness settled upon mankind. Though individuals survived the desperate apostasy, the darkness was general and constantly intensifying.

Only divine intervention could save the world from a total spiritual blackout. It was evident that man had neither the intention, motivation nor ability to find out God by his own searching. It is into this most serious situation that God wrote a bold "But God!" into human history.

THE UNIQUENESS OF THE NATIONAL RELIGION

The protevangelium (Gen 3:15) becomes the illuminating star out of the darkness and despair, and Genesis 12 — the call of Abraham — is the beginning of a divine counterculture designed both to arrest evil and unfold the gracious plan, salvation and purpose of God. It is a new ray of hope for the world. This is more fully revealed in the Old Testament. Let us, therefore, look more in detail at this new beginning and further unfolding, considering briefly the uniqueness and significance of the national (Israelitish) religion in light of the development of the history of religions as such.

In keeping with the general tenor of Scripture, which we believe to be both historical and factual, three general principles can be perceived from the sources of the Old Testament:

1. *The beginning of the national religion of Israel rests in the supernatural act and revelation of God.* In the beginning God! This was so in creation; it is so in salvation. Abraham did not seek God; rather, God, the God of glory, pierced the heavens and miraculously broke into history to seek Abraham. He appeared to him when the latter dwelt safely and securely in Ur of the Chaldees in a home where idolatry was practiced (Josh 24:2). Here the God of glory invaded time and space and summoned Abraham to separate from his country and kin. He was ordered to follow the Lord into an unknown land and a new beginning. Here sovereign grace displayed itself on behalf of mankind. Nowhere in the Scriptures do we learn why God called Abraham and not someone else. The purpose is however definite.

We state again: Man is not reaching up; God is reaching down. God interposed in time and space. The origin of the national religion of Israel through Abraham is not the result of cultural development. It is not the outflow of a great enlightenment achieved by human concentration. It is not the fruit of ethnic evolution. It is not the product of an earnest God-searcher. It is not the rational and progressive synthesis of selective borrowing and skillful adaptation. It is not the invention of a great religious genius and intense religious consciousness. Human sources are not credited with its origin nor are they adequate to account for it. Neither does the origin lie in a distant and unknown past gradually evolving from Semitism and enriching itself from neighboring religions. It does not root in natural sources and the religious instinct of man.

Man is not the originator of the Old Testament revelational religion. Rather, it roots in a supernatural act and revelation of God at a specific place at a particular time and to a singular person whose name was Abraham. The man lived in Ur of the Chaldees some two thousand years before the Christian era. Thus its origin is divinely, historically, personally and geographically oriented. It is neither myth nor legend but history.

The above negatives, of course, must not be construed to imply that God brought down from heaven for Abraham a religion — dogma, cultus and culture — tailor-made in quantity as well as quality and completely distinct from or unrelated to the cultural milieu of Abraham's time and heritage. This would be contrary to all of God's workings. The biblical record does not make such claims. Neither does it deny that Abraham was a religious genius with a keen and susceptible religious consciousness and a man of special religious aptitude. God used all of these natural means. However, no one of them, or all combined, accounts for *the qualitative uniqueness* of Abraham's new religion and life. A new religious quality appears in religious history which is born not of blood (racially), nor of the will of the flesh (sociologically), nor of the will of man (psychologically), but of God. It roots in an act and revelation of God.

2. *The beginning of the national religion constitutes a definite turning point in the history of religions.* Religious history is not an even flow. Religion has fluctuated a great deal between progress and retrogression, reform and decay, evolution and devolution, renaissance and distintegration. The forces of dynamism and death are at work everywhere, and religion is not exempted. Only some decades ago we spoke of the decadence of the non-Christian religious systems; today we are troubled by their dynamism and resurgence. Rajah B. Manikam mentions four main types of resurgent movements: "Reform,

Revival, Renaissance, and Revolt."[2] He could have added "messianism" and "missiology."

Biblical history agrees with the general trend of religious instability and tensions but notes that degeneration, disintegration and decay have prevailed along the upward pull. The process of death has triumphed historically over positive and constructive religious dynamism.

From the biblical records we gain the impression that mankind was free from idolatry at least up to the Tower of Babel experience. No mention of idols, images or gods is found in the first eleven chapters of Genesis. The buried and silent centuries between chapters 11 and 12 of Genesis can only be disclosed to us by archeology, and that only in part. References to Abraham and the time preceding his call are recorded in Joshua 24:2 and Isaiah 51:1-2. Neither reference is complimentary.

While no idolatry has been mentioned thus far, we know that in the home of Terah, the ancestor of Abraham, idolatry prevailed (Josh 24:2). This seems to have been the general practice in Chaldea, as archeology substantiates. That this practice continued in the clan is proven by the record which says that Laban in Haran had house gods (Gen 31:19, 32, 34), which eventually affected the household of Jacob while he was residing there (Gen 35:2, 4).

We have already noted that Paul gives a theological interpretation in Romans 1:18-32 concerning the general religious deterioration of this period and that this is the beginning of the great historical religious systems. Mankind is on the road downward in its history of religion and is moving rapidly away from God into self-devised systems of religion. "Professing themselves to be wise, they became fools, and changed the glory of the incorruptible God into an image made like to corruptible man, and to birds, and fourfooted beasts, and creeping things."

Commenting on Romans 1:23, James M. Stifler says:

> The glory of God, that admirable and effulgent representation of himself which glowed in all that he had made, this they changed in the likeness of an image — "the incorruptible God into an image made like to corruptible man." The odiousness of idolatry is not alone in the immorality to which it leads, but that it is a caricature of God and a slander. It belongs to his glory that he is imperishable.

He was likened to that which is corruptible. The very material of the image was a dishonor, as if one should erect a statue to a distinguished man today not in marble or bronze but in chalk or putty. To liken God to man is idolatry. Men were to make no image of him. Had they served their original conception of him they would not have attempted it. In due time he gave an image of himself in a sinless being who was animated with eternal life, "the brightness of his glory, and the express image of his person" (Heb. 1:3). If Jesus were not more than a mortal, he was an idol.

These professed sages did not stop with likening God to man; they figured him as a bird, then as a quadruped, and finally as a reptile. There was the Apollo of the Greeks, the eagle of the Romans, the bull of the Egyptians, and the serpent of the Assyrians. Paul may be giving in this verse the historical development of idolatry, from its highest phase to its worst; or he may be setting it forth in climactic form; but certain it is that all these phases of the sin existed.[3]

Paul outlines the wrath of God which is revealed from heaven against this kind of ungodliness manifested in the general history of mankind. In contrast to the wrath of God in history, the call of Abraham speaks in concrete historical form of the grace of God. God was not willing that mankind should totally and forever bury itself beyond repair and God-awareness in utter superstition, idolatry and false religions. And while mankind collectively did not listen to His voice, Abraham, the individual, did. At Babel, mankind had attempted in united strength to withstand the purpose of the Most High. Therefore the divine principle of separation and division had to be introduced to counteract the ungodly confederacy of mankind.

Thus a new beginning was divinely initiated, a beginning which constituted a definite turning point in the history of religion and divine operation. However, it was not a change in the ultimate design and divine purpose of God.

a. The methodology of divine operation calls for a particularism in revelation and operation. God is limiting Himself in His unique revelation to one people and operates uniquely in and through Israel. Here *Heilgeschichte* (salvation story) in a peculiar and particularistic sense is born. Secular and sacred history are taking on separate courses. The history of Israel is distinct because God is watching over it and enriching it in many ways, especially with His own self-disclosures. In the history of Israel, God is uniquely present, distinguishing it not only quantitatively but qualitatively from the general flow of history.

b. The principle of divine operation calls for a mediatorial people. Israel is made the mediator between God and the nations. It is to be a kingdom of priests and a holy nation to mediate the unique revelation of God which it is to receive. Israel is called to be a channel, not a storehouse, of blessings.

The ultimate design of divine operation remains the human race. Universality is not canceled out but rather enhanced by the method of particularism and the principle of mediatorship.

> The singling out of Abraham was indeed necessary to slow down the general advance of salvation, but so much the more would it, with fulness of wisdom, facilitate it and all the more surely lead it to its goal. It was designed specially with a view to the universal aspect, the detail to the whole, the small to the great. The limiting of the revelation at first to Abraham was only the divine method to serve the ultimate universality of the salvation. The restriction was there, but its appointment had its own removal as its object. God turned away His salvation from the nations so as to be able all the more certainly to give it back to them glorified.[4]

3. *The beginning of the national religion marks a new epoch for the creation of a moral and religious consciousness and ideal that transcends all human experiences and speculations.* It is, indeed, a divinely instituted protest movement against the evils of the old and developing world. It is a witness to God and the truth by raising up moral and absolutistic religious ideals.

In order to bring this point into focus we must review briefly the history of religion in pre-Abrahamic times. The history of mankind from the scriptural point of view is not too pleasant and inspiring. It is nothing to be proud of because it is a history of sin abounding.

In brief, Genesis 3 — 11 presents the following sequence of events:

First, the entrance of sin into the human race (Gen 3). The Bible does not unfold to us clearly the origin of sin; nevertheless, sin meets us as stark reality in chapter 3 and cunningly invades the race, From here on we have a history marred by sin, degeneration, destruction and death.

Second, the development and main patterns of sin. It is instructive to note that the first sin outside paradise reveals itself in the religious life.

The sacrifice of Cain typifies his self-styled religion of redemption. Religious perversion and self-styled redemption lie at the root of all evil in the world. Religion is the "cement" that holds culture together. Religion separated from God is a major source of evil in culture because inadequate views of God inevitably lead to inadequate views of man, sin and nature. Thus religion is a source for good or a source for evil, depending upon its concept of God.

With religion gone wrong, brutality quickly followed. Cain slew Abel. Forsaking the presence of God, Cain turned not only to his self-redemption, but to the attempted redemption of the cursed earth by the development of a godless civilization which fostered polygamy and the evil of blood-revenge. There is in Cain not merely the beginning of a religion of self-redemption, but also the ambition to become the redeemer of the earth and to build his own paradise in which self-will, lust and power will reign. Justice is dethroned and grace rejected. The natural results are immorality and sensuality, incest in the full sense of the word as witnessed in Genesis 6:1-5. Additional patterns of sin display themselves later.

Third, the divine intervention and judgment upon sin are recorded in Genesis 6 and 7. I accept the historicity of the record of the flood and read it as a chapter on the severity of God. I am not interested in a debate about all its details. Divine judgment eventually becomes a necessity, not only a possibility. Let no man trifle with sin, for he that sows to his flesh shall of the flesh reap corruption and destruction.

Fourth, the revival of sin is seen in the appearance of a new pattern of degeneration: the sin of intemperance. And what a universal sin it is! The use of intoxicating liquor and its consequent drunkenness are practically universal, except where religion strictly prohibits it (Islam) and by force inhibits it. Intemperance led to immodesty first in Noah and then in Ham.

Fifth, the culmination of sin (Gen 11:1-9). Here direct rebellion against God and His purpose came to a climax. Setting aside the purpose of God to populate, cultivate and dominate the earth, man defiantly built a confederation for his own glorification. He sought his own deification and set the final pattern of that age. The satanic idea to become like God, which was implanted in Eve and Adam, has never left mankind. Eventually it will be the crowning sin of mankind, climaxing in the Antichrist.

The first chapter of human history spanning several millenniums can thus be summarized in the following phrases:

the invasion of sin (Gen 3)

the evolution of sin (Gen 4 — 5)

the divine retribution for sin (Gen 6 — 7)

the revival of sin (Gen 9)

the culmination of sin (Gen 10)

All this manifests itself in:

the sin of unbelief and disobedience (Adam)

the sin of self-redemption (Cain)

the sin of brutality (Cain)

the sin of polygamy (Lamech)

the sin of blood-revenge (Lamech)

the sin of incest (Antedeluvians)

the sin of intemperance (Noah)

the sin of immodesty (Ham)

the sin of rebellion (Tower of Babel builders)

the sin of self-glorification and self-deification (tower builders).

To this list we may add the abominable sin of idolatry with all its accompanying evils which surfaces somewhere before chapter 12.

All these sins can be traced in the history of the nations as we meet them on the pages of the Old Testament or in the records of secular history. A study of Arnold Toynbee's twenty-one perished civilizations is proof of sin's degradation.

Against the background of such deplorable conditions, the call of Abraham and the religious history of Israel must be evaluated. Israel's history is not a history of arbitrary election, of favoritism, of narrow particularism, and nationalism. It is an act of sovereign and gracious election to preserve the race and the temporal and eternal destiny of mankind.

THE IDEALISM OF THE NATIONAL RELIGION

To perform His gracious ministry God initiates a protest movement against the prevailing evils. He upholds moral and religious ideals to preserve, deepen, and define the moral and religious consciousness in order to lead Israel and mankind to bankruptcy in self-redemption and prepare the world for the salvation of God in Christ Jesus.

In order to accomplish the divine mission, the Old Testament displays a relentless protest against the prevailing religions and evil cultures. Revelation becomes the judge of all ethnic religions. Condemnation is pronounced against divination, soothsaying and necromancy as sources of divine knowledge and prognostication; against witchcraft, magic, sorcerers and sorceresses as religious practitioners; against idolatry and imagery which are strictly prohibited throughout the Old Testament and are not to be tolerated by the people of God either in private or public worship; against human sacrifices and temple prostitution as enticement and appeasement of deities; against immorality, sensuality, and other evil practices which are condemned in explicit terms.

Judgment is exercised to demonstrate the seriousness of sin and transgression and to cultivate a sin-awareness. Upon many of these evils the sentence of death had been specifically pronounced, which greatly expanded the guilt consciousness and death penalty.

After pronouncing judgment on sin, the Old Testament constantly reiterates social, moral and religious ideals and practices. This is done for two reasons: first, to awaken and intensify the moral consciousness in man lest he fall into utter moral decay and death; second, to create moral and religious conditions where decent life would be possible and the salvation of God an eventual reality for all mankind.

Thus we find:

1. Divine declaration through the Decalogue of God's unprecedented religious, moral and social ideals. These ideals transcend all human experiences, speculations, religious intuitions and moral decisions. The Ten Commandments stand unparalleled in the history of mankind. They are not unique in pattern but are absolutely unique in moral and spiritual grandeur, glory and severity.

2. Rigid precepts and inclusive laws established for the control and discipline of the people of God.

3. An emphasis on the seriousness of a breach of the commandments, severe penalties attached to disobedience, and executions of judgments meted out according to divine prescriptions.

4. A strong stand by various individuals for moral and religious ideals in the name of their religion and their God — first the judges, later the schools of the prophets, and finally the individual prophets specially called of God and qualified by Him to be His mouthpiece and representatives.

5. Numerous and minute religious institutions which the people of God were called upon to observe and obey without fully understanding all their implications and signification.

6. The elaborate sacrificial system, with its tabernacle and furniture, to atone for sin, to keep open the way to God, to teach a life of separation and devotion to God, and to worship Him in a pure, dignified and meaningful manner. To this were added the annual festivities of social and religious significance. These were commemorative, instructive and predictive on the one hand, and expensive and interruptive on the other. Thus they tested Israel's loyalty, devotion and obedience to God in the routine of life and work.

It must never be imagined that the religion of Israel was an inexpensive experience designed by the natural man for the convenience of the people. It was a trying obligation, testing to the utmost their faith and love for God. God's work is never inexpensive and convenient. Becoming His faithful servant is always a trying experience bound up with sacrifice, devotion and obedience.

It must also emphatically be stated and clearly grasped that we are dealing here with revelational idealism and not with human aspirations. Repeatedly the Old Testament witnesses to a sharp cleavage between revelational idealism and Israel's actual experience. Not infrequently folk morality and religion stole their allegiance. Influenced by human propensities and environment, such thinking deprived the people of the blessings of God, provoked sharp denunciations, and often resulted in physical and material judgment. Unless this dualism between divinely revealed idealism and experiential historic realism is observed in the Old Testament, conflicts and discrepancies seem to appear on its pages.

THE SOURCES OF MORAL AND RELIGIOUS STRENGTH OF ISRAEL'S NATIONAL RELIGION

The above-mentioned counterculture and idealism were not lightly assumed and superficially discharged. They required deep and assuring foundations, clear-cut convictions, divinely wrought persuasions, and a courage and loyalty that falter neither in danger, criticism, enmity, nor suffering. None of this is lacking in the Old Testament society of believers — at least not in the responsible advocates and leaders. These sources of motivation and inspiration are deep and enduring. Let us consider each of them in detail.

1. *A deep consciousness of a unique covenantal and existential relationship between God and Israel.* God is known as the God of Abraham, Isaac and Jacob — the God of the fathers. He is also known as the God of Israel, the Creator, King, Shepherd, Saviour of His servant Israel. Israel is known as God's peculiar people, the sheep of His fold, the people of His making, the apple of His eye. Israel is uniquely the people of God.

God has bound Himself to Israel in several unconditional covenants which neither time nor circumstances change. Though their actual fulfillment can be interrupted and delayed, the covenants are abiding because of God's immutability and moral fidelity. His divine "I will" is their guarantee. The covenants are assured to a people of faith. God remains the covenant God of Israel. These sacred covenants place tremendous responsibilities upon this people. Indeed, so central and dynamic is the covenant idea that it becomes pivotal in the interpretation of the Old Testament economy. God and Israel are irrevocably bound together in covenant relationship. God is the God of Israel; Israel is the people of God.

2. *A deep consciousness of a unique revelation which has come to Israel.* The religion of Israel began in a singular revelation of God. The God of glory appeared. In this extraordinary revelatory message, God issued a summons and offered a promise to Abraham in Ur of the Chaldees. God assured him in His emphatic "I will" that sovereignty and grace operated on Abraham's behalf in the midst of loneliness, danger, tests and perplexities. God did not fail in personal visits and assuring promises to lighten the burden and brighten the path of the weary and lonely pilgrim.

The blessing which was promised to Abraham as a reward for his obedience to the call is so frequently mentioned that it runs like a refrain through all the story of the patriarch's life. This blessing has three main features, each of which is mentioned repeatedly with more or less detail and firmly anchored in the divine "I will" and confirmed in sacred covenants.

    a. the seed — a numerous and unique seed (Gen 12:2; 13:16; 15:5; 16:10; 17:2, 4-6; 18:18; 22:18)

    b. the land — (Gen 12:1, 7; 13:15, 17; 15:7, 18; 17:8; 24:7)

    c. the nation — (Gen 12:2; 18:18; 22:18).

The covenants and promises of God with and to Abraham were later transferred and confirmed to Isaac (Gen 26:2-4) and to Jacob (28:13-15), the fathers of the people of Israel. Abraham, Isaac and Jacob walked in the assurance that God had spoken. They did not follow cunningly devised fables, myths, dreams or instincts, for their assurance of faith rested in the infallible revelation of God.

From this point on, revelation expands the message of God to Israel. The phrases "thus saith the Lord" or "the word of the Lord came" are found in almost monotonous repetition in the Old Testament. Men risked their lives to speak of the assurance and authority of God. Never once were there serious doubts about whether God had disclosed Himself. Revelation was not questioned in Israel. In fact, so general and so thorough was the faith in God's revelatory activity that false prophets and charlatans capitalized on it to make personal gain, exploiting and misleading the people.

Israel lived and worshiped in the knowledge that they were in possession of a peculiarly revealed and distinct message of God. Because of this, Moses and the prophets carefully wrote down their message under the inspiration of the Holy Spirit, insisting that it was the Word of God to man and thus inerrant, authoritative and normative. As such, the Old Testament has been accepted and respected by the Jewish people and was acknowledged and proclaimed by our Master, Jesus Christ. It served as His own inspiration and pattern for life. It became the charter and program for His ministry. He never doubted the revelatory nature and quality of the Old Testament.

    3. *A deep consciousness of a true and unique knowledge of God and His purpose.* The most distinct quality of the national religion is its concept of deity. This lofty and distinct concept of God became Israel's greatest contribution to the development of religion. Well does J. Philip Hyatt say,

> The prophets were not systematic theologians (and this goes for Moses and the fathers — Abraham, Isaac and Jacob — as

well). They were God-intoxicated men whose religion was God-centered. God was for them not an object of thought and speculation, but an object of intimately personal experience. Their teachings about deity do not constitute a carefully worked out system but are the result of insights that came to them in great moments of revelation.[5]

The God concept of a people determines the quality and character of religion and life, the progress or stagnation of culture. It is central, foundational, and directive in all philosophies of religion and world and life views.

It lies at the basis of everything good and bad in the beliefs, activities and destiny of man. For example, the doctrine of God determines laws, types of government, international relations, institutions of learning and beneficence, systems of finance, commerce and agriculture, science, art, literature, music, etc. The doctrine of God held by a people makes or unmakes these and other such things, whether or not called strictly religious.

In things strictly religious the doctrine of God molds and shapes the forms of life and activity. Religious institutions and agencies are based on the doctrine of God.

Man's character and destiny here and hereafter rest upon the same doctrine. The thing then of supreme importance is to know the truth about God's revelation of himself and concerning himself. Who and what is God?[6]

Thus all religious contributions must be evaluated by the concept of God from which they spring and/or to which they logically or experientially lead. What, then, is the God concept of Israel?

BASIC PRESUPPOSITIONS

Before presenting an outline of the Old Testament's God concept, we refer to three basic presuppositions which are fundamental to the approach of the Old Testament message concerning God:

1. The Old Testament writers do not belong to a speculative school of philosophical theology. They were neither interested in presenting elaborate proofs for the existence of God nor in speculative definitions on the being of God. The reality of God in their experience and in the history of the people of Israel was sufficient proof for them. God lived in their midst and unfolded Himself to them, and they experienced Him and worshiped Him.

2. The Old Testament writers operate on the assumption that God cannot be found out by human reason, by unaided human intuition and mystical insight, or by human religious experience. They presuppose that any true understanding of God must come from God Himself and that only revelation can bestow this upon man. Thus all true knowledge of God comes by supernatural revelation, God encountering man and explaining its nature and meaning.

3. Finally, the Old Testament writers assume that God in infinite grace has unveiled Himself to them and thus He can be known, approached, and His message understood. He is not the "unknown God" of Athens or the unknowable and undefinable Brahma of India. God dwells with His people. By speaking and acting He makes Himself known to them.

THE DEITY CONCEPT

In a study of the nature and quality of the God of Abraham, Isaac and Jacob, and the God of Israel — Moses, Elijah and David, and the prophets — we find many witnesses but the same portrait, many emphases but the same God, many definitive designations but the same "name" (or being). Loyalty to the Old Testament sources does not permit me to accept the evolutionary principle that the patriarchs — Abraham, Isaac, Jacob — were polytheists, each worshiping his own god at a specific place. It does not teach either that Moses developed monolatry and that the prophets finally reached ethical monotheism.

No change in the fundamental position of, and relationship to, the God-concept is evident in Old Testament sources. The God of Genesis is the "I AM THAT I AM" who appeared to Moses; the sources inform us (Ex 3:6-17; cf. 4:5; 6:2). He summoned Moses and sent him back to "my people which are in Egypt." Later He covenanted with Israel at Sinai and constituted a nation by means of a living hope, an organized system of worship, and an abiding moral law. The God of the patriarchs and the God of Moses are bound together in Old Testament sources and in the heart and mind of Israel. In the redemption of Israel from Egypt, God is but fulfilling a promise to Abraham (Ex 6:2-9). Nowhere does Moses cast doubt on this certainty, though, as Elmer A. Leslie reminds us, "He gave Israel its national consciousness, its distinctive religious bent, and its enduring religious passion"[7] and thus made a tremendous personal contribution to his own people. As far as the prophets are concerned, "the great classic interpreters of Jahweh's nature and requirements of the eighth century B. C. either expressly or by inference pointed back to the epoch of Moses and the wilderness as the normative period of Israelite religion (Ho 11:1 and 13:4ff). To it, as to a refreshing and purging fountain, the prophets were convinced that the Isarel of their day must return. By the spirit of that epoch, Israel's religious trends must be checked and corrected."[8] They believed "that they were largely summoning Israel back to the religion of the Mosaic era, but like all reformers they presented ideas that were both old and new. Their mission was actually not so much to present new ideas of God as to correct at some points mistaken notions and to deepen and widen the Hebrew understanding of God's nature. They wished to deepen the Hebrew experience of God and to widen the area of life over which the Hebrews would recognize His sovereignty."[9]

Whatever modern scholarship may say to the contrary, the Old Testament writers were unanimous and uniform in their testimony concerning God. Nowhere do they betray any evolution from polytheism to monolatry, to ethical monotheism. The God of Israel was the "I am" (Jehovah) of Moses, the God of Abraham, Isaac and Jacob. *Elohim* with its various definitive enrichments and *Yahweh* with its various combinations were qualitative descriptions of the same God, the God who created the world, who called Abraham, and who covenanted with Israel. There is continuity in revelational monotheism from Abraham throughout the whole Old Testament. This ideal was not reached progressively but rather was clung to fervently, defended staunchly, and proclaimed boldly. The doctrine of the *schema* (the Hebrew word for "hear" with which Deu 6:4 begins: "Hear, O Israel: The LORD our God is one LORD") is foundational, central and determining for the national religion of Israel from the very beginning. It is its theological leitmotif from which all other doctrines derive their quality and meaning.

The nature and character of the God of Israel can be defined according to His names, which certainly have a qualitative meaning in the Old Testament. The divine character can also be studied from the explicit statements about God, and it may also be deduced from His acts in the history of mankind (Gen 1 — 11) and in the history of Israel (Gen 12 ff.). In His essential being, the God of Israel is personal, spiritual, one, infinite, eternal, self-existent, omnipotent, omniscient and omnipresent. He is God in the absolute sense of the word.

In relation to the universe and history, He is the Creator, the ground and source of all existence, and the supreme and benevolent Lord and Governor, sovereign Saviour and Judge of the universe and mankind who is both immanent and transcendent.

Qualitatively, God is characterized as holy, with the attributes of majesty, glory, righteousness, truth and veracity involved. He is love with the resultant attributes of goodness, grace, loving-kindness, mercy, tenderness, compassion, patience, long-suffering and forgiveness. His wrath with justice and judgment is implicit.

Such is the God of the Old Testament, the God of the patriarchs, of Moses, and of the prophets. As such, He disclosed Himself to His people.

It must be repeated, however, that not all people knew Him experientially in His fullness. It is evident from the pages of the Old Testament that at numerous occasions Israel fell far short of the revelational ideal and sank into the religious and idolatrous morass of the Egyptians, the Canaanites, and other nations. Kings, priests and false prophets often led the way into apostasy and debauchery, drawing the severe judgment of God upon themselves. Yet, the revelational ideal remained constant. God always raised up mighty champions of His cause who courageously stood in the gap.

This apparent dichotomy must not obstruct us from seeing the unity and majesty of the revelation and the consciousness which broke through again and again, indicating that Israel was the possessor of a true and unique knowledge of God.

4. *A deep consciousness of a relationhsip between human sin and human suffering.* This consciousness expresses itself in a most realistic, persistent and consistent manner throughout the entire Old Testament. Thus the numerous judgments are not recorded as evil acts of deities invading the earth or as natural consequences of nature, but as the moral acts of God in response to man's sins, individually and collectively. Sickness, natural calamities, wars and all suffering are interpreted in a similar way.

Human sin is a terrifying reality in the Old Testament, appearing with a frightening cutting edge. It is more than ignorance or a mistake, it is unbelief in God. It is ignoring and disobeying God's law, rebellion against God, confronting Him in self-will. It involves man and the moral government of God and thus results in guilt, judgment and penalty.

God as the absolute and moral Governor of the universe exerts universal judgment, using all means to execute the needed punishment. Therefore, suffering logically demonstrates God's moral government, correcting the sufferer and warning others.

Penalty and suffering, however, are not naturally bound up with sin, as *karma* would imply, with no way out of the consequences. In the Old Testament no mechanical law automatically decides and inescapably executes. Rather, a Governor morally measures sin and guilt, and in moral responsibility and justice metes out penalty. Not the universe but the Governor is moral. Because of this there is a way of escape, for genuine repentance and moral transformation may be substituted for suffering. Therefore, one of the most significant words in the Old Testament is the word *repentance* and its positive synonym, *conversion*.

The logic of the sin-suffering relationship, however, is not absolute. This is clearly set forth in the book and story of Job, where suffering, indeed, is a mystery to Job and becomes such to his comforters. It may be the refiner's fire or the proof of genuineness. Also, suffering may be substitutionary, as Isaiah 53 so clearly reveals.

However, in the main, the thesis stands that there is a consequent and moral relationship between suffering and sin. God is the God of justice and judgment whose moral wrath abides upon evil and the evildoer. God, who will never wink at sin nor can be deceived by it, can only be atoned in order that He might forgive.

5. *A deep consciousness and living hope of divine salvation from sin, the destruction of evil, and the triumph of righteousness and glory.*

The Old Testament is a book of hope. There is no room for the cyclical view of history with its endless repetition of misery. History is moving toward a goal of salvation and glory.

Salvation in the Old Testament is characterized in a unique way:

1. It is always the salvation of God. God is a God of salvation. The redemption of Israel from Egypt is the classic example. Self-redemption has no place in the religious history of Israel.

2. It is a salvation from sin and its consequences. God is able to save from sin, stain, enemy, tragedy and suffering.

3. It is total salvation of the individual, nation, race and universe. It is a total redemption resulting in a moral transformation of the individual and of society. It is a radical renovation of the cosmos to yield its plenty and riches to mankind.

4. It is a salvation that will result in the total conquest of evil and the complete triumph of peace, prosperity, righteousness and glory in a blessed fellowship between God and His people.

5. It is a salvation based upon atonement by substitutionary suffering, as is so vividly demonstrated in the continuous and varied sacrifices.

Such are the sources of moral and religious strength of Israel's religion. If truly experienced, they constitute an overwhelming missionary attraction and/or motivation.

THE UNIVERSALITY OF THE NATIONAL RELIGION

The national religion is the trumpet sound of hope for an eventual triumph of a renewed religious universality which will reconcile mankind in shared blessings and unified worship of the one true and living God, the Creator, Lord and Saviour of mankind.

Such a statement may seem contradictory. How can something national imply universality? As noted in the previous discussion, the national particular relates to methodology while universality is the principle and purpose.

Much havoc has been created by interpreting the Old Testament as nationalistic in design rather than in methodology. Universality is written with such bold letters into the Old Testament that no unprejudiced reader can avoid sensing it. Universality presents itself at least in five ways by implication and by explication:

1. *The consistent emphasis upon monotheism in the Old Testament reveals God as the sole Creator and benevolent Ruler of the universe.* Nowhere is there a hint that God "shares" His dominion with another God. There is neither a pantheon nor a henotheism in revelational history. God is the sole God.

I am well familiar with the evolutionary hypothesis of the history of religion, its Troeltshian interpretation and modern refinements and change, as well as with the Wellhausen school of Old Testament interpretation and its theory of various Old Testament documents. Its roots, of course, are found in Hegelian idealism. The latter has had to die a rather violent death in the brutality of two world wars; the former, however, has survived. I must leave the evaluations and refutation to Old Testament scholarship. Personally, I find it more confusing than helpful. Neither is it based upon history exegesis. It is not an honest theology derived from the Old Testament, but rather, speculation which is based upon David Humes' premise that the perfect is a development of the imperfect. Such a premise is totally unacceptable to the Bible which begins and ends with monotheism.

2. *The insistence upon God as the Lord of hosts who remains the Ruler and Judge of the nations and who actually uses them as His instruments for judgment in advancing His cause.* Much confusion has been created by an interpretation of history which casts a shadow upon God. I refer to a seeming narrow and false view of the Pauline statement in Romans 1:24, 26, 28 that "God gave them up." Certainly Paul does not mean that God completely disassociated Himself from the nations to set them free from all restraint, for this would set at nought His Creator-relationship, His promise to and covenant relationship with them (Gen 1 − 2; 9:8-17, 25-37). It would violate His moral governorship of the universe and disclaim His omnipresence in the world. Total divine abandonment of the nations could have resulted only in total chaos where eventual salvation would become an impossibility. Thus, whatever "God gave them up" may imply, it cannot mean total divine disassociation from the nations and absolute abandonment.

To the contrary, the universal presence of God and His unhindered operation are evident everywhere in the Old Testament. He is neither the God of one tribe or people nor the God of one locale, even though ancient folk religion often sought to make Him such. He was present in Ur of the Chaldees to call Abraham, and later in Haran to summon him. He proved His saving power in Egypt and His sufficiency in the desert, accompanying Israel through the territory of the various nations. He was with them in Palestine and later in Babylon, raising up prophets in both places.

However, His people are not the only ones in His presence, for His watchful eye is upon the world. He knows in detail the sins of the nations; He sets their bounds and time and pronounces and executes judgment upon them (compare such passages as Amos 1:3 − 2:3; Ob

1; Is 10:5-34; 13:1 — 23:18; Jer 42 — 51; Eze 25 — 32, 38 — 39; Dan 2:1-45; 7:1-28; 9:20-27; 11:1-45).

God is not localized in His interests and activities; He is the God of the nations. No one escapes His provisions, though nations may grossly misuse such. None evades His moral government. He is present in a certain sense everywhere, even though He has chosen to limit His unique disclosures to and through a particular people. Thus universality and particularism are not mutually exclusive.

It is also evident from the pages of the Bible that God uses the nations as His instruments. He saw fit to lead Israel to Egypt, not only to provide for her physically in the midst of famine, but also to preserve her as a distinct nation and to enrich her culturally. Egypt thus became God's handmaid in serving His people.

God calls Nebuchadnezzar "my servant" (Jer 25:9; 27:6; 43:10), and likewise does He name Cyrus "my shepherd" and "His anointed" with a most remarkable prophecy to follow (Is 44:28 — 45:13). He speaks of the Assyrian as "the rod of mine anger" and declares "the staff in their hand is mine indignation" (Is 10:5). The "kings of the Medes" are his "battle axe and weapons of war" in the destruction of Babylon (Jer 51:11, 20). Thus God's hand is moving in the affairs of the nations.

The most beautiful presentation of God's relation to the nations is found in the book of Jonah. Nineveh is completely outside the bounds of particularistic revelation, but it is still within the bounds of God's care and concern, to the degree that He sends them a messenger, grants them grace for repentance, and spares the city from destruction, much to the digust of nationalist and particularist Jonah. It is evident that the prophet was unable to see God's universalistic design of salvation behind particularistic revelation. Thus he was unwilling and unable to enter into God's gracious relationship to the nations beyond particularistic revelation.

3. *The pronounced and condemning attitude toward the development and practices of religion outside the sphere of particularistic revelation.* Nowhere does God approve the nonrevelational religions or consider them as the legitimate religions of the nations of the world. He is not indifferent toward the religion and worship of the nations; to the contrary, a consistent critical and condemning attitude of the Old Testament persists toward all religions outside of particularistic revela-

tion. This criticism is one of the most difficult aspects of the Old Testament for modern man. It seems to be too separatistic, too self-assertive, too intolerant, too imperialistic. There is no room for dialogue. The Old Testament knows nothing about the "logos" or "fulfillment" theory. Neither is the "way of synthesis" or the "way of reconception" acceptable. It knows only the "way of radical displacement," whether congenial to modern man or not.

4. *The clear pronouncements and inclusive promises of the Old Testament.* The material in this area is so abundant that only a meager selection can be listed. There is no doubt that the central thrust of the salvation of God as envisaged in the Old Testament is racial rather than national, universal rather than particular. This does not mean that Israel subjectively interpreted it as such. Objective revelation makes the constant promise an abiding thrust of the Old Testament. This is evident at all epochal events and crucial moments of Old Testament history and revelation.

We have already pointed out the universal and irrevocable racial promise of the protevangelium (Gen 3:15), the morning star of "primitivism." We have spoken of the universality of the covenant of God with Noah and the prophetic pronouncements of Noah (Gen 9:8-17; 9:25-27). All three of these events are within the "racial revelation" of God and are, therefore, universal in significance. As this is the central thrust in "racial revelation," it remains constant throughout "national revelation."

The universality of God's intent is clearly implied in the promises to Abraham (Gen 12:3) and in the prelude to the covenant with Israel (Ex 19:3-6). It is given prominence in the Psalms and included by Solomon in his dedicatory prayer of the temple (2 Ch 6:32-33). And most certainly the promise is present in Isaiah 53. Old Testament salvation is not particularistic in promise and outlook, a fact which is established later in detail.

5. *The solemn and unique calling of Israel to be God's witness and God's priesthood as instituted under Moses and developed by the prophets.* Little needs to be said on this subject. In no uncertain terms had God commanded Israel to be His royal priesthood (Ex 19:5-6), to be His servant and His witness (Is 40-53) and to show forth His praises among the nations (Is 43:21). Later Christ speaks

of His people as the salt of the earth and the light of the world (Mt 5:13-15). Israel was a peculiar, singular people with a glorious calling and mission (Deu 7:6; 14:2; 26:18-19).

The divine calling was accompanied by tremendous divine graces and enrichings. These, in turn were matched by equally weighty responsibilities. Somehow the world's religious fate was bound up with Israel's faithfulness and self-giving. Their calling demanded more than animal sacrifices. It required the dedication of the nation to the service of God for the welfare of the world.

MISSIONARY UNFOLDING IN THE PATRIARCHAL AGE

The first cluster of promises given to Abraham, who was perhaps yet in Ur of the Chaldees, includes a promise to the world. Indeed, this is the fullest of all the promises. It is great to receive a blessing, but it is greater to dispense a blessing. Thus Abraham is assured that "in thee shall all families of the earth be blessed" (Gen 12:3). This promise and assurance are repeated in Genesis 18:19; 22:19 (cf. Ac 3:25; Gal 3:8).

It makes little difference whether we accept the above translation or the suggested reading, "by you all the families of the earth shall bless themselves" (RSV). The difference is one of methodology and not of principle.

The central and significant fact is that the call of Abraham is not personal favoritism of a particularistic god to establish a local religion in practice and design. It originates in the God of glory and is designed for the welfare of mankind. Just as God does not call His minister for the minister's sake but for the sake of the congregation, the community and the world, so He did not call Abraham for Abraham's sake. The world was in view, and mankind was the goal, whatever the methodology. This promise, with its design of universal intention, was transferred in due time to the patriarchs, Isaac (Gen 26:4) and Jacob (28:14). In a somewhat different form, both enriched and more specific, Judah inherited it from Jacob (49:10) and became the standard-bearer of Israel, though Levi was chosen for the priesthood. Thus there is no weakening of universality in the patriarchal time. God's universal design and intent were emphatically spelled out to them.

MISSIONARY UNFOLDING IN THE MOSAIC AGE

The Mosaic stage enriched the religion of the Israelites in many ways, making it a religion of miraculous redemption, positive monotheism, devoted consecration, dynamic ethics, responsive faith, love and obedience, organized worship, unified law and a great hope. Although it did not add many references to universality, it did emphasize inclusiveness in the memorable prelude, which precedes the inauguration of Israel as a nation, the giving of the Decalogue and the covenant. If this prelude were properly grasped, it would be of revolutionary and enlivening significance to Israel by giving her history meaning, purpose and direction. Says the almighty God to His people about to be covenanted and to be constituted into a nation, "Ye have seen what I did unto the Egyptians, and how I bare you on eagles' wings, and brought you unto myself. Now therefore, if ye will obey my voice indeed, and keep my covenant, then ye shall be a peculiar treasure unto me above all the people: *for all the earth is mine:* and ye shall be unto me a kingdom of priests, and an holy nation. These are the words which thou shalt speak unto the children of Israel" (Ex 19:4-6).

Much human speculation has surrounded the interpretation of this passage. It has been inferred that Israel in this decisive moment of her history left the basis of grace and promise (the dispensation of promise divinely initiated in Abraham) and entered a new epoch — the dispensation of the law. Such interpretation, however, does not do justice to the scriptural significance of this event as interpreted by Moses, the prophets, and Paul. Neither does it properly set forth the meaning of the Mosaic covenant and law, especially the Ten Commandments. Nowhere does Moses think in terms of a new dispensation or of himself as the founder of a new epoch in the history of religion. The prophets never interpret the event in terms of newness, though in many ways normative. The covenant with and the promises to Abraham are the prophets' stay and consolation throughout history. The people know themselves as heirs both of the Abrahamic covenant and promises. They are the rightful children of the fathers, Abraham, Isaac and Jacob. Paul joins them in this interpretation in Galatians 3, pointing out that the two covenants run parallel from Sinai to Calvary, where the Sinaitic covenant ends and the Abrahamic covenant — at least in part — finds fulfillment.

The passage from Exodus 19 quoted above must be interpreted in terms of servanthood. *The Abrahamic covenant makes Israel the people of God while the Mosaic covenant makes Israel a nation and servant of God.* The Mosaic covenant is not related to salvation nor to Israel's becoming God's possession because they already were such in Egypt, which was the reason God delivered them. Rather, it constitutes Israel as a nation of *unique position among the nations* of the world as through Abraham they had received a *peculiar relationship.* Here responsibility is matched with privilege.

At this moment God is most emphatic that all the earth, nations included, is His. Israel is not His only possession. In this, Israel is not essentially unique. It is unique, however, in its position and mission. It is to be, God says, "my own possession," living in extraordinary relationship to Him and above all people; it is to be "a kingdom of priests" mediating between God and the nations in order to share richly with the nations and to manifest God's glory. Israel is to live in the "environment of God" while living in the midst of the nations.

This high calling of Israel, of course, places tremendous demands upon the people which manifest themselves in high religious (Tablet I of the Ten Commandments) and moral ideals (Tablet II), rigid discipline (the rules and regulations), solemn commitments (the covenant), unique source of strength (worship — tabernacle, sacrifices, priesthood, annual festivities). Israel became the *people of God* in the sovereign and gracious call of Abraham without any conditions attached to it. To become the *servant of God* to the nations of the world, however, is circumscribed by rigid divine regulations and conditioned by absolute and voluntary commitment and by implicit obedience.

This servanthood of Israel is most fully described in Isaiah 40 — 55. Repeatedly Israel is described as "my servant." The words "my servant" are used eighteen times in this portion.

Thrice God speaks of Israel as "my witnesses" (43:10, 12; 44:8). The legitimate question is, A witness to whom? Explicitly the Lord declares, "This people have I formed for myself; they shall shew forth my praise" (43:21). Show forth His praise to whom? Verse 9 gives us the direction: "Let all the nations be gathered together, and let the people be assembled." Here is the audience of Israel. Here is her mission!

This servanthood concept is not weakened by the fact that four servant songs are uniquely devoted to that "ideal Servant" of God who is Christ Himself, as we show later. The servanthood of Israel is clearly set forth. Israel has a mission to perform, a service to render. The words of Paul echo the true calling of Israel in the Old Testament: "I am a debtor both to the Greeks, and the Barbarians; both to the wise and to the unwise" (Ro 1:14). That Israel did not recognize this servanthood position and serve mankind does not destroy the Old Testament ideal for, and calling of, the nation.

As we keep in mind this twofold position and relationship of Israel, much of the Scriptures will gain a new perspective and deeper meaning. Never does Israel cease to be the people of God, though because of failure she is rejected temporarily as the servant of God. She remains disqualified until genuine repentance will restore her again. Such restoration is both promised by the grace of God and demanded by the justice and faithfulness of God.

The explicit and implicit universality of the Exodus passage is evident. God explicitly states that all of the earth is His. As Creator He is its rightful Possessor. Israel must keep this in mind and think of God neither in local geographical terms nor in tribal or national terms. He is the God of all the earth, all mankind included. In the terms of Melchizedek to Abraham, He is the "Most High God," the Possessor of heaven and earth, the *El Elyon*. Israels' position is not of sole possessor of God.

Having made this explicit pronouncement as a reminder to Israel for Israel's humiliation and gratitude, God declares Israel's position in the midst of His total possession. Israel is to be His "peculiar treasure among all people," "a kingdom of priests" and "a holy nation."

We realize the variations of translations that are possible here, but these matter little for our purpose. The fact is that here God defines Israel's threefold relationship:

Her relationship to Jehovah. Israel is a peculiar treasure among the nations, variously translated as "my own treasure," denoting singularly "personal property," or "you will be privileged for me among all the peoples." Whatever translation we choose, the meaning is clear: Israel is to be uniquely related to the Lord.

Her relation to the nations. Israel is to be a kingdom of priests, again variously translated as a "royal priesthood" (Septuagint), "a priestly kingdom" (Vulgate), "kingdom of priests" (Peshitto), and "kings and priests" (Targum). Again, whatever translation we may prefer, the fact is clear that Israel is God's priest and is to perform a priestly ministry in the world. She is to be God's mediator. No priest exists unto himself; he has value and meaning only as a mediator.

Her relation to herself. Israel is to be a holy nation, a nation separated from worldly defilement, insulated against sin, and dedicated to God in wholehearted devotion and joyous service. Only so will Israel be able to be the receptacle of God and the dispenser for God. Thus universality in design is written into the preamble of the national covenant and charter of Israel.

In the light of the above divine statements, a study of the attitude and relationship of the Israelite to the stranger is most illuminating. No other religion regulates this matter as carefully as does the Old Testament and no other religion enjoins similar practices or expresses similar concerns. The references in the Pentateuch are too numerous to study in detail. I select a few more significant injunctions and regulations to illustrate the Old Testament position.

The stranger is expected to join Israel on an equal basis and observe the Passover (Ex 12:48; Num 9:14); he shall not be vexed or oppressed by the Israelite (Ex 22:21); he is informed that his offering will be acceptable (Num 15:14); he shall receive righteous judgment before the judges (Deu 1:16); he is assured of the loving care of the Lord along with the widows and orphans (Deu 10:18); he may freely share in the covenant with Jehovah and stand before the Lord (Deu 29:11); he shall be gathered with the rest of the people to receive the instruction of the law (Deu 31:12).

Such are some of the injunctions and privileges of the stranger. Old Testament revelation was not a closed national religion; it held its doors wide open. It had its theological, moral and ceremonial restrictions, but it was neither racially nor nationally a closed system. The stranger was welcome, and his acceptance on equal status was assured.

MISSIONARY UNFOLDING IN THE DAVIDIC AGE

The impact of David upon the religious life of Israel is not often treated separately. Yet it is well to think of David as the initiator of renewal and enrichment in the history of Israel. While there may not be a new beginning, there is a high level of worship introduced which makes Israel an exclusively worshiping community. It is apparent that the life and service of David were of tremendous significance not only in building Israel into a unified kingdom but also in giving Israel a politico-religious center (Jerusalem) and an ordered and beautiful worship service. Though he was not permitted to build the temple, David made all the plans and preparations for it. His son Solomon had only to execute the plan.

For our purpose we point to two important factors: The message and usage of the Psalms; and the prayer of dedication of the temple by Solomon.

The message and usage of the Psalms. The Psalms are probably the richest religious literature in the world. Reflecting the religious experiences of the saints, they are existential in their content, speech and form. They speak to the hearts of people, and continued blessings flow from them.

While the authors of some psalms are unknown and the dates of others are late, seventy-three are assigned to David. Thus nearly half the Psalter comes to us from "the sweet psalmist of Israel." No doubt they were designed partly for use in private devotion but mainly in public worship, as the superscriptions of Asaph and Korahitic psalms indicate. It must be said that these latter two added some twenty-four psalms to the list of David's composition.

Speaking of the usage of the Psalms, Dr. Robert Martin-Achard of Geneva says:

> The major preoccupation of the psalmists was not with propaganda for *Yaweh* directed to the heathen. Their psalms were designed to be used by the Jerusalemite community and concerned Israel and not the nations. They voice the chosen peoples faith and in so doing, they strengthened it. The hymnody of the Old Testament originates in the Temple and is intended for the use of the believers assembled at Jerusalem.
>
> The sole purpose of the writers of the psalms is to praise the God of Israel. . . . Yaweh deserves the praise of the whole creation; this is the thought that is voiced in more than one psalm. It is not only the nations that are to be summoned by the faithful among the chosen people. The heavens, the earth, the rivers, and even the sea must also applaud the God of Israel. It is by reason of their belonging to the realm of creation and not because they are called to share Israel's faith, that the heathen must glorify God.[10]

This, however, is only relatively true. It is a profound fact that "the hymn of praise is missionary preaching par excellence," especially when we realize that such missionary preaching is supported in the Psalms by more than 175 references of a universalistic note relating to the nations of the world. Many of them bring hope of salvation to the nations.

This was a most astounding discovery for me some years ago. The believer will be greatly enriched in his missionary thinking by reading through the Psalms and underlining all references relating to the nations of the earth. Indeed, the Psalter is one of the greatest missionary books in the world, though seldom seen from that point of view. Not only are the Psalms permeated with references of universal connotation, but whole psalms are missionary messages and challenges. Study carefully Psalm 2, 33, 66, 72, 98, 117, 145.

The impact of such hymnody must have been profound upon a spiritually minded people. What must it have meant to the pious Hebrew heart when he heard the choral chant accompanied by musical instruments:

> All nations whom thou hast made
> Shall come and worship before thee, O Lord;
> And they shall glorify thy name.
> For thou art great and doest wondrous things:
> Thou art God alone.
>
> God be merciful unto us, and bless us;
> And cause his face to shine upon us;
> That thy way may be known upon earth,
> Thy salvation among all nations.
> Let the peoples praise thee, O God;
> Oh let the nations be glad and sing for joy;
> For thou wilt judge the peoples with equity,
> And govern the nations upon earth.
> Let the peoples praise thee, O God;
> Let all the peoples praise thee.
> The earth hath yielded its increase:
> God, even our own God, will bless us.
> God will bless us;
> And all the ends of the earth shall fear him.
> PSALM 86:9-10; 67:1-7, ASV

Universality is pronounced and consistent in the Psalms.

Prayer of dedication. The building and dedication of the temple were of great national and religious significance to the people of God in the Old Testament. The temple ushered in a new era in the outer order of worship. Its design was to unify the nation and to symbolize the unity and glory of Jehovah. Israel was to have only one temple and one central place of worship, even as it worshiped only one God.

The dedicatory performances were elaborate and imposing. While we wonder at the almost numberless sacrifices, we admire the dedicatory prayer of King Solomon which represents the spiritual heart of all rites, ceremonies and liturgy. We are on sacred ground in this prayer. It is more than a man's prayer; it expresses more than a man's desires and yearnings. The imprint of the Holy Spirit is evident in it. Solomon, as the representative of the people of God, prayed under the inspiration and direction of the Holy Spirit and thus expressed the design of God for His people. From this point of view we must read this prayer. And as we do so, we find a marvelous unfolding of the thoughts of God.

It is well to note the comprehensiveness and inclusiveness of the prayer. Solomon, mindful of the various needs of his people and his land, humbly petitioned the Lord to be gracious to the people when they would cry to Him in the various circumstances of life and history.

Having made his prayer for the people, Solomon was led by the Spirit to anticipate the coming of the stranger to pray at the temple. Thus he included the stranger in his petitions that he too might find an open door into the presence of the Lord.

In summary, he then stated the *missionary purpose* of it all: "That all people of the earth may know thy name, to fear thee, as do thy people Israel; and that they [the nations] may know that this house, which I have builded, is called by thy name" (1 Ki 8:43).

Once more Solomon reviews the needs of his people and in supplication presents them to the Lord. And once more he expresses *the missionary design* of it all: "That all the people of the earth may know that the LORD is God, and that there is none else" (1 Ki 8:60).

We may seriously question whether Solomon realized the full implication of his prayer. Nevertheless, the Holy Spirit directed him to include the stranger in his prayer and to point out the missionary significance of the temple. The temple was God's monument of His relationship to the earth and of the accessibility to God by all nations.

As such, Isaiah saw the temple (Is 56:7). Here God was making Himself known in an extraordinary manner to all people.

MISSIONARY UNFOLDING IN THE PROPHETIC AGE

The rabbi (prophet) phenomenon was not peculiar to the revelational religion of Israel, for it was widespread and may be found throughout Asia. Thus considerable study has engaged both the Old Testament scholars as well as the students of comparative religions to delineate between the revelational and nonrevelational, or biblical and extrabiblical prophets.

The liberal scholar is ready to evaluate everything according to the principle of continuity and sees merely a difference in degree of inspiration between the various prophets. The conservative Christian is not inclined to accept such a position and seeks for the qualitative distinctness in broad historical terms.

It may be helpful to think of four concentric circles. The innermost circle represents the authentic prophets of God in the Old Testament. The next circle encompasses a large number of prophets mentioned or unmentioned in the Old Testament and characterized as false prophets. The 450 prophets of Baal (1 Ki 18:22) are examples of this movement. They are numerous and widespread, deceived and deceiving, ever ready and ever active.

The third circle represents the prophets of the neighboring nations of Israel. Here, too, men were voicing oracles and speaking for their gods.

The fourth and widest circle in our studies would include the prophets of Persia — Zoroaster (600-583 B.C.), the founder of Zoroastrianism, also known as the religion of the Parsis; India — Mahavira (Vardhamana) (599-527 B.C.), founder of Jainism of India; Gautama (Buddha) (560-480 B.C.) founder of Buddhism; China — Lao-tzu (604-517 B.C.), founder of Taoism of China; Confucius (551-479 B.C.), founder of Confucianism of China.

The most astounding factor of this phenomenon is the fact of their contemporaneousness, though Zoroaster of Persia preceded the men of India and China somewhat.

The phenomenon has raised the question whether, indeed, the prophetic movement was peculiar to Israel or whether it was a movement of the time and culture.

Dr. Edward J. Young has submitted this question to serious examination and presents his thesis for the uniqueness of Israel's prophets in his book entitled *My Servants the Prophets,* an able apologetic for the uniqueness and authenticity of the biblical prophets of Jehovah which will answer many questions. In his appendix, Dr. Young compares biblical and "extra-biblical prophecy" in the ancient world and concludes that there are "certain formal similarities" with "great difference in content." It is "evident that they were separated by a wide gulf. They were different one from another as day is from night."[11]

Authenticating marks of the prophets of God. The world phenomenon of "prophecy" and "prophets" raises the question of the authenticity of a prophet of Jehovah. What are his distinguishing qualities? How can we differentiate the genuine from the pretender? Here are six characteristics of a prophet of Jehovah:

1. The prophet and his singular personality and integrity. The prophet of God makes no claims to authority, wisdom, insight, or superior intelligence. His absolute independence of man and circumstances makes objectivity possible. He seeks neither favor nor pleasure, position nor wealth. He proclaims objective truth, much of which he has subjectively experienced and digested. Much of it has gone beyond his experience except for his having received it. Integrity of character marks his service, message and relationship.

2. The prophet and his imperturbable consciousness of divine commission. He comes in the name of Jehovah and speaks in the authority of his Lord. He considers himself sent and commissioned. "Thus saith the Lord" or "the Word of the Lord came" is his authority and commission. He knows himself to be a spokesman for God.

3. The prophet and his inner authentication by the Spirit of the Lord. "Thus saith the Lord" rings out in fullest assurance, authenticated in his own mind by the presence of the Holy Spirit. Thus his message came not in word only but also in power and in the Holy Ghost and in much assurance.

4. The prophet and his incorruptible verdict and value judgment. The pronouncements of the prophets are clear-cut and decisive. Above all, they are objective and according to truth. Their standard is the plumbline of the Lord, the absolute law of God.

5. The prophet and his sense of unworthiness and deep conflict in service. The fact of unworthiness is expressed by the prophets repeat-

edly, and their sufferings and conflicts are well summarized by the writer of the book of Hebrews (11:37-38).

6. The prophet and his triumphant expectations and visions of faith. Though speaking by revelation to the people of their times and to the conditions of their day and forecasting gloom and judgment upon the people, their God inspires hope and forecasts ultimate triumph.

The message of the prophets of God. The message of the revelational prophets arises out of immediate circumstances and speaks to the immediate conditions and emergencies. In this sense it was experiential and historical. To limit it to this platform, however, is to rob it of its distinctly divine quality, origination and orientation. The messages of Lao-tzu, Confucius, Gautama (Buddha) and other "prophets" also arose out of distinct local needs and circumstances and spoke to the people of their time. The messages of the latter, however, lack that deeper level of continued contemporaneousness, the present-tenseness, that abidingness. They do not have that special Messianic forecast, vision, hope and inspiration.

The message of the prophet of God has at least a threefold significance:

1. It speaks to the "immediate" society and circumstances: *it is historical.*

2. It speaks to the "contemporary" society and circumstances. It has spoken through the centuries and it speaks to us today; *it is existential.*

3. It speaks to the "Messianic" society and circumstances. It forecasts events and happenings and calls upon other "prophets" to do likewise. It points to this quality as a divinely authenticating characteristic (see Is 43:9; 41:22; 44:7). *It is prophetic* in the profoundest sense.

The missionary thrust of the prophets. The voice of the prophets regarding the missionary thrust of divine purpose and salvation is clear and pronounced. For the purpose of our studies we group the prophets in the following manner: postexilic prophets — Haggai, Zechariah, Malachi; exilic prophets — Jeremiah, Ezekiel, Daniel; preexilic prophets — Obadiah, Jonah, Nahum, three prophets who direct their entire messages to non-Israelitish nations, Edom and Nineveh respectively. Two are messages of judgment; one is a message of salvation. This leaves seven preexilic prophets: Joel, Amos, Hosea, Isaiah, Micah, Zephaniah, Habakkuk. These come up for our first consideration.

The preexilic prophets. It is well to note two points regarding the preexilic prophets. First, these prophets of God ministered in a span of time of approximately 175 years (800-625 B.C.). Thus they speak very much to the same people and circumstances. It may be expected that their message and the thought forms of their message would be much alike, making room, of course, for personality differences and other factors. Further, it can be expected that there would be considerable duplication which seems like conscious or unconscious borrowing.

Second, all these prophets have at least a note of universality. *Zephaniah* has perhaps the briefest word on universality since he is addressing Judah on the coming judgments of God (cf. 1:2-3 — the face of the earth; 2:11 — all the lands of the nations; 3:8 — all the earth shall be consumed; 3:20 — among all the peoples of the earth).

Thus as the judgments of God on the day of the Lord shall affect all the nations of the earth (1:2-3; 3:8), so shall all revere the Lord (2:11), and all shall know of His saving power (3:19-20).

Habakkuk lays down three basic principles of universal significance:

1. a universal principle of justification by faith (2:4)
2. a universal knowledge of the glory of the Lord (2:14)
3. a universal worship of the Lord (2:20)

Thus he qualifies well as a universalist behind a national particularism.

Joel, in addressing Judah and warning the land of the awful judgment in the day of the Lord, also tells of blessings to follow. As the judgments of God will be upon all nations (Joel names at least seven of them, 2:20; 3:4, 6, 8-9, and speaks of "all nations," 3:9, 11-12), so will all nations share in the gift of the Spirit (2:28, "all flesh") and in the peace that will follow the judgment of the day of the Lord (3:9-12).

Amos, a thunderous voice at Bethel — is vibrant with a heart of conviction and passion. He is more than a preacher, he is a prophet of social justice based upon personal righteousness. Though seemingly an unlearned man of humble occupation, Amos is one of the most observant students of history and world affairs. His detailed knowledge of the life and sins of the nation is as astounding as is his boldness in proclaiming the sweeping judgments.

His universality is more implicit than explicit. Yet, the very fact that God is the universal Judge would include the principle that God is also the universal Saviour. He is the God of the nations, and no one escapes His observations, care and judgment. This thought is expressed in the restoration message which concludes Amos' book (9:7-15, particularly v. 12). Here hope for all nations illuminates the darkness of the book. In the restoration hope of Israel lies the salvation hope of the nations.

God's universality is reinforced by His cosmic control and rule, as the prophet boldly declares it (5:8-9; 9:5-6).

Hosea, perhaps a contemporary of Amos or his close follower, is a son of the Northern Kingdom and speaks as a "home missionary" to his own people. In tender love and warm compassion he pours out his heart and life for the revival of his land. His scathing pronouncements of judgment upon Israel as well as upon Judah are comprehensive and without respect of persons, although expressed in tender sympathy and expectation of repentance. The hope of restoration illuminates the dark skies of judgment and promises a sunrise for his nation. However, Hosea does not go beyond his people. Thus his whole message of warning, judgment and hope relates to Israel. No note of universality is expressed.

The very limited view of universality on the part of Amos and Hosea may not be due to their prophetic vision but rather to the people whom they address. Both found their field of labor in the northern ten tribes, the people of Israel. The Old Testament, however, makes it abundantly clear that God never sanctioned the rupture, nor was there a "future" for Israel as a ten-tribe nation. Their future restoration and their being a blessing were linked with reunification with Judah. Only with Judah will Israel be restored to its proper place in the economy of God. Thus the note of universality is much more pronounced in the prophets of Judah, as we will see in Micah and Isaiah.

Isaiah and Micah were contemporaries and may be considered together. It has well been stated that Isaiah is the great evangel prophet and prince of Old Testament seers. A great internationalist and a prophet of cosmic vision and dimension, he sees not only Israel and the nations renewed, but the heavens and earth as well.

It has become almost common practice to divide the book of

Isaiah into two main sections, chapters 1 — 39 and 40 — 66, and to speak of the latter part as Deutero-Isaiah. I do not hold this view, but consider the book a basic unity written by the same author. For study purposes, however, we adopt the above division of the book.

In the first section (chaps. 1 — 39) Isaiah, the prophet-statesman, addresses not only Judah but also the nations of the world. His philosophy of history assumes them all as under the sovereign rule of the holy One of Israel and under the just judgment of the righteousness of God. No gods of the nations can interfere with His sovereignty and power and save from His judgments. Thus the nations are warned of God (chaps. 10 and 13 — 23). The power of God over the nations is further established in His intervention and specific judgment upon the Assyrians (chaps. 36 — 37). The nations, however, are also included in the great promises of blessing which Isaiah prophesied, according to the following references: 2:1-4; 11:3-4, 9-10; 25:6-9.

The climax of all prophecy in the Old Testament is found in the second section of Isaiah, a rich mine from which interpreters have drawn much precious gold, but also much wood, hay and stubble. Debate over the authorship and unity has often clouded the deep treasures unveiled there, but the fact remains that the treasure is there to be enjoyed by all who accept the message as from God.

No doubt the second division of Isaiah is the most Messianic segment of Old Testament writings. Also the most emphatic assertion of absolute monotheism, it contains the most scathing pronouncement of the "nothingness and folly" of idolatry and presents the sharpest focusing upon servanthood to be found in the Old Testament.

Our study here is confined to the "servanthood" as unfolded in this section, especially in chapters 40 — 53. In these chapters God is addressing Israel in a most intimate manner. He speaks of her as "my people," "Israel whom I have chosen," "Israel my chosen," "my nation" and "my messenger." The most frequent designation is "my servant," which occurs thirteen times (41:8-9; 42:1, 19; 43:10; 44:1-2, 21, 26; 45:4; 49:3, 6; 52:13). To this must be added "the servant of the Lord" (42:19), "his servant" (44:26; 49:5; 50:10), and "his servant Jacob" (48:20). Thus a total of eighteen references speak of servanthood. This is most significant for a section of material which is so highly Messianic. Is the Messianic hope on the deepest level a hope of blessings to be experienced and enjoyed, or a servantship to be rendered?

Within this portion are four particular passages commonly known as the "servant songs" (Is 42:1-9; 49:1-13; 50:4-9; 52:13 — 53:12), depicting the "ideal Servant of Jehovah." Isaiah thus seems to speak of two different servants: Israel as a servant of Jehovah, and an ideal man as a Servant of Jehovah.

H. Wheeler Robinson, after submitting the section to a careful comparative study, concludes that the "servant" of the servant songs must be distinguished from the nation of Israel as a servant of Jehovah because "on the one hand, the general character of the Servant in the Songs is different from that in the rest of Deutero-Isaiah, and on the other, there are passages which suggest a mission to, rather than of, Israel."[12] These are important points deserving careful attention.

We turn our attention first to *Israel as the servant of Jehovah*. What is the major responsibility of Israel as a servant of Jehovah, according to Isaiah? It seems to me that the primary mission is expressed in two phrases recurring several times. They are, "Ye are my witnesses" (43:10, 12; 44:8) and "My [His] messenger" (42:19; 44:26). Israel had a message to declare in this world. This was the servant's supreme responsibility.

Three truths surround this mission:

1. Israel's mission is a God-appointed mission. God is explicit in His emphasis that He is the source and Originator of this mission. He created Jacob, He formed Israel, He redeemed His people; He is the Creator and Redeemer, the King and holy One of Israel. Over and over these phrases and designations recur. Israel is not a self-made people, nor a nation of a self-appointed destiny; Israel is "the people whom I formed for myself that they might declare my praise" (43:21). Israel does not belong to herself but is peculiarly God's people for a uniquely divine mission and purpose. Her origin rests in God, even as her destiny and purpose belong to God. He is the beginning and He must be the end of Israel. Israel must place herself at the disposal of God and live for Him. He will not alter His choice nor will Israel find rest and meaning in life until the nation will yield herself to God.

2. Israel's mission is a God-centered mission. As God is the Originator of the mission of Israel, so He is its center and content. Israel existed principally in Old Testament times for the purpose of *upholding ethical monotheism* in opposition to, and in the midst of, a sea of henotheism, polytheism, and philosophical monism. The last-named

had neither absolute ethical principles, ethical purpose, nor a God-ward direction of life. Spiritual complacency and indifference are the main results of their impact.

The God-centered mission is evident from the continuous emphasis upon the sole Godhead of God: "I am the first, and I am the last; and beside me there is no God" (Is 44:6, see also 44:8; 45:5, 6, 21). Thus the absoluteness, unity and singularity of God are stated over and over again. It should be noted here that because of this fact, and to make this truth vivid to Israel and the nations, worship was permitted and sanctioned only at one place in Israel. Israel was to have only one temple.

In keeping with this emphasis, God presented Himself as the only Creator by whom and in whom the whole universe exists. Besides Him there is no creator.

He is the only Redeemer "and beside me there is no saviour . . . there is none who can deliver from my hand." Also, He is the only God of true prophecy. He alone unveils the mysteries of the post-creation and the secrets of things to come. This is one of the important arguments for the Godhead (Is 41:22; 43:10; 44:7; 45:21; 46:10; 48:3, 5).

This is the positive witness Israel is to uphold in this world. In the midst of religious humanism and idolatrous apostasy, God's people are to uphold ethical monotheism.

God through Isaiah also clearly expresses His attitude toward idolatry with pronouncements and scathing remarks. In various ways God seeks to divert the attention and affections of Israel from idolatry and to redeem her from this evil to make her a witness to Himself in an idolatrous environment.

a. God repeatedly calls to mind His great deeds of redemption and protection which He has wrought in behalf of Israel. This should keep Israel humble and grateful and close to the Lord. His challenge is: "Remember."

b. God employs the mental weapon of irony, pointing to the folly of idolatry. Dr. H. R. Ironside comments on 46:1,

> When Cyrus attacked Babylon and the city fell, the idolatrous priests loaded their helpless gods upon carts to wheel them away

and set them up somewhere else. Idols who could not deliver their worshipers had to be delivered by them from absolute destruction.

God had satirized the making of gods out of the trees of the forest (compare 44:9-20). Now He ridicules those who make graven images out of the various metals. The goldsmith takes the metal, fashions and works over it and then sets it up and says, "This is god." But it is immovable. It cannot walk. It cannot see. It cannot hear. It cannot do anything, and in time of danger it needs someone to protect it. What a God![13]

This is the irony of idolatry. How different is our God! He assures us of the certainty of His care (46:3-4), the certainty of His purpose (46:9-11), and the certainty of His salvation (46:12-13).

c. God combats idolatry by exercising severe judgments upon idolatrous nations. History is replete with examples of vanished nations, ruins of ancient idolatrous empires and decayed cultures. If Babylon is singled out in Isaiah, it may well be because Babylon is usually considered the fountainhead of all idolatry. According to history, idolatry had its origin in Babylon. We find idolatry here in all its pomp, its lasciviousness, its boastings, and its outright defiance of God. Today Babylon is practically obliterated from the face of the earth. This is God's warning to idolatrous nations.

Of course, idolatry does not only mean the worship of molten images. It may also include the worship of great ideas, systems, institutions and personalities. While Hinduism and Buddhism have their countless images, the West has a far more subtle idolatry: a worship of scientism, psychologism, spiritism, etc. God will tolerate no form of idolatry.

d. God upholds before Israel His unchanging love, His assuring presence and boundless promises. Chapters 40 – 48 present some of the greatest and most quoted promises of God which should draw us away from all other gods and bind us in confidence, devotion and faithfulness to God.

e. God appeals to the intellect and raises such questions as: "To whom then will ye liken me, or shall I be equal?" (40:18, 25; 46:5). Note the repeated "Who?" and other challenges to consider the matter soberly and to realize the intellectual folly of idolatry.

f. Finally, note His clear and bold assertions of His uniqueness, supremacy, sovereignty and absoluteness (41:4; 43:13; 44:8-10; 45:22-

23; 46:9-11; 48:12-13). He rules supreme in heaven and on earth. All nations are under His control and judgment, and all must look to Him for salvation. None can resist Him. Thus God confronts idolatry and the idolator and seeks to win us for Himself.

3. Israel's mission is a mission to the nations. Isaiah has some of the finest missionary texts of the Old Testament (cf. 40:5; 42:1, 6-7, 10; 45:22-23; 49:6, 26; 51:4-5; 52:10, 15). Israel exists for the nations and finds true meaning only in world mission.

Though judgment upon unsubmissive nations and kings is implied and idolatry and irreligion are not to be tolerated, salvation is to be for all mankind and is to be offered to all nations on equal terms with equal privileges and blessings. In this great and glorious task Israel is to be God's instrument and mediator.

This mission of Israel was not discovered by religious genius or selfish ambitions and voluntarily assumed. It was divinely bestowed. This is the calling and purpose of Israel. She is not to live to self and self-aggrandizement. Jacob, the supplanter, must give way to Israel, the prince of God, and become God's mediator between God and the nations of the world.

The ideal Servant. All this is magnified and enriched while much is added to the ideal Servant of Jehovah in the four servant songs. Isaiah portrays the servant as the ideal, yet publicly rejected, man. He suffers innocently, voluntarily, sublimely, prayerfully and silently. His sufferings unto death are vicarious, redemptive and atoning because they are God-ordained. However, death gives way to resurrection, and His triumph is complete (Is 52:13 – 53:12).

The three other songs magnify many of these features and all make it clear that this Servant has universal significance. We are told in the first song:

> He will bring forth justice to the nations. . . .
> He will not fail or be discouraged till he
> has established justice in the earth.
> [He will be] a covenant to the people,
> a light to the nations,
> to open the eyes that are blind,
> to bring out the prisoners from the dungeon,
> from the prison those who sit in darkness
> (42:1, 4, 6-7, RSV).

The second song is addressed to the coastlands and the people from afar:

It is too light a thing that you should be my servant
to raise up the tribes of Jacob
and to restore the preserved of Israel;
I will give you as a light to the nations,
that my salvation may reach to the end of the earth
                              (49:6, RSV).

The fourth song informs us:

So shall he startle many nations; kings shall shut their mouths
because of him;
for that which has not been told them they shall see,
and that which they have not heard they shall understand
                              (52:15, RSV).

Thus Israel as the servant of Jehovah and the Messiah as the ideal Servant both have universal significance and find their full meaning only in world service.

The last section of Isaiah (chaps. 55 — 66) deals mainly with the restoration of Israel. Yet, even in the light of this major concern, the note of universality does not diminish. Beautiful promises of rich blessings for the nations are upheld in the midst of glory for Israel. The reader should carefully study such passages as 55:4-5; 56:3-7; 59:19; 60:10-16; 61:5-11. Of special significance is 66:18-21. Although some commentators seek to make this a judgment scene, it is not necessarily so. The evangelization of the entire earth is here expressed perhaps more emphatically than anywhere else in the Old Testament. Here uniquely the Lord promises to take people from among the nations for His peculiar service.

The nations shall not only see His glory; they shall also declare it. And "some of them also [the nations] I will take for priests and for Levites, says the LORD" (66:21, RSV).

Thus, not only is there an equal sharing in salvation blessings, but also in responsible ministry, in equality of position, and in privilege of honor. This is the very pinnacle of Old Testament universality.

The perfect harmony of Micah with Isaiah is seen in the following quote from Micah 4:1-4:

But in the last days it shall come to pass, that the mountain of the house of the LORD shall be established in the top of the mountains, and it shall be exalted above the hills; and people shall flow unto it. And many nations shall come, and say, Come, and let us go up to the mountain of the LORD, and to the house of the God of Jacob; and he will teach us of his ways, and we will walk in his paths: for the law shall go forth of Zion, and the word of the LORD from Jerusalem. And he shall judge among many people, and rebuke strong nations afar off; and they shall beat their swords into plowshares, and their spears into pruninghooks: nation shall not lift up a sword against nation, neither shall they learn war anymore. But they shall sit every man under his vine and under his fig tree; and none shall make them afraid: for the mouth of the LORD of hosts hath spoken it.

The exilic prophets — Jeremiah, Ezekiel, Daniel — and the post-exilic prophets — Haggai, Zechariah, Malachi — do not add or enlarge upon the vision of Isaiah. Neither do they subtract, modify or contradict Isaiah's description of the ministry of Israel and the ideal Servant of Jehovah. Isaiah's universality, therefore, remains constant and normative.

The latter group of prophets, however, labors hard to preserve Israel as a peculiar people and to mold her into the servant of Jehovah. Jeremiah seeks to preserve the sin-consciousness, Ezekiel the God-awareness, Daniel the kingdom-consciousness, and Haggai, Zechariah and Malachi the consciousness of Israel as peculiarly God's people.

CONCLUSION

Thus universality of salvation pervades the entire Old Testament. It is not peripheral but rather constitutes the intent of Old Testament revelation because it constitutes the dominant purpose of the call, life and ministry of Israel.

The Old Testament does not contain missions; it is itself "missions" in the world. Like a lonely voice in the wilderness the Old Testament boldly proclaims revelational ethical monotheism in protest to Greek, Egyptian, and early Indian henotheism — the multitudinous systems of surrounding polytheism and incipient philosophical Eastern monism. Raised up by God to declare normative religion, it has been assailed from its beginning and repeatedly threatened with destruction and corruption, but God has graciously and miraculously preserved both the books of its content (the Old Testament) and the people as its bearer (Israel). Indeed the Old Testament is a missionary book and Israel a missionary people.

In Christ the true interpretation and fulfillment of the Old Testament blossomed forth to the healing of the nations of the world. Indeed, the New Testament is the normative interpretation of the Old Testament while at the same time it abrogates and modifies many practices, and transforms, enlarges and completes the revelation of God. Man can now find perfect satisfaction for his spiritual and moral needs and fulfillment of his potentialities. It is this fact that lays upon us the missionary responsibility to the entire world and to each individual.

4

Missionary Theology and the New Testament

THE MISSIONARY THEOLOGY of the New Testament (outside of the gospels) is not difficult to establish. We need only remind ourselves of the fact that the book of Acts is the authentic missionary record of the apostles and the early church and that all epistles were written to churches established through missionary endeavors. Were Christianity not a missionary religion and had the apostles not been missionaries, we would have no book of Acts and no epistles. With the exception of Matthew, even the gospels were written to missionary churches. The New Testament is a missionary book in address, content, spirit and design. This is a simple fact but it also is a fact of reality and profound significance. The New Testament is theology in motion more than it is theology in reason and concept. It is "missionary theology."

To establish the theology of missions in the New Testament one simply accepts the New Testament for what it is. No reader can remain untouched by its missionary thrust and design. There is perhaps little theology of missions as such in the New Testament because it is in its totality a missionary theology, the theology of a group of missionaries and a theology in missionary movement. Thus it does not present a theology of missions; it *is* a missionary theology. Read the New Testament from that point of view.

It has been reasoned that the apostles did not give world evangelization or missions a high priority since they seem to be saying relatively little about it in their epistles. This seems like a logical deduction except that it rests upon a superficial reading of the New Testament writings and on a misunderstanding of the mind of the apostles.

131

It is true that the apostles do not state or restate Christ's commission in the epistles. It must be kept in mind, however, that the so-called Great Commission as recorded in the various gospels belongs to the *living tradition* of the church of the apostles. The very fact that all the writers of the gospels cite it in one form or another is clear evidence that its existence and content were quite universally known. This is clearly established by Luke as he writes about things "which have been fully established among us" (Lk 1:1, ASV marg.). This, of course, includes the commission to evangelize the world, which Luke states in greater detail than the other writers.

Again, in keeping with the practice of their Master, the apostles upheld great principles of faith and conduct, implanting great ideals of missions into the life of the churches. They trusted that the Holy Spirit in His own time would transform these ideals into dynamic motivation. This had been their own experience. In this manner world evangelism would become a living and dynamic ideal of the churches rather than a "command" in letters to be legally obeyed or submitted to. Thus while the apostles did not command missions, the great ideals in the epistles imply it most emphatically.

This emphasis becomes most pronounced in the writings of the apostle Paul, as might be expected. Is not God the God of all nations? Did not Christ die for all mankind? Is it not stated that God is not willing that any should perish? Are not Christians exhorted to pray for the salvation of all men? Is Paul not definite on his call to be a missionary to the nations? Does he not accept this as a special grace from the Lord? Is not the church to be gathered from among the nations? Is Paul not specific that the ignorant and unbelieving shall perish from the presence of God? Does Paul not uphold certain missionary churches as special examples to other churches? Is Paul not raising a series of startling questions in Romans 10:14-15? Is the apostle not training a large core of faithful workers to carry on the missionary work which he had begun? Such are some of the great New Testament missionary ideals. It is amazing how much of missionary ideology there is in the epistles.

On the other hand, we need to keep in mind that the New Testament presents a twofold movement: the vertical and the horizontal. The latter dominates the Acts of the apostles, the former the epistles.

Together they constitute a divine unit which brings balance to Christianity and to the churches. We must always keep them together.

We must also remember that every church found itself in a mission setting in a very peculiar sense. Every church was surrounded by multitudes without God, without hope. Here was their first challenge, as Paul tells the church at Philippi (Phil 2:12-16). Similar words are spoken to the churches at Corinth, Ephesus, Thessalonica and Colosse.

Again, Paul commends the churches at Rome and Thessalonica for their efforts in evangelizing their communities and beyond their borders (Ro 1:8; 1 Th 1:8). The apostle admonishes the church of Corinth to abound in the work of the Lord (1 Co 15:58), that is, they are to excel, to go beyond their usual bounds, to spill over and do the unusual. The apostle also praises the Philippians for having an active part in his ministry (Phil 4:10). It must be remembered that the Philippian church had a missionary out in the field (Phil 2:25).

Paul expects that his own example will inspire others to follow in his train. He calls upon the churches to follow him even as he follows Christ (1 Co 11:1; 4:16; Phil 3:17; 1 Th 1:6; 2 Th 3:6-7). He makes it clear that his supreme mission is evangelism (1 Co 1:17, "For Christ sent me not to baptize, but to preach the gospel [evangelize]"). He speaks in no uncertain terms of his mission to evangelize (1 Co 9:16-18). To follow Paul meant to pursue the path of evangelism.

Finally, the writings of Paul present some of the greatest missionary texts and thoughts. We cannot read Romans 10:12-18 and not think missions. Second Corinthians 5:9-21 remains a standard missionary text, and no doubt these verses have inspired thousands to an active participation in missions. Ephesians 3:1-12 rings with a missionary challenge. This is true also of such passages as Romans 1:13-17; 1 Corinthians 9:16-18; Philippians 2:14-16; 1 Timothy 2:1-7. Many others could be listed. Paul says much about missions and evangelism. Supremely an exponent and propagator of the gospel, he expected the early churches to be of like kind.

Missions is not peripheral in the New Testament. The apostles knew the value of missions in their own experiences. They actively enlisted newly founded churches in the missionary enterprise, soliciting their prayers, accepting their contributions, and drawing their co-laborers almost exclusively from them. This is especially true of the apostle Paul, who wrote no prayer letters to his home churches; nor did he call upon them to send additional funds and laborers. He found all the needed resources in the new churches. They shared in the practical universality of the apostles and became missionary churches by nature, design, calling and practice.

In order to present missionary theology of the New Testament, we shall briefly survey the basic missionary concepts which underlie the misisonary activities of the twelve. We shall also look at the missionary theology of Paul.

THE TWELVE

The gospels report very few of the sayings of the apostles. Here they were observers, followers, learners, disciples. To know their mind and learn their theology we must hear them speak and read their writings. Our main sources, therefore, are the book of Acts and those epistles written by apostles.

In the book of Acts we see the apostles at work, first as missionaries to their own people and later as ambassadors of Christ to the nations of the world, though we do not have the accounts of the various members of the apostolate. Retrospectively Mark writes, "And they [the apostles] went forth, and preached every where, the Lord working with them, and confirming the word with signs following" (Mk 16:20). The exact locations and geographical areas we are unable to establish with certainty. From the course of history of Christianity in apostolic times, we are justified to conclude that all of them were effective evangelists and missionaries. According to tradition, most of them laid down their lives as martyrs in the mission fields of the world. The rapid and far-flung spread of Christianity within a few decades is our best commentary on the zeal and labors of the apostles.

We have valuable insight into the motivation of these men in this missionary thrust. Implicit and explicit theology becomes evident.

The great dividing line in the lives of the twelve is Pentecost, the watershed of evangelical missions. Here New Testament missions began a progressive course of realization. Therefore, the missionary significance of Pentecost is beyond human estimation. The presence of the Holy Spirit in the lives of the apostles made all the difference, for it fashioned them into men of God and apostles. Boldly they confessed that they were witnesses of God's redemptive event in Christ, emphasizing particularly the death and resurrection of Jesus Christ. To the Jews at Jerusalem they witnessed supremely of the resurrection of Christ. Boldly they taught that in the resurrection God had vindicated all the claims of Christ, had consummated redemption, and had established Christ as Lord, Christ (Messiah), Saviour and Judge (Ac 2:32, 36; 3:15, 26; 4:10-11, 33; 5:31-32; 7:52, 56). Emphatically they declared that Christ alone is the Saviour of mankind and that there is no salvation in any other, "for there is none other name under heaven given among men, whereby we must be saved" (Ac 4:12). Courageously they told the high court about their inner compulsion to obey God rather than any court order. Bravely they stated, "Whether it be right in the sight of God to hearken unto you more than unto God, judge ye." And again, "We ought to obey God rather than men" (Ac 4:19; 5:29). The lordship of Christ controlled their lives; His will and word were their command. The inner glow of their experiences could not be contained; they had to speak the things they had seen and heard.

Therefore, we gather that their missionary theology sprang from a deep well with roots in eternal verities which became their earthly experiences. There is no other reasonable explanation for their missionary glow and go. The great missionary ideals which Christ had lived and taught came to their fruition in God's time and under the gracious ministry of the Holy Spirit. The Holy Spirit did not operate in hearts devoid of truth and reality.

As we trace the missionary theology of the apostles, we come to the depth of their missionary motivation. Let us define several areas which relate to their missionary thrust.

APOSTOLIC MISSIONARY MOTIVATION

It is never easy to do justice in an analysis of motivations. They are not singular but become dynamic in constellations. Some are evident while others remain hidden and unrecognized. Some surface and become dominant at one occasion and others at another time. Thus even the best analysis is a penetration only in part.

We are assisted in our study of the apostles by some clear statements on their part as other men sought to probe their motivations. This puts us at least in the right path in our pursuit and should also enable us to understand and interpret the apostles correctly even if not completely.

I present a series of summary statements which seem to underlie the great movement of apostolic times and which express at least in part the motivation of the men who turned the world upside down.

THE APOSTLES WERE GRIPPED BY GOD'S GREAT AND SOVEREIGN
REDEMPTIVE ACT ROOTED IN HIS ETERNAL COUNSEL

This act which had taken place in Christ Jesus, the man of Nazareth, had been accomplished in history — in the here and now, in time and space. Taking place according to prophecy, it was completed for the benefit of all mankind. It must be appropriated by faith in Jesus Christ, and such faith is experientially related to repentance from sin.

The apostles knew God had acted. He had acted sovereignly, decisively and redemptively. Though not exonerating the Jews of their guilt in crucifying Christ, Peter unhesitatingly states that Christ was delivered up by the determinate counsel and foreknowledge of God (Ac 2:23; 4:28). The rejection and crucifixion of Christ were not only due to the sin of Israel, for somehow God had acted in them according to His gracious purpose and plan of salvation. Thus the sending of Christ and the resurrection of Christ are consistently ascribed to God; they are the acts of God. Later Peter fully substantiates this position when he writes of Christ as the Lamb without blemish and spot, "who verily was foreordained before the foundation of the world" (I Pe 1:20).

In a similar vein, John writes, "In this was manifested the love of God toward us, because that God sent his only begotten Son into the world, that we might live through him. Herein is love, not that we loved God, but that he loved us, and sent his Son to be the propitiation for our sins." And, again: "The Father sent the Son to be the Saviour of the world." And, once more: "God sent his Son" (1 Jn 4:9-10, 14).

The God of eternal love has acted in a very concrete, decisive, appropriate and effective manner. Though evil hands had crucified the Lord of glory, this was not contrary to the eternal purpose of God. Nor was it independent of His plan, for, in the ultimate sense, God had acted. He gave His Son; He sent His Son. He manifested His love.

Thus God was not frustrated by the rejection and crucifixion of

Christ, because His plan and purpose had not been brought to nought. Rather, the sin and wrath of man served to fulfill the plan of God. Herein lay the hope of forgiveness upon repentance toward God and faith in Christ. Despair and condemnation do not radiate from the cross, but rather, hope and forgiveness.

The apostles were convinced that the decisive, redemptive act of God had taken place in Christ Jesus, the man of Nazareth. Although the act of God was sovereign, it was not without mediation. God's redemptive act was indissolubly linked with Christ. He is the Servant Jesus, the holy One, and the Just, the Prince of life, the Lord of glory (Ac 3:13-15; Ja 2:1). He is Lord, Messiah and Saviour. In the words of Paul, "God was in Christ, reconciling the world unto himself" (2 Co 5:19). The apostles know of no salvation apart from Christ. Only "he that hath the Son hath life" (1 Jn 5:12). They were borne along by the deep conviction of the *sole saviorhood* of Christ crucified and raised. They knew Him and they declared Him boldly as both Saviour and Lord to the Jew as well as to the nations (Ac 2:36; 4:12; 10:36).

Triumphantly Peter declared on the day of Pentecost: "Therefore let all the house of Israel know assuredly, that God hath made that same Jesus, whom ye have crucified, both Lord and Christ" (Ac 2:36). It is most remarkable, almost startling, that Peter commands the convicted and inquiring multitude to "repent, and be baptized . . . in the name of Jesus Christ for the remission of sins" (Ac 2:38). Had not Christ commanded the disciples to baptize "in the name of the Father, and of the Son, and of the *Holy* Ghost" (Mt 28:19)? Why does Peter at Pentecost modify the formula to the name of Jesus Christ?

May I suggest that it was not Peter who modified the formula. It was the directive of the Holy Spirit, and it was done to emphasize the *sole saviorhood* of Jesus Christ. Very similarly, the saviorhood of Christ is lifted up in Acts 3:20; 4:12; 5:31. When asked by what power or by what name the miracle of healing the lame man had been wrought, Peter knows of only one name. Thus "by the *name* of Jesus Christ of Nazareth, whom ye crucified, whom God raised from the dead, even by him doth this man stand here before you whole." And again: "Neither is there salvation in any other: for there is none other *name* under heaven given among men, whereby we must be saved" (Ac 4:10, 12). Emphatically Peter declared, "To him [Christ, the historic Person, slain and raised from the dead and ordained of God to be the

Judge of the quick and the dead] give all the prophets witness, that through his *name* whosoever believeth in him shall receive remission of sins" (Ac 10:43).

Many years later Peter wrote: "Ye know that ye were not redeemed with corruptible things, as silver and gold, from your vain . . . [manner of life] received by tradition from your fathers; but with the precious blood of Christ, as of a lamb without blemish and without spot" (1 Pe 1:18-19). No less does the apostle write a little later, "Christ also hath once suffered for sins, the just for the unjust, that he might bring us to God, being put to death in the flesh, but quickened by the Spirit" (1 Pe 3:18).

No other witness in the New Testament is more emphatic on the sole saviorhood of Christ than is John. Christ is "the propitiation for our sins: and not for our's only, but also for the sins of the whole world." Clearly John states: "Whosoever denieth the Son, the same hath not the Father: [but] he that acknowledgeth the Son hath the Father also." The apostle informs us that "this is his commandment, That we should believe on the name of his Son Jesus Christ." "And this is the record, that God hath given to us eternal life, and this life is in his Son. He that hath the Son hath life; and he that hath not the Son of God hath not life." "The Father sent the Son to be the Saviour of the world," and cleansing from sin is found only in the blood of Jesus Christ (1 Jn 2:2, 23; 3:8; 3:23; 5:11-12; 4:14; 1:7).

According to the witness of John, there is no propitiation, cleansing from sin, deliverance, eternal life, no Father-son relationship without the saviorhood of Christ. This is the solemn declaration of the apostle John in his first epistle.

The harmony of the apostles in this fundamental truth is obvious throughout the New Testament. Jesus Christ is both Saviour and Lord. In Him, God has acted once for all — conclusively, decisively and adequately for all mankind.

The apostles were convinced that the act of God in procuring salvation was a historical event with consequent historical results. It was eternal and spiritual reality manifested in time and in space. It is not "faith-belief" (illusion). It is not mythology or a dream of ecstatics. It is reality concrete and datable. It happened to a historical Person — "Jesus of Nazareth a man approved of God among you by miracles and wonders and signs, which God did by him in the midst of you, as ye yourselves also know" (Ac 2:22; cf. 10:38). It took place in a geo-graphical setting and in a historical city, Jerusalem (Ac 2:14). It occurred under a specific Roman procurator in Palestine, Pilate (Ac 3:13). These are historical facts and cannot be denied. God acted in history, in the here and now.

Therefore Christianity offers a historical salvation, a salvation which is personal and social. It could have become national had Israel as a nation obeyed the gospel. It is real "here and now" in personal experience, offering forgiveness of sin and cleansing from sins and bestowing eternal life which is a present possession. It upholds a trans-forming power in the Holy Spirit, inviting man to share peace, joy, assurance, hope, godliness and fellowship with God through Christ Jesus as present and abiding experiences. It is not merely "pie in the sky." Most certainly history cannot exhaust the fullness and abiding-ness of salvation, but neither can history shut out salvation. Its fullness in human experience is limited only by ignorance, unbelief, sin in our life, and our common human limitations. It is available to all now upon repentance of sin and faith in Christ Jesus. This is the gospel, the good news of God in Christ Jesus. It must be proclaimed now because it operates in the great and gracious *now* of God. This is the day of salvation. The present-day reality of the salvation of God in Christ Jesus is the central theme of the book of Hebrews. At the same time it presents the supremacy and the finality of Christianity.

The apostles were convinced that all that had happened was in perfect harmony with the prediction of Old Testament prophecy. Pentecost had transformed their vision. They saw the chain of events not as tragic failures and disappointments of history but as fulfilling the prophecies of the Old Testament. Thrice Peter refers to Old Testa-ment predictions in his great Pentecostal sermon (Ac 2:16, 25, 34). He also reminds his hearers that "the promise is unto you, and to your children," telling them that "those things, which God before had shewed by the mouth of all his prophets, that Christ should suffer, he hath so fulfilled" (Ac 2:39; 3:18). He further refers to "the times of refreshings" and "the times of restitution of all things, which God hath spoken by the mouth of all his holy prophets since the world began" (Ac 3:19, 21). Peter knows of the prophecy of Moses and expresses a most comprehensive view of fulfilled prophecy in Acts 3:24. The apostle knows Jesus as "the stone which was set at nought

of you builders, which is become the head of the corner" (Ac 4:11;
cf. 1 Pe 2:6; Is 28:16). No less convincing was the reasoning of
Stephen in the synagogue (Ac 6:9) and the words of James at the
stormy Jerusalem council meeting when he freely quoted from the
writings of Old Testament prophecy (Ac 15:15-18).

The full scope of the usage of the Old Testament by the early
church is best illustrated by the gospel of Matthew, who himself
was an apostle, the book of Hebrews, and the preaching of Paul in
the synagogues as Luke records it in the second half of the book of
Acts. The Old Testament was their Scriptures. They found it fulfilled
in Christ Jesus.

It was the settled conviction of the apostles that God had acted
in perfect harmony with His predetermined counsel and His plan as
unfolded in the writings of the Old Testament. This conviction gave
steadiness to them in the midst of storm and stress, pressure and
tensions, threats and persecution, suffering and martyrdom.

*The apostles were convinced that the redemptive act of God in
Christ was for the benefit of all mankind.* Peter explicitly states on the
day of Pentecost, after having exhorted the people to repent and be
baptized, "For the promise is unto you, and to your children, and to
all that are afar off, even as many as the Lord our God shall call" (Ac
2:39). Considerably later he declares that "God is no respecter of
persons: but in every nation he that feareth him, and worketh righteousness, is accepted with him" (10:34-35). And as Peter reported his
experience to some contentious brethren in Jerusalem (11:4), Luke
informs us, "When they heard these things, they held their peace and
glorified God, saying, Then hath God also to the . . . nations granted
repentance unto life" (11:18).

John joins in the universality of Peter and plainly declares that
Christ "is the propitiation for our sins: and not for our's only, but also
for the sins of the whole world" (1 Jn 2:2). And again he says, "The
Father sent the Son to be the Saviour of the world" (1 Jn 4:14).
Nationalistic particularism may have lived in the sentiments of the
disciples, but it had no place in the inspired theology of the apostles.

Jude knows of the "common salvation." In his brief epistle he is
most inclusive in his embrace of salvation and judgment in history.
Certainly he is not a nationalistic particularist in his doctrine of salvation. And even James exhorts his readers to "have not the faith of

our Lord Jesus Christ, the Lord of glory, with respect of persons" (Ja 2:1), and he opened the door of the church to believing Gentiles without conditions and restrictions (Ac 15:13-20).

Thus the voices of the writers unite in the fact that God has acted decisively and graciously in Christ Jesus for the benefit of all mankind. The universality of salvation ideally held and proclaimed by Christ comes to practical and dynamic fruition in the apostles.

The apostles were convinced that repentance and faith were the God-ordained way to enter into the salvation of God. The salvation of God in Christ Jesus is available to all people, but it must be consciously and voluntarily appropriated by faith in Jesus Christ. Such faith is essentially related to repentance from sin. It may be noted that faith is the positive and repentance the negative aspect of that living and dynamic relationship which relates man savingly to Christ. Both aspects are emphasized by the apostles.

It is evident from the preaching of the apostles that they were not merely announcing the good news of God's salvation. They were prevailing upon men and women to repent of their sins and to believe in the Lord Jesus Christ. The call to repentance rings out distinctly, loudly and repeatedly (Ac 2:38; 3:19; 8:22; 11:18).

While repentance is a gift of God (Ac 5:31; 11:18), man must appropriate and exercise it in order to benefit by it. It is man's part to repent.

No less emphatic is the challenge to faith. Man must by faith receive what God has provided in Christ Jesus. Faith is all-important (Ac 2:44; 3:16; 4:4, 32; 6:5, 7-8; 8:12-13, 37; 9:42; 10:43; 11:17, 21, 24). Without faith it is impossible to please God and to experience His gracious provisions.

There is a clear line in apostolic teaching separating people into two distinct groups. On the one side are the believers who experience the salvation of God in Christ; they are the children of God. On the other side are the unbelievers and disobedient who do not possess the salvation of God. Thus apostolic preaching aims at persuasion as well as at dispensing information. The apostles sought to move men and women to repentance from sin and faith in Christ Jesus. They were convinced that apart from such a relationship there is no experience nor possession of eternal life. God commands all men everywhere to repent, and He commands that men should believe on the name of

His Son Jesus Christ (Ac 17:30; 1 Jn 3:23). This is the unanimous voice of the apostles. In this they agree with the emphasis of all other writers of the Bible and the spokesmen of God. Repentance and faith are the God-ordained way into the spiritual riches in Christ Jesus.

The outlined cluster of theological convictions is reinforced by personal commitment in obedience to their Lord and the experience in their hearts.

THE APOSTLES WERE IMPELLED IN THEIR MISSIONARY ENDEAVOR
BY THE COMMITMENT IN OBEDIENCE TO THEIR LORD

They were urged forward by the persuasion in their hearts that they must obey God and fulfill His blessed will regardless of difficulties and cost. Twice Peter set the will of God over against the authority and orders of the priestly court boldly telling the Jewish authorities that it behooved them to obey God rather than men. This was more than human audacity; this was divine persuasion. Logically the court may have agreed with Peter but was not the voice of the high priest the voice of God? Here is the fatality of the blindness and confusion of the natural man. The apostles had the spiritual discernment to distinguish human interpretation from divine inspiration and revelation.

Most certainly the apostles were going against all tradition and practices of Jewry when they refused to obey the rulings of the high court. However, they had the spiritual stamina to endure the consequences and in the end to triumph in all sufferings. The impressive words of John have been fully justified in history: "He that doeth the will of God abideth for ever" (1 Jn 2:17).

Obedience is a key word to understand the operation of the apostles; it became prominent in their vocabulary. Emphatically Peter links obedience to the gift of the Holy Spirit (Ac 5:32). On several occasions the apostle uses the words *faith* and *obedience* interchangeably, thus indicating the experiential unity of these two basic Christian concepts (1 Pe 1:2, 22; 2:7-8; 3:20; 4:17). Obedience is held up as a cardinal Christian virtue and a proof of belonging to God, keeping and doing the commandments of God (1 Jn 2:3-4; 2:29; 3:7, 24; 5:2-4). To the apostles, obedience is not optional; it is occupational. It occupies all of their life and commits them in obedience and loyalty to their Lord and Master.

THE APOSTLES WERE MOTIVATED BY THE
EXPERIENCE OF THE LIVING CHRIST

The apostles were irresistibly inspired by the glow of their personal experience of the living Christ indwelling their lives through the Holy Spirit. The reality of Christ in human experience became their blessed portion; it was their sustaining and impelling power. They knew Christ had been raised from the dead. And even though they had seen Him ascend on high and disappear in the clouds, they were conscious of His presence in their lives. He was not a distant Christ to them. With Paul they could confess, "Christ liveth in me." Christian experience was meaningful and dynamic to them.

Joyfully Peter exclaims, "We cannot but speak the things which we have seen and heard." Repeatedly the apostles refer to the resurrection of Christ Jesus. He was an ever present reality to them (Ac 2:32; 3:15; 4:10, 33; 5:29-32). The experience of the risen Lord was indelible, transforming, overwhelming, constantly refreshing, abidingly inspiring, gloriously triumphing. Confidently John writes, "That which was from the beginning, which we have heard, which we have seen with our eyes, which we have looked upon, and our hands have handled, of the Word of life . . . that which we have seen and heard declare we unto you, that ye also may have fellowship with us and truly our fellowship is with the Father and with His Son Jesus Christ" (1 Jn 1:1-3). Peter ascribes our regeneration and also our salvation to the resurrection of the Lord (1 Pe 1:3; 3:21).

Here was *reality-experience*. This was more than vague, subjective mysticism. Here was more than mere "resurrection faith." Here was faith in the resurrected One, faith substantiated by reality experience. Such faith could not be silenced. It had to obey, it had to speak. The inner glow of the living Lord generated an irresistible dynamic that led to the great witnessing explosion which followed Pentecost.

The language of the apostles betrays the fact that they were unable to get away from *the glory* of the resurrected One. His glory was reflected in their experiences, which may be seen in their repeated usage of the word *glory*. It constitutes a prominent part in their vocabulary. Stephen speaks of "the God of glory" (Ac 7:2). James knows "the Lord of glory" (Ja 2:1). Peter refers to "the spirit of glory" (1 Pe 4:14). We are informed that the Christians are called to glory (2 Pe

1:3; 1 Pe 5:10), are to receive a crown of glory (1 Pe 5:4), are partakers "of the glory that shall be revealed" (1 Pe 5:1), are to "rejoice with joy unspeakable and full of glory" (1 Pe 1:8). In his dying moments Stephen saw the glory of God (Ac 7:55). There was glory in the experience of the apostles. Here were glory, glow and go.

THE APOSTLES LIVED AND LABORED IN THE CONSCIOUSNESS OF
BEING POSSESSED BY THE HOLY SPIRIT

The experiences of the living and glorious Lord were mediated through *the Holy Spirit.* Thus there is a strong and consistent emphasis upon the Holy Spirit in apostolic teaching and experiences.

The presence of the Holy Spirit was proof of the divine work in the lives of the people (1 Jn 3:24; 4:13). The gift of the Holy Spirit is underscored on the day of Pentecost (Ac 2:17). It is withheld from all who obey not the gospel of God (Ac 5:32), but the Spirit is given to believing Jews, Samaritans and Gentiles (Ac 2:4; 6:5; 8:17; 9:17, 31; 13:1-2). God is no respecter of persons; His gift of the Spirit is bestowed upon all who meet His requirements.

The Holy Spirit is the dynamic in their ministry, and to be filled by the Spirit is essential for effective and acceptable service (Ac 2:4; 4:8, 31; 6:3, 5, 10; 7:55; 8:29, 39; 10:19; 1 Pe 1:12; 2 Pe 1:21). The Holy Spirit is also the adequate source of power and comfort in suffering and martyrdom.

The apostles knew experientially the significance of the Holy Spirit. Without Him their lives would have remained less than Christian, less than normal, for He mediated life, dynamic, meaning, direction and glory. It was because of His presence in their lives that the glory of the risen Lord radiated forth from the apostles and impelled them in their missionary endeavor.

APOSTOLIC MISSIONARY VISION

FULLEST MISSIONARY PRESENTATION

The fullest missionary presentation is made by John in the book of Revelation where most dramatically God is presented as the God of the cosmos — the God of all the earth and of all the nations, no realm excluded. His majestic, radiant throne is high and lifted up above all, and from it the lines of rulership go out in every direction.

[God is in continuous governmental relationship with the world as progressively as well as catastrophically His rulership is extended over the whole earth. All people must stand before Him in judgment.] No other god is acknowledged or shares in His power and authority. He alone is the God of the universe, the God of the nations, the God in whom salvation and refuge are found, the God who is the sole, sovereign and righteous Judge of mankind. His authority and power must and will prevail, and His standard of right and wrong will be acknowledged by all. Finally, He alone will be worshiped by redeemed mankind upon a new earth and in a new heaven. His victory is complete and His worship unrivaled. All other gods have been cast out, all rebellion has been overcome, and all power has submitted to Him. God is all and in all.

Similarly John sees the Lamb of God in the book of Revelation. He portrays the Lamb not as bearing the sin of the world but as having triumphed over sin, hell, Satan and the grave. He does not behold the Lamb as operating among the Jews and in Palestine; instead, the Lamb is walking among the churches in Asia and in pagan cities. Jerusalem and Mount Zion are not in sight in the beginning of the book.

In his second major vision, John sees the Lamb at the right hand of God in glory preparing for world operations in judgment and gospel expansion. Certainly there is nothing limiting or particularistic about the visions of the Lamb in His relationships.

In the closing scenes John sees the Lamb triumphing over all systems of the world, the religious included. As the new heavens and the new earth appear, the Lamb shares in the glory and worship of the Father while the *nations* enjoy the blessings that flow from the abounding throne of the Lamb. Such is the missionary vision of John, and we may well assume that John speaks representatively. The twelve are in accord with Him. God is redemptively related to the world through Christ Jesus. The Holy Spirit is operating in the name of the Father and the Son to make the good news of God's redemptive love and act in Christ known to the world by means of gospel communication. This He does by mobilizing and energizing the church as God's chosen instrument.

CONCLUSION

These blessed realities, facts and truths in the consciousness of the twelve became the source of the missionary motivations and thrust of the apostles as well as the cornerstone of their missionary theology. Little is said of the example of Christ, although He went about doing good, healing all who were oppressed of the devil. No direct reference is made to His Great Commission, although we must not conclude that it played no role in the early church. The fact that in some form it is found in every gospel is sufficient evidence that it was part of the living tradition and teaching of the early church.

The missionary theology of the apostles, however, was rooted more deeply than in a command. It was anchored in the foundation which made the command of world evangelism an evangelical and spiritual imperative, an outflow of life rather than an imposition. Thus, they became missionaries not as slaves but as bondslaves. Missions became their life, their all-absorbing interest, their all-consuming passion to which their lives were joyfully dedicated.

Only three of the twelve have left us writings: Matthew, John, Peter (whether the writer of the book of Jude was the apostle Jude is indefinite). Certainly there is no particularism to be found in their presentations, for the missionary thrust overcame all particularism, nationalism and Jewish ethnocentrism.

In conclusion, let us note the interesting fact that no one of the twelve felt himself out of harmony with his Master in his missionary outreach. Nor did he feel himself in conflict with the Old Testament. Somehow all felt themselves working out the unchanging purpose of God which gives unity to all revelation.

> A glorious band, the chosen few
> On whom the Spirit came,
> Twelve valiant saints,
> Their hope they knew,
> And mocked the cross and flame:
> They met the tyrant's brandished steel,
> The lion's gory mane;
> They bowed their necks the death to feel:
> Who follows in their train?
> REGINALD HEBER

THE APOSTLE PAUL

Of all the apostles, Paul stands out as the central figure in the interpretation and propagation of Christianity. We can hardly imagine Christianity without him, but he is not a cofounder, an innovator or a rival to Christ. Christ remains the fountain, foundation, cornerstone and content of Christianity.

Paul clearly expresses his position in this matter in 1 Corinthians 3:11 when he says, "For other foundation can no man lay than that is laid, which is Jesus Christ." Earlier he wrote, "And I, brethren, when I came to you, came not with excellency of speech or of wisdom [philosophical speculations and niceties], declaring unto you the testimony of God. For I determined not to know any thing among you, save Jesus Christ, and him crucified" (1 Co 2:1-2). However, Paul is the fullest exponent, the foremost theological representative, the greatest evangelical apologist, and the most ardent advocate of Christianity. Therefore, we present his thought on universality and, where needed, correlate the teaching of the other apostles to that of Paul.

We need not project an elaborate apologetic for the universality of Paul in God's provision of salvation for all mankind (*ideal* universality) and in God's purpose to have His gospel universally proclaimed (*practical* universality). Both are too obvious in the life and teaching of Paul. He is the concrete incarnation of ideal and practical universality. In vain students search the New Testament for *realized* universality within the scope of history or post-history. There is no indication in the New Testament that all people will be saved. Clearly and emphatically the New Testament teaches that this is not the case and that people will actually be lost eternally from the presence of the Lord.

THE IDEAL UNIVERSALITY OF PAUL

As the great exponent of Christ and Christianity, Paul traveled extensively, as Luke records in the book of Acts. Energetically he preached in synagogues, marketplaces, public halls, private homes, and other places as opportunity afforded it. He wrote prolifically, as his letters indicate. The mind of Paul is laid open before the world, so no one need be a stranger to his ambition, goal, motive and purpose.

Paul has indelibly impressed many truths upon the world, foremost among which is the fact that "God was in Christ, reconciling the world unto himself." In other words, God has provided in Christ a salvation adequate to save man from his total and eternal lostness unto a glory unspeakable and indescribable. Paul stressed that God has provided a Saviour and salvation sufficient for all mankind. Again, Paul emphasized that God fervently desires that this gospel be made known to all men everywhere for the purpose that man might believe and subjectively possess what God has wrought objectively in Christ. The details of this glorious message we can only follow later in outline.

I am well acquainted with the so-called theory of limited atonement as implied in the teachings of Calvin and explicitly advanced by some schools of theology. As I search for its roots, content, implications and authority, they seem to be far from the general tenor of the Scriptures and in clear conflict with so many direct biblical statements that I must consider them fabrications (I cannot avoid this expression) to accommodate and bolster certain Neoplatonic and Aristotelian premises in election and predestination that seem strange to the Bible and would have bewildered Paul. They seem like tragic importations from philosophy rather than Pauline exegesis. The racial purpose of God so clearly evident on the pages of revelation, the absolute and ethical monotheism of the Scriptures which makes God the sole, righteous and good God, the organic unity of the race and Christ's identification with the race in order to deal with the principle of sin and His effective dealing with it, God's impartial, holy and righteous love manifested and fully expressed in Christ, as well as specific references — all these forbid me to take the theory of limited atonement seriously. These arguments derived from the Old Testament and the life of Christ are implicitly or explicitly expressed by Paul and the apostles. I simply find no biblical basis for the theory of limited atonement. Paul's comprehensive statement is sufficient proof against it: "Therefore as by the offence of one judgment came upon all men to condemnation; even so by the righteousness of one the free gift came upon *all men* unto justification of life" (Ro 5:18). And again, "For this is good and acceptable in the sight of God our Saviour; who will have *all men* to be saved, and to come unto the knowledge of the truth. For there is one God, and one mediator between God and men, the man Christ Jesus; who gave himself a ransom *for all*, to be testified in due time" (1 Ti 2:3-6). John heartily endorses this position when he writes, "And he [Jesus Christ the righteous] is the propitiation for our sins [the sins of the believers]: and not for our's only, but also for the sins of the whole world" (1 Jn 2:2). These were dynamic truths that lived in the mind of Paul. Like a mighty, onrushing torrent, they bore him on in his ambitious purpose to preach the gospel where Christ had not been named. There were no national or cultural bounds in the missionary thinking of Paul because he found no such bounds in the purpose of God and in the sufficiency of Calvary.

In a logical and convincing manner Paul presents a series of great missionary thoughts in his most doctrinal epistle, the epistle to the Romans. Perfectly fusing theology and missions, his logic is as follows:

1. The whole universe is the creation of God. It is manifesting God, is under His sovereign rule, and is therefore responsible to Him (Ro 1:18 ff.).

2. The whole human race is an organismic unit created in Adam. The organic unity of the entire human race is never questioned in the Bible. Paul firmly holds to it (Ro 5:12-21).

3. The whole human race fell in Adam and became sinful because of this (Ro 5:12-21).

4. The whole human race followed a course of sin and therefore became guilty before God (Ro 1:18-21).

5. The whole human race was represented in Christ, and in Him salvation was provided for all mankind not only by substitution but by identification and representation (Ro 5:12-21).

6. God has provided only one way of salvation — the way of justification by faith in Jesus Christ. This holds true for the Jew as well as for the Gentile (Ro 3:21 — 5:21).

7. God's way of salvation is not discovered by man. It comes to him by revelation, and it must be preached to him from the revealed Word of God. "Faith cometh by hearing, and hearing by the Word of God" (Ro 10:8-17; cf. 16:25-26).

8. Paul knew himself called of God and separated unto the gospel of God to bring men and nations to obedience of faith. This was his apostleship; for this he labored, always pressing onward. For this he suffered, and in this he gloried (Ro 1:1, 5, 14; 11:13, 25; 15:15-16, 18-23; 16:25-27).

There are no arguments anywhere by any of the apostles in the New Testament to conflict with the thinking of Paul.

IMPLICATIONS OF PAUL'S IDEAL UNIVERSALITY

The implications of Paul's universality are far-reaching. They caused most serious disturbances even within the early church and brought to Paul much misunderstanding, difficult theological struggles, and bitter persecutions. However, Paul survived them all, as did his great and eternal ideals, the ideals of God's gracious purpose in Christ Jesus.

In this ideal universality Paul sees all mankind assuming equal position before God as sinners, whether they be Jew or Gentile (Ro 1:18 – 3:20; Eph 2:1-3); being under equal condemnation and in need of salvation from the present and eternal wrath of God (Ro 1:18 – 3:20); experiencing justification on equal terms, by faith in Christ as God's provision and propitiation (Ro 3:21 – 5:21); receiving equal status in the church of Jesus Christ as members of the body of Christ (Eph 2:11 – 3:12); enjoying equal relationship with God as Father in the household of God (Eph 2:19; Ro 8:15; Gal 3:26); sharing equal privileges and riches as heirs of God and joint-heirs of Jesus Christ (Eph 3:6; Ro 8:17).

The latter thoughts are most fully developed in the epistle to the Ephesians, a writing which is filled with the universality of the Christian gospel and equality of all believers. The whole epistle is built up around the metaphor of the temple. In this case the imagery does not refer to the temple in Jerusalem but to the temple in Ephesus, the magnificent temple dedicated to its patron goddess. The Greeks called her Artemis and the Romans, Diana. The temple was the workmanship or masterpiece of man and was recorded as one of the seven wonders of the ancient world.

In contrast to this man-made temple, Paul presents the church of Jesus Christ as the workmanship or masterpiece of God, the temple of the living God. The logic of its presentation is as follows:

the foundation of the temple – the triune God, 1:3-21
the material of the temple, 2:1-10
the formation of the temple, 2:11-21
the unveiling of the temple, 3:1-13
the dedication of the temple, 3:14-21
the ministry in the temple, 4:1 – 6:9
the warfare in behalf of the temple, 6:10-20.

The epistle allows for no Jew-Gentile division. A new dividing line is being emphasized. Paul divides all mankind into two classes: those "in Christ" and those "not in Christ." This becomes his wall of partition. Those in Christ constitute the body of Christ (1:23; 3:6; 4:4, 12, 16; 5:23, 30). They are the household and the family of God (2:19; 3:15); they are the temple and the habitation of God (2:21-22); they are the new man (2:15); they are fellow citizens and fellow heirs (2:19; 3:6). Together they share one Father (1:3, 17; 2:18; 3:14; 4:6; 5:20; 6:23); they are children of God (5:1). The concepts of unity and equality of all who are in Christ permeate the whole epistle. There is no privileged people in our dispensation as there was in the Old Testament, for all who are in Christ share equal experiences, relationships, rights, privileges and responsibilities (2:4-10, 13-22). At the same time Paul emphasizes that the privilege to be in Christ is extended on equal terms to all nations (3:6, 8-9), and all of this is according to the eternal purpose of God as He purposed it in Christ Jesus (3:11).

Such are the thoughts of Paul in relation to the universality of the gospel of Jesus Christ and equality of all believers. These great truths drove Paul to a dynamic and effective intraracialism which prompted him to preach the gospel to all nations.

It was Paul's identification with God in His eternal purpose in behalf of the human race, his identification with Christ who had come to redeem the race, his identification with the Holy Spirit who operated on behalf of the salvation of the race, and his identification with the kingdom of God which is to embrace the total race that enabled him to rise above nationalistic particularism and Judaism and become the gospel champion in the interest of the race. Paul is a race-man as well as a Christ-man. Thus he became the world missionary, and his ideal universality triumphed in practical universality.

His course as the world missionary took him on his several missionary journeys over land and sea, from city to city, and from one people to another people. Neither perils nor sufferings could halt him. Triumphantly he could write after some twenty-five years of hard labors and at the close of a very fruitful life, "I have fought a good fight, I have finished my course, I have kept the faith: henceforth there is laid up for me a crown of righteousness, which the Lord, the righteous judge, shall give me at that day: and not to me only, but unto all them also that love his appearing" (2 Ti 4:7-8). With this, his labors and his life were concluded.

THE DEFENSE OF PAUL'S IDEAL UNIVERSALITY

In his own letters the apostle presents and/or defends universality by at least six arguments:

1. *Ethical monotheism, which he presents in the form of rhetorical questions.* "Is he the God of the Jews only? Is he not also of the Gentiles? Yes, of the Gentiles also: seeing it is one God" (Ro 3:29-30). To Paul it seemed logical that if God is God at all, He is the God of all. Ethical monotheism banishes particularism. God cannot be the God of some and not of others. As the Creator, God is related to the race as well as to the individual. The very God concept of Paul demands ideal universality. His promise to mankind in Genesis 3:15 demands that God would provide salvation for all mankind. God is not the God of one people only.

It is on the basis of ethical monotheism that Paul builds up the great doctrine of justification by faith in Christ Jesus recorded in Romans 3 – 5. The same God who is God of all also justifies all on equal grounds. Ethical monotheism provides Paul a strong and sound basis for practical universality.

2. *The justification of Abraham while yet a Gentile.* Paul begins his argument where God began with Abraham. It is evident that Abraham had not always been a Hebrew; there was a time he was a Gentile. In fact he first became a Hebrew in Genesis 17 through the covenantal act of circumcision of his entire household. Until then he had been a Gentile from every theological point of view. God found him as a Gentile, called him out, led him all the way, bestowed the greatest promises upon him, entered into a covenant with him, and all the while Abraham was a Gentile.

3. *The sin of Israel in rejecting the Messiah.* This argument is expanded with force and logic in Romans 9 – 11. Paul reasons that God has not totally, absolutely and finally cast away His people and that restoration is awaiting Israel. However, because of their sins, God has temporarily set Israel aside as His unique instrument to bless the nations. Israel's lot is that of waiting, wandering and suffering until the fullness of the nations is come in (Ro 11:25). Thus at the present time God is gathering directly out from among the nations a people unto His name. Since this is not the time for Israel to be used

as God's instrument, Paul must go directly to the nations and make known the unsearchable riches of Christ.

Romans 9 and 10 are Paul's argument against the hypothetical or real question of God's *right* and *authority*. The basic question is whether God has a *right* to call a nation from among the nations and set Israel aside. Has He not commited Himself to Israel in an unconditional covenant? Is He not obligated to remain bound to Israel? Paul's answer is that if God has the *right* to choose Israel from among the nations and set aside the nations (chap. 1), the same God has the *right* to set aside Israel and choose another nation. In view of the most grievous sin of Israel, God is setting Israel aside. Grace and sovereignty are never in conflict; neither does the one take precedence over the other. They find their beautiful blending and harmony in the mind and wisdom of the eternal God. Let no man play with sin and hide behind grace.

4. *The incompleted revelation of the Old Testament.* A careful study of Paul's attitude toward the Old Testament will reveal at least three facts:

First, he accepted the Old Testament as the Word of God revealed and written. He revered it, believed it, preached it.

Second, he based his doctrine of salvation upon it. He fully and completely defended such major doctrines as justification, sanctification, the unity of the race, the coming of Christ, and the atonement from the Old Testament. He did not claim to bring anything new in these vital doctrines but merely claimed to interpret the Old Testament Christologically. He preached Christ in the synagogues from the Old Testament, reasoning with and confounding the Jews with it. He stood squarely upon Moses and the prophets in the doctrine of salvation.

Third, he went beyond the Old Testament in the doctrine of the church as the body of Christ with equal rights, position and privilege for all, whether Jew or Gentile, in the household of God and the priesthood of all believers. In this he not only went beyond Judaism but also beyond the Old Testament. For this he claimed special revelation (Eph 2:11 – 3:12).

Paul went to the first great block-section of revelation (Gen 1 – 11) in order to establish the racial basis of the salvation which he proclaimed. In Romans 5 he leads us past Abraham to Adam, the father of all mankind. Christ is not likened to Abraham but to Adam.

As in Adam all mankind lost its position before God and became equally guilty, so in Christ the possibility exists for all to be restored on an equal basis and with equal privileges.

Thus while Paul accepted all of the Old Testament, he did not hesitate to express his position that he believed that the Old Testament did not unfold the whole counsel and total plan and purpose of God. The "mystery of the church" had come to him not as a result of Old Testament studies but as special revelation of God (Ro 11:25; Eph 3:1-12). The church revelation was a part of that eternal counsel in Christ which was progressively unfolded and concluded in the New Testament.

5. *The nature and composition of the church.* While Paul would have loved to work among his own people, this privilege was not granted him. His love and concern for the Jews never failed, but he found his field of labor among the Gentiles. Paul's labors and writings make it abundantly clear that he was convinced the gospel was to be preached to all nations and that the church of Christ was to be composed of an international body of people gathered from among all nations. Not only is there no distinction in the body of Christ between Jew and non-Jew, but there *must* be a universal representation in the church (Ro 11:25; Rev 5:9). Thus Paul is ready to divide his field of labor with Peter, the latter becoming a special missionary to the dispersion while Paul is a special missionary to the Gentiles. He becomes a "debtor both to the Greeks, and to the Barbarians; both to the wise, and to the unwise." "To the weak became I as weak, that I might gain the weak: I am made all things to all men, that I might by all means save some" (Ro 1:14; 1 Co 9:22).

Paul informs us in Romans that he glories in his office as an apostle to the nations (Ro 11:13), and in Ephesians he attributes this calling to a unique grace of God upon his life (Eph 3:2, 7-8; Ro 15:15-17). The depth of the conviction that the church must be gathered from among the nations is well illustrated in Paul's missionary journeys.

6. *Paul's certainty of his apostolic commission.* Knowing himself to be an apostle appointed by the Lord, Paul's certainty of his calling rings through his personal testimonies in Acts and in his writings. There was no room for questioning or doubting. The impact of the vision of the glory of the Lord on the road to Damascus that smote him down and the voice of Christ were indelibly impressed upon Paul.

His missionary commission was clear, precise, irrevocable and irresistible on theological, experiential and spiritual grounds. Not even sacrifice, suffering and martyrdom could alter his course or dissuade him from his missionary endeavor. He speaks of himself to be an apostle of Jesus Christ by the will of God, defending his apostolic position vigorously before the Corinthians as well as before the Galatians. His apostolic commission was a settled conviction.

However, not only was Paul certain of his apostolic calling; he was also certain of his commission *to be an apostle to the nations.* These convictions permeated his being and determined his work (Ac 26:23; Ro 1:1, 5; 11:13; 15:15-16; Gal 1:16; 2:8-9; Eph 3:1, 4-8; 1 Ti 2:7; 2 Ti 1:11). The assurance of his calling and commission sustained him in all difficulties, hardships, disappointments, misrepresentations and sufferings. He neither dared nor desired to be disobedient to his Master or to fail in that which had been committed to him. He was persuaded of God, and no man could dissuade him concerning his own commissioning *as an apostle to the nations.* This may seem to be logic based upon experience. However, with Paul it became a blessed certainty and dynamic motivation in world evangelism.

A word must be said about the commission of Paul as he reports it to Agrippa (Ac 26:15-18). Much emphasis has been placed upon the obedience of Paul, and verse 18 has been cited as one which spells out the details of Paul's mission: to open eyes, turn to light and to God, etc. These are worthy and timely emphases. Seldom, however, is the scope of the commission noted. Paul is sent to the people and nations. It is well to note that the word *nations* is plural. Paul was not sent to one nation but to the "nations" or "peoples."

Underscore the personal pronouns *their, they* and *them* in verse 18. These words speak of nations or peoples. Paul was not only to preach the gospel he was to preach it to the nations; he was to open the eyes of nations in order to turn them from darkness to light; he was to turn nations from the power of Satan to God; nations were to receive forgiveness of sin, and nations were to be among those who are sanctified by faith in Christ. Such is the scope of Paul's mission. God's plan and program are greater than the individual. He thinks, plans and commissions in terms of families, tribes, peoples and nations.

Therefore, Paul, assured of the will and purpose of God, courageously carried his crusades into cities and towns, provinces and states, to the educated, to the free and the slaves. Total evangelization was his ambition. All must hear, all must have an opportunity to know the gospel, all must have representation in the church of Jesus Christ which is to be gathered from the nations (Ro 11:25; Ac 15:14). The book of Acts is the authentic record that myriads of Jews (Ac 21:20) and multitudes from among the nations responded to the gospel, that the apostolic church was made up of Jews, Samaritans, Greeks, Romans, Galatians, Cretes, Arabs, Egyptians, and we may well add Indians, Spaniards and various conglomerate people of Asia Minor and the Middle East.

International and interracism were more than an ideal; they became blessed reality in the church. Their full realization is seen in Revelation 5:8-10 where the raptured church before the throne is composed of representatives "of every kindred, and tongue, and people, and nation."

Part II

BIBLICAL DELINEATION
OF
MISSIONS

5

The Missionary Task

THE MISSIONARY TASK bears within it something of the nature of the ultimate, something that neither centuries, circumstances nor cultures change. There is such a thing as a "changeless task." There is, also, that within the task of missions which bears the nature of the relative, something that demands adaptation. Unless these two aspects are clearly seen and kept in mind, the missionary cause will seem confusing and the assignment indefinite. I present four aspects of the changeless nature of the missionary task:

THE MISSIONARY TASK IS A SPIRITUAL TASK

Essentially and ultimately the missionary task is committed unto the Holy Spirit. As salvation originated in the eternal counsel of God, as salvation was procured historically in the person and work of Christ, the eternal Son of God, so the administration and actualizations of salvation have been committed unto the Holy Spirit. Only the Holy Spirit can make real experientially the salvation procured on Calvary. He is the present Administrator, not only of salvation but also of missions, the propagation of the precious gospel of God concerning Jesus Christ.

This is apparent in the book of Acts, as we shall see more fully later. His instrument is the Word of God, and His agents are the church of Christ and individual believers called out for specific mission services.

The fact that missions essentially is a ministry of the Holy Spirit is both a comfort and a challenge to us   a comfort in that we may trust Him fully to accomplish His work, a challenge in that only Spirit-filled people, Spirit-sanctioned means, and Spirit-approved methods

can be used effectively in mission ministries. There is no greater lesson
to be learned for a missionary candidate than the lesson of how to live
a Spirit-filled life, how to walk in the Spirit, and how to minister in
the Spirit. A spiritual task can be performed only by the Holy Spirit
who works through a spiritually minded person. The final struggle
and battle are in the realm of the spirit. This can never be emphasized
too strongly, though it may be stressed too one-sidedly.

THE MISSIONARY TASK IS A BIBLICAL TASK

The previous pages of this book have sought to establish the
premise that the missionary task is a biblical task. A thorough acquaintance with the whole counsel of God will inevitably lead to a
missionary thrust, and a biblical theology will be a missionary theology.
A sound Bible teacher will also be a missions teacher, for missions is
imbedded in the total thrust of the Word of God. A genuine revival of
missions, therefore, can come only from a genuine revival of biblical
theology, properly interpreted according to the counsel of God. Missions not founded upon sound biblical interpretation will be sporadic
and erratic.

What holds true for missions, as such, is certainly applicable to
the missionary. We are not sent forth as missionaries merely for friendship purposes or to demonstrate the oneness of Christians in the body
of Christ. These are precious truths and belong in the realm of true
Christian living, but we are sent forth primarily to share with the
world the great benefits of Christianity. We are witnesses of Christ;
we are ambassadors of Christ; we are preachers of the gospel of God
and bearers of God's message to mankind. Our message is contained
in a book, the Bible. Gladly we bear the scorn of the world that we
are people of one Book, the messengers of an ancient message. The
challenge of the believer is to be a "missionary," a "sent one," sent by
the Holy Spirit through the church (Ac 13:4) to bear witness to Christ
and proclaim the revealed message of God's redeeming act in Christ
Jesus. This, of course, requires thorough knowledge of the message
as deposited in the Bible, and intimate personal acquaintance with
Christ.

As our message is derived from and determined by the Bible,
so also is our assignment. Much confusion exists today in relation to
the preparation of missionaries because our assignment has become
hazy and blurred. In the words of the late missionary statesman, Dr.

Samuel Zwemer, there is a great deal of "grey thinking" about missions. One of the major causes of this indefiniteness is the fact that we are not delineating clearly between the biblical assignment to the church and the biblical responsibility of missions. It is here that we need a new and penetrating study of the Great Commission. Only here can we find our theological and practical orientation regarding missions. The Great Commision does not set forth the complete divine assignment to the church, as we will see later. This is found in the entire New Testament. But the Great Commission does set forth the basic framework and essentials of our missionary assignment. We find our directions for missions not in the needs of mankind as they appear to us, for they are limitless, ever growing, ever changing. We receive our assignment from our Captain in His changeless Word. Here is our beacon light in the midst of human fog and conjectures. Thus we are thrown back upon the Bible as our unfailing guide which presupposes a thorough knowledge of the Bible. We find both our message and our assignment in God's Word because the missionary task is a biblical task.

THE MISSIONARY TASK IS A TASK OF FAITH

God has ordained that Christianity be a religion of faith. From the objective point of view Christianity is a religion of supernatural revelation. From the subjective point of view it is a religion of faith. Faith is the spiritual eye that beholds God, that perceives in Christ the Saviour and Lord, that understands the Bible to be the Word of God, that accepts the missionary task as the purpose and will of God, that discovers missions as the natural result of the work of Christ, and that missions is an inherent element of the call unto salvation and the obedient compliance to the promptings of the Holy Spirit. Without faith it is impossible to please God; faith is fundamental to all Christian life and endeavor. There is no truly spiritual work which is not also faith work.

Though man through the fall has been transformed from a faith being into a being of unbelief, yet through the operation of the Holy Spirit he can be re-created into a faith being. By faith he accepts the offered salvation in Christ. Paul tells us that we walk by faith and not by sight. The Christian life is from beginning to end a life of faith; so also is the missionary task. Here our love for the Lord and for others is tried. So is our faith. Do we actually believe the cardinal pronouncements and doctrines of the Bible regarding the marvelous person and purpose of God, the depth of being and height of possibility for man, the absoluteness, finality exclusiveness, universality and individuality of the gospel of God, the temporal and eternal issue as disclosed in the Book? These are faith issues based upon revelation rather than human reason or experience. No human sentimentalism or goodwill is sufficient to sustain the burdens, frustrations and disappointments of the missionary task. We need deeper resources. Only a heart set aflame by the Holy Spirit through deep and stirring faith-convictions in eternal verities will uphold us in the heat of the battle and the depth and length of sacrifices.

> Faith is not only a means of obeying, but a principal act of obedience; not only an altar on which to sacrifice, but a sacrifice itself, and perhaps, of all, the greatest. It is a submission of our understandings; an oblation of our idolized reason to God, which he requires so indispensably, that our whole will and affections, though seemingly a larger sacrifice, will not, without it, be received at his hands.[1]

True and successful missionary work, therefore, can only be done by men of faith, men who know God and have learned to appropriate the promises of God, to whom answers to prayer do not come as pleasant surprises but rather as from a God who is true to His Word and who cannot lie, men who know their God and who are able without hesitation or fear of heart to undertake tasks for God humanly impossible.

It is well to realize that today's new situation demands new tests of faith. Such testing will determine whether the faith of the church is wholly and solidly rooted in the apostolic gospel. Dr. Visser't Hooft put it thus:

> A church which is not deeply penetrated by the faith that the crucial center of all human history is what God has done, in and through Christ, will hardly undertake a sustained missionary effort, and its witness will never have the toughness and resiliency, the patience and the endurance without which missions cannot accomplish their task. It is only those who offer real News about divine deeds who will stand the test in the day of trouble.[2]

Such faith, though a work of the Holy Spirit, does not come to man overnight, nor does it come automatically or mechanically. It grows only in a certain atmosphere and must be carefully cultivated. This takes time, discipline, patience, much humble waiting in the presence of God, an abiding in Christ, and an absorbing interest in the Word of God. It is no surprise that Paul spent three years in Arabia soon after his conversion, and somewhat later, five to seven years in Tarsus. He needed time and solitude for theological orientation, biblical solidification, as well as spiritual maturation before he became the greatest missionary of the Christian era. Men of faith are not grown in a theological hotbed or an ecclesiastical organization, but neither do they come up in a vacuum. They prosper only in the presence of God, in a walk with God, and in the battles of life. Men of this quality are rare, yet they are desperately needed. Only men of genuine faith can do real faith work and will leave their mark in a world of unbelief. Faith, world-overcoming faith, is a quality demanded of the modern missionary task at home and abroad. Only faith will lead to triumphs in Christ.

THE MISSIONARY TASK IS A HUMAN TASK

God has chosen human instruments to accomplish His task in human hearts within a human society surrounded by human environment. Humanism and theological liberalism, no doubt, have overemphasized this factor and have made missions almost totally anthropocentric and philanthropic. Evangelical Christianity to a great extent has underestimated this vital fact. Man does not live in isolation or in a vacuum; he lives in society and within a culture. His culture is his physical, mental, psychological and religious atmosphere, which he breathes for himself, his own survival and advancement, and which he values for what it does.

Man is an interacting being. He is acted upon most successfully and effectively, however, by agents of unicultural relationships. He most readily follows the leader of the in-groups and submits to the authority of his own groups. If man is to be reached, he must be reached within his own culture.

A tragic dualism often plagues the evangelical missionary. It is not necessarily his love for Westernism that troubles him, for such love he left behind when he yielded to the Master for service abroad. It is far more his fear that through identification he may endanger his testimony of the uniqueness of Christianity or that he may become a participant in the many sins bound up in the culture of the people he has come to serve, and that the principle of Christian separation and separateness may be blurred by his life.

This is a legitimate fear which must not be dismissed lightly. Yet, it is a fear which may enlarge upon us, make the necessary cultural adaptation for identification and integration impossible, and thus paralyze the effectiveness of our ministry. Much weakness in evangelical mission work and mission churches is due to the fact that the missionaries have not been able or willing to make such cultural adaptation, social integration, psychological penetration, and spiritual identification as to make spiritual fellowship deep, lasting, contagious and vital. Somehow the wall of separation was not broken down. Isolationism developed or continued, and real effectiveness did not bless the work. There was no real communication or communion with the people he came to serve. The cultural worlds, though existing side by side, never really met and melted together. The missionary never "sat where they sat," though he sacrificed much and put forth great effort to communicate to them a message so precious to himself.

It is not my intention to enter into a discussion of cultural anthropology and the basic demands upon missionaries for effective communication. Suffice it to say that missionary work is a human task and can be accomplished only when human relationships between the missionary and the people are truly ideal and fully human and when communication takes place according to divinely created human channels of communication which include far more than the knowledge of the national language.

With the cross-cultural problems, two other difficulties have developed in recent decades — the cross-racial barrier (a barrier loaded with emotions to no small degree) and the cross-organization barrier. The missionary has failed to integrate with the church he has planted. He feels there are good reasons for not integrating. Rightly or wrongly a dichotomy has arisen which is separating a fellowship rather than marking a division of labor.

The human aspect of the missionary task is best demonstrated by our Lord and Saviour Himself. Paul vividly presents it:

> Let this mind be in you, which was also in Christ Jesus: who, being in the form of God, thought it not robbery to be equal with

God: but made himself of no reputation, and took upon him the form of a servant, and was made in the likeness of men: and being found in fashion as a man, he humbled himself, and became obedient unto death, even the death of the cross. Wherefore God also hath highly exalted him, and given him a name which is above every name: that at the name of Jesus every knee should bow, of things in heaven, and things in earth, and things under the earth; and that every tongue should confess that Jesus Christ is Lord, to the glory of God the Father (Phil 2:5-11).

Christ came to minister and to identify Himself with the people. Well does A. R. Hay say,

To find men He became a man; to win the Jew He became a Jew, lived as a Jew and observed Jewish customs, except where principle was involved. He lived their life with them and gave Himself unreservedly for them. He did not stand apart or hold Himself unreservedly from them. He identified Himself with the people as a whole and not with any particular class. He did not live a sheltered life or a life of ease and comfort but faced life with its toil and hardness.[3]

Similarly, Paul recognized that missions was a human task involving man in his total relationships and in his national, social and cultural identity. Thus he sought to identify himself as nearly as possible with the national and social strata of mankind in order to present the gospel intelligibly and acceptably. He tells us,

For I take no special pride in the fact that I preach the gospel. I feel compelled to do so; I should be utterly miserable if I failed to preach it. If I do this work because I choose to do so then I am entitled to a reward. But if it is no choice of mine, but a sacred responsibility put upon me, what can I expect in the way of reward? This, that when I preach the gospel, I can make it absolutely free of charge, and need not claim what is my rightful due as a preacher. For though I am no man's slave yet I have made myself everyone's slave, that I might win more men to Christ. To the Jews I was a Jew that I might win the Jews. To those who were under the Law I put myself in the position of being under the Law (although in fact I stand free of it), that I might win those who are under the Law. To the weak I became a weak man, that I might win the weak. I have, in short, been all things to all sorts of men that by every possible means I might win some to God. I do all this for the sake of the gospel; I want to play my part in it properly (1 Co 9:16-23, Phillips).

Missions does call for sacrifices in many ways. It is no "cheap business." The demands of missions are as discouraging to the unspiritual as they are challenging to the spiritual. Missions operates totally within human milieu. Therefore God can use significantly only those human beings who can operate with Him within such milieu.

Therefore we pray: *"Lord, make us intensely human that we might be used greatly!"*

THE TWOFOLD MANDATE

There is a fundamental twofold mandate of God to man set forth in the Bible which we must grasp clearly in order to define the missionary assignment of the church precisely. This twofold mandate is given at the beginning of each Testament and to each humanity: the humanity in the first Adam, and the humanity in the second Adam, Christ.

It must be noted that the second mandate does not negate, supersede, duplicate, or absorb the first mandate. While it closely relates itself to it, it is unique. It is not dependent upon it, since it is a distinct mandate arising out of different circumstances and serving different needs and purposes.

DELINEATION OF THE TWO MANDATES

The first mandate was spoken to Adam as representative of the race and involves the whole realm of human culture. In its widest sense it includes religion. It serves man in his need as a socio-religio-cultural creature. It includes the natural and social aspects of man such as habitat, agriculture, industrialization, commerce, politics, social and moral order, academic and scientific advancement, health, education and physical care. In simple words, it is the qualitative and quantitative improvement of culture on the basis of the revelational theism manifested in creation. Such culture was to benefit man and glorify God. The Bible expresses it in the following terms: to populate, to subjugate, to dominate, to cultivate, and to preserve (Gen 1:28; 2:15). Here are the basic concepts and directives for an ordered and progressive society based on principles of sound morality and ethical monotheism. The Bible does concern itself with social and cultural welfare. It has ethical principles for society and nations which form the cornerstone of God's judgment of the nations.

It is man's responsibility to build a wholesome culture in which man can live as a true human being according to the moral order and creative purposes of God. While this program was severely interrupted by sin and made extremely difficult by man's depravity due to the fall, the mandate remains in power and still rests upon man. Indeed, the fall made it even more imperative if man is to survive as a human being. This is evident from the message of God to Noah after the flood, as recorded in Genesis 8:15 – 9:17. It is also evident from the strong denunciatory messages of the prophets directed against Israel and the nations of the world whenever they violated the moral order and basic human rights. God has never absolved man from his divinely ordained mission and moral responsibility. Here is the clue to the vanished civilizatons of the past and to the vanishing cultures of the present.

It should be noted that this responsibility is heightened and intensified by the high ideals which the New Testament sets forth for the governments of the nations. Paul enjoins us in Romans 13 to be obedient to the governments and to the ideals of the governments. Clearly these are for the welfare and order of society. Man remains man even after the fall. He is a culture-creature and remains within the providential care of God, responsible to God for the moral and social structure of society and behavior as well as the culture he develops. Man has the privilege to destroy himself or advance himself according to the moral quality of culture he develops.

The second mandate was spoken to the apostles as representatives of the church of Jesus Christ, involving the whole realm of the gospel. It majors in the spiritual liberation and restoration of man although it does not overlook his physical and social welfare. In modern terminology, it means that the gospel is designed to make man whole, to restore his personality that he might function as man. It is seen in the prayer of a saint who said something like, "Lord make me intensely spiritual that I might be genuinely human."

The second mandate is carried forward by evangelization, discipleship training, church-planting, church care, and benevolent ministries. We find this substantiated and outlined in: (1) the sending of the twelve (Mt 10:1-20; Mk 3:13-19; Lk 6:12-16); (2) the sending of the seventy (Lk 10:1-20); (3) the further sending of the twelve (Mt 16:14-18; Lk 24:36-49; Jn 20:19-23; Ac 1:7-8); and (4) the sending of Paul (Ac 9:15-16; 26:14-20).

In every instance the spiritual dominates. The second mandate deals principally with the problem of sin and guilt. It proclaims the good news that in Christ forgiveness of sins may be found, that Christ can make a man whole and restore him to his original purpose and mission.

Thus there is first a mandate to man as *man* and as a member of the human race; and second, there is a mandate to the Christian as *Christian* and as a member of the church of Jesus Christ.

It must be emphasized that both mandates originated in God and are designed to serve mankind. Together they meet every need of man. It may sound irreligious but it nevertheless is a fact that the gospel does not serve all the needs of mankind. It was never designed to do so. While metaphysically it is true that all good originates in God, existentially and practically it does not all emanate directly from the gospel. When man is hungry he needs bread; when he is naked he needs clothes; when he has a serious infection he needs antibiotics first of all to remedy the situation. Man needs culture as well as the gospel; there is urgent need for both. Without culture, man could not survive nor could the gospel be proclaimed because man would soon perish. Both mandates are required to meet man's total needs.

Care must be taken, however, not to confuse the two mandates. If the two are disassociated unnaturally and unhealthily, a dichotomy arises which will work negatively upon society. If the mandates are too closely interrelated or blended, a culture-religion arises (Ritschlian *Kultur-Christentum,* and all ethnic religions). The gospel suffers, divine priorities become blurred, and man's spiritual welfare is imperiled. The last-named is the case in the social gospel and liberalism where biblical evangelism is practically eclipsed. Evangelical social action, the social implication of the gospel, Christian service and welfare programs must remain under the judgment of the Word lest they become Christian priorities or gospel substitutes.

THE CHRISTIAN AND THE TWO MANDATES

Christians, as the salt of the earth and the light of the world, should seek to make their contribution according to the first mandate through societal channels as much as possible, instead of setting up separate arms or agencies for the church and thus duplicating functioning organizations and confusing the issues. The situation changes when governmental or humanitarian agencies do not permit a Christian witness to accompany the service.

In these matters the Christian church needs to think soberly and reevaluate its program and unique contributions. We need more biblical thinking on the slogan of the late archbishop, William Temple: "Let the Church be the Church."[4]

According to my knowledge, the Lord never charged His Old Testament elect, the people of Israel, with the mission to make special contributions to the first mandate as the people of God. This did not constitute their divine calling and mission, though as members of mankind they were not exempt from such responsibilities. Indeed, Israel did give to the world one of the seven wonders — the Solomonic temple, a tremendous religiocultural contribution.

Neither do I find anywhere in the New Testament that the church of Jesus Christ as a church is charged with the mission of special cultural contributions, though every member as a member of mankind has a contribution to make. Also, we need to remind ourselves that it is profoundly Christian to distinguish a Christian in a qualitatively unique service wherever he finds himself in this world and whatever his service may be.

Israel, however, did have the responsibility of raising a most serious prophetic voice against the evils of the nations. Prophets like Amos, Isaiah, Jeremiah, Ezekiel, Obadiah, Zephaniah and others did not only speak to their own nation; they spoke boldly to the nations of the world, warning them of and threatening them with the sure and severe judgments of God. Fearlessly they trumpeted the principles of ethical monotheism and called upon the nations to turn from their evil, to practice righteousness, and to bow before God. Jonah clearly expressed a great Old Testament principle when he went to Nineveh and preached judgment and repentance. Thus the prophets of God functioned as a conscience in their society and in the world.

Today we are pathetically confused, believing that social action is to replace the feeble prophetic voice of the church. Placations rather than prophecy mark the voice of the church. We seek to be peacemakers by appeasement rather than the voice of God for righteousness and justice, the true pillars of peace. The world needs a bold prophetic church speaking out in a ringing tone the great principles of ethical monotheism. Social action as carried on at the present by the church will sooner or later find itself in competition with the welfare state which more and more takes on the care of the people. Not so the evangelical herald of the good news and the church with a sound prophetic voice. Man will always need both the gospel to save him and a conscience to guide him.

PRESENT-DAY CONFUSION OF THE TWOFOLD MANDATE

I do not find anywhere in the Bible that the first mandate comes under the biblical category of missions. It is man's assignment as man and is to be fulfilled on the human level. It is not implied in the Great Commission of our Lord to His disciples, nor do any of the spiritual gifts (charismata) as presented in the Scriptures relate to it. It is therefore unscriptural to confuse these two mandates and speak of them on equal terms as missions and church ministries. Only the second mandate is considered missions in the strict biblical sense. The first mandate is philanthropic and humanitarian service rendered by man to man on the human level and as from members of the same "family" (Gal 6:10; Lk 10:25-37). It should not be downgraded as unworthy or secular service, though it is not missionary service in a technical sense.

Because the two mandates have not been distinguished, serious confusion has resulted in our assignment, work and the choice of workers for the mission fields. Much mission work resembles an export company. It is busily occupied with exporting cultural fruit from the West to other lands while little effort is being put forth to take the gospel to the people and plant indigenous "trees" (churches) and cultivate them to produce indigenous fruit. Our cultural fruit has sprung up in a specific soil under the impact of the gospel and has grown up in a church-conditioned atmosphere which is conducive to the fruit. While we may export our cultural fruit, it is naive to expect that it will reproduce itself without the appropriate soil and atmosphere having been cultivated by the gospel and the church. The question therefore arises, Is it the assignment of missions to sow the seed and plant trees (preach the gospel and plant churches) that in due time will bear fruit? Or are we sent forth to export fruit, hoping that in due time it will reproduce itself?

It is imperative to distinguish missions from the whole scope of "cultural fruit" that has grown up under the wholesome impact of the gospel and in the shadow of the church. It remains a fact that:

> There is no force in the world so powerful to accomplish accessory results as the work of missions. Wherever it goes it plants in the hearts of men forces that produce new lives; it plants among communities of men forces that create new social combinations. It is impossible that any human tyranny should live where Jesus Christ is King.
>
> All these things the foreign mission movement accomplishes; it does not aim to accomplish them. I read in a missionary paper a little while ago that the foreign mission that was to accomplish results of permanent value, must aim at the total reorganization of the whole social value, must aim at the total reorganization of the whole social fabric. This is a mischievous doctrine.
>
> We learn nothing from human history, from the experience of the Christian Church, from the example of our Lord and His apostles to justify it. They did not aim directly at such an end. They were content to aim at implanting the life of Christ in the hearts of men, and were willing to leave the consequences to the care of God. The results of Christianity are most comprehensive and complete.[5]

We need to face these issues on the deepest level, especially when the Peace Corps is being considered as a substitute for missionary service and the churches of America are eager to compete with the government in social service to prove their worth and value in the world as well as to express an incarnational gospel. It must be kept in mind that missions has a singular purpose and a specific task. Cultural fruit is to be sought where the church has been planted and it is maturing to assume its dutiful place in society. To merely export it from the West is not the biblical responsibility of missions in its regular and biblical assignment.

With these brief and summary remarks we must discontinue our consideration of the first mandate, since it is neither the mandate of the church, as such, nor does it constitute missions in the proper sense of the word. We turn our attention to mandate two.

THE GREAT COMMISSION

INTEGRITY

⸤The authenticity and genuineness of the Great Commission passages, especially as found in Matthew and Mark, have been assailed by representatives of nationalism and higher criticism, the former on a theological and the latter on a documentary basis.⸥ Evangelical scholarship, however, has staunchly defended both the genuineness as well as the authenticity of the passages and has held its position well on the basis of internal and external evidences.

I am confident that we have here the words as spoken by the Lord and as recorded by the gospel writers. Also, I am aware of the fact that the ending of Mark (16:9-20) is much debated and that several good ancient manuscripts do not record the verses. However, it is just as clear that Mark did not end with verse 8 and that the present ending is well documented from second- and third-century writings. Thus the debate continues.

INTERPRETATION

⸤The interpretation of the Great Commission passages has differed greatly through the centuries and has caused a great deal of discussion. Debate has revolved around the address of the words. Were they spoken to the disciples as apostles of Jesus Christ? Did they constitute a part of the unique assignment of the apostolic office? Were they addressed to the apostles as representatives of the church of Jesus Christ and thus exist as a part of the church's commission unto the end of the age? Again, what is the interrelationship between baptizing and teaching? Is the latter a coordinate with or a subordinate to the former since the conjunctive *and* is missing? Or is teaching associated with baptizing and not merely subsequent to the latter? And how are baptizing and teaching related to making disciples? What is the real meaning of baptizing "into" (*eis*) the name? Why is the word "name" used in the singular when it is followed by an enumeration of the three Persons of the Godhead?

Such are some of the ecclesiastical and theological questions that have been raised and debated in relation to the Great Commission passages and meaning.

Evangelical scholarship has sought to answer some of these questions, believing that the commission is addressed to the church and must be obeyed unto the end of the age and that it must be interpreted in the light of total revelation. Few commentators deal exhaustively with the Great Commission passages. Recently two exegetical studies of note have appeared. The first by Dr. Karl Barth is in *The Theology of the Christian Mission*,[6] while the second comes from the pen of Dr. R. D. Culver and was published in the *Bulletin of the Evangelical Theological Society*, and later by *Bibliotheca Sacra*.[7] Both men, however, fail to see the total scope of the Great Commission and limit their studies to the gospel of Matthew. Thus, at the best, they are only a partial presentation of the Great Commission. It is tragic that the Great Commission has been more debated than it has been obeyed in church history.

RELATIONSHIP TO CHRISTIANITY

The Great Commission is not an isolated command arbitrarily imposed upon Christianity. It is a logical summation and natural outflow of the character of God as He is revealed in the Scriptures, of the missionary purpose and thrust of God as unfolded in the Old Testament and historically incarnated in the calling of Israel, of the life, theology and saving work of Christ as disclosed in the gospels, of the nature and work of the Holy Spirit as predicted by our Lord and manifested on and after Pentecost, and of the nature and design of the church of Jesus Christ as made known in the Acts of the apostles and the epistles. It forms an organic unit and an integral part within that revelation and receives its true meaning and force only if seen in this larger relationship.

The Great Commission does not make Christianity a missionary religion. The latter is such because of its source, nature and total design. The apostles became missionaries not because of a commission but because Christianity is what it is and because of the indwelling Holy Spirit who is an outgoing and witnessing Spirit. Christ Himself speaks of the mission of the Holy Spirit as a witnessing mission (Jn 15:26; 16:8-15). Thus, if the particular words of the Great Commission had never been recorded or preserved, the missionary thrust and responsibility of the church would not be in the least affected. It prospers wherever Christianity is truly known, thoroughly believed, genuinely experienced, and implicitly obeyed.

VALUE

Having said this, we must still emphasize that it is of immense value that the Great Commission has been spoken by our Lord and recorded by the Holy Spirit in the gospels. While it does not create new duties for Christianity, it sharply focuses the missionary thrust and responsibility of Christianity beyond reasonable doubt and disputing. Again, its singularity as a command of the risen Lord marks it off as unique among His words and makes it more than just one commission among many commands to the disciples. Its restatement by every one of the gospel writers witnesses to its living tradition in the early church. The book of Acts demonstrates its dynamic in the original movement of Christianity.

COMPOSITE NATURE

The Great Commission is a composite commission. Its record in all four gospels and in Acts is unique among the words of Christ. It points up its significance in the mind of each writer, its richness and fullness of content, and the unity of purpose and design of each of the gospels. They all culminate in the Great Commission and point in a common direction. Christianity is centrifugal in nature and thrust.

It has become necessary to emphasize the composite nature of the Great Commission. The fact that each of the four evangelists gives it in one form or another needs to be noted. No one of them gives it in its completeness, but they beautifully supplement each other. While each of the evangelists presents it from his own point of view and with his own unique emphasis, together they make a complete whole, as the following outline shows:

Matthew — the authority, all-inclusive goal and the time-extension of the work

Mark — the urgency, method and geographical scope of the work

Luke — the Christocentric message and universality of the work

John — the spiritual equipment and the spiritual nature of the work

Only as we see the whole outline as presented in the four gospels do we see the total Great Commission.

SCOPE AND PATTERN

As we analyze the Great Commission we discover two imperatives that give direction to the commission. These are found in Matthew and Mark in the words "make disciples" and "preach the gospel."

Thus we have in the Great Commission an ellipse with a twofold focus. While in former decades the emphasis was upon the Markan focus ("preach the gospel") and evangelism was the all-out thrust, the emphasis today is upon Matthew's focus ("make disciples") and church-planting has come to the foreground. The Bible emphasizes both and keeps them in proper balance. The imperatives are supplemented by the participles "going," "baptizing," "teaching."

There are no imperative verbs in either Luke and John. However, there is a scriptural ("thus it is written") and spiritual ("receive ye the Holy Ghost") force back of these words. Therefore, an imperative verb is not necessary; indeed, it would seem out of place. The dynamic of the Word and the Spirit takes the place of the imperative.

As we consider the composite Great Commission as recorded in all four gospels, we gather the following fact: the all-inclusive goal is "make disciples" of all nations. In order to accomplish this purpose, we must do the following:

1. We must engage in an intensive and extensive heralding of the gospel among all nations, communicating meaningfully and persuasively the gospel of God as recorded in the Scriptures.

2. We must lead people into an experience of the grace of God made available through the death and resurrection of Jesus Christ, and offering forgiveness of sin in His name to all who will believe the gospel.

3. We must separate people from the old relationships and establishments and build them into the new congregation of God through the practice of baptism preceded by and followed by teaching.

4. We must teach them the value and greatness of the gift and gifts of the Holy Spirit and lead them out in a walk and ministry in obedience to and in dependence upon the Holy Spirit.

5. We must indoctrinate them in the precepts of the Master and thus, by the renewing of their minds, mold them into true Christian discipleship.

Such is the pattern of our ministry according to the Great Commission. None of these elements may be omitted or neglected.

THEOLOGICAL SIGNIFICANCE

The Great Commission is more than just one commission among many commands of Christ. It is lifted out because of its singularity as a command of the risen Lord and of its restatement in one form or another by the four evangelists, each presenting it from his own point of view and with his own unique emphasis.

Most significant, however, is the Great Commission because of its theological comprehensiveness. It establishes the following facts:

1. The sovereignty of the Lord of the Christian gospel — "All power [authority] is given unto me" (Mt 28:18; cf. Phil 2:9-11; Rev 3:7).

2. The imperative of the Christian gospel (Mt 28:18-20; Mk 16:15-16; Lk 24:44-47).

3. The universality of the Christian gospel (Mt 28:18-20; Mk 16:15-16; Lk 24:44-47; Ac 1:8).

4. The nature of the Christian gospel (Lk 24:46-47; Jn 20:23; Ac 26:15-23; cf. 1 Co 15:1-3).

5. The human instrumentality in the proclamation of the Christian gospel (Mt 16:15-16; Lk 24:48; Ac 1:8; 26:16).

6. The need of spiritual equipment to minister successfully in the Christian gospel (Lk 28:49; Jn 20:22; Ac 1:8).

Thus the Great Commission is made dynamic by a great theological substructure.

PSYCHOLOGICAL SIGNIFICANCE

The Great Commission does not make Christianity a missionary religion; it is such because of the character and purpose of God. Neither is it the dynamic of missions, for this resides in the Holy Spirit alone. Yet, it is of great significance that the Great Commission was formulated by our Lord and reported to us by the evangelists.

Its importance is seen when we realize that it is the Word which gives concepts to our mind, conditions our hearts to obedience, and gives objective directives to our lives. The Word is a lamp unto our feet and a light unto our path. Without the Word the ministry of the Holy Spirit would remain a vague, mystical and undefined dynamic in our lives. While the Holy Spirit is the subjective inspiration and enablement, the Word is the objective light and directive. We cannot dispense with either. There is a beautiful coordination of the Holy Spirit and the Word of God in the making and directing of the believer. We may compare the human mind and soul to a field needing irrigation. In order to accomplish this, we need water but we also need a canal system. Irrigation would be impossible without the first and extremely difficult without the other.

The water may be compared to the work of the Holy Spirit. He does the irrigating of our soul as He inspires, fructifies and energizes the believer. The "canal" system is prepared in our minds and hearts by the Word, God's instrument in conditioning our hearts and minds. An objective instrument is needed to accomplish the subjective ministry and to impress an image and pattern upon our minds. The more specific the Word, the more specific the conditioning and the image and pattern. The more often the Word is repeated, the more abiding the conditioning, and the more lasting the engraving, even if the words sink into the subconsciousness. This is no doubt why Christ repeated the Great Commission at least five times in the hearing of the apostles. At last it registered.

Even though it took some years in the lives of the apostles until the Great Commission became practically effective, it did break through. Though it is not quoted officially in the Acts of the apostles and in the epistles, the apostles' minds had absorbed it and had been conditioned by it, for all of them became missionaries, except James who was martyred before he left Jerusalem. That the Great Commission was a living tradition in the early church is evident from the facts that all four evangelists record it and that the first church was, indeed, a missionary church. It should be noted that Luke reports the Great Commission at the greatest length after carefully researching the subject.

It would be wrong, however, to infer that the apostles and the early church were a missionary movement because of the Great Commission. The Great Commission gave them merely a design and pattern in missions, as we shall see momentarily. They were missionaries because Christianity is what it is and because of the indwelling Holy Spirit who is the Spirit of missions (Jn 15:26; 16:8-15).

It would be well for the church to realize the psychological significance and add the Great Commission of our Lord to the Apostles' Creed which is confessed every Sunday in numerous churches. This could have wholesome results in the lives of many believers, engraving in the hearts and minds of the participants a direction of life as well as a commission and responsibility.

PURPOSE

The Great Commission is given to us by each of the four evangelists (Mt 28:18-20; Mk 16:15-16; Lk 24:46-49; Jn 20:21-22) and in the Acts of the apostles (Ac 1:8). It is reiterated in the charge to Paul as recorded in Acts 26:13-18. To Bible believers it has far-reaching implications. It constitutes an identification of the believers with Christ in accomplishing the divine purpose as unfolded in the missionary thrust of the Old Testament and incarnated in the Lord. It is the command to preach the gospel to every creature, the marching orders to evangelize the world, the divine authorization to be ambassadors of Christ to every nation of the world. The cumulative force of this reiterated command is evident, leaving no doubt in the mind of the believing and obeying disciple of Jesus Christ that the evangelization of the world is the unquestioned will and plan of the Lord. It is the divine imperative written in bold letters into the nature of Christianity and defined in a plain commandment by the Lord Himself. Such is the first impact of a study of the Great Commission. The Great Commission authoritatively states the Christian duty of world evangelization. I repeat, the Great Commission does not make Christianity a missionary religion, for no command could ever do this. The missionary nature of Christianity does not originate in a command; the command merely focuses it. The missionary nature itself springs from the God who is the source of Christianity.

The Great Commission does not create new duties; it merely defines original ones. Christian duties flow from the character of Christianity and their relation to the Lord.

This, however, is not the whole story of the Great Commission. The primary historical significance of the Great Commission lies in the fact that it gives to the church the pattern and purpose of missions. It defines and delineates the missionary task. We have in the Great Commission a compass, a charter, and a plan. A comparative study of the parallel passages is most illuminating and instructive. It yields precious truths and principles to guide the church in world evangelism and to define in specific terms the missionary aspect of the churches' ministry.

The sixfold command in the gospels and Acts expresses one central concern of Christ: the concern of world evangelization; it declares one central purpose: the purpose of gathering a people for the name of the Lord from among the nations to constitute the church, the body and the bride of Christ, the temple and household of God; it prescribes one central strategy: the heralding of the gospel of Jesus Christ by Spirit-equipped witnesses making disciples among all nations. In addition to this common core, each one of the evangelists emphasizes a unique aspect or several aspects of the missions' activity and movement.

Let us view these as recorded by each writer.

THE GREAT COMMISSION AND THE COMMISSIONS

When I have spoken of the *Great Commission,* in all such cases I have not referred to specific passages in the gospels. I have sought to draw a distinction between the Great Commission as a composite directive from the Lord and what is recorded of the Great Commission by each of the gospel writers.

It is of great significance to note this distinction, as mentioned earlier. Too often a narrow view of our commission is presented because we lift out the emphasis of only one of the gospel writers. The fact that the Holy Spirit has seen fit to preserve for us the various versions is important, and the composite nature must be emphasized if a proper balance is to be maintained.

On the other hand, it is also important to study and note the individual traditions as preserved in the several gospels. Therefore, we turn now to an interpretation of the commissions in each of the four gospels.

THE COMMISSION ACCORDING TO MATTHEW

The historical setting of the commission. The scene of this manifestation of Christ was a mountain in Galilee where Jesus had asked His disciples to meet Him. The mountain is not specified; it could be the same one on which Peter, James and John had experienced the transfiguration scene, or the mount on which the disciples had heard

Him declare His "new law," the Sermon on the Mount. I am inclined
to think of the latter mountain.

As Christ had here declared His "new order," so here He proclaimed a "new program," the discipling of the people from among
all nations. Though Matthew mentions only the eleven, it is most
probable that Christ was seen at this occasion by about five hundred
brethren. In favor of this supposition is the fact that this is the only
occasion on which there was a meeting by appointment between the
risen Lord and the disciples. It is most probable that as many as
possible would come out to see and meet the Lord.

The reason for the appointment is not given. It is not improbable
that Christ had summoned His disciples to the mountain in order to
declare His authority, issue a new mandate, and make known His new
program. This conclusion is substantiated by the emphasis of the commission as seen from an analysis of the words.

The outline of the commission. The commission can be outlined
as follows:

1. The power (sovereignty) of the King — "all authority."
2. The purpose of the King — "make disciples."
3. The precept of the King — "going . . . baptizing . . .
   teaching."
4. The presence of the King — "I am with you."

Matthew introduces the Great Commission with the majestic
declaration of Christ, saying: "*All authority* is given unto me in heaven
and on earth." Thus the sovereignty, finality and absoluteness of
Christ in all spheres are declared. He is the sovereign and sole Lord
of history and geography, the chief Commander who has power and
authority to send His ambassadors forth to proclaim the good news
wherever He as Sovereign sees fit, as well as to make known the rights
and rules of Himself as the Lord of lords. The Lord Himself in His
person, word, work and position is the authority for Christian missions.
This is not the place for a full treatise on the authority behind missions.
Here we merely emphasize that Christ in His Great Commission,
according to Matthew, boldly declares Himself as the sovereign Lord
who has the authority to send His ambassadors into all the world
without geographical limitations.

Peter tells us in Acts 2:36, "Therefore let all the house of Israel
know assuredly, that God hath made that same Jesus, whom ye have

crucified, both Lord and Christ." In a similar manner Paul declares, "For to this end Christ both died, and rose, and revived, that he might be Lord both of the dead and living" (Ro 14:9). Repeatedly the Bible declares that Christ is seated at the right hand of God, seated on the throne of God, the place of highest, supreme, sovereign authority. Presenting Himself to the church in Philadelphia, our Lord declares, "And to the angel of the church in Philadelphia write; These things saith he that is holy, he that is true, he that hath the *key of David,* he that openeth, and no man shutteth; and shutteth, and no man openeth" (Rev 3:7).

G. Campbell Morgan, commenting on the above verse, says:

> Let it be most particularly noted that Jesus did not say, "He that can open and none can shut, and that can shut, and none openeth." That is obviously true. But He said something far stronger. He did not make a declaration of ability, but of activity. Not merely that He held an executive position, but that He was executing the work. "He that openeth, and none shall shut, and that shutteth and none openeth." This is not a distinction without a difference but a difference with a distinction. . . .
>
> These words should bring to us a great sense of confidence and safety, notwithstanding all the appearances which appall us. He is God's King today, and though for a while man rejects him, He nevertheless holds the reins of government, sitting upon the holy hill of Zion, King by right of character, King as witness the key of office which He holds. He moreover acts in perpetual administration. He opens to-day, and He shuts to-day. Amid all the fret and restlessness of the age He is moving toward the final order, and that through the mysteries that enwrap us. Let us ever comfort our hearts also with the threefold truth of His character, "He that is holy, He that is true"; of His official position, "He that hath the key of David"; and of His actual administration, "He that openeth and none shall shut, and that shutteth and none openeth."[8]

Thus our Lord never stands helplessly before closed mission doors. He opens as He pleases. He can remove the most stubborn dictator and the most determined opposition. Neither need we fret when doors close on us. He has the keys.

The authority of our Lord is both our comfort and our dread. It is our comfort insofar as we rest assured that when our Lord calls and sends, He assumes the responsibility for His servants. Certainly He is able to supply all needs, not only materially but also physically and spiritually. He can preserve His ambassadors in all dangers and can send legions of angels to rescue them from perils as well as send ravens to supply their needs. The sovereignty and authority of our Lord are also our dread because we know in our conscience that we owe Him absolute obedience and submission and that some day we must face Him to answer Him as our Lord.

The focus of the mandate according to Matthew is to "make disciples." In order to penetrate to the heart of the mandate and discover the facts involved in it, we do well to analyze the commission.

Analysis of the commission. There are four key verb forms in this command which we must understand if we want to interpret the mind of the Master as expressed in this commission. These forms are "go," "teach" (actually "disciple"), "baptizing" and "teaching." Of these four words, the verb "disciple," which may be translated "make disciples," is central and is the only one which is an imperative. It expresses the core of the commission. The other three verbs are participles which are involved in the central commission as ways and methods of accomplishing the commission. They supplement the main verb.

Dr. Leavell summarizes his findings in these words:

> In this commission there is one dominant and controlling imperative, while all the other verb forms are participles. In the original Greek the central verb is formed on the noun for "disciple" and should be translated "make disciples" as it is in the American Standard Version. It is a first aorist imperative, second person plural. The word translated "go" is a participle and could be translated "going" or "as ye go." Likewise the words translated "baptizing" and "teaching" are participles. While these participles are immensely important the imperative "make disciples" is of superlative importance.[9]

Robert D. Culver makes the following analysis:

> Πορευθέντες is a nominative plural masculine participle, first aorist of πορεύομαι a deponent verb meaning to "pass from one place to another, *to go.*" It is not an imperative form and as an aorist participle would naturally be rendered either "having gone" or "as ye go." It is inflected in agreement with the understood subject of

the imperative verb which follows immediately. This word is now presented.

Μαθητεύσατε is second person plural, first aorist imperative active of μαθητεύω. This verb is somewhat anomalous here, for it is ordinarily intransitive, meaning "to be a disciple." Yet it is here used in a transitive sense and must be translated, "make disciples!" It is imperative in form and meaning – the only imperative verbal form in the entire paragraph beginning with verse 16.

Βαπτίζοντες is a nominative plural masculine participle, present active of βαπτίζω. This participle is likewise in agreement with the finite imperative verb μαθητεύσατε. It is not imperative in form, though because of its position and relationship to the imperative verb which controls it, it is in much better position to convey an imperative idea nevertheless, as shall be seen. It means *to baptize* – a controversial word we will define no further on this occasion.

Διδάσκοντες. This word is to be analyzed exactly the same as the preceding, except that it is derived from διδάσκω which has the meaning *to teach*. It is in agreement also with μαθητεύσατε, yet is also grammatically and syntactically connected with βαπτίζοντες as dependent, not strictly co-ordinate, as is sometimes assumed. The justification for this statement is the absence of καὶ *"and,"* the coordinate conjunction. That is, the "teaching" is associated with the "baptizing," not merely subsequent to it.

A certain structural relationship now clearly emerges. There is only one basic element in the commission μαθητεύσατε πάντα τά ἔθνη, "make disciples of all the nations." Presupposed by this basic command is the fact that Christian believers are already to be deployed on the scene of their missionary labors – πορευθέντες, *having gone*, or, *as ye go*. Two activities will be involved in making disciples of the nations, not successively, but somehow contemporaneously, βαπτίζοντες, "baptizing," and διδάσκοντες, "teaching."

The critical commentaries, i.e., those on the Greek text, present a reassuring consensus on these basic facts of exegesis. Not that every one of them consulted presents all these points, but they do not disagree, while supplementing one another. This survey, while not exhaustive, included many of the best recognized exegetical authorities.[10]

The issue is clear and the proceedings are specific. The church needs to rethink the commission to make disciples.

Several facts emerge from this analysis:

First, making disciples is focal. The doctrine of Christian discipleship is focal in our commission and in the New Testament, and it must become focal in the church of Jesus Christ. There are 270 references to it in the gospels and the book of Acts. In the epistles it is replaced by the word *saints*, which is used very frequently by Paul.

Christian discipleship is a vital expression of the Christian life. To teach it is imperative; to neglect it is tragic.

The pattern of Christian discipleship is found in the life and teaching of Jesus Christ. He calls men to follow Him. We are challenged by the apostles to consider Him, to remember Him, to emulate Him, and to cultivate the mind of Christ in us. Peter tells us that Christ left us an example that we should follow in His steps. Our path of sanctification is one of being "changed into the same image from glory to glory, even as by the Spirit of the Lord" (2 Co 3:18). The Christian hope culminates in the glorious expectation of being transformed into the likeness of Jesus Christ (1 Jn 3:2).

With such emphasis in the New Testament, may it not be true that the Christian church at home and abroad is betraying weakness because she has neglected the heart of the commission of Christ? We evangelize, make converts and church members, but we fail to make disciples.

Christian discipleship was focal in the ministry of our Lord while He was here upon the earth. This becomes very evident as we read carefully the accounts of the gospels. Few students have followed the comprehensive study of A. B. Bruce in his classic *The Training of the Twelve* with the subtitle *Exhibiting the Twelve Disciples of Jesus Christ under Discipline for Apostleship.* I believe this to be a worthy approach to the study of the gospel records and the ministry of Christ, our Lord. We turn to the gospels to search for the meaning and making of disciples.

Christ is the Maker of disciples. The call to discipleship sounds like a clarion call through the gospels and came repeatedly from the lips of our Lord as He walked the paths of Palestine. It is presented in the gospels in a threefold manner: (1) the historical records of the call of the individual followers of Christ (the call of Matthew is an illustration), (2) the repeated address of Christ to individuals in the words, "Follow me," and (3) the expression of Christ in several instances, "Take up the [or his] cross."

1. The historical record of the call of individuals. We need not delay ourselves with a study of these recorded incidents, for they tell their own story. It is important, however, to distinguish between the call to discipleship and the appointment to the apostleship. The former we see in passages like Matthew 4:19-21 and 9:9, while the latter is stated in Mark 3:13-19 and Luke 6:12-16.

2. The repeated address of Christ to individuals in the words, "Follow me." The words "follow," "follow me," and "come after me" come to us from the lips of the Master more than twenty times. They are addressed to various individuals as the following passages illustrate: Simon and Andrew (Mt 4:19; Mk 1:17); James and John (Mt 4:21; Mk 1:20, implied in these passages); Matthew (Mt 9:9; Mk 2:14; Lk 5:27); Philip (Jn 1:43); Peter (Jn 21:19, 22); the rich young ruler (Mt 19:21; Mk 10:21; Lk 18:22); another of His disciples (Mt 8:22); any man (Mt 16:24; Mk 8:34; Lk 9:23; Jn 12:26). Paul speaks of himself as a follower of Christ and calls upon the Corinthians to follow him (1 Co 11:1). So also his exhortation goes forth to the Ephesians, Philippians and Thessalonians (Eph 5:1; Phil 3:17; 1 Th 1:6).

The biblical concept of the word *follower* is pregnant with meaning which is best seen from its various usages. *Cruden's Unabridged Concordance* introduces the word *follow* with this brief study:

FOLLOW signifies: (1) *To come after one that goeth before, as servants come after their masters*, 1 Sam. 25. 27. . . . (2) *To imitate, or do as another gives us an example*, Mat. 16. 24. . . . 1 Co. 11. 1. . . . (3) *To believe and obey*, Jn. 10. 27. *And in all passages where men are said to follow strange gods*, it signifies, *to put trust in them, to rely upon them, and yield them service*. 1 Kings 18. 21. . . . Judg. 2. 12). . . . (4) *To side, or take part with*, 2 Sam. 2. 10. 2 Kings 11. 16. (5) *To endeavour after . . . and pursue with great desire and diligence*. Phil. 3. 12. . . . (6) *To die with one*. John 13. 36.

Edvin Larson in his new book, *Christus als Vorbild* (Christ as Example), carefully studies the concept *Nachfolge* (following) and points to the fact that *Nachfolge* originates in the initiative of Christ.[11] He calls His own *Nachfolger* (followers) to decisive and radical separation from former relationships, positions and way of life; to concrete association with Christ in daily living; to humble submission to Christ in a life of instruction; to ready obedience to the command of the Master in all matters of life; to conscious imitation of the Master in His life and teaching. He is the pattern in all things, attitude and relationships; readiness to suffer with Him is expressed in the words of cross-bearing.

Our previously cited passages and incidents readily establish these basic principles. We therefore conclude that to follow Christ means to identify ourselves daily in the totality of our life with the totality of the life of Christ. This indeed is true, biblical, Christian discipleship. To this we are called with a holy calling.

3. The expression of Christ on several occasions — "Take up the cross." It must be emphasized again that the call to discipleship extends to every believer. No Christian is exempt. *All* are to be disciples of Christ. *All* are to own Him as Lord as well as Saviour. *All* are called upon to bear the cross and follow Christ. Thus the call of Christ goes forth: "And he said unto *them all*, If any man will come after me, let him deny himself, and *take up his cross daily*, and follow me. For whosoever will save his life shall lose it: but whosoever will lose his life for my sake, the same shall save it" (Lk 9:23-24; cf. Mt 10:38-39; 16:24-25; Mk 8:34; Lk 14:27).

To clarify the concept of cross-bearing, we do well to distinguish it from the Pauline "thorn in the flesh" and the common expression of "burdens of life." Too often these various concepts are being confused.

A study of Paul's "thorn in the flesh" will soon convince us that, whatever Paul meant by these words, the affliction indicated had not been voluntarily assumed by Paul. In fact, he besought the Lord thrice to deliver him from it. The Lord's reply, "My grace is sufficient for thee," finally gave Paul peace but not deliverance. The "thorn in the flesh" was something highly personal in the life of Paul, afflicting him from time to time to keep him humble in his revelations and success, and dependent upon the Lord in his ministry. Thus each servant of God needs and has a "thorn in the flesh" to preserve him for divine usefulness. This is not the cross.

The "burdens of life" are common to all men. They are not our errors. They are the afflictions, trials, disappointments and depressions due to our membership in a sinful race and living in a sinful world. Thus the Christian is not exempt from the common misfortunes of life which are due to sin in general. He shares in such burdens of life as illness, accidents, fire, and nature hazards. Numerous experiences are burdensome and may become depressive if we do not find the proper fortitude to uphold us in life.

In contrast to the "thorn in the flesh" and the "burdens of life" is the experience of cross-bearing. Note five basic principles of cross-bearing: (1) Cross-bearing is voluntary — "if any man will." (2) Cross-bearing is continuous — "daily." (3) Cross-bearing is absolutely necessary to discipleship — "Whosoever doth not bear his cross, and come after me, cannot be my disciple." (4) Cross-bearing is not pleasing to our natural self for it is basically associated with self-denial — "deny himself." (5) Cross-bearing is taken up for the sake of Christ — "my disciple."

Larson, referring to a study by A. Friedrichsen, points out the fact that the expression "cross-bearing" was a contemporary metaphor indicating "radical social isolation and humiliation."[18]

Whatever else cross-bearing may mean, it certainly implies such voluntary identification with the Lord that He absorbs our love, devotion, time, talent and strength to such a degree that nothing and no one else matters in our life except the Lord. Self-interest, plans, pleasures, position and relations have been denied; self is dethroned and delivered to the Spirit to be crucified. Discipline, limitations and dependence are accepted to follow the Master at every cost and at any expense, even the expense of life. Such is implied in cross-bearing. Here we come to the heart of Christian discipleship. Rutherford is supposed to have said that there are some who would have Christ cheap, who would have Him without His cross, but the price will not come down. These are weighty words, leading us to the very heart of the theology of Christian discipleship and speaking of a depth of Christian experience difficult to fathom and rarely to be witnessed.

A Christian disciple is more than a believer. A disciple is more than a learner in the ordinary sense of the word. A disciple is more than a follower and imitator of Christ, more than a holy enthusiast for Christ, yea even more than one who lives in full devotion to the Lord. A disciple is a believing person living a life of conscious and constant identification with the Lord in life, death and resurrection through words, behavior, attitudes, motives and purpose, fully realizing Christ's absolute ownership of his life, joyfully embracing the saviorhood of Christ, delighting in the lordship of Christ, and living by the abiding, indwelling resources of Christ according to the imprinted pattern and purpose of Christ for the chief end of glorifying his Lord and Saviour. There are divine fullness and content in the concept of discipleship which we must not limit.

By analyzing the above definition of a true disciple, we find the basic qualities of a disciple of Christ outlined as follows:

A disciple of Christ is a believing person:

1. living a life of conscious and constant *identification* with Christ
    a. in life, death and resurrection
    b. in words, behavior, attitudes, motives and purposes
2. fully realizing Christ's absolute *ownership* of his life
3. joyfully embracing the *saviorhood* of Christ
4. delighting in the *lordship* of Christ
5. living by the abiding, indwelling *resources* of Christ
6. according to the imprinted *pattern* and *purpose* of Christ
7. for the chief end of *glorifying* his Lord and Saviour.

Thus we have salvation, dedication, liberation, enthronement, enrichment, content and a goal.

The biblical concept of Christian discipleship must always be interpreted to involve humble following, constant fellowship, sanctified openmindedness, undisputed obedience, ready submission, heroic faith, arduous labor, unselfish service, self-renunciation, patient suffering, painful sacrifice, and cross-bearing. It is the bringing of all of life under the lordship of Christ. This is not only the purpose of salvation but the fullness of salvation — redemption from self and devotion to the Lord. And to this every Christian is called.

Too often, however, Christian discipleship has been detached from the everyday life of every believer and thought of in terms of the great and the heroic, with a peculiar sense of saintliness being attached to it, instead of it being lived out daily in the ordinary affairs of life and relationships.

Second, disciples are to be made of all nations. The commission forbids nationalism, ethnocentrism, provincialism and particularism. Our Lord thinks in terms of the nations of the world, with no particular nation to be preferred. God is not a respecter of persons. Christians must learn to think internationally, interracially and interculturally if they are to fulfill the commission of the Lord.

This fact is well presented by Luke in the book of Acts. Here the gospel of Jesus Christ crosses all barriers and boundaries — geographical, national, cultural, linguistic, religious and racial. The church in the Acts of the apostles is indeed multiracial, international, and multicultural, as well as embracing people of varied social strata and professions. While evangelism and church growth may follow social and cultural relationships, the church of the Acts of the apostles developed into an intrasocial and intracultural organism, an ideal which the church must never surrender.

Third, to make disciples involves a process of Christian development through fellowship and instruction. Christian disciples are not produced in moments of time, in isolation and in a doctrinal vacuum. Time, fellowship and teaching are not only important; they are essential.

In fact, we must keep in mind that discipleship is a *path* rather than an achievement. While there is growth and grading among the disciples, there are no graduated disciples. Discipleship is a perpetual school which may lead from one degree to another but does not graduate its scholars. Therefore, the beginner is a disciple as well as the advanced individual. The ideals of completed discipleship are too high. No one ever achieves them completely as no one achieves completed sanctification. Discipleship is a unique and continuous experience, a growth in grace and in the knowledge of the Lord Jesus Christ.

This factor is well illustrated in the church of the first chapters of the book of Acts. Contrary to much popular thinking, it must be stated that Pentecost did not immediately produce a "witnessing church." Nothing is said of the believers in the first five chapters except that they were diligent in their studies of the Word, regular in their fellowship, fervent in their prayers, liberal in their contributions, and unsparing in their hospitality. Witnessing, teaching and preaching seemingly were carried forward by the apostles. Only after the new believers had established themselves in the new way of life, in the teaching of the apostles and in the bond of fellowship, were they prepared to become effective witnesses in a world of opposition and indifference. It takes time to produce disciples.

THE COMMISSION ACCORDING TO MARK

Historical setting of the commission. It is difficult to determine the setting and the occasion of the manifestations of the risen Lord. It is possible that Mark relates one of the last appearances of Christ, as the word "afterward" (16:14) could imply. The summary report of Mark, however, makes it difficult to determine the exact time. One fact is evident: the commission was given by the risen Lord to His disciples sometime during the forty-day period preceding His ascension to the right hand of God. The emphasis of the commission is clear, as the exposition will establish.

The outline of the commission. The outline of the commission is as follows:

1. The method of missions — preaching.
2. The scope of missions — the world.
3. The message of missions — the gospel.

The *method* of missions according to Mark is the oral proclamation of the gospel of Jesus Christ. Ours is the commission to preach the good tidings of great joy, which shall be to all people.

Mark adds, most significantly, an emphasis upon the *scope* of missions by instructing us that such preaching is to be done in all the world and to every creature.

God is the God of all the world. Never once does the Bible deviate from the great truth that God is the Creator of the universe and of mankind, that He is the only and absolute God, that He is the living and redeeming God, that His redemption is as wide as His creation reaches, as deep as the need requires, and as high as His glory demands.

It is evident that the command of Christ obligates His church to preach the gospel in all the world for a witness to all nations. The world is the scope of our commission, while the bounds of the earth are the church's only limitations. The gospel must be published among all nations, and every tribe and tongue must hear; such is the explicit will of the risen Lord. We dare not rest before this is accomplished.

The "message" of missions is presented later.

THE COMMISSION ACCORDING TO LUKE

The historical setting of the commission. Luke's report of the commission seems to come from the meeting of our Lord with His disciples on the very day of His resurrection. The disciples had gathered in the evening behind closed doors, trembling with fear because of the enemies. They wondered with amazement about the strange messages received from several individuals. While waiting in blurred anticipation for new light, hope and directives, the disciples saw the Lord in their midst.

It is evident that the minds of the disciples were not prepared to accept and retain many things. These men were mentally and emotionally disturbed, disappointed and depressed, with affections paralyzed and imagination perplexed. Their dreams had been crushed and their hopes destroyed. They were broken in heart. Their plans were shattered. Life had lost its meaning, direction and glow. Their future had faded like a mirage. They faced nothing but animosity. Into this situation came the Lord with His greeting, "Peace be unto you!"

Having restored their mental and emotional equilibrium, He unfolded to them His program of action for world evangelization.

The outline of the commission. The outline of the commission is as follows:

1. The revelational foundation of the gospel — the Scriptures, the law of Moses, the prophets, the Psalms.
2. The content of the gospel — the death and resurrection of Christ.
3. The charge of the gospel — repentance and remission of sins should be preached.
4. The scope of the gospel — among the nations.
5. The instrument of the gospel — ye are witnesses.
6. The dynamic of the gospel — the promise of the Father and the Holy Spirit.

The message of the commission. Luke presents the command of Christ from a unique point of view. The Holy Spirit sees fit to emphasize through Luke the message which the church is to carry into the world.

Christianity is to a certain extent a book religion. The Christian missionary goes forth with a book, the Bible. He does not trust his own wisdom and inventions to meet the religious quest and the moral and spiritual needs of the world. Neither does he go forth to preach the message of his own "encounter." He has a message from the

very heart of God, revealed and inscribed in the Bible. Having had
his understanding opened to the message of the Bible and having
believed and obeyed it, he goes forth with the Scriptures to make the
message of God known.

In particular, the Christian missionary centers his message on
three significant facts:

1. That it behooved Christ to suffer, and to rise from the dead
the third day. This is a biblical summary statement of the wonderful
salvation God has wrought for mankind through Christ Jesus our
Saviour and Lord. It is fully expounded in the book of Acts and in the
epistles, especially in the epistle to the Romans and in the letter to
the Hebrews. The cross and the resurrection of Christ forever remain
central in the Christian proclamation, showing what God has done for
the redemption of mankind as they speak of the free grace of God and
present the objective aspect of the saving work of God in Christ.

2. That repentance and remission of sins should be preached in
His (Christ's) name among all nations. Here is the subjective aspect
of salvation. Christ has not only done something *for* us, He is ready
to do something *in* us. He is able and willing to forgive our sins and
to cleanse us from all unrighteousness.

The doctrine of forgiveness of sins is written in bold letters across
the pages of the Bible and is one of the fundamental doctrines of
Christianity. Though we will never grasp the full meaning and significance of this marvelous doctrine, we have the privilege to experience the forgiveness of sins and to preach it among all nations. Whatever else the doctrine may imply and the experience may mean, it
brings to the soul a consciousness of blessedness, liberty and fellowship, as well as a certainty that the sins have been removed, the soul
has been cleansed, the personality liberated, and the favor and fellowship of God have been restored.

We must never forget that this experiential aspect of salvation is
possible only because of the cross and resurrection of Christ. The
subjective is rooted and grounded in the objective. The cross and
resurrection remain fundamental.

3. The Scriptures make it abundantly clear that the Christian life
can be lived only in and through the Holy Spirit. The Bible does not
belittle the difficulties a believer and disciple will meet while living
in a world basically hostile to Christ and Christianity. Rather, it

speaks freely of suffering, persecution, distresses and reproaches for Christ's sake. The world, Satan and the flesh are deadly enemies of Christ and the Christian. The prospects of hardships could frighten and discourage the Christian were it not for the blessed gift of the Holy Spirit in the heart of the individual believer, which is the secret of his endurance, perseverance and victory. "Greater is he that is in you, than he that is in the world" (1 Jn 4:4).

Such is the message we are privileged to carry into a sin-sick, sin-burdened, crushed and enslaved world. It is a glorious message indeed.

THE COMMISSION ACCORDING TO JOHN

The historical setting of the commission. John informs us that it was "the same evening" (in all probability the resurrection day) when the disciples were assembled. The scene is the same as we found in Luke. John reports one experience while Luke observes another happening of the same evening. Here, too, we find the blessed and familiar greeting: "Peace be unto you." Having given them physical proof of His resurrection and restored their joy, Christ commissions them for their most comprehensive ministry.

The outline of the commission. The commission is outlined as follows:

1. Orientation — "As the Father hath sent. . . ."
2. Commissioning — "So send I you."
3. Equipment — "Receive ye the Holy Spirit."
4. Mission — "Remit sins."

The message of the commission.

John majors on the spiritual emphasis. Having spoken peace unto the disciples, and having shown them His wounds in His hands and side and dispelled all doubt and fear, our Lord commissions His disciples to go forth into the world as He Himself has been sent forth into the world by the Father. These truths stand out:

1. The mission implies a spiritual identification of the disciples with their Lord in a work which is delegated to Him by the Father. "As my Father hath sent me, even so send I you." It might appear that Christ is now withdrawing from His work and is delegating it to His disciples, but such is not the case. Christ has never and will

never withdraw from the work before it is completed, for the task of world evangelism is His as truly as is world redemption. The perfect tense of the verb in "hath sent me" clearly indicates the abiding mission of Christ.

Bishop Westcott has made a rather detailed and comparative study of the Johannine use of aorist and perfect tenses of the word "sent" and "send" and the use of the two words translated "sent" (*apostello* and *pempo*). He makes the following remarks: "The general result of the examination of these facts seems to be that in this charge the Lord presents His Own Mission as the one abiding Mission of the Father; this He fulfills through His church. His disciples receive no new commission, but carry out His. Compare Matthew 28:20; Hebrews 3:1."[13]

Again the bishop writes, "The mission of Christ is here regarded not in the point of its historical fulfillment (sent), but in the permanence of its effects ('hath sent'). The form of the fulfillment of Christ's mission itself was still continued and still effective. The apostles were commissioned to carry on Christ's work, and not to begin a new one. Their office was an application of His office according to the needs of men."[14]

Dr. Ellicott most succinctly states:

As spoken here to the disciples they are the identification of them with Himself in His mediatorial work. He is the great Apostle (Heb. 3:1); they are ambassadors for Christ, to whom He commits the ministry of reconciliation (2 Cor. 5:18ff). He stands in the same relation to the Father as that in which they stand to Him. He declares to them, and they in His name are to declare to the world, the fulness of the Father's love, and the peace between man and God, witnessed to in His life and death. He and they stand also in the same relation to the world. At this very moment they are assembled with shut doors, for fear of the Jews, who are triumphing over Him as dead. But to that world, which will hate, persecute, and kill them as it had hated, persecuted, and killed Him, they are sent as He was sent; they are to declare forgiveness, mercy, love, peace, as He declared them, to every heart that does not harden itself against them; and they are to find in His presence, as He had ever found in the Father's presence, the support which will ever bring peace to their own hearts (chap. 14:27).[15]

It is of tremendous significance to realize that we are not doing mission work *for* Christ but rather *with* Christ. This fact is in keeping with the promise of Christ when He says, "And lo, I am *with* you alway, even unto the end of the age" (Mt 28:20, marg.). Mark puts it beautifully in the closing verse of his gospel: "And they [the disciples] went forth, and preached every where, the Lord working *with them*, and confirming the word with signs following." Paul expresses the same truth in speaking of himself as "laborers together with God," or "We are God's fellow-workers" (1 Co 3:9, ASV).

The charge is a charge to spiritual and purposive identification of the disciples with their Saviour and Lord in salvation as well as in mission. In their lives Christ is to live. In their sending, Christ continuously is expressing and experiencing His sending forth from the Father. As Paul expresses the believer's identification with Christ for justification, life and holiness, so John is expressing here the believer's identification with Christ in a world mission. His vision, motive, compassion, purpose and obedience express themselves through His disciples. In the words of Lyman Abbot:

> Full weight is to be given to the phrase *as, i. e., in like manner as (kathos)*. This is the most weighty and solemn declaration of the mission of the disciple, I think, in the New Testament, albeit it corresponds with the universal teaching of both Gospel and Epistle, viz., that Christ is the first born among many brethren, and that those who are his disciples are also to be *in all things* his followers; like him *teachers of the truth;* like him *manifesting the life and character of God* in the world, by the divine life begotten in them from above; like him *bearing the sins of others in their own person,* and so filling up what is behind of the sufferings of Christ (Phil. 3:10; Col. 1:24; 1 Peter 4:12, but not in a substitutionary, atoning manner). Christ does not merely *leave* his disciples in the world, he *sends* them into it, as he was sent, each disciple in his narrower sphere a savior of others, and the whole discipleship to be the body of an everliving, ever-incarnate, ever-teaching, and ever-atoning Lord. Thus, too, not only because they are *left alone,* but yet more because they are *sent forth* to complete his work, does the Son ask the Father to be to them what he has been to their Lord in his earthly mission.[16]

2. The mission is possible and effective only if done in and

through the Holy Spirit — "Receive ye the Holy Spirit." Numerous and various explanations have been offered to make plain the significance of our Lord's breathing on the disciples, saying, "Receive ye the Holy Ghost!" We cannot accept the position which sees this merely as a promise to be fulfilled at Pentecost. Nor can we share the position that at that time the disciples received the Holy Spirit, and that later on the day of Pentecost they received the power and the gifts of the Holy Spirit. The first thesis is unrealistic, and the second is devisive and untrue to the Scriptures. In the words of a commentator,

> These words are not, on the one hand, to be understood as simply a promise of the future gift of the Holy Ghost, for they are a definite imperative, referring to the moment when they were spoken; nor are they, on the other hand, to be taken as the promised advent of the Paraclete (John 16:7), for the gift of the Holy Spirit was not yet, because Jesus was not yet glorified (John 7:39). The meaning is that He then gave to them a sign, which was itself to faithful hearts as the firstfruits of that which was to come. His act was sacramental, and with the outer and visible sign there was the inward and spiritual grace.[17]

It seems reasonable and scriptural to believe that Christ bestowed upon His disciples the Holy Spirit in the Old Testament order to enable them to stand the pressure of the pre-Pentecostal trials and dangers as well as to wait in Jerusalem for the fulfillment of the promise of the Father. Certainly the disciples did not carry on the pre-Pentecostal prayer meetings in human strength and expectation. They did so by the same Spirit who had enabled the Old Testament saints to wait for the salvation of God and to suffer as a people of God. This same Spirit had inspired the holy prophets to speak in the name of the Lord and to write the Old Testament Scriptures.

With a clear view of the gift of the Holy Spirit prior to Pentecost, at Pentecost and thereafter, the passage should present no special difficulty of interpretation. As the believers today receive the Holy Spirit as an earnest of a full reality to come, so the disciples received the Holy Spirit, as recorded by John, for their enabling as an earnest of a Pentecostal fullness to come.

It is important, however, to realize that the passage in John is a less dogmatic statement. It is spoken to the disciples to teach the valuable lesson that the whole of Christian life and especially the Christian's commission can be accomplished only in and through the Holy Spirit. As Christ lived, spoke, worked and died by the Spirit, so must the disciple of Jesus Christ. A spiritual life — a spiritual ministry — a spiritual warfare for the believer can be realized only in the Spirit of the Lord.

Already in the Old Testament it had been taught, "Not by might, nor by power, but by my spirit, saith the Lord of hosts" (Zech 4:6). The life of our Lord was a demonstration of this divine principle, and so eventually were the lives and ministries of His disciples. How fully this was realized is well portrayed in the book of Acts, the book which has often been called the book of the Acts of the Holy Spirit.

3. The mission will involve the disciples in the deepest spiritual conflict and the greatest ministry to be rendered to mankind. Thus the Lord declares, "Whose soever sins ye remit, they are remitted unto them; and whose soever sins ye retain, they are retained."

I am well aware of the conflicting interpretations which exist on this passage and the extravagant claims that are being made on the basis of these words. Satan has never failed to pervert the most sacred truths and to degrade the most solemn prerogatives.

Upon careful exegesis of the passage and in keeping with the teaching of the Bible as a whole, I dogmatically assert that the disciples did not receive power to forgive sins as our Lord had exercised it. Such power and authority belong to God alone. Theirs was a mediatorial ministry, for to them was committed the ministry of reconciliation. Theirs was the blessed privilege and solemn responsibility to preach the gospel of God in all the world and thus bring within reach of every hearing and believing heart, the possibility to experience forgiveness of sins and a liberation of life. No doubt the key to the kingdom of God committed to the disciples is the Gospel of Jesus Christ. This must be preached among all nations, for without this message the way of release cannot be found. Such confidence we have in the gospel, which we rely on as God's means for man's salvation.

Thus the church today holds within its power the possibility of remitting and retaining sins. Its faithfulness in preaching the gospel of Jesus Christ will result in the joy of remitting the sins of numerous repenting and believing people. But if the church fails to discharge the solemn obligation, she will retain the sins of the people.

Here is the sacred and tremendous responsibility of the church toward the world. If the church fails to preach God's way of forgiveness of sins, no one else will and the world will remain in sin and therefore separated from God and in the bondage of the evil one.

Because the church is God's instrument in preaching the gospel, she finds herself either bitterly opposed by all evil forces or she is tempted to be sidetracked into all kinds of secondary and social services which in themselves may be good and uplifting, but they do not constitute the essential ministry of the church. Satan never minds a busy church, but he hates a holy and gospel-preaching church because the gospel is "the power of God unto salvation to every one that believeth." In the words of Christ, "Ye shall know the truth, and the truth shall make you free." In the gospel of Christ alone lies the power to release man from sin, liberate his life, and restore him to divine position and fellowship.

Such then is the spiritual aspect of our mission according to John. It requires *identification* with the Lord in His mission, *dependence* upon the Holy Spirit for the mission, and *reliance* upon the gospel of Jesus Christ to accomplish the mission.

SUMMARY

The Great Commission as reported by the four writers of the gospels presents a comprehensive and detailed pattern of our missionary assignment. I repeat, the Great Commission does not spell out all the duties of the church in this world or the total mission of the church. It concerns itself primarily with the outreach of the church into the world of the nonchurch people, whoever and wherever they may be. It is the great charter for world evangelization and not a program of world Christianization, not even a prescription for church edification. The emphasis, therefore, is to make disciples and evangelize the nations. These two imperatives must be held in constant tension and in proper balance and historical perspective until the total world has had the opportunity to hear the good news of the salvation of God in Christ Jesus.

6

The Church and Missions

WORLD EVANGELISM is the *imperative* of the New Testament. "The
gospel must first be proclaimed [heralded] among all nations" (Mk 13:
10, free trans.). The Paraclete to accomplish the task is the Holy
Spirit, while the divinely chosen agency for the proclamation is the
church of Jesus Christ. These are sobering and scriptural assertions.

Even a superficial reading of the New Testament will convince
the reader of the importance of the church in the present economy of
God. We read that Christ loved the church and gave Himself for
her. We are assured that at present He is building His church and
that eventually He will "present it to himself a glorious church, not
having spot or wrinkle, or any such thing; but . . . holy and without
blemish." All this is according to the eternal purpose which God purposed in Christ Jesus our Lord, "to the intent that now unto the principalities and powers in heavenly places might be known by the
church the manifold wisdom of God" (Eph 5:25-27; 3:10-11).

The church is God's chosen generation, royal priesthood, holy
nation, purchased people. The purpose of this high calling is that the
church should show forth the virtues of Him who called her out of
darkness into His marvelous light. The church is a purposive creation
in Christ Jesus; she is the body of Christ (His visible manifestation)
and the temple of the Holy Spirit. She was created on the day of
Pentecost to serve as the embodiment of the Holy Spirit for the accomplishing of the purpose of God in this world.

In order to clarify the muddled thinking about the church, I first
present a brief biblical study on the nature of the church of Christ.
Following this we shall consider the church's missionary task.

199

THE CHURCH OF JESUS CHRIST

Missions is not an imposition upon the church for it belongs to her nature and should be as natural to her as grapes are natural to branches that abide in the vine. Missions flows from the inner constitution, character, calling and design of the church. Therefore, what is the church?

To define the nature of the church from the biblical point of view, we turn to the study of the word *church (ekklesia)*, to the metaphors used to describe the church, and to the designations of the church.

A STUDY OF THE WORD "CHURCH"

The New Testament uses the word *ekklesia* to convey the concept of the church. The word itself is a compound taken from *kaleo*, "to call," and *ek*, "out from." The compound verb therefore means "to call out from," and the noun should mean "the called-out ones." However, the usage in the New Testament has more the meaning of "called unto." The word *ekklesia*, which always has a positive implication, refers to an assembly of people who are related to God and obey God, rather than a negative conception of those called away from the world.

From its use in classical Greek, the Septuagint and the New Testament, we may deduce the following basic qualities of the word *ekklesia:*

1. It was a *called-out* and *called unto* people.
2. It was a people of a *special kind*.
3. It was a people called out and called together *for* a *specific purpose.*
4. It was a people conducting their affairs on *principles of equality and brotherhood.*
5. It was a people *uniquely related to God* (a new aspect introduced by the Septuagint and New Testament; (Ac 7:38; Heb 2:12).

Turning to the New Testament we note that the word is used three ways:

1. Five times it is used in its classical Greek meaning of assembly. Two out of these five references (Ac 19:32, 39, 41; 7:38; Heb 2:12) represent the Septuagint usage, denoting the assembly of Israel (Ac 7:38; Heb 2:12).

2. The prevailing and fundamental idea of *ekklesia* is that of a local body organized on principles of brotherhood for purposes of pro-

clamation, fellowship, worship and service. Of the 115 occurrences of the term in the New Testament, some 85 may be assigned to the local congregation.

3. A special use of the term by Christ (Mt 16:18) and Paul does represent the idea of the church in an ideal sense, often spoken of as the church universal of which all believers in Christ are a part. Paul uses the term in this sense at least twelve times; most occurrences are in Ephesians and Colossians.

A STUDY OF THE METAPHORS USED TO EXPRESS
THE NATURE OF THE CHURCH

The symbols which the Bible employs to present the church in its nature, function, relationship and position are as follows:

1. a new man (Eph 2:14-15)
2. the body of Christ (Eph 1:22-23; 5:30; 1 Co 12:27)
3. the temple of God (Eph 2:21-22; 1 Co 3:9, 16; 1 Ti 3:15; 1 Pe 2:5)
4. a royal priesthood (1 Pe 2:5, 9; Rev 1:6; 5:10)
5. the bride of Christ (2 Co 11:2; Mt 25:6)
6. the household of God (Eph 2:19)
7. the flock of God (Jn 10:1-29; 1 Pe 5:3-4; Heb 13:20; Ac 20:28)

Some authorities would add several other symbols.

THE DESIGNATIONS OF THE CHURCH

The church of Jesus Christ is given several titles which indicate her unique position. The church is called:

1. The church of God (Ac 20:28; 1 Co 1:2; 10:32; 11:22; 15:9; 1 Ti 3:5; 1 Th 2:14)
2. The church of the living God (1 Ti 3:15)
3. the church of Christ (Ro 16:16)
4. the church of the firstborn (Heb 12:23)
5. the church of the saints (1 Co 14:33)

It should be noted that while the word *ekklesia* refers principally to the local body of believers or the local church, the symbols express more the idea of the church universal, the church ideal, the church of Jesus Christ as a whole. It is not wholesome to emphasize one idea at the expense of the other. We must further note that every one of the symbols expresses the basic idea of relationship and function rather than organization. No one can study the symbolic presentation of the church without being deeply impressed by the truth of inter-dependence. While the Bible upholds the autonomy of a local assembly, it knows nothing of *independence* in the absolute sense of the word. Biblical independence is always balanced by absolute *dependence* upon the Lord and *interdependence* among the churches. Thus denominationalism is not contrary to the Bible. Denominationalism in the sense of larger fellowships, closer cooperation and mutual exchange and assistance of churches is fully within the framework of biblical teaching and is clearly implied in the symbolic presentations of the church.

Definition of the church ideal. In light of the above material, I define the church ideal as that body of people which has been called unto God by means of the gospel of Jesus Christ, brought into a life relationship with Jesus Christ by faith, and baptized into the body of Jesus Christ by the Holy Spirit. It is the temple of God indwelt by the Holy Spirit, constituting a brotherhood in the household of God, a peculiar people to serve a unique purpose of God in this age with a blessed hope of occupying a unique position with the Lord in the ages to come.

Definition of the local church. A local church may be defined as that ordered body of professing baptized believers who, on the basis of common experiences of the Lord and convictions of the Word, in the bond of mutual love and understanding, in the interest of common concerns and causes, and for the purposes of mutual spiritual benefits and fellowship, assemble themselves together according to the Word of God, conduct worship services in an organized and orderly manner, observe the Lord's ordinances, perform such functions as they deem advantageous to themselves and their community according to the Word of God, and discharge such other responsibilities as they judge their duty before God and man.

The basic *qualities* of a biblical local church expressing the functional nature of the local church may be summarized in several statements:

The church is the gathering together of baptized believers.
The church is an ordered (structured) body of believers.
The church is a united body of believers.

The church is a brotherhood of believers.
The church is a disciplined fellowship of believers.
The church is a witnessing fellowship of believers.
The church is a proclaiming and serving fellowship of believers.
The church is a worshiping fellowship of believers.

Thus worship, fellowship, unity, fraternity, discipleship, proclamations, witnessing and serving remain the great and distinct marks of a true and biblical local church.

Underlying and determining principles. Without dwelling upon the many practical implications, I limit myself to deducing certain underlying and determining principles. Let me state them in outline:

1. First, the church is a divine creation. It is not a product of spontaneous development in history, nor is it a construction of the natural genius of man. It is not a human invention. It does not belong to the natural order of history or nature of things. Neither has it evolved out of historical precedents. It is a continuously existing dynamic, purposive event which found its origin in a decisive and histtorical act of God on the day of Pentecost by the coming of the Holy Spirit. It is a new creation, indeed, the "masterpiece" of God (Eph 2:10) in which the manifold wisdom of God is being made manifest unto the principalities and powers in heavenly places (Eph 3:10). And this is "according to the eternal purpose [of God] which he purposed in Christ Jesus our Lord" (Eph 3:11).

2. Second, the church is God's unique possession. It is the church of God, the church of Christ, the household of God, the habitation of God. The preposition *of* is significant. Well does Deissmann say,

> It has not yet been generally recognized that St. Paul's use of the genitive "of Jesus Christ" is altogether very peculiar. There are a number of passages in St. Paul in which the ordinary grammatical scheme of "subjective genitive" and "objective genitive" prove sufficient. Later Greek possessed in addition to these a genitival use, sometimes rather remarkable which to some extent is the result of the survival of a very ancient type. So too, in St. Paul it would be possible to establish a peculiar type of genitive, which we might call the *"mystic genitive"* because it expresses the mystic fellowship. "Of Jesus Christ" is here in the main identical with "in Christ."[1]

The mystic-realistic relationship between the church and Jesus Christ and through Jesus Christ with God the Father makes the church, in a very unique sense, God's own possession. This Peter declares when he writes, "Ye are . . . a people for God's own possession" (1 Pe 2:9, ASV). Paul tells us that we are not our own because we have been bought with a price (1 Co 6:19-20). Neither passage could be applied to the world in the same manner.

While I readily admit that all creation belongs to God, there does exist a unique relationship between the church and God which makes the church peculiarly His possession. The world is not the body of Christ nor the habitation of God in the same manner as the church.

3. Third, the church is principally divine functionalism and relationship. The church must be defined in terms of relationship and dynamism at least as much as in terms of idealistic concepts and structure. Not that the church exists apart from or in opposition to form and structure. Rather, the latter are not a part of the nature of the church. While they may be inseparably related *to* the church, they are not *of* the church. It never has been true and it never will be true that where the bishop is, there the church is. The church is not principally a visible, hierarchical, institutional structure; it is a living organism. The church is intelligent purpose rather than structure, energetic wisdom rather than institution, living fellowship rather than hierarchy, dynamic idealism rather than defined constitution, vibrant organism rather than mere orderly relatedness or organization, the incarnation of the mind, ideals and will of Christ under the headship of Christ rather than theological formulations, philosophical systems, creeds or dogmas. It is purposive, dynamic existence in an orderly and existential pattern and with an eternal mission and destiny.

4. Fourth, the church is a divinely ordered or structured society. This may at first seem to contradict the previous paragraph. In reality it does not. It is an addition which must neither be identified nor confused with the truth stated above. Nevertheless, it is a vital fact of biblical revelation. The church is the temple of God, a divine household, a royal priesthood, a body functioning in an orderly, coordinated manner. Every metaphor of the church speaks of order and design. Paul appointed elders or overseers in the churches and charged them with heavy responsibilities. He commanded Titus to "set in order" the things in the churches in Crete. Timothy received instruction that he might know how it behooves to behave in the household of God (Titus 1:5; 1 Ti 3:15).

We may well think of the church as "structural community" (Rahner), or "spiritual community" (Tillich), or "company of the committed" (Trueblood). Whatever designation we may choose, a church is more than a conglomeration of believers or a loosely knit group of believing people or an occasional gathering of the people of God. A church has form, structure, configuration and order.

We may not be able to define conclusively the form and structure, nor design a form and structure for all times and cultures, but it is a certainty that no organism exists without form, structure and organization, no matter how different and adaptable the latter may be.

The *ekklesia* of the New Testament is the people of God called unto God to be His marching army, His worshiping and serving priesthood, His proclaiming heralds. All this presupposes and implies order and structure. Without such, neither instruction, building, discipline nor continued fellowship can result.

Dynamic functionalism and divinely ordained order, therefore, must be kept in biblical tensions for the welfare of the church in its ministry and progress.

THE CHURCH AND HISTORIC REALISM

The biblical ideals of the *ekklesia* of God as outlined above are not always clearly discernible in the church. Time and history were harsh and oppressing forces, and not always did the church come through unscarred and unmarred. Accommodation was too often a way of life rather than just a way in or out of situations.

Though the history of the church is a marvel and her preservation through the centuries in a hostile world can be attributed only to her divine origin, design and destiny, the elements of time, space and human sinfulness have left their marks. Historical realism must be distinguished from biblical idealism. It has never been possible to equate the *ekklesia* of God with the visible church or Christendom, be that the Roman Catholic Church, the Greek Orthodox Church, the Anglican Church, the great denominational churches that sprung from the Protestant Reformation, or even the independent church movements. The chaff has always mingled with the wheat, and not seldom have the "weeds" (theological, ecclesiastical, social or moral evils) threatened to choke out the genuinely divine plants. And even though waves of renewal have swept over the church, the evil within her has never been overcome.

Failure of human leadership. It is a sad fact of history that human leadership in the church has often failed to recognize the true nature and character of the church. In consequence, the church has often been dealt with much like an institution, a corporation, an organization, a structured society for secular purposes, or even a state. Therefore, she has been misdirected in purpose and mission and misused for purely social or selfish ends. From the perspective of history, the church in her visible or organized form portrays little divineness. In many ways she is a religious power structure and an embodiment of just another religion with her cathedrals and other sacred edifices and places, altars, priesthood, clergy and holy orders, ordinances, rites, sacraments, symbols, liturgy, ceremonies, relics, holidays and feasts. The church has become structured Christendom, an all-embracing, all-inclusive entity which is little more than a society for religious practices. Divisiveness, dissension, worldly ambition, dominance, rulership mentality and worldliness have often characterized the institutionalized church and hierarchy. Though waves of renewal have swept over parts of the church, it cannot be said that the church as a whole has ever permitted the reviving power of the Holy Spirit to penetrate, reform, transform and redirect her total life and ministry. And when waves of revival have graciously descended, they have either been resisted or redirected and rechanneled, as is the case at present with the ecumenical movement and the charismatic experiences. This is, indeed, a humiliating story.

Great impact and contribution. Nevertheless, Christianity has made a tremendous impact and wholesome contributions. It has not been a failure. It cannot be! It has released an unparalleled and humanly unaccountable amount of noble ambitions, unselfish service and heroic sacrifices, and has created humane institutions, philanthropic movements and worldwide missionary endeavors to the benefit of mankind. Besides bringing the deepest spiritual experiences and values to countless multitudes, it has deeply affected, transformed and greatly enriched culture and values in the Western world, where it has been most believed and obeyed. Its impact is immeasurable. No student of comparative cultures will deny this fact. The Bible and the Christian presence in the West have made an impressive difference.

Faithful remnant. It is also true that the Lord has always had His faithful remnant, a people born anew by the Spirit of God and obeying the Word of God. This people constitutes the true *ekklesia* of God in this world. Genuine Christianity has always survived in the midst of nominal Christendom, and the real *ekklesia* of God has always persisted within the framework of the "church." Neither time, circumstances nor error within Christendom has been able to choke out the true life and light completely. The *ekklesia* of God is a present and blessed reality. It is composed of individual believers within the stream of Christendom, believing local congregations, and even denominations which have remained true to the gospel and the Lord Jesus Christ. We need to recognize this, take heart, and thank the Lord for it. Our Lord has always had His "seven thousand" that have not bowed their knees before Baal. Individual people, local congregations and some denominations are true to the gospel and the purpose of God.

These evangelical churches and denominations may not always approximate the biblical ideals absolutely, nor do they resemble each other very closely. Their outward form and structure may differ, and they will have their peculiar emphases and characteristics. This, however, may be due more to human limitations in experience, time, culture, psychology and tradition than to true biblicity and spirituality or relationship to their Lord and His Word. This should not disturb us severely. God needs various vessels to express the fullness of His gospel and to appeal to the various peoples of the world with His message.

Today's ideas and endeavors. Our present-day ecumenical endeavors on the one hand and antiestablishment mentality on the other hand easily blind us against that which is real and genuine in churches and denominations which seek to preserve and propagate "the faith which was once delivered unto the saints" (Jude 3). It must be remembered that the Bible does not foster the present-day ecumenical ambitions nor design. Neither does it support antiestablishment, antidenominationalism or antichurch attitudes. The Bible is *for* the gospel and *for* the church that is *for* the gospel. The believing individual, the evangelical congregation or a grouping of like-minded churches bound together by the Word of God, a common faith and experiences, biblical purpose, a spiritual sense of belongingness, relatedness and togetherness are present-day historical realities which God uses to.be the light of the world and the salt of the earth. They are God's channel for the propagation of the gospel of our Lord Jesus Christ.

It may not be easy to blend or harmonize biblical idealism and historic realism in relation to the church; yet the *ekklesia* of God is a blessed reality, and Christ Himself assures her triumph and consummation (Mt 16:18).

THE MISSIONARY TASK OF THE CHURCH

Because the church is God's unique creation and not the result of historical and natural processes, and because she is God's unique possession through Jesus Christ, it is to be expected that she has been designed for a unique purpose and mission.

The mission and purpose of the church are not exhausted in the general movements of history. It is as dangerous to identify her mission with the movements and events of history as it is to isolate her from them. The church is *in* history, yet not *of* history; she is *in* history, yet *apart from* history, yes, *above* and *beyond* history. She performs her mission in history, yet finds her origin, sustenance, final authority, deepest motives, ideal design, true purpose, ultimate destiny and final goal outside of and beyond history. She is *in* time, yet she is *of* eternity; she is *for* man, yet she is *of* God.

This is both the reality and the mystery of the nature and task of the church. While human in appearance, she is suprahuman in being and design; while historic in operation, she is suprahistoric in mission, purpose and goal. She is not enigma but mystery and revelation. Her design, mission and purpose constitute her *task*. To this we must turn and formulate.

THE TASK IN GENERAL TERMS

The reader of the Bible will soon become convinced that the responsibility which rests upon the church corresponds in weight and measure to the riches bestowed upon the saints. While the yoke is easy and the burden is light, and while the way is illumined and the provision is bounteous, the task is multiple and the demands are radical. The task of the church is both glorious and challenging, inviting and frightening. It is a labor in the Lord which is both refreshing and exhausting. To define it is not an easy assignment.

The late Henry C. Thiessen puts the mission of the church in seven statements upon which he then elaborates. He says that the purpose of the church is "to glorify God, to edify itself, to purify itself, to educate its constituency, to evangelize the world, to act as a restraining and enlightening force in the world, to promote all that is good."[2]

This seems a fair summary of biblical teaching. From the teaching of the New Testament it is easily perceived that the church operates in three relationships: *upward* to God in worship and glorification; *inward* to herself in edification, purification, education and discipline; *outward* to the world in evangelization and service ministries. For our purpose we need to concentrate on the outward relationship and movement of the church.

It is evident that *evangelization* refers more to the oral or verbal communication of the good news of God to man, whereas the *diakonia* aspect denotes more the implementation and demonstration of the practical implications of the gospel of God. There is a service aspect to the gospel as well as a proclamation aspect. In our days we need to see clearly what the implications and explications of evangelization are.

In a most original manner, Hugh Thomson Kerr puts the emphasis where it ought to be:

> We are sent not to preach sociology but salvation; not economics but evangelism; not reform but redemption; not culture but conversion; not progress but pardon; not a new social order but a new birth; not revolution but regeneration; not renovation but revival; not resuscitation but resurrection; not a new organization but a new creation; not democracy but the gospel; not civilization but Christ; we are ambassadors not diplomats.[3]

THE THRUST OF THE NEW TESTAMENT

[We are moving within the center stream of the New Testament when I assert that the principal task of the church is to communicate intelligibly and effectively a divine message to the world in order to bring man to a living relationship with Christ by faith. The gospel — the good news of God in Christ — constitutes the heart and the core of the Christian possession.] The preservation, interpretation and the intelligible and persuasive communication of the good news, with the

fixed intent of leading men to a knowledge of Christ as the only
Saviour and a resolute commitment to Him as Lord, remain forever
the church's supreme and primary task. Here is the heart of Christian
missions. Such emphasis may sound strange, old-fashioned, outdated
and irrelevant to an activistic and irritated generation bent more upon
social action than upon gospel proclamation. It may also seem peculiar
to a pietistic mentality where *being* a Christian has been much emphasized. However, that proclamation is central and therefore practical and relevant, according to the New Testament.

The above emphasis does not deny the significance of social action, the need for Christian influence in society, and the desirability of
advancement in civilization. Most certainly Christians ought to be
deeply involved in the social ills and struggles of society and to be
energetically striving to bring reconciliation, remedy and assistance to
mankind. Social welfare and advancement are significant and desirable; however, such services are not the mission of the church. Neither are they focal in the New Testament. New Testament Christian
social ethics is personal, not ecclesiastical.

It must also be stated emphatically that the New Testament does
not foresee the conversion of the world to Jesus Christ in this dispensation. It is clearly implied in the teachings of our Lord and the
apostles that the church will remain a "gathered out" people and thus
constitute only a minority unto the end of the age. We are, however,
commanded to *evangelize* the world and make the gospel available to
every creature. *And evangelization is the intelligible, attractive,
meaningful, purposive and persuasive presentation of the gospel.* This
remains our determining ministry and continuing thrust. This is our
supreme and primary calling.

Christian presence and Christian proclamation. It is a fact of
history that God became incarnated in order to draw near unto man,
unveil Himself in moral, social and spiritual grandeur, and fully and
completely accomplish His eternal purpose of salvation for man.
Propositional revelation in the Old Testament, as perfect and unerring
as it was, could not fully and satisfactorily unveil God to man because
of man's limited and dulled sense of perception. Sin has darkened
man's mind, especially in spiritual and eternal matters. Thus "Christian presence" in the incarnation of the Word was a necessity and
became a reality. Emmanuel, "God with us," is not only an eternal

and spiritual idea, it became a historical reality. The Word became flesh and dwelt among us.

It is not fair, however, to stop with the fact. We must ascertain the biblical content and purpose of the fact. Was the incarnation for incarnation's sake? What lies behind and what lies ahead of the fact? Into this we must inquire diligently and honestly.

Christ is the wisest of all philosophers. He is the wisdom of God, yet He founded no philosophical school. Christ is the greatest of all scholars and educators, yet He instituted no educational system. Christ is the greatest benefactor and philanthropist, yet He founded no social welfare society, institutions or philanthropic foundations. Christ was "Christian presence" with deepest concerns for freedom, social uplift, equality, moral reformation, and economic justice. Yet Christ founded no organizations or institutions to initiate, propagate or implement the ideals which He incarnated. He poured out His life's energies to give man a true concept of God and finally shed His blood to make a way for man to approach God. His fundamental task was to build a bridge between God and man, to become the Mediator between a holy God and ruined sinners.

"Christian presence," the Word as flesh, is a historical reality, but it is a reality of a unique kind and quality. Christ did not become involved in processions against Roman overlords, slavery, social and economic injustices, or marches for civil rights, higher wages, or better education. He was no "riot" leader or social revolutionary. He authorized no one to be such. Not in riot or revolution but in redemption on Calvary's cross, incarnation found its supreme expression and consummation. Calvary became its crowning moment and event. "Christian presence"? Yes! But what kind? What purpose?

Christ, the Teacher and Preacher. Christ was not known to His contemporaries and disciples as "Christian presence" or "divine incarnation." Rather, He was known as the Teacher and Preacher setting forth great and majestic spiritual truths, ideals and patterns. He declares Himself, "The Spirit of the Lord is upon me, because He hath anointed me to *evangelize* the poor; He hath sent me to *proclaim* release to captives and sight to blind, to send away the crushed ones in release, to *proclaim* a year of the Lord acceptable (Lk 4:18-19, free trans.).

Forty-eight times Christ is called *Teacher* in the gospels, and more than one hundred times His ministry is described in terms of teaching, preaching and evangelizing. Paul, too, knew himself as a preacher, apostle, and teacher. All this emphasizes the importance of verbal communication of the message of God committed unto us.

The emphasis in the New Testament is on evangelism by the communication of the message of God — the gospel — committed unto us. More than 140 times the New Testament uses such words as *diaggello,* to announce; *kataggello,* to tell thoroughly; *euaggelizo,* to spread good news; *laleo,* to talk or speak; and *kerusso,* to herald or proclaim.

At this time there is much debate about the significance of *Christian presence* versus *Christian proclamation* or verbal communication. In reality this is a debate about meaning and priorities. No believer in the Bible will question the importance of *Christian presence* if the expression is given biblical content. The problem is that today *Christian presence* is taken out of its biblical context and given primarily social, religious, economic and political content. Thus it has lost its true Christian meaning and significance.

It is not a question of Christian presence *or* Christian proclamation. It is not an either/or proposition. It is a matter of both/and. To be sent *(apostello)* invariably implies presence, but presence is not primary or an end in itself, it is purposive. The apostles of Jesus Christ were not commissioned to the *present* in the world, they were men under orders with a message. They were sent forth to *proclaim* the gospel of their blessed Lord. This mission necessitated their presence, but their presence did not constitute their mission. To be an apostle in the biblical sense of the word demanded a message to be announced. Thus *Christian presence* in itself does not exhaust the biblical concept of being sent. Neither does it do justice to the biblical concept, "The Word became flesh." Christ was more than mere *presence.*

THE SPECIFICS OF THE CHURCH'S TASK

In order to focus clearly, we need to define the church's task as much as possible in specifics. In the Great Commission as reported to us in the four gospels we have the divine charter of Christian missions. While the Great Commission does *not* fully describe the *total task* of the church, as we have stated before, it does charter the church's responsibility in her *outward* or mission relationship. The Great Commission is silent regarding the upward ministry in worship and only slightly touches upon the inward responsibilities of the church. It is clear and exhaustive in the outward ministries of the church. It is commanding, defining and limiting. It is imperative and indicative. It presents full-orbed "missions," not the total mission. To the Great Commission we must turn to find our orientation, authority and directives. It is the "royal charter" of missions.

As we review the mandate of the Great Commission, we may summarize the task of the church in several statements which present the pattern and purpose of missions. The Great Commission emphatically declares the sovereignty of the Lord and throughout assumes the uniqueness, finality, sufficiency, absoluteness, inclusiveness, exclusiveness and universality of the gospel of our Lord Jesus Christ.

The Christian church is placed under the solemn obligation to do the following:

1. To present Christ vividly, intelligibly, attractively, effectively and persuasively to the world and to the individual as the Saviour of God, the sovereign Lord of the universe, and the coming Judge of mankind.

2. To lead people into a faith relationship with Jesus Christ in order that they might experience forgiveness of sins and newness of life. Man must be born again if he is to inherit eternal life and eternal fellowship with God.

3. To segregate and congregate believers through the administration of baptism and build them into functioning Christian churches. Christian fellowship constitutes a vital part of the Christian life.

4. To establish the believers in Christian doctrine, principles and practices of Christian living, Christian fellowship and Christian service, teaching them to observe all things. This is indoctrination, the making of Christian disciples, the Christianization of the individual.

5. To train them in a life of the Holy Spirit. Since the Christian life is charged with supernatural ideals and demands, it can only be lived in absolute reliance on the Holy Spirit. Unless the lessons are learned early, the Christian life becomes beset with frustrations and numbness; apathy sets in, or people become conditioned to an abnormal and subnormal Christian life. This is the tragedy of countless believers who do not even expect to live up to the biblical ideals.

It is clearly implied and understood from the context and the general tenor of the Bible that such a task can be carried through only in the power of the Holy Spirit. He is the great Superintendent, the Energizer and Sustainer of His church. The church's task, in the final end, is a supernatural task which demands supernatural resources. Because these are available in the Holy Spirit, we must lean hard upon Him. The church's task is glorious, urgent, demanding, unique. We dare not surrender, neglect, secularize or popularize it. It is of God, even as the church is of God. We are His unique creations and His unique possession, and we are His for a unique task.

We must move from mission into missions to fulfill the purpose of God and live in the fullness of His blessings.

The Church in Missions

The history of the church in missions is in the main the history of great personalities and of missionary societies. Only in exceptional cases has it been the church in missions. The present-day slogan, The Church in Mission, is a rather late by-product of Christian missions or a late awakening of the Christian conscience.

Five reasons seemingly are responsible for this unfortunate and abnormal historic development which has produced autonomus, missionless churches on the one hand and autonomous churchless missionary societies on the other hand. While the latter claim to be "servants" of the churches, they are autonomous, legislative and administrative bodies with their independent charters and thus at least able to operate independently. What is the history behind such a phenomenon?

REASONS FOR HISTORICAL ABNORMALITIES

The theology of the Reformation. The sixteenth-century Protestant Reformation gave birth to the missionary message and released a spiritual and potential missionary dynamic which eventually resulted in a vigorous missionary movement. Just how far the missionary pattern and direct missionary motivation may be attributed to the great Reformers is a matter of debate. No one of them was so blind that he did not see the evangelistic implications of the Christian gospel and salvation experience. All of them, however, seem to have been so preoccupied with their immediate needs and pressures that time was not available to make a systematic and convincing presentation of the foreign missionary cause. Paradoxical statements may be discovered, and both positive and negative implications have been deduced.

Luther has been decried as a man of no missionary vision in whom the missionary idea was not only totally lacking, but who explicitly denied its validity. On the other hand, he has been lauded as a man of a superlative missionary vision. Thus praise and blame have been heaped upon the leaders of the Reformation for their attitudes and statements. In recent years, serious attempts have been made to reconstruct the image of Luther and portray him as an advocate of missions. None of the presentations is really convincing if the "quotes" are viewed within their context, the purpose for which they were spoken, and the occasion which called them forth. The debate continues and should continue. The existential, causal and occasional approach of Luther to life, ethics and theology, however, will make it difficult to become dogmatic and conclusive in this question.

While we respect the Reformers as truly great men of God and want to grant them as much credit as possible, this much remains a fact: The churches which resulted from their labor were not missionary churches in the modern sense of the word, and the theologians who followed them and claimed to be their true successors and interpreters did not advance the missionary idea and motivation. A negative theology did dominate the official Protestant church following the Reformation for some two centuries. While noble individuals spoke and acted in protest, the "missionary status quo" in continental theology was only effectively broken through German Pietism and the resultant revivalism which succeeded in permeating part of the church and arousing the missionary impetus at least in the "church within the church."

We must not lose sight of the fact, however, that the Reformation gave men a new spiritual vision, a new objective, a new dynamic, and a new fellowship which eventually but inevitably resulted in a worldwide missionary outreach.

The relation of the church to the state. Due to an inadequate view of the church according to the New Testament, the great Reformers of the sixteenth century did not develop a free church in a free state. Rather, they preserved and perpetuated the concept of a state church. This made the church dependent upon the state in many ways, of which finances were not the least. Thus, while the state provided finances for the support of the church at home, no such funds were available for the expansion of the church in mission territories, except in a few exceptional cases and in a limited manner. Before the church could become actively involved in mission, the church had to learn to walk alone and independently of the state in finances, organization and administration.

The lack of readiness on the part of the church to launch out in missions. It is rather a serious indictment to say the church was not ready to begin missions, but it would be difficult to deny the fact. This is evident from the fact that most missions began as societies which functioned according to the pattern of the corporations, some of them with annual dues contributed by all voting members. The churches were not prepared to assume the responsibilities for large expansions. The reason for such lack was due in part to the low spiritual level in the churches which lacked spiritual vitality and ambition.

The misconception that missions was the responsibility of individuals rather than the obligation of the churches. This erroneous idea, advocated by Zwingli and his successors, has only gradually and in part been overcome in recent decades. Zwingli maintained that missions is the business of specially called apostles, and that the church as such has nothing to do with missions. This same idea carried over later into Pietism and became dominant in much of Western Protestantism. It still survives due to the inertness of many churches and their inability to organize effectively for missions on the one hand and the strong and vital individualism of some leaders on the other hand.

Thus individuals have felt called to follow in the steps of the apostles and to pioneer for Christ in mission lands independently of the churches and church direction. As a result, many churches as such have remained practically uninvolved in missions while individuals or small groups from within the churches have aggressively carried on foreign mission work. Such abnormalities became the regular experience and pattern in the large churches of the Continent and of Great Britain.

While this was not the original pattern in most American denominations, it was only gradually and in part overcome in the free churches in Great Britain and the Continent. This also accounts for the fact that most early British and continental missionary societies were organized originally on an interdenominational basis or only loosely related to a denomination. Only gradually did they gravitate toward denominationalism. The trading companies rather than ecclesiastical bodies became the pattern of organization, legislation and operation. Such development was most unfortunate and worked itself out negatively in at least three ways:

First, it left many of the larger churches passive and uninvolved in missions.

Second, it set up a trade-company type of mission administration and complex with the mission societies becoming autonomous agencies alongside autonomous church bodies, thus introducing a dichotomy on the home base.

Third, it related the churches of the mission lands to a missionary society rather than to a mother or sister church of the sending countries.

Strong personalities knew themselves called of God but were not acceptable to ecclesiastical authority and existing sending agencies. This may be true, either because of personality makeup, academic qualifications, or lack of such qualifications or the choice of the field of their labor. Thus Hudson Taylor was pressing for inland China but was not able to induce any of the existing agencies to move aggressively forward. Rowland V. Bingham similarly pleaded to be sent into the interior of the Sudan. Both men were compelled to create new agencies to realize this calling of God. Many others could be cited. As a result, new sending agencies were developed.

Through the decades the sending agencies have multiplied until today they are too numerous to list. The justification of such proliferation we must leave to history.

With the development of a deeper and purer concept of the church and an awakening within the churches to a mission responsibility and the essential missionary nature of the New Testament church, the whole question of missionary society has come under critical review. The right to existence of the missionary society as historically developed has been seriously questioned if not outrightly denied. It is the church in missions rather than a missionary society, we are told. The tensions are increased by strained relationships of the missionary societies and the younger churches in the mission fields. The latter desire to relate themselves to churches rather than to missionary societies. Thus the slogan is dominant, The Church Is Mission, which makes the societies seem superfluous.

The existing situations throw us back upon the Scriptures. Fully aware of the fact that the Bible does not present to us a fixed and ready-made pattern in these matters, the question is legitimate: Does the Bible present some guidelines in these most crucial matters? Is there a possibility to relate autonomous missionary societies to autonomous churches and church bodies to the satisfaction of both parties? In order to answer these questions we consider first, the responsibility of the church; second, the rights of the missionary society; and third, some patterns of relationships between missions and the younger churches.

THE NEW TESTAMENT CHURCH AS THE MEDIATING SENDING AUTHORITY

In speaking of the sending authority, we are fully aware of the fact that ultimate sending authority rests in Christ who states, "All authority is given unto me in heaven and on earth." This authority is exercised and administered ultimately by the Holy Spirit; The book of Acts leaves no doubt in this matter. From the pages of the New Testament we deduce that the church, the local congregation, becomes the mediating sending authority as the missionary society becomes the mediating sending agency. To this we turn our attention.

In our consideration of the New Testament church as the mediating sending authority, we shall point to the centrality of the church in the New Testament and her relationship to the Lord who is the Head of the church, to the apostolic succession of the church, the interrelationship of the authority of the church and the individual priesthood of the believer, which includes a consideration of the significance of the rite of laying on of hands, and the relationship of some apostles to the churches.

The centrality of the church in the New Testament. Ours is the dispensation of the church of Jesus Christ as the Old Testament was the dispensation of Israel. Even a casual reading of the Acts of the apostles and the epistles will direct our attention to the fact that the New Testament places the church in a central position. The very fact that the church is mentioned 115 times speaks for her significance. It is worthy of note that the larger portion of these references refers to the local congregation of believers. We observe further that the local assembly becomes an authoritative creation of Christ in nearly every respect of doctrine, life, discipline and ministry (cf. 1 Co 12-14; Eph 4:11-16). The church is the "house of God" and the "pillar and ground of the truth" (1 Ti 3:15). Also, the church is the manifestation of "the manifold wisdom of God" (Eph 3:10).

Paul says most significantly that "Christ is the . . . saviour of the body" and that "Christ also loved the church, and gave himself for it" (Eph 5:23, 25). To this he adds the words that he, too, rejoices in his sufferings to "fill up that which is behind of the afflictions of Christ in my flesh for his body's sake, which is the church" (Col 1:21). Wherever Paul went to preach the gospel he founded a church. Of course, it was not a church merely for a church's sake. Paul evangelized to plant living cells that would become evangelizing centers in that community.

We believe that we are not out of line with New Testament thinking if we state that the local congregation of believers stands in a unique relationship to Christ and that the local assembly becomes the mediating and authoritative sending body of the New Testament missionary. This is a vital, biblical principle and we dare not weaken, minimize nor disregard it.

The "apostolic succession" of the church in the New Testament. The concept "apostolic succession" has been much debated in the history of the Christian church. It is not our intention to enter into the pros and cons of the debate. However, we are interested in continuities of responsibilities and ministries. It may be of value to consider the concept from two aspects. There is in the New Testament an apostleship as an office of authority and position and also an apostleship as a function or a ministry. The former is clearly confined to the twelve and Paul with perhaps James, the brother of Christ (see Gal 1:19), and comes to an end with the death of the bearers of this office. The latter is more general and continues in the church as teachers, evangelists and missionaries after the twelve and Paul have passed from the scene. To speak of apostolic succession, therefore, is rather difficult. Yet there is a continuity of responsibility and ministry. This continuity we find in the church rather than in any official of the church. We see the church in apostolic succession. This position we deduce from five facts:

1. Paul informs us that the church is "built upon the foundation of the apostles and prophets, Jesus Christ himself being the chief

corner stone" (Eph 2:20). It should be noted that this is not a salvation passage, for no apostles and prophets stand between Christ and the individual believer in salvation relationship. In salvation, Christ is the direct and immediate foundation (1 Co 3:11). Paul has dealt with salvation in Ephesians 1:3 — 2:10, linking the believer directly to Christ. This passage is a position passage in which a divine order of historical succession of priority in ministry is indicated. Thus, if there is any apostolic succession, the line of succession is as follows: from the Father to the Son, from the Son to the apostles, and from the apostles to the church. This seems to be the divine order indicated by the passage. The church rather than the individual minister, as such, lives in the apostolic succession.

The historic dictum of Cyprian, "Where the bishop is, the church is," finds its reversal in the biblical order, "Where the church is, the bishop [overseer] is," or, "There is no bishop [overseer] where there is no church." The church makes the bishop and not the bishop the church. The church is God's priority. It may not be so in human organizations.

2. Such an order is also in perfect harmony with the great and glorious truth that Christ is the Head of the church, and the church is the body of Christ. Christ is the Bridegroom of the church, and the church joined together with Christ constitute "the Christ" (cf. 1 Co 12:12 in the original).

3. As we turn to the Great Commission according to Matthew, we find Christian responsibility defined as making disciples, which includes baptism and teaching. We have no doubt that this commission was first addressed to the apostles, but the question presses upon us as to who inherits the mantle of the apostles — the church or individual Christians? Too frequently the words are being addressed only to individuals as Christ's special challenge to missions. While they have such force and implication, the fact remains that it is the church's responsibility to baptize and to teach. This is evident from the practice and teaching of Paul.

The church is God's creation for the observance of the divine ordinances, and it is God's institution for teaching purposes. Since the church is the pillar and ground of truth, the Great Commission falls principally upon her. She inherits the Great Commission from the apostles of Christ and becomes responsible for its realization. Too long has pietistic individualism dominated the mind and scene of Protestantism in relation to the Great Commission while the church was left asleep.

4. The soundness of the above reasoning is further evident from the fact that several of the "general apostles" mentioned in the Scriptures are spoken of as apostles of the churches. This is true of Epaphras (Phil 2:25) and also of the "brethren" referred to in 2 Corinthians 8:23. Such designation is significant. While the twelve and Paul are apostles of Jesus Christ, the others become apostles of the churches, that is, they are receiving their commissioning and authority from the churches. The church becomes Christ's mediating agency to constitute apostles. We do well to heed and respect this biblical order.

5. It is symbolized by the rite of laying on of hands by the church upon the missionary. The biblical rite of laying on of hands is a symbol of deep spiritual and soteriological significance. In relation to ordination, it is an event of serious consequence to the church as well as to the recipient. In this relationship the ordinance points at least in two directions. On the one hand, it speaks of the priority and authority of the church as the mediating sending agency of God. It presents the church as the responsible missionary body assuming her position and place in missions under the authority of Christ.

On the other hand, the rite speaks of authentication, identification, and the creation of a representative by delegation. By this rite the church is publicly authenticating the call of God; she is constituting a rightful and responsible representative, and she is declaring her identification with the representative in his call and ministry. In the person of the ordained individual, the church by substitution goes forth into the ministry.

By the laying on of hands, the church and the individual missionary become bound in a bond of common purpose and mutual responsibility. It is thus not only a privilege and service; it is also the exercise of an authority and the acceptance of a tremendous responsibility. The identification of the church with the sent-forth representative is inclusive doctrinally, spiritually, physically and materially. It is the constituting of a rightful representative who will be able and who is responsible to function as a representative of the church. The church, therefore, by the laying on of hands, declares herself ready to stand by and make such representation possible. This should include the prayers and the finances required for such a representative ministry.

It is my solid conviction that the proper exercise of this biblical principle by the churches would do more to boost the morale of our missionaries and the flow of missionary candidates than many other factors combined. Should our young people realize that not only does "my church go with me, but my church goes in my person, stands with me, prays with me, sacrifices with me, and underwrites my support," the challenge would become inescapable. Here is the church's real opportunity, responsibility and challenge to herself and to the young people. Laying on of hands is not a favor we extend, but a divine authority we exercise and a responsibility we assume. A church should think soberly before it performs the act.

The same principle, however, holds true also for the one who receives the laying on of hands. He recognizes the delegating authority of the church, identifies himself with the church, submits himself to the direction and discipline of the church, and commits himself to be a true and responsible representative of the church. He operates within the doctrinal framework and spirit of the church, conscious of the fact that he is a representative of his Lord as well as of his church, to whom he also acknowledges accountability. Any deviation would be made only by mutual understanding and agreement.

Such relationship of mutual identification and loyal representation would certainly do much for missions. It would prove rewarding for the church, the missionary, and the work. It would involve the church more directly in missions, and it would bind the missionary to the church in a healthy and bolstering manner. He would feel neither "independent" nor "forsaken," knowing that he has a home church that has "gone with him into the field," while the church would know that she is actively involved in missions in a representative manner. Returning from the field, the missionary would find a home for his family and a place where he could enrich his life while making a contribution to his home church.

The priesthood of the believer and the mediating sending authority of the church. We must be careful, however, not to interpret the above truth in an absolutistic manner and put the congregation as an organization between Christ and the individual believer in such a manner that it destroys the precious doctrine of the personal relationship and individual priesthood of the believer. The Christ-church-individual relationship is not a salvation relationship, as indicated before; it is an authority relationship and refers to service rather than salvation. But neither must the individual priesthood of the believer be elevated above the church as the mystic body of Christ or local congregation of believers. One danger is as perilous as the other.

We have reached here another one of the New Testament's seeming paradoxes where only the spiritual mind can deliver us from contradictions and frustrations. The local assembly and the individual believer belong organically together, and they must function harmoniously if the full biblical truth is to be manifested. While there is governmental autonomy of the local church, there is no such governmental autonomy of the individual believer. Neither is there governmental autonomy of the individual missionary when it relates to his service. The missionary is always a sent one and remains under authority of the church or church-delegated agency. He is always only a representative of authority, never an authority in himself. The authority of Christ seems to be delegated and transferred to the local congregation of believers. No one lives unto himself nor is anyone a law or authority unto himself.

Thus, while the call of Christ comes directly to the individual and there is a sending forth by Christ Himself, a spiritual church will also sense the call either directly or indirectly. And, a humble and spiritually minded individual will gladly submit to the authoritive commissioning by the local assembly as the representative body of Christ and sustain a responsible relationship to the sending authority. Neither should a church hesitate to pray for missionaries and expect men and women to respond to the challenge (Mt 9:38). Nor is it unscriptural personally to contact and challenge young people with the need and ministry of missions (Ac 1:24-25; 6:2-3). This, however, deeply involves the local congregation in missions. The church, too, must be able to say, "Lo, we are with you."

The absolute need for identification of the local church with her missionaries is great, and it is most rewarding.

The Missionary Society as the Sending Agency

In seeking to establish the thesis that the church is the divinely ordained mediating sending authority, the analysis and conclusions have raised these questions: Have missions operated on an unscriptural basis by creating special missionary sending agencies? Have the missionary societies imposed upon the churches and robbed them of their scriptural prerogative? Have the missionary societies a scriptural right to exist? Can we justify their continued existence and ministry?

These questions deserve careful study. The answer, however, is not difficult to find. [While we must contend that the church is the mediating sending authority, the manner in which the local church exercises such authority depends upon circumstances and convictions. The church may do so directly or by delegation, establishing or relating herself to a special sending agency commonly known as a missionary society.] Many congregations exercise their prerogative through denominational agencies, others prefer an interdenominational sending organization, while some few congregations prefer to act directly as a sending agency. In our days of numerous complications and far-reaching involvements of missions, the latter method does not seem advisable or practicable.

The advantages of being a member of a respectable missionary society are so numerous and so evident that we strongly urge young people to associate themselves with a missionary sending agency. It must be stated, however, that to become dogmatic in this area and seek to establish exegetically the biblicism of a missionary society seems to be going beyond clear scriptural evidence. The Bible presents broad organizational principles but not defined organizational patterns. These broad principles certainly provide authority for the organization of missionary societies and justify their continued function.

THE PRINCIPLE OF ORGANIZATION FOR EFFICIENCY AND EFFECTIVENESS

The church had been moving on as a spontaneously expanding body without taking care of efficient organization. Due to this negligence, difficulties arose. Acts 6 is not so much concerned with the creation of a new office in the church as it is concerned with adequate organization for efficient function and effective service. The central lesson here is not the divine institution of the diaconate. Rather, the emphasis must be placed upon efficiency of organization for effective service.

The same truth is taught in 1 Corinthians 12:4-13, 28-31. The ministrations mentioned here are not necessarily exhaustive. Rather, they are illustrative and representative, indicating that God provides qualified men to operate His church effectively as time and circumstances demand it. The same truth is expressed in the metaphoric designations of the church as the body of Christ, the temple of God, the building of God, the household of God, and the priesthood of God. In each case there is order because definite laws and principles are at work and govern the interrelationships for smooth and efficient functioning. There are cooperation, coordination and subordination. There is structure. It should be mentioned that, while the true church is an organism, all organisms are organized. They do not function in a chaotic manner but embody principles of harmony, structure and symmetry as well as dynamics. Organization is not a substitute for organism, but neither is it necessarily the opposite of it. The principle of organization for efficiency and effectiveness in service is imbedded in the Bible and needs new emphasis in evangelical circles.

THE PRINCIPLES OF CORPORATE ACTION, OR THE ASSOCIATION OF CHURCHES FOR JOINT ACTION AND SERVICE

The principles of corporate action are well illustrated in Acts 15 and in the metaphors of the church as mentioned above. The independence of the local church is beautifully balanced by the interdependence of the churches and members as so well expressed by the metaphors of body, temple, building, priesthood and household. No local church is the complete body, temple, building, priesthood or household. Indeed, no one liveth to himself, not even the local church. There is strength in the proper mobilization and coordination of our interdependence which results in unity of purpose and action. This needs to be emphasized again and again. Individualism asserts itself not only in the individual but also in the absolutization of the independence and autonomy of the local church and the individual missionary organization.

For strength, order, efficiency and unity there must be organization, even within the priesthood of the believers.

THE PRINCIPLE OF DELEGATED AUTHORITY

The principle of delegation is well known in the Bible. Christ delegated His disciples, while His disciples delegated various ministries to others (cf. Mt 10:1; Mk 3:13-15; Ac 6:6). Paul, too, practiced delegation extensively, sending Titus, Timothy, Silvanus, Luke and other colaborers to churches and to cities on special assignments. The symbol of transfer, delegation and identification is the laying on of hands as indicated above.

The church thus finds herself within biblical tradition if she delegates the sending forth and the direction of missionaries to missionary societies with which she is in doctrinal agreement, united in purpose, and one in assignment. This delegation, however, does not relieve the church of the responsibility to care for the missionary. The missionary remains the representative of the church first and foremost, only secondarily that of the society. The church does not sign over the missionary to a society. She delegates the sending forth to a society to whom she is related. The missionary remains a rightful member of the church whom he represents.

THE PRINCIPLE OF SELECTIVE APPOINTMENT

In cases where the church as a corporate body fails to carry out the purpose and the mandate of God, He is not frustrated but raises up individuals who will respond to His mandate. This principle is well established in Scripture and in history. In fact, this is how most missionary sending agencies came into being. Few were born within their churches or denominations, for they are mainly the creation of individual men or small groups of men who had the vision and passion of Christ re-created in their hearts.

The fact remains that the historic missionary societies arose in this manner. When the Baptist ministerial association of Great Britain failed to launch out upon the challenge of William Carey, thirteen believing men formed a society and courageously launched the great pioneering Baptist Society. So also the London Missionary Society was formed, as well as the Church Missionary Society. Almost all of the continental societies were the result of one or several men who believed God and acted in obedience to His Word. Factors militated against the church and bound her to herself and her soil. Thus the principle of selective appointment became the order of the modern missionary movement and has proved to be a blessing when the corporate body failed God.

Here is the legitimate basis of the so-called faith missions. I have already mentioned the China Inland Mission and the Sudan Interior Mission. We could recount the story of other founders of missionary societies. No doubt many of them are the direct result of God's sovereign act of selective appointment to move ahead where the church and church-related bodies feared or failed.

The sovereignty of God's selective appointment is written indelibly into the history of missions as it is also found in the Bible. It is as evident as are His grace and faithfulness.

When the human race refused to submit to God and heeded not His word, He chose one man, Abraham, and began a new work through him on behalf of the world. When Israel — the people, the priesthood, and the kings — failed, God raised up prophets. There was no prophetic institution or order, yet God raised them up again and again, one by one. In all cases selective appointment was operative.

God raised up John the Baptist, who did not fit into an established order of his time. He was a lonely voice crying in the wilderness, but he was the voice of God.

God raised up the church when Israel refused to accept His mandate, and individuals within the church when the church failed to move in keeping with His Word and purpose.

No one will deny that God raised up Luther, or Calvin, or John Knox, or John Wesley, or George Whitefield, or Jonathan Edwards, or William Carey, or Hudson Taylor, or Rowland Bingham, and on and on. The sovereignty of God is not frustrated by failure of corporate action, nor is it necessarily impeded by approved but stagnant institutions. The principle of selective appointment is well anchored both biblically and historically.

Let the church hear and heed: the Lord who constituted the church to serve as a mediating sending authority is a sovereign Lord. As He had the authority to choose and authorize, He has the authority to withdraw and to set aside as He has warned He will do (Rev 3:14-22). It is futile to argue with a sovereign Lord as the Jews did, disputing the right of God to set His chosen nation aside and choose the church as His instrument (Ro 9 — 11). Let the church cease disputing with God concerning His right to use certain institutions and missionary agencies which seemingly do not fit into the humanly structured situation, and let the church repent over failure, spiritual bankruptcy, and theological apostasy. God may bring about drastic revolutions which no one of us can predict or foresee. Until then, however, He will use either His church or such representatives of the church who are united with Him in the supreme purpose of our age — the evangelization of the world and the gathering out of His church. If the "regular and ideal" channel fails, it does not mean that God is frustrated or that He cannot create new channels for His glory and for accomplishing His purpose. Not the church but the Lord is sovereign. This is clearly taught, illustrated and predicted in the Scriptures. Before Him we stand in humble submission, ready obedience, and joyous adoration. His plan will be carried out.

A word of caution must be sounded here. The principle of selective appointment is no license for anyone to sit in judgment over the church and to begin a new organization as he sees fit. We hardly know how to control our emotions and select our words in speaking about this matter, trembling that we might hurt the cause of Christ. Yet we must sound a note of alarm at the proliferation of organizations. Consider all the personnel that is being tied up in the home office administration, and the overhead expense the people of God are asked to pay. We can only commit this to the Lord and to the judgment of history, hoping that eventually sobriety will overcome all personal and historical obstacles and that integration, coordination and amalgamation will take place to facilitate, function and create greater efficiency.

CONCLUSION

The Bible provides us with broad and basic principles. It does not, however, spell out the detailed organizational patterns. This is a matter of Christian wisdom, culture, expediency, efficiency and possibility. There is no question in my mind that our times and culture demand mission organization and missionary societies. God will have ways and means to maintain and/or to raise up such agencies. He is a God of order, and He demands orderliness and efficiency in missions. This requires organization under the guidance of the Holy

Spirit in keeping with cultural patterns which today call for more and more specialization. God has set His seal of approval upon the mission societies thus far.

It must be recognized, however, that ideally the church and not the missionary sending agency, as such, is God's authority and creation for sending forth missionaries. It may well have been stated that the church's mission truly belongs to the church and not to isolated missionary societies. The mission agency ought to be the church's provision, instrument, and arm to efficiently expedite her task. It can neither displace nor replace the church, though it may be called upon to act in the place of the church.

To establish and maintain the proper relationship between the local congregation and the sending agency is of the utmost importance. Mutual respect, confidence, consistency and loyalty must characterize this relationship.

As we return to our subject, permit me to summarize it as follows: As long as there is a need for missionaries and such are available and as long as the churches and/or individual men will retain the missionary vision and passion, so long will there be need for missionary sending agencies. However, the missionary, the local congregation, and the missionary society belong organically together and must function in a harmonious cooperative manner to further the work of God, whether they are bound together organizationally or not. The relationship of these home and sending agencies to the receiving churches on the fields of the world forms another important section.

Missions-Church Relationships

Mission societies are institutions, or accidents of history, called into being by churches or individuals to serve an urgent, divine mission in this world. They have tremendous functional significance for the ongoing of world evangelism and church expansion. It must be stated, however, that they are not of biblical origin, for they are not divine institutions of the same order as churches. They gain historic and biblical significance from the mission they perform. Therefore, they are not of necessity permanent forms of Christian manifestation.

Above I have sought to establish the fact that missions is a limited task, yet an abiding task. It is my contention that as long as the church is alive and alert and as long as world evangelism will remain an ordered movement, there will be a place for mission organizations and societies.

Today the God-blessed movement finds itself at crossroads which seem to threaten the very existence of the mission societies. With the church becoming more universal in the sense of being present in every country, with the rise of nationalism arousing a deep sense of self-identity in the national churches, with the national churches gaining more experiences and maturity, with the concepts and philosophy of socialism penetrating every strata of society and determining our thinking, and with the Christian concept of brotherhood of mutuality and equality permeating our consciousness, two vital questions are raised:

First, have the time and usefulness of mission societies expired, at least in their traditional sense? I fully support the idea that the functional aspect of such societies needs thorough review, and that operational changes are necessary. Adjustments are needed, and times will bring them about. However, such functional transmutations do not eliminate the societies as such. It is my position that the time of the mission societies has not expired and that their usefulness is not exhausted.

Second, what is the relationship of the mission societies to the churches they have established among the various peoples and in the different countries and climes? While this is a natural question, it is not easily answered. Diligently historians have searched the pages of the history of the Christian church, the missiologists have studied the story of missions, and the exegetes have examined the pages of the Bible to find patterns to regulate the mission-church relationships. Thus far no universally satisfactory philosophy has been propounded, and no pattern has been designed.

In a situation near desperation it is frequently observed that the Bible does not prescribe specific patterns of relationship between mission and churches. It seems to be open to history, circumstances and human wisdom. Such statements, however, must be accepted with caution and must not be interpreted to mean that the Bible does not offer decisive and abiding *guiding principles* in this issue. It seems but reasonable to expect that the Lord of missions and the churches would not leave the people of God without guidance in such important matters and that Paul, the master builder of churches and missions would give some direction to the churches and his successors.

Our problem must be found elsewhere. Our predicament seems to rest in our limitations and historic developments rather than in the lack of revealed, guiding principles. Several blindfolds seem to obscure our ability of comprehension:

First, the church-mission relationship on the home base has become seriously blurred and is not biblically defined nor clearly understood. A serious dichotomy between church and mission societies has developed in a rather abnormal history of the church (see fig. 3).

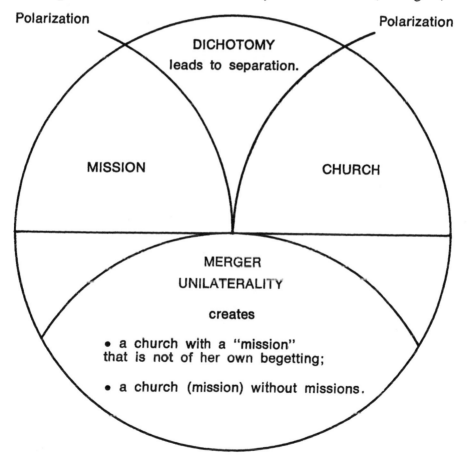

Fig. 3. Church-Mission Relationship

Therefore, we have today many missionless churches and many churchless mission societies.

Because of this nonrelationship between many churches and mission societies on the home base and an abnormal dichotomy in our situation, the relationship on the field is not fully understood and thus suffers in its deepest levels. The abnormality of the home base (perhaps the best we were able to create under given circumstances) carries itself over to the field of operation and reflects itself in abnormalities and tensions in the new situation.

Second, the depth and nature of the underlying issues of the mission-church relationship are not fully grasped and dealt with in concrete, realistic terms. Ideologies, sentiments, tradition, nationalism (in the mission and in the church), immaturity, inflexibility, organizational identity and/or organizational dominance are all involved in beclouding the issues of the dilemma. Not least is a peculiar concept of the indigenousness of the church which many a missionary carries with him and seeks to practice.

It is difficult to penetrate to the core and define the real issues of the mission-church tensions. It must also be recognized that the concerns differ with missions, churches, peoples and times. Thus denominational missions do not face the same problems as do the interdenominational missions. Neither are the problems in former colonial areas the same as they are in countries that have not gone through this experience. Tribal areas differ greatly from city churches. All of this must be taken into consideration.

Third, the great variations in mission and church organizations, the background, training, home church relationship and the theological church concepts of the missionaries, differing early practices in the fields by different missions and missionaries, and the nonrelationship mentality of numerous missionaries combine in creating difficulties in recognizing guiding principles laid down in the Scriptures. Together these blindfolds constitute formidable obstacles to permit the Holy Spirit to guide us into His perfect way. Only a divine breakthrough in missions and the churches can lead us through the maze which history, psychology and a warped missiology have cast upon us. In this situation let us look at Paul and learn some guiding principles from him.

Paul speaks of himself as a master builder (1 Co 3:10). We recognize Paul's *missionary principles* as revelation-related and therefore normative for all times; however, it is important to distinguish his principles from his *missionary practices* and *patterns*. The latter are not necessarily normative for all times and people. His practices and patterns are culture-related and therefore relative. Paul, who was creative, flexible and adaptable, was also people- and culture-related, as he explains in 1 Corinthians 9:19-23. Thus, there are both the constant and the adaptable in the operation of Paul. He never changed his message, goal, and principles in his mission ministries, but he did change his approaches, methods, practices and patterns. His basic concerns were the gospel and the people, and only secondarily, the forms, methods, patterns and structures.

Most certainly mission-church relationships are involved in missionary principles. Therefore we have a right to look to Paul and the Scriptures for guidance in this important and urgent matter.

PAULINE MISSIONARY-CHURCH RELATIONSHIP

Paul expresses his missionary-church relationship in the brief but meaningful phrase: "Your fellowship [*koinonia*] in the gospel from the first day until now" (Phil 1:5). A closely related passage is found in Romans 15:24 where Paul expresses the expectation that the church in Rome will set him forward with gifts and companions on his way to Spain. The key word for our studies is the word *koinonia*, a beautiful word and a concept rich in meaning. Thayer translates it as fellowship, association, community, communion, joint participation, intercourse. Vine gives partnership, partner, partaker, fellowship, communion, contribution. Benseler makes it to mean *Gemeinschaft*, *Anteil*, *Teilnahme*, *Verbindung*, *Vereinigung*, *Umgang*. William Barclay speaks of it as a sharing of friendship, practical sharing with those less fortunate, partnership in the work of Christ.

Paul uses the word *koinonia* four times in Philippians: fellowship in the gospel (1:5), fellowship in the Spirit (2:1), fellowship in His sufferings (3:10), fellowship of my affliction (4:14). In 4:15 a related word is used to express the fact of financial sharing in Paul's life and ministry.

The fullness of the concept of *koinonia* becomes evident if we consider its usage in the New Testament, especially in Paul's vocabulary. Therefore, Vincent speaks of our passage as "sympathetic participation." Wuest translates: "Your joint-participation [with me] in the furtherance of the good news." The Amplified New Testament reads: "Your sympathetic co-operation and contributions and partnership in advancing the good news."

However we may interpret the working methods and practices of Paul, his missionary-church relationship principle is clear: *It is a relationship of partnership* in the full sense of the word (see fig. 4). His relationship would not fit into the modern patterns of parallelism or of merger. Paul never thought of himself as "separate" from the churches he had founded. Spiritual, theological, cultural, ecclesiastical or organizational dichotomy would have seemed strange to him and totally unacceptable. He was too closely related to and too intimately bound up in the life of the churches. But Paul was not so completely merged with the churches and submerged in church ministries that his divine calling and commission as a missionary to the nations were imperiled. Beautifully Phillips translates Romans 15:23:

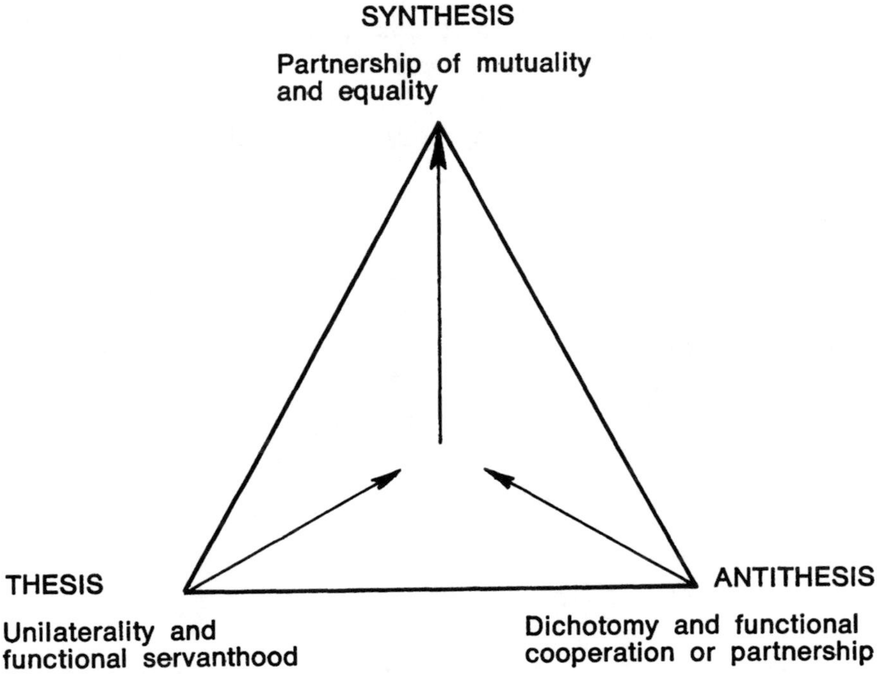

SYNTHESIS

Partnership of mutuality and equality

THESIS

Unilaterality and functional servanthood

ANTITHESIS

Dichotomy and functional cooperation or partnership

Fig. 4. Partnership

"But now since my work in these places no longer needs my presence." Paul felt his time had come to move on. The apostle avoided both extremes. Neither dichotomy (parallelism) nor merger would have fitted his pattern; he labored in *partnership* with the churches.

Paul's partnership relationship was one of full participation in the life of the churches and in their mobilization and enlistment in prayer, personnel and finances in evangelism. Paul discovered the resources for all his advances in evangelism and church expansion in the churches he planted. Thus the churches became involved with Paul from the very beginning in an aggressive program of evangelism and church multiplication. This is very evident from such reports of gospel outreach and gospel triumphs as Luke records in Acts 13:49; 19:10, 20, 26. Such reports could not have been written had Paul operated as a mission society apart from the churches. Neither could Paul ever have written that he had fully preach the gospel from Jerusalem to Illyricum (modern Yugoslavia) had he not fully mobilized the churches in partnership in evangelism (Ro 15:19). It is also evident that the churches remained in such partnership throughout the life of the apostle. It never became a question which ministries and projects belonged to the mission and which to the churches, for it was a total partnership ministry from the very beginning. No transfer ever became necessary.

PAULINE PRINCIPLES

Several guiding principles evolve out of our statement and from the epistle to the Philippians. Paul and the churches labored in partnership in the gospel of Jesus Christ. The churches were involved in the struggles and prayers of the apostle (Phil 1:5; 4:14; Ro 15:30-32; Eph 6:18-20; Col 4:2-4).

Free sharing of resources. Partnership included the free sharing of all resources for the proclamation of the gospel and the evangelization of the communities. Paul's finances all came from the mission fields (Phil 2:25; 4:15; Ro 15:24). The New English Bible translates the latter passage: "For I hope to see you as I travel through, and to be sent there [Spain] with your support after having enjoyed your company for a while." All of Paul's associates came from the churches he founded, and it can be assumed that they were sustained by the churches. Most probably they were all or mostly all Paul's own converts. The only exception may be Silas, the Silvanus of the epistles, who joined Paul in Jerusalem. However, Silas, too, was a Roman citizen, as Acts 16:37 indicates.

Natural partnership. Because it was introduced from the very beginning of the ministries, partnership was natural. Thus evangelism was caught by the churches as much as it was taught to them. Paul was not working for them but rather with them, and from the very beginning the churches were schools of practical evangelism (Phil 1:5).

Continual partnership. Partnership continued throughout the lifetime of the apostle. Paul remained related to the churches, and their care was upon him continuously. The epistle of Philippians is evidence of this fact. Paul wrote it from the prison in Rome (Phil 4:18; 2 Co 11:8).

No lording over one another. Partnership excluded the lording of one party over the other. Never did Paul demand or legislate the partnership of the churches, but he solicited and elicited their partnership in missions. Paul's attitude in partnership in missions must not be confused with his authoritative pronouncements in doctrine and his legislation in moral matters and discipline in moral and doctrinal matters. Such authority was his because of his divine calling to the apostleship. He did not exercise such authority in missionary partnership. Here he was a humble brother and energetic leader among fellow laborers, and a dynamic and exemplary force in the churches in evangelism and church expansion.

Relationship grew from fellowship. Partnership relationship in missions between Paul and the churches grew out of deeper levels of fellowship — fellowship in the Spirit, fellowship in His sufferings, fellowship in the apostle's afflictions. Paul's complete identification with the churches in love, life and ministries made fellowship possible on the deepest level and resulted in a natural partnership in missions. It would have seemed strange practice to Paul to find in a common field of labor a "fellowship of the mission" and a "fellowship of the national churches." Such dichotomy Paul could have never tolerated, no matter how well meant and how ideally defended. Fellowship and partnership grow out of the same root, and they feed from the same source: Christ Jesus our common Lord and our mutual fellowship with *him*.

No complete merger or subservience. Partnership in missions excluded the demand of the churches for complete merger of the missionaries with the churches and the subservience of one party to the other. The common goal of world evangelism forbade the capturing of the mission and missionaries by the churches. Outreach, not inreach, was the dominant note and thrust. Partnership meant the "let go" (Ac 13:3) of the workers as well as cooperation in the labors.

PAULINE PREMISES

Such a partnership relationship, however, rested upon specific premises, which are evident from the book of Acts and the Pauline epistles.

Churches recognized. Paul recognized the churches as duly constituted churches of Jesus Christ from the very beginning. He respected them as churches and expected them to function as the church of God in their specific communities. There came a time for the missionary (and the mission) to move on (Ro 15:15-24).

Spiritual gifts recognized. Paul recognized the spiritual gifts of the Holy Spirit and believed that the Holy Spirit would enable and qualify every constituted church to function adequately without the importation of special help from the outside. Temporary teaching and organizing help may be wise, and some follow-up ministry is required. However, Paul expected the churches to function under the lordship of Christ and the direction of the Holy Spirit as self-sufficient units.

Truly Christian and evangelizing churches. Paul was less concerned about establishing churches which were autonomous and indigenous, which were peripheral concepts, than he was about establishing truly Christian and evangelizing churches. He labored strenuously and incessantly for the latter. In this he was remarkably successful, as the seven churches around Ephesus (Rev 2 – 3) and the evangelizing efforts of the church in Thessalonica show.

Positive view. Paul's view of service and missionary partnership is wholly positive. Service in the New Testament is as much a divine means of Christian growth as it is the result of Christian maturity. Missions is not an optional enterprise; it is the life-flow of the church. The church exists by missions as fire exists by fuel. Missionary partnership must be built into the church from the very beginning, for without it no church will reach its full maturity. Service is not only for the perfect; it is a means for the perfecting of the saints.

Dependence. Paul depended upon the gospel of the universal love of God, the greatness of the work of Christ, and the abiding presence of the Holy Spirit to motivate and direct the churches in their gospel partnership.

Expectation. Paul expected that his own example would set the evangelizing pattern for the churches and lead them on in their evangelistic outreach and missionary partnership. Unhesitatingly he called upon the churches to follow him as he was following Christ (1 Co 11:1; 4:16; 1 Th 1:6).

APPLICATION FOR TODAY

In our days of tensions, gropings and searchings, we do well to look more closely and confidently to Paul as an example and to the Holy Spirit to show us some of His guiding principles of partnership in missions. We will not find it easy to enter into true partnership, for partnership eliminates the over-against, the side-by-side, the one over the other, and the one submerging in the other. Partnership in missions is a sacred and comprehensive concept of equals bound together in mutual confidence, unified purpose and united effort, accepting equal responsibilities, authority, praise and blame; sharing burdens, joys, sorrows, victories and defeats. It means joint planning, joint legislation, joint programming, and involves the sending and receiving churches on an equal basis. Only the closest bond in Christ, savored by a rich measure of humility, love, confidence and self-giving, will actualize partnership. Partnership of equality and mutuality in missions is as much an attitude, a spiritual, social and theological relationship, a philosophy of ministry, a way of life and missions, as it is a defined pattern of church-mission relationship for administration and legislation.

I am not blind to the fact that the transition from the Pauline world and mission to our time, situation and ministry is not easily made. The mission world and circumstances of Paul differed greatly from our mission world.

A situation like it prevailed in the Greco-Roman world with a dominant Hellenism, cross-cultural fertilization, economic prosperity, relative safety, philosophical bankruptcy, cross-racial movements, religious ferment — to mention only a few factors — but such a situation has never been duplicated in history. The combined factors constituted unique circumstances for the flow and reception of the gospel of Jesus Christ. Only a few of the mentioned factors are making themselves felt in our modern days.

Paul was a citizen of the world in which he labored and not a guest in a foreign country as most of today's missionaries are, enjoying the hospitality of a government under specific conditions. The apostle was born in a mission field, so he had no cultural barriers to overcome and no language to learn. He was a part of the world in which he labored. Neither did he have cultural and economic advantages to offer to an underprivileged people.

The Scriptures had been translated into a language understood by large sections of the population. Monotheism was widespread and much respected, and Old Testament ethical principles had been widely advocated by Jewish writers and the synagogues. Most of Paul's churches were founded in cities where Jews, proselytes and God-fearers constituted a goodly portion of the people. Seldom did Paul come to communities where he did not have some previous contacts. He was therefore able to find accommodation and begin his ministry with some friends or acquaintances.

It is evident that Paul had tremendous advantages from many points of view. From a practical point of comparison, Paul operated in a home mission field. It is therefore difficult to carry over Paul's methods, practices and patterns in totality and without qualifications into our situation and into our times. We must make allowance for many variables. The beautiful idea "to do as Paul did it" may betray more naiveté than wisdom, more idealism than realism. We must remain sober and balanced.

The fact remains, however, that the principle of partnership is not affected by these variables, for this principle does not rest in culture, times or circumstances. Partnership is a relationship which has its roots in our identification with the churches on the deepest levels and in our fellowship in the Spirit, in His suffering and in our mutual burdens, interests, purposes and goals. Partnership is not circumstantial; it is a matter of life, health and relationship. It belongs to the nature of Christianity. It is not optional; it is bound up in Christian fellowship and progress.

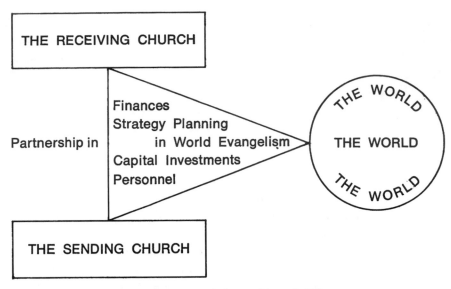

Fig. 5*a*.　Partnership — United Effort

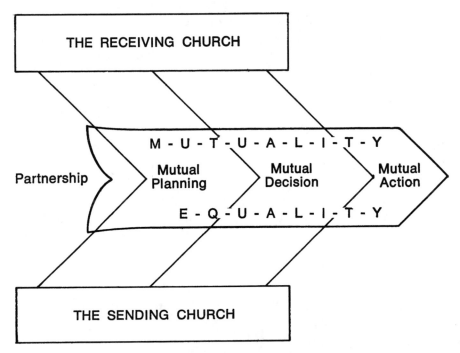

Fig. 5*b*.　Partnership — Joint Programming

Source: Adapted from *Japan Christian Quarterly*, Winter 1971.

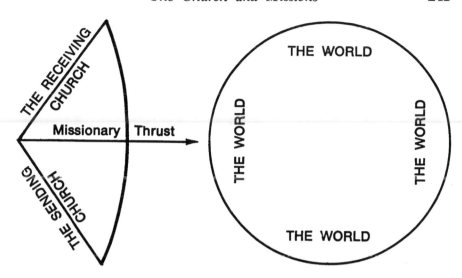

SOURCE: Adapted from *Japan Christian Quarterly*, Winter 1971.

Fig. 5c.   Partnership — Equality and Mutuality

The working out of the principle of partnership may take on variant patterns. However, while the patterns are the phenomena of which partnership is the *pneumena* — and the two must not be confused — it is very evident that the patterns will be determined by the principle of partnership. The patterns cannot conflict with the principle because there must be formal and functional harmony and symmetry between the outer and the inner, the body and the spirit. Somehow the patterns must portray partnership.

The principle of partnership is comprehensive and becomes determining in programming, planning, financing and personnel appointment and assignments as these factors relate to the mission outreach and as they involve the mission and churches in the task of evangelism and other mutually agreed upon projects and endeavors. In all things it behooves us to keep the unity of the Spirit in the bond of peace and demonstrate our mutuality and equality in Christ and in His cause before the world.

Part III

BIBLICAL
INSTRUMENTS AND DYNAMICS
OF
MISSIONS

7

The Instruments of Missions

APOSTLESHIP AND THE MODERN MISSIONARY

CONCERNING THE SPIRITUAL CARE and advancement of the church of Jesus Christ, Paul mentions five ministries in Ephesians 4:11 — apostles, prophets, evangelists, pastors, and teachers. In a similar list elsewhere he enumerates seven gifts bestowed upon the church for its ministration (1 Co 12:28-30; Ro 12:3-8). In 1 Corinthians 12:8-11, nine gifts are mentioned. In other epistles he speaks frequently of bishops and presbyters and also mentions deacons. Thus there is diversity as well as sufficiency in the gifts.

A comparison of the various passages in Acts and the epistles indicates that Paul and the other apostles speak on the one hand of the church in universal terms, the church as the body and bride of Jesus Christ, the temple and household of God, and on the other hand as the local assembly of believers, the church in a geographical localized sense. This must be kept in mind in the study of the ministries.

THREE SIGNIFICANT PRINCIPLES

According to the New Testament, three principles seem to govern the ministry in the church of Jesus Christ:

1. The New Testament assigns certain ministries to the local church and certain to the church universal. In keeping with this principle, it is within the framework of the Scriptures (Eph 4:11 ff.) to think of apostles, prophets and evangelists, pastors and teachers as belonging to the whole body of Christ, and bishops and presbyters as ministering to the local congregation. A teacher may be considered as belonging to either realm, as is evident from the word's usage in several passages (cf. Ac 13:1; 1 Co 12:28-29; 1 Ti 2:7; 2 Ti 1:11;

4:3; Heb 5:12; Ja 3:1). Later history justifies the assumption that the concept of teacher does describe a person with a universal ministry as well as a local ministry.

2. Paul ascribes the distribution of the gifts to the sovereignty of the Holy Spirit, grounded in His wisdom and loving care for the church (cf. 1 Co 12:11; Eph 4:11). The Holy Spirit knows the needs of the church and graciously supplies those needs.

3. Paul does not speak in final terms when he lists the various gifts bestowed upon the church, and neither does he present an exhaustive enumeration. His recounting is representative rather than conclusive and final, which is evident from a comparative study of the various passages in his epistles (1 Co 12:8-11, 28-30; Eph 4:11). The principal emphasis is upon the fact that the Holy Spirit meets the complete need of the church at any time or place. He remains the sufficiency of the church. In this the church finds certainty in an ever changing world with ever increasing demands in ever growing opposition and complexity.

PRELIMINARY DELINEATION

As we turn to the subject of the missionary, we omit from our study the ministry in the local church, which narrows our investigation considerably. Five major concepts need to be dealt with: apostle, prophet, evangelist, pastors, teachers — concepts which imply universal rather than local ministries.

It is a common practice among expositors to separate these concepts into two groups, listing first, apostles and prophets; and second, evangelists, pastors and teachers. In most instances they write off the former as falling into New Testament times and having come to a close at the end of the apostolic period, while the evangelists, pastors and teachers have persisted in history.

Such summary dismissal of the former and the unqualified adoption of the latter are superficial and not warranted by the Scriptures or by history. It is more accurate to combine these concepts in a different manner and again think of them as two and two, changing the groupings into (1) apostles and evangelist, and (2) prophets and pastor-teacher. The second concept in each case becomes the successor of the first and perpetuates not the authoritative office of the former but his gift and function.

A careful study leads to the conclusion that a New Testament evangelist is an apostle, fully responsible for the apostolic function minus the apostolic office and original authority. Thus the evangelist continues the function of being the *sent one* for the same purpose the apostles were sent — to preach the gospel, preach the Word, evangelize communities and establish churches — but he does not possess the original apostolic office, authority and rank. The latter, the authority, is objectively vested in the writings of the apostles and subjectively in the local congregation, not their personal followers, the evangelists.

Again, the prophet and pastor-teacher seem to merge, with the pastor-teacher becoming the functional successor to the prophet minus the special gift for being "preachers and expounders under the immediate influences of the Spirit."[1] In this the prophet is distinguished from the pastor-teacher. Westcott speaks of the prophet as "an inspired teacher."[2]

The distinction between original authority and immediate spiritual ministries of apostles and prophets and the lack of such by their successors is most essential. No servant of God since the apostles can claim for himself their original authority. In this matter their teaching, not their example, becomes our guide. We must keep in mind that the apostles had no New Testament to guide and control them. New Testament doctrine and principles came to them directly by the Spirit of God. They did not have the written Word as we have it, except for the Old Testament. Thus they combined in one person the inspirational and original authority as well as evangelistic, pastoral and teaching ministry. The former is today embodied in the New Testament, and only the latter is being inherited by men following in the train of the apostles and prophets.

It is therefore not correct for a missionary to exercise authority over the churches which he establishes in the same manner as Paul did. Neither does he have the same superintending authority Paul exercised. Our authority rests in the Word and not in an office, a fact which we too often forget in our mission and church administration, especially on the mission fields. Too readily we appeal to the example of Paul, forgetting that he was an apostle performing apostolic functions in apostolic authority bestowed upon him. We are evangelists — missionaries — performing apostolic functions without original apostolic authority. The only right and recourse we have is to appeal to apostolic authority as recorded in the New Testament. It behooves us therefore to be careful and very humble.

Thus the authoritative and original offices of the apostles and prophets were discontinued with the first-generation Christians. The apostolic and prophetic gifts, functions and ministries, however, continue in the evangelists and pastor-teachers serving the church universal. This thesis we shall seek to establish.

A PRELIMINARY DEFINITION OF "A MISSIONARY"

To the question, "Who really is a missionary?" we receive various definitions. In these days of generalizations, almost everything is missions and almost everyone is a missionary. The idea that every Christian has a missionary obligation must not be minimized, for it expresses an important biblical fact and is in perfect harmony with the basic biblical doctrine of the priesthood of all believers and the essential missionary nature of the church.

Most certainly, every believer has a vital spiritual ministry to fulfill. This must be said again and again. For clarity's sake, however, we need to distinguish between the technical, biblical missionary function and the general missionary involvement of all believers which springs out of the missionary nature of the church.

A careful study of three Greek words must be made here: *martureo* — to witness, to testify, give evidence of, or present proof; *euaggelizo* — to announce good news or bring good tidings; *kerusso* — to preach, proclaim, herald. These greatly help us to set off the specific from the general, noting that the first and second Greek words are general terms applicable to *all* believers, while the latter is a more technical term applicable to specifically designated individuals.

The Bible does not offer a formal definition of missions or the missionary. But according to the Scriptures (study carefully the Great Commission: Mt 28:18-20; Mk 16:14-20; Lk 24:44-48; Jn 20:19-23; Ac 1:8; 26:13-20), a missionary is a messenger with a message from God, sent forth by divine authority for the definite purpose of evangelism, church-founding and church edification.

In the technical and traditional sense of the word, a missionary is a Christian messenger of the gospel of Jesus Christ, sent forth by the authority of the Lord and the church to cross national borders and/or cultural and religious lines in order to occupy new frontiers for Christ, to preach the gospel of redemption in Christ Jesus unto the salvation of people, to make disciples and to establish functioning and evangelizing Christian churches according to the command of Christ and the example of the apostles.

There are at least three essential qualities of a missionary: He is a believer sent forth, a messenger, a herald of the Lord, and he has a definite assignment to fulfill — the preaching of the gospel and the planting of churches; he is to collaborate with these churches to fulfill the divine purpose in that community and in the world.

Thus not everyone is a "missionary" in the technical and biblical sense of the word. While all Christians are *witnesses* to Christ and gospelers of the good news, not all Christians are "missionaries," just as not all Christians are preachers of the gospel or pastor-teachers of the churches.

With this basic idea in mind, let us return to our study and establish the biblicism of the missionary office, gift and function. We are considering it from four points of view: the missionary as one sent forth, the New Testament apostleship, the New Testament office of evangelism, and the New Testament office of teaching.

THE MISSIONARY IS ONE SENT FORTH

The word *missionary* is not found in our English Bible. It comes to us from the Latin word *mitto* — "I send" — and thus is closely related to the New Testament *apostello* — "to send." Any reader of the Bible quickly realizes that the words "sent" and "send" occupy a prominent place, especially in the gospels. The Greek words *apostello* and *pempo*, both meaning "to send," occur in the New Testament 215 times — *apostello*, 135 times, and *pempo*, 80 times. The vast majority of them appear in the gospels and in the Acts of the apostles — *apostello*, 123 times, and *pempo*, 50 times.

Both Greek words are used of Christ as well as of the apostles. There is, however, some difference in emphasis and depth. While *pempo* emphasizes more the act of sending and expresses the relation of the sender to the sent, *apostello* also involves the idea of authoritative sending with a mission. The latter includes a definite purpose in the sending. Vincent says about *apostello*: "The verb carries the sense of sending an envoy with a special commission. Hence it is

used of the mission of the Son of God, and of His apostles; the word
apostle being directly derived from it. It is thus distinguished from
pempo, 'to send,' which denotes simply the relation of the sender to
the sent."

Dr. Vincent writes:

> The contrast between the verbs (*apostello, pempo*) is obviously
> significant. Both verbs are used of the mission of the Son, and of
> the mission of believers, but with distinct meanings. The former
> (*apostello*) corresponds with the idea of our own words "dispatch"
> and "envoy" and conveys the accessory notions of a special com-
> mission and so far of delegated authority in the person sent. The
> simple verb *pempo* marks nothing more than the immediate relation
> of the sender to the sent.[3]

It is significant to note that *pempo* is never used in relation to
God in the synoptics nor by Paul. *Apostello* is not used in relation to
the sending of the Holy Spirit. Even in John the two words are not
absolute synonyms. A fine distinction prevails throughout the Scriptures.

The common factor in both words is the fact that they point to
an authority beyond the sent one. There is an authority, a Sender
beyond the messenger. The messenger himself is not an authority;
he merely represents an authority.

On the other hand, it is readily seen that the word *apostle* finds
its roots in *apostello* and thus means a person authoritatively sent
forth with a message and on a mission.

CHRIST, THE SENT ONE

Turning back to the record of Scripture, we discover that Christ
spoke of Himself at numerous occasions as the sent one. He walked,
worked and suffered in the deep consciousness of having been sent
into the world (cf. especially John's gospel, chaps. 6 – 8). He was,
indeed, an apostle, one sent forth (cf. Heb 3:1).

His own words reveal clearly that He walked in blessed fellowship with the Father who had sent Him, that the Father's authority
was resting upon Him, and that the Father was sharing in His ministry. There was authorization as well as companionship in the experience of having been sent. This illumined His path and lightened
the burdens of the way. In submission to and in fellowship with the

Father who had sent Him, He withstood all opposition, pressures and criticism. He endured suffering, shame and death, triumphing in it all.

THE DISCIPLES, THE SENT ONES

As we turn to the disciples we discover similar experiences. They, too, were sent ones — messengers, ambassadors, apostles. On several occasions Christ sent them forth into ministries. In fact, He chose them that they might be called apostles, or "sent ones" (Lk 6:13).

Though the discipleship aspect is more prevalent in the gospels, the consciousness of apostleship is not lacking. Nine times they are called apostles in the gospels. In the Acts of the apostles, discipleship gives way to apostleship. Thus, they too walked and worked in the full consciousness of having been sent into the world for a specific purpose and with a definite message.

In the sending forth of the disciples there is, however, one absolute distinction from the sending of our Lord. They are never said to have been sent by the Father. To the contrary, twice it is explicitly stated that they are being sent by Christ (Jn 17:18; 20:21). Previous to this, Christ had sent them out in His own name (cf. Mt 10:1 ff.; Mk 3:13-19; 6:6-13; Lk 9:1-6; 10:1-20). Thus while Christ is the Apostle of the Father, the disciples became apostles of Jesus Christ. Paul designates himself repeatedly as "Paul an apostle of Jesus Christ," and Peter does likewise. Christ became their sending authority and their authorization. He also shared in their ministry. He was their authority and their Companion.

The apostles were fully conscious of their source of authority. When Peter was asked by the rulers, "By what authority [or by what name] have ye done this?" he was quick to inform them that there is only one name (cf. Ac 4:5-12). Christ's companionship is explicitly stated in His blessed promise in Matthew 28:20 when He says, "Lo, I am with you alway, even unto the end [or consummation] of the age" (ASV marg.). The same truth is reiterated in Mark 16:20, where we read, "And they [the apostles] went forth, and preached every where, *the Lord working with them*, and confirming the word with signs following." This is also beautifully reflected in the words of Christ in John 20:21.

Bishop Westcott, having made a rather detailed and comprehensive study of various words and tenses in the gospel of John, makes the following remarks: "The general results of an examination of these facts seems to be that in this charge the Lord presents His own mission as the one abiding Mission of the Father; this He fulfills through His Church. His disciples receive no new commission, but carry out His (cf. Math. 28:20; Heb. 3:1)."[4]

Thus the sending Agent becomes the closest Companion in the ministry. The apostles were not asked to do mission work *for* Christ but rather *with* Christ. This is, indeed, true partnership in missions. Paul could speak with inner satisfaction as being a colaborer with God. There is an identification of Christ with His sent ones that sweetens all bitterness and drives away the shadows through His blessed smile. His presence and companionship are their constant experience and abiding heritage. Their great need is to practice constantly the consciousness of His presence.

THE MISSIONARY, A SENT ONE

The missionary today is a "sent one" if he is a missionary in the biblical sense of the word. A missionary is not one who has *gone* out, but one who has been *sent* out. It is the sending that makes all the difference. And unless he can walk in the blessed assurance that he has been sent forth, he will be unable to bear the strain and frustrations, the pressures and the disappointments of missionary life. However, the consciousness of having been sent forth will uphold him in his trials and failures and will most certainly lead him to triumph and success. The crucial question, therefore, is: Who sends the modern missionary? Who is his sending authority? It is evident that the missionary today does not experience the sending forth as the apostles did, for Christ is not present in the same manner today as He was when He walked the paths of Palestine. Is there a further delegation of the sending authority? This is a serious question which deserves our careful and prayerful attention.

Our times are beset by two extremes: on the one hand is the independence of the individual, growing out of Western individualism rather than out of the individual priesthood of the believer with its resultant independence; on the other hand is the hierarchical system with its tight centralized organization in which the individual has little or no freedom of movement. Under these circumstances we need to assure ourselves of scriptural foundations and directives.

Certain facts in the New Testament may keep us from either extreme and give us the needed directives in this vital matter. These facts relate to the apostleship of the New Testament on the one hand and the significance of the church on the other hand.

New Testament Apostleship

We have stated above that the word *missionary* comes to us through the Latin and from the Greek word for sending — *apostello* ("to send"). The words *apostello* and *apostolos* ("apostle") have a common root. There is a certain relationship etymologically between the biblical concept of an apostle and a modern missionary. This relationship we must discover and define, if possible.

APPLIED TO CHRIST

The word *apostle* is applied to our Lord by the writer of Hebrews, where Christ is spoken of as "The Apostle and High Priest of our confession" (3:1, marg.). This statement, which is unique in the New Testament, declares that Christ was sent forth into the world as an Envoy or Paraclete of God. In word and deed He did set forth the general framework of the Christian confession; therefore He is the chief cornerstone in revelation and work. In Him the Old Testament finds its fulfillment and its unveiling. In Him also the New Testament finds its criteria, content and unfolding. He is the Apostle *par excellence*.

USED FOR HIS DISCIPLES

The word *apostle* is used repeatedly as the common designation of the followers of Christ known to us as His disciples. They are called on numerous occasions "the apostles," without reference to position, mission or function. Such is its main usage in the gospels and the Acts (cf. Ac 1:2; 2:37, 42-43; 4:33, 35-37; 5:2, 12, 18, 29, 40).

USED IN OFFICIAL SENSE

It is used in an official sense to indicate the office, position, delegation and authority of the twelve, of Paul, and perhaps of James, the brother of the Lord (Gal 1:19; cf. Ro 1:1; 1 Co 1:1; 2 Co 1:1; Gal 1:1; Eph 1:1; Col 1:1; 1 Ti 1:1; 2 Ti 1:1; Titus 1:1; 1 Pe 1:

1; 2 Pe 1:1; 1 Co 12:28; Eph 2:20; 3:5; 4:11). The apostles are dis-
dinguished from the elders and the brethren. Several references indicate this usage (Ac 15:2, 4, 6, 23). Here apostleship is based upon
personal discipleship in the narrowest sense concerning men chosen
and personally instructed by the Lord, Paul receiving his instruction
by special revelation. This is the *apostolic office* in a restricted sense
which came to an end with the death of the apostles of Jesus Christ.

The apostolic office is unique in calling, comprehensiveness
and authority and is bestowed by the Lord upon His peculiar and
original band of men. This thesis is supported in several ways in the
New Testament.

First, the original twelve and Paul alone are known in the New
Testament as "apostles of Jesus Christ." Only this original band holds
this official title. They were called in a very personal manner by the
Lord to be apostles. They were uniquely authorized for their ministry, and they were authenticated by "signs of the apostles" in a
peculiar manner (Mt 10:1-2; 2 Co 12:12). The remainder are
"apostles," delegated or sent ones of the churches, or they are
associates of the apostles (2 Co 8:23; Phil 2:25; 1 Co 4:6, 9).

Second, the original twelve and Paul are constituted "witnesses"
in a peculiar sense. There are a ministry and an apostleship which
are restricted in their application. This is evident from the words
of Peter in Acts 1:17, 20*b*, 22, 25-26. From verse 21 we may gather
that Matthias was well acquainted with the life and ministry of
Jesus Christ. In a certain sense he was an ear- and eye-witness of
Christ. Yet, according to verse 22, he is to be chosen *to become* a
witness of the resurrection of Christ together with the eleven (vv.
22, 26). It is this official functioning as a witness which is spoken
of as "this ministry and apostleship" (vv. 25-26). It is also in the
light of this fact that the emphasis of Peter in being witnesses must
be interpreted (Ac 2:32; 3:15; 5:32; 10:39).

Similarly Paul emphasizes his apostleship as a unique ministry
and position (Ro 1:5; 1 Co 9:1-2; 2 Co 12:12; Gal 2:8). His call to
be a witness is clear (Ac 22:15; 26:16).

In a very special manner the twelve and Paul were the unique
witnesses of Jesus Christ, especially as it relates to His resurrection.
Well does Dr. H. N. Ridderbos express the significance and uniqueness
of this ministry:

All that "Jesus began to do and teach" (Acts 1:1) is continued and confirmed by the witness of the apostles. Thus they receive their own special place in the history of salvation. Not only the great deeds of God in Christ Jesus themselves, but also their *proclamation* by God's appointed witnesses, belong to the execution of God's plan of salvation. Therefore the written record of the words and deeds of the apostles as set down in the Acts of the Apostles is not merely meant as biography of the apostles or a sketch of the history of the early Church — the Acts is far too fragmentary and incomplete for such a purpose — but as evidence of the certainty of the Christian faith (Luke 1:4) and of the foundation of the Church in the whole world. The "uniqueness" (*Einmaligkeit*) of the apostolate is thereby of special significance. The number of the apostles is limited because the apostolate is inseparably linked with being an ear- and eyewitness and because the certainty and foundation of the faith lie in their ministry. Therefore the apostolate is *genus suum*, and apostolic succession in the personal sense of the term is in conflict with the peculiar place of the apostles in the history of salvation, and a contradiction in terms. The apostolic witness is much rather the canon of the New Testament Church, the delimited standard of Christian preaching and Christian life.[5]

It must be kept in mind that the apostolic office has not been delegated to successors. To make such claims is completely unfounded scripturally. There is not the slightest hint that Paul transferred his apostleship to Timothy and confirmed him in it. Neither does Peter refer to such action. Specifically Paul charges Timothy to "do *the work of an evangelist.*" He does not communicate the apostleship to him (2 Ti 4:5).

The apostles of Jesus Christ did not deposit their authority and witness in an office to be perpetuated, but in a *scriptura* which is to become the objective guide and authority of the church of Jesus Christ. This *scriptura* constitutes our New Testament, our apostolic witness, and our authority in doctrine and practice.

There is a theory which would like to raise the modern missionary movement into a certain type of "apostolate," a successor to the apostolic band, and make its ministry independent of church association, direction and control. This may be a noble aspiration, at times much desirable, and under certain circumstances it may even become necessary. It must be stated emphatically, however, that such a *theory* is extrabiblical. It roots more in an independent mentality of missions and missionaries who do not see fully the biblical place and perspective of the local congregation or who have lost confidence in the church. It is also noteworthy that this theory is verbalized more at a time when the pressures from many national churches are upon missions and missionaries to identify more fully or even merge with the national church and submit to the direction of this body.

USED IN WIDER SENSE

There is, however, a wider usage of the word in the New Testament. It is applied to Barnabas in Acts 14:4, 14; to Epaphroditus in Philippians 2:25; to some unnamed brethren in 2 Corinthians 8:23. By implication it was applied to Silvanus and Timothy in the epistles to the Thessalonians (note the greetings in 1 Th 1:1 followed by the plural pronouns "we," "our" and the consequent plural "apostles" in 1 Th 2:6). Paul seems to include Apollos along with himself as being among apostles who are made a spectacle to the world (1 Co 4:6, 9).

It is evident that there were false brethren who claimed the title of apostle for themselves who were not of the twelve or among the associates of Paul (cf. 2 Co 11:13; Rev 2:2). "Had the number [of apostles] been definitely restricted, the claims of these interlopers would have been self-condemned"[6]

After a careful examination of the biblical data, James Hastings in his *Dictionary of the Apostolic Church* comes to the following conclusion:

> The cumulative effect of the facts and probabilities stated above is very strong — so strong that we are justified in affirming that in the New Testament there are persons other than the Twelve and St. Paul who were called apostles, and in conjecturing that they were rather numerous. All who seemed to be called by Christ or the Spirit to do missionary work would be thought worthy to the title, especially such as had been in personal contact with the Master."[7]

J. C. Lambert writes: "The very fact that the name 'Apostle' means what it does would point to the impossibility of confining it within the limits of the twelve."[8]

The above conclusions are substantiated by the usage of the word *apostle* for itinerant ministers in the subapostolic age. In this wider application it is known to Irenaeus, Tertullian and Origen who apply the designation also to the seventy whom Christ sent out.

The *Epistle of Barnabas* (v. 9) speaks of the Lord's choice of His own apostles and therefore seems to know of some other apostles (perhaps Jewish apostles). Four passages in *Hermas* make it perfectly clear that the author had a wide circle of messengers in mind in using the designation of apostle (cf. Vis. 3; 6; Sim. 9; 15; 4. 12, 5; 25. 2). Similarly, the *Didache* knows a wide circle of apostles (11. 3).

Harnack notes that "during the second century it became more rare than ever to confer the title of 'apostle' on any except the biblical apostles or persons mentioned as apostles in the Bible. But Clement of Rome is called an apostle by Clement of Alexandria (Strom. IV. XVII 105) and Quadratus is once called by this name."[9]

The New Testament and apostolic history both distinguish between the authoritative *apostolic office* — in a restricted sense — bestowed upon the twelve and Paul by the Lord Himself, and the *apostolic function* which relates to the unique ministry of brethren designated and delegated by the apostles and/or by local churches for ministries outside of the established churches. As noted above, none of these later apostles is designated as an "Apostle of Jesus Christ." That title, which is carefully reserved for the twelve and for Paul, is an official designation. The other apostles are related to the churches. Epaphroditus is mentioned as "your apostle" (messenger), that is, the messenger of the church at Philippi, while Barnabas was "sent forth" by the church at Antioch (cf. Ac 13:1-3).

We must also bear in mind that the concept of apostleship, though not appearing in the Bible before the gospel records, was nevertheless a historically established ministry of Judaism which also had its "apostles." This is well established in extrabiblical literature, as proven by Harnack in his studies.[10] The functions of these "apostles" have been outlined as follows:

1. They were consecrated persons of a very high rank.
2. They were sent out into the Diaspora (dispersion) to collect tribute for headquarters.
3. They brought encyclical letters with them, kept the Diaspora in touch with the center and informed of the intentions of the latter (or of the patriarch), received orders about any dangerous movement, and had to organize resistance to it.

4. They exercised certain powers of surveillance and discipline in the Diaspora.
5. They formed a sort of council as they returned to their own country which aided the patriarch (of Judaism) in supervising the interests of the law.[11]

There is thus *an apostolic function* which was inherent in the apostolic office and which is continuing in the church of Jesus Christ. It is the function of *evangelism* and *the pastor-teacher ministry*. Paul not only demonstrates that his apostleship makes him supremely an evangelist. He explicitly states it. He tells us, "Christ sent me not to baptize but to evangelize" (1 Co 1:17, free trans.). In the same letter he writes, "If I evangelize, I have nothing to boast of, for necessity is laid upon me; for woe is me if I evangelize not" (1 Co 9:16, free trans.). These statements are in perfect harmony with the commission of the Lord to Paul: "But rise, and stand upon thy feet: for I have appeared unto thee for this purpose, to make thee a minister and a witness both of these things which thou hast seen, and of those things in the which I will appear unto thee; delivering thee from the people, and from the Gentiles [nations], unto whom now I send thee, to open their eyes, and to turn them from darkness to light, and from the power of Satan unto God, that they may receive forgiveness of sins, and inheritance among them which are sanctified by faith that is in me" (Ac 26:16-18). Evangelism is not only central in the apostleship; it is essential to this New Testament office and constitutes a crucial aspect of the function of apostleship. He also emphasizes his pastor-teacher ministry.

We therefore turn to a study of the interrelationship of the ministry of the apostles and the evangelist and pastor-teacher. The latter two functions, we believe, constitute the missionary function of the church of Jesus Christ and are expressing themselves in the modern missionary movement throughout the world.

New Testament Office of Evangelist

The gospel is the heart of the New Testament, and the gospel-bearers are of central significance. Thus the New Testament makes much of "gospeling" (evangelizing). Fifty-five references bear upon this important ministry, and it is binding upon all believers just as witnessing is.

In addition to this generalized ministry of gospeling and evangelizing is the work of the evangelist, who is the bearer of the evangel or the gospel in a specialized manner. This is his special vocation and his absorbing ministry. To bring out this neglected truth, Conybeare and Howson make the following comment on 2 Timothy 4:5: "The term Evangelist is applied to those missionaries who, like Philip and Timothy, travelled from place to place, to bear the glad-tidings of Christ to unbelieving nations or individuals. Hence it follows that the Apostles were all evangelists, although there were also evangelists who were not apostles." Thus Conybeare translates 1 Corinthians 9:18 and makes Paul say, "It is to make the glad-tidings free of cost where I carry it, that I may forego my right as an evangelist." And in a note on that translation he comments, "The passage may be literally rendered: 'it is, that I should, while evangelizing make the evangel free of cost, that I may not fully use my right in the evangelist.' "[12]

Vincent comments briefly on Ephesians 4:11 and speaks of evangelists as "traveling missionaries."[13] In 2 Timothy 4:5 he describes one as "a traveling minister, whose work was not confined to a particular church . . . a helper of the apostles."[14]

Bishop Westcott writes: "The work of the evangelist was probably that of a missionary to the unbelieving."[15] Plummer, writing in the *Dictionary of the Apostolic Church,* draws our attention to the fact that "evangelist" comes from the verb "to evangelize" and remarks: "There is at any rate some evidence that those who acted as missionaries to the heathen were called evangelists. . . . Philip was called 'the evangelist' because of his good work in preaching to the heathen."[16] *The Bishops Commentary* identifies the evangelist with the modern missionary.

Vine writes: "Evangelist, literally a messenger of good, denotes a preacher of the gospel. Acts 21:8 and Ephesians 4:11 make clear the distinctive functions in the churches. . . . Missionaries are evangelists, as being essentially preachers of the Gospel."[17]

Fausset comments on evangelists as follows: "The Evangelist founded the church; the teacher built it up in the faith. . . . They [evangelists] traveled almost freely where their services were needed, either to propagate the Gospel or to inspect and strengthen congregations already formed."[18]

This is in keeping with Theodoret who describes the evangelists as traveling missionaries. Augustine, though applying the word mainly to the writers of the gospels, is not unaware of its wider usage. Writing at the time of Trajan, Eusebius says:

> They preached the gospel more and more widely and scattered the saving seed of the Kingdom of Heaven broadly throughout the whole world. For, indeed, most of the disciples of that time, animated by the divine word with a more ardent love for philosophy, had already fulfilled the command of the Savior, and had distributed their goods to the needy. Then starting out upon long journeys they performed the office of evangelists, being filled with the desire to preach Christ to those who had not yet heard the word of faith, and to deliver to them the divine Gospels. And when they had only laid the foundations of the faith in foreign places, they appointed others as pastors, and entrusted them with the nurture of those that had recently been brought in, while they themselves went on again to other countries and nations, with the grace and the cooperation of God.[19]

Later history has changed the meaning and usage of the word and made something extrabiblical out of it.

The word *evangelist* occurs only three times in the New Testament (Ac 21:8; Eph 4:11; 2 Ti 4:5). This should not belittle its significance. The title *bishop* or *overseer* is found in only three passages, while *deacon* is mentioned only twice and *pastor* only once. In two of the three references, *evangelist* refers to persons of traveling and pioneer ministries rather than to those serving a local and established congregation. In the third passage it indicates a specific function within the total framework of the church.

The word *evangelist* must not be interpreted in too narrow a sense as conditioned by its present-day usage. Its biblical significance is much wider, and its usage in the first centuries is much fuller.

Kittel in his *Theologisches Woerterbuch Zum Neuen Testament (Theological Dictionary of the New Testament)*, after considerable studies, comes to the conclusion that evangelists were assistants to the apostles and their rightful successors.[20] They performed a comparable task, minus the apostolic dignity and authority. Thus their major task was to herald the gospel in unevangelized territories, congregate believers into rightful assemblies, and establish them in faith, doctrine and life. The term "to evangelize" includes all of these phases and not merely the idea of acquainting people with the gospel and leading them to a decision for Christ. Thus the evangelist is a successor to the apostle and prophet, and a predecessor of the teacher and pastor, though temporarily he may have to function as evangelist, teacher and pastor as Timothy had to do in Ephesus and as Titus had to do in Crete. However, the evangelist does not settle down to a permanent position. When he does so, he changes his status from evangelist (missionary in the technical sense of the word) to that of a teacher or pastor, which may be perfectly legitimate and in keeping with God's will and order for him.

When we combine the root meaning of the word *evangelist*, the comments of the various commentators, the unique function of the evangelist within the church ministries, and its historical meaning as indicated by Eusebius and other church Fathers, we believe we have a right to identify our present-day missionary with the biblical designation of evangelist. This gives us the following portrait of a missionary:

The missionary is: (1) one sent forth — a messenger, a herald, a sent one, a man on the go; (2) he is an apostle, or one sent forth through the church by divine authority on a specific mission; (3) he is an evangelist — one who bears the good news, a gospel-bearer. Beautifully the three definitions confirm our description of a missionary.

New Testament Office of Pastor-Teacher

Closely related to the work of the evangelist is the ministry of the pastor-teacher. Christ Himself is supremely a Teacher. Christ commands His disciples *to proclaim* the gospel (evangelize) and *to teach* believers to observe all things (cf. Mk 16:15; Mt 28:19). Paul speaks of himself in the same verse as a preacher, an apostle, a teacher of the Gentiles in faith and verity (cf. 1 Ti 2:7; 2 Ti 1:11). It is of interest to note that Paul never speaks of himself as a prophet, perhaps because the apostolic office included the special gift of a prophet. Most probably, however, it was because the Lord instituted a special prophetic office, the function of which continued in the pastor-teacher ministry of the missionary movement.

NOT NEW OFFICE AND FUNCTION

The office and function of the prophet are not new to the New Testament. As an institution, this office was well rooted in the history of the Old Testament. Then it was revived in John the Baptist. Christ in His ministry stands in the biblical line of the prophets. It is our impression that the prophetic ministry in its dual capacity of revelation and teaching under the direct influence and inspiration of the Holy Spirit continued until "revelation" was completed in the New Testament. From here the teaching ministry alone continues.

UNIVERSAL TEACHING MINISTRY

While the ministry of the pastor-teacher in part belongs to the local church (Ac 13:1; Heb 5:12; Ja 3:1; 1 Ti 3:2; 5:17; 2 Ti 2:2, 24), there is a teaching ministry of a universal character (1 Co 12:8, 28-29; Eph 4:11; 1 Ti 2:7; 2 Ti 1:11).

The best evidence of this principle is in the life and ministry of Apollos. Though he is mentioned only occasionally in the book of Acts and the epistles (Ac 18:24-28; 19:1; 1 Co 1 — 4; 16:12; Titus 3:13), important lessons can be gleaned from his life. As the embodiment of this very important missionary principle, his description in the Scriptures is significant. He is an Alexandrian Jew, a learned man, mighty in the Scriptures, a man instructed in the way of the Lord, fervent in Spirit, skillful and diligent in his teaching, both powerful and convincing in his speech. Yet, in spite of such qualifications, he was a fellow worker, a team worker. He does not seem to have been a pioneer evangelistic missionary; he was a confirming pastor-teacher-missionary. Thus the brethren of Ephesus recommended him to the disciples of Achaia. When Apollos arrived he "helped them *which had believed* through grace." We find him ministering next in the church at Corinth (Ac 19:1; 1 Co 1 — 4), where he was *watering* that which Paul had planted. In all probability he returned from Corinth to Ephesus (1 Co 16:12), where seemingly he labored together with Paul for some time. Much later he visited the churches on the island of Crete (Titus 1:5; 3:13), establishing believers.

PRINCIPLES FROM APOLLOS' MINISTRY

Certain principles evolve from the ministry of Apollos:

1. He was a traveling minister of the Word of God, a pastor-teacher not bound to a local congregation.

2. He was a pastor-teacher, a missionary of the Word of God whose ministry was directed to the believers and younger churches rather than to the world in evangelism. He confirmed and watered that which others had planted.

3. He was able to fit his ministry into the framework laid down by the pioneer evangelists. Thus he greatly complemented their ministries and enriched the churches without discrediting or disrupting former ministries.

The ministry of the pastor-teacher is complementary to the work of the evangelist. While the latter functions mainly outside of the church in evangelism and church-planting, constantly expanding the frontiers of the church, the pastor-teacher nurtures and establishes the church in faith and life. Thus he continues the work of the evangelist while supplementing the ministry of the officers, the bishops and presbyters, in the local church.

The continuation of the function of teaching as a ministry to the universal church is well established in history. Adolf Harnack quotes extensively from the apostolic fathers and church Fathers to establish this fact.[21] He summarizes his findings:

> One early source of Acts, Paul, Hermas and the author of the Didache, all attest the fact that in the earliest Christian Churches "those who spoke the word of God" occupied the highest position, and that they were subdivided into apostles, prophets, and teachers. They also bear evidence to the fact that these apostles, prophets, and teachers were not esteemed as officials of an individual community, but were honored as preachers who had been appointed by God and assigned to the church as *a whole*. . . .
>
> By means of this feature Christendom possessed, amid all its scattered fragments, a certain cohesion and a bond of unity which have often been underestimated. These apostles and prophets wandered from place to place, and were received by every community with the utmost respect. This serves to explain how the development of the church in different provinces and under very different conditions could preserve, as it did, such a degree of homogeneity.[22]

THREE FUNCTIONS IN CHURCH LIFE

The pastor-teacher served three ways in the life of the church:

1. He traveled from church to church for the purpose of teaching the Word of God for the edification and inspiration of the saints to guide them into the counsel and purpose of God.

2. He founded schools for the training of the ministry. The most prominent of such schools arose in Alexandria, which became an early missionary training center.

3. The pastor-teacher became the early literary defender of Christianity and is known as the early Christian apologist. As such, he often preceded the evangelists in their ministry. His relentless attacks upon the emptiness and evils of paganism and idolatry served as a preparation for the preaching of the saving gospel of God. We do well to take note of the apologetic aspect of preaching in the first several centuries. It did much to undermine the philosophical and religious foundations of the religious systems of the day and is greatly needed today in the fields of the younger churches.

CONCLUSION

With the above facts before us, I draw the following conclusions:

The missionary world calls especially for two types of ministries: the evangelist and the pastor-teacher.

1. The evangelist engages in missions. As Dr. T. Watson Street explains, "Missions are specific missionary, or evangelistic, expeditions across the frontier of faith and no faith."[23] Or in the words of Stephen Neill, "Missions are concerned with pressing forward into the world of the heathen."[24] While his work may be church-based, it is not church-centered. He operates mainly in nonchurch territory, seeking the conversion of non-Christians and gathering them together into churches.

2. The pastor-teacher follows in the train of the evangelist, relates himself closely to the converted groups, and seeks to build them up into self-functioning, self-sufficient churches who are able to enter actively into the life and ministry of the church universal in order to experience the wider fellowship and to fulfill the purpose of God for our age. It is evident that the work of the pastor-teacher is not only church-based but also church-centered. He bears a different relation to the churches than the evangelist does. He is a part *in* the movement, not only *of* the movement as the evangelist is.

The contribution of the churches to the world is the evangelist. The contribution of the older churches to the younger churches is the pastor-teacher. This activity is one of the great needs of today.

THE PERMANENCY OF THE MISSIONARY ORDER

Having defined and established the biblical order of the missionary, we must now inquire into the time element of the missionary designation.

Are the missionary order and function permanent or transitory biblical establishments? Do they fall into the category of the "apostles and prophets" which has gradually vanished in history after the church of Jesus Christ had established itself within the social structure and the ongoing stream of life? Or is it a permanent establishment within the total ministry of the church until the evangelization of the world is completed and the church has been gathered out from among all (not some) nations of the world?

These are not vain questions. They are being asked by sincere and honest men who are deeply exercised by and involved in world evangelism. We dare not dismiss them lightly. It is a great and glorious fact that the church of Jesus Christ has been established at least as a beachhead on every continent and in every nation. A great task has been accomplished. But, with the establishment of the church, has the missionary task as biblically defined and practiced been completed?

The thesis that the missionary era has passed may sound reasonable. To some it may be even welcome news. However, is such a position scriptural or even practical? Indeed, I must reject it as being contrary to the general thrust of the New Testament as well as being in conflict with specific concepts and statements. From the Scriptures I am persuaded of the permanency of the missionary order. Here are four reasons for this position:

THE SILENCE OF THE NEW TESTAMENT ON THE TERMINATION OF SUCH A MINISTRY

In an unmistakable manner our Lord commanded His disciples to disciple all nations, not merely some people among the nations. Two most significant principles are embedded in this commission:

The discipling is to continue until "the nation" has been reached with the message of God. Our Lord does not limit the missionary command and activity to the establishing of a "beachhead" church in that nation. The process must continue until the nation has been saturated with the gospel of Jesus Christ. Paul is bidden to go *to the nations,* to open *their* eyes, that *they* may receive forgiveness of sins (Ac 26:17-18). Even stronger is the emphasis of Mark when the Lord commands His disciples to preach the gospel to *every creature.* Thus it is evident that there is no terminal point in the Great Commission on *the scope* of the ministry.

Our Lord presupposes that the evangelizing program will continue to the end of the age. Thus He promises to His discipling apostles that He will be with them until the end of the age. Again, there is no terminal point on time. In fact, the words of our Lord, "And, lo, I am with you alway, even unto the end of the age," definitely imply that the missionary task will continue to the end of our dispensation. Similar are the implications of the command: "Occupy till I come!" (Mt 28:20; Lk 19:13).

We do well to note the silence of the Lord on the termination of our missionary assignment. It just was not in His mind and program. In fact, neither its scope nor its time has termination. For Christ there is no postmissionary era.

THE NATURE AND VASTNESS OF THE ASSIGNMENT
IN THE GREAT COMMISSION

The Master is clear in His pronouncements that the gospel must be preached to every creature, that repentance and remission of sins must be proclaimed in His name among all nations, that evangelization must be carried to the uttermost part of the earth, and that the ministry will not be completed until all nations have been discipled. (The relationship of this ministry to the church is established later.)

The concept "all nations" is a uniquely pregnant concept which continues to call for "the foreign missionary." It is well known that the word translated here as "nations" is the Greek word *ethnos* from which our present-day anthropological designation *ethnology* comes. According to Thayer, it "designates a multitude living together, a multitude of individuals of the same nature or genus, a race or nation, foreign nations not worshiping the true God, pagans, Gentiles. . . ."

Today we speak of ethnic groups of people, indicating those people who are bound together by a common culture. It has little to do with national or geographical boundaries of nations in the modern sense of the word.

It is evident that the Great Commission remains in force, at least until the last ethnic group has heard the gospel of Jesus Christ. As long as there are groups of people who are not worshiping the true God, and until the gospel message has been presented to every creature, there will be a demand for missionaries. Christ indicates that this will take until the end of the age, either because of the assignment or because of new generations coming up to whom the gospel must be preached. In the light of the population explosion and the unreached masses of people, there is greater demand for missionaries today than ever before. So, practical reason and the Scriptures would seem to imply that more missionaries than ever are needed.

The practical carrying out of the Great Commission remains the responsibility of the apostles (in the generalized sense) and of the evangelists as sent forth through the churches by the Holy Spirit.

THE PERMANENCY OF THE ORDER OF "EVANGELISTS"

Some people may question the permanency of the order of evangelists; however, they would constitute a very small minority in the Christian church. Somehow the Christian church has always believed in evangelism and in evangelists. In fact, the paucity of the latter has often disturbed and even alarmed the church. Peculiarly, a general feeling that evangelists are needed and wanted has characterized the church. We ask ourselves the searching questions: Why has this feeling moved the people of God to ask God to send a man divinely endowed with the gift of evangelism? Is there not a Spirit within the church hoping that the gospel might prevail, the church expand, and the world be evangelized?

This is in perfect accord with the Word of God. Nowhere is there an indication that the office of the evangelist will ever terminate or that the function of the apostle in the general sense of the term will come to a close. These are functions established by the Holy Spirit. The design is that the church might grow quantitatively as well as qualitatively, and the nations of the world might hear the gospel and be saved. There is no command or indication that world evangelism will terminate before the end of the age. The foreclosure of the world evangelist or missionary cannot be deduced from biblical commands, exegesis, biblical examples, or biblical anticipations. To speak of the end of the missionary era and the termination of the missionary order is not to speak from the Bible or from the point of view of biblical realism or idealism. Here the order of the evangelist-missionary is as permanent as the mission of the church is abiding. Both will terminate at the end of the age.

AN ABIDING PRINCIPLE: "SO SEND I YOU!"

Generally, Christians believe that the Great Commission has abiding validity. It is therefore important that we pay close attention to its wording. It is of interest to compare two passages in the gospel of John which deal directly with the sending forth of the apostles. While in John 17:18 the word "sent" is in the aorist tense and indicates an act of sending, the verb in John 20:21 does not have such a form. It is stated in the present active indicative form and may be taken to express the idea of a process of sending or continuous sending.

Though we would not want to build conclusively upon such a distinction and form, we believe that, by implication, John 20:21 expresses an abiding principle of sending which continues throughout this age.

Dr. Westcott in his "Additional Notes on 20:21," after detailing the various passages in John dealing with the sending of the Son and the apostles and observing the two tenses of aorist and perfect of *apostello* and *pempo*, observes, "In all cases [where aorist is used] it will be found that the exact force of the teaching lies in the actual fact of Christ's mission." To the contrary, "the use of the perfect tense elsewhere is sufficiently frequent to show that it preserves its proper sense, and describes a mission which continues in its present effects."[25]

Then turning to John 20:21, he remarks, "The mission of Christ is here regarded not in the point of its historical fulfillment (sent) but in the permanence of its effects (hath sent). The form of the fulfillment of Christ's mission was now to be changed, but the mission itself was still continued and still effective. The apostles were com-the Bible there are at least four absolute qualities or principles inherent in the call to the ministry of the Word. To these we turn next.

BIBLICAL IMPLICATIONS OF THE CALL OF GOD
TO THE MINISTRY OF THE WORD

The Word of God must remain our guide in this most important matter. The ministry of the Word of God cannot be lightly assumed, for it is a ministry which God portions out and one which must remain under His sovereign jurisdiction. The Bible attaches definite qualities to such a ministry and calling.

IT IS A CALL SOVEREIGNLY EXERCISED BY THE HOLY SPIRIT

The fact that God's call is sovereignly exercised by the Holy Spirit is clearly demonstrated in the choice of the twelve by the Lord. Thus we read of Christ: "And he goeth up into a mountain, and calleth unto him *whom he would:* and they came unto him. And he ordained twelve, that they should be with him" (Mk 3:13-14). Later in life, Christ reminded His disciples of this and told them: "Ye have not chosen me, but I have chosen you, and ordained you" (Jn 15:16).

The same authority was exercised by the Holy Spirit when He spoke to the leaders in Antioch and said, "Separate me Barnabas and Saul for the work whereunto I have called them" (Ac 13:2). Paul, who never was able to get away from this solemn fact in his life, obediently and humbly acknowledged the sovereignty of the Holy Spirit in his own life and call. Moreover, he gloried in the position and ministry. His experience grew into a conviction and theology which he clearly expresses in his epistles. At least five times he speaks of his calling as having been bestowed upon him by the grace of God (Eph 3:2, 7-8; Ro 15:15; 12:3). He was made a minister (Eph 3:7; Col 1:23, 25), and he was put into the ministry (1 Ti 1:12). It was neither just a choice on the part of Paul, nor was it a burden he felt he must bear. He gloried and suffered in it with joy (Ro 15:15-19).

In a statement he informs us of the operation of this principle as a permanent principle in the church of Christ. Thus we read, "And he gave some to be apostles; and some, prophets; and some, evangelists; and some, pastors and teachers" (Eph 4:11, ASV). And again, having enumerated the various gifts for the ministries in the

missioned to carry on Christ's work and not to begin a new one. Their office was an application of His office according to the needs of man."[26]

The fact stands: the principle of sending is as abiding as the effects of the work of Christ and the needs of men. The principle can also be substantiated by Romans 10:12-15, where the sending becomes most crucial and where it expresses a principle rather than just an individual act. Thus, if not by direct command, by implication and necessity the function of the missionary remains a permanent order within the general framework of the ministry of the church.

The idea that we are living in the postmission era is not borne out by the Scriptures, the need of the world, the expectations of the younger churches, or by the Christian. The fact remains that the needs are staggering, the demands are pressing, the possibilities are overwhelming, and the response is unprecedented. God is at work as never before. This is not the time to doubt or question, or to be bewildered, confused and hesitant. This is the time to be brave and daring — to undertake greater things for God than ever, to be out in the harvest and battlefield.

But this is also the time for special measures of God's wisdom in missionary strategy, brotherliness in cooperation, humility in adaptations to the need and demands in the fields, Christian sympathy and understanding toward the younger churches in the lands of vast unreached masses and non-Christian governments, of deep insights into the subtle movements of syncretism and sly maneuverings of structured opposition. We are living in dangerous times where opportunities unredeemed may become our fiercest tragedies, where needs unmet may become our future oppression, where sin-bound slaves unloosened may become our future masters.

Our times demand absolute loyalty to the Word, complete devotion to our God, unreserved obedience to and reliance upon the Holy Spirit, unflinching determination to complete the evangelization of the world according to the purpose of God and command of our Lord, and radical thinking and drastic revamping to bring missions up-to-date and to accomplish our task.

THE CALL OF GOD AND THE MINISTRY OF THE WORD

The words *call, called* and *calling* are used in the New Testament in numerous relationships. This may be seen from the following quotations: "called . . . by his grace" (Gal 1:15); "called . . . by our gospel" (2 Th 2:14); "called . . . with an holy calling" (2 Ti 1:9); "called according to his purpose" (Ro 8:28); "eternal life, whereunto thou art also called" (1 Ti 6:12); "called the sons of God" (1 Jn 3:1); "called to be saints" (Ro 1:7; 1 Co 1:2); "called unto the fellowship of his Son Jesus Christ our Lord" (1 Co 1:9); "called unto liberty" (Gal 5:13); "called . . . to peace" (1 Co 7:15); "called . . . to glory and virtue" (2 Pe 1:3); "called, that ye should inherit a blessing" (1 Pe 3:9); "called . . . unto his kingdom and glory" (1 Th 2:12).

This list could be extended considerably to show that the calling of God is most inclusive in a Christian's life. We believe, however, that we do no violence to the Scriptures when we state that basically the Bible confronts us with a threefold call: the call to salvation, the call to discipleship, and the call to the ministry of the Word. Let us consider the call of God in this order for our own spiritual orientation and to make our calling and election sure.

THE CALL TO SALVATION

The divine call to salvation, according to the Bible, comes in the form of invitations, promises and commands. As an *invitation* we hear the voice of the Spirit in such familiar passages as Isaiah 1:18; 45:22; 55:1-3; Matthew 11:28-30; John 7:37-39; Revelation 22:17.

The numerous *promises* call us and assure us of the great salvation of God. Thus the Lord upholds before us such beautiful promises as John 3:14-18; 36; 5:24; 6:37; Romans 10:9-13; Revelation 3:20.

The Bible, however, confronts us also with *commands*, calling upon us to repent, believe, commit, trust, return and be converted. We refer to such passages as Isaiah 55:6-7; Jeremiah 3:12; Matthew 3:1-3; 4:17; Mark 1:2-3, 15; Luke 3:3-4; Acts 2:38; 17:30; Romans 16:26; 2 Thessalonians 1:6, 8.

We are not interested at this time in entering upon a theological differentiation of a universal and specific call, a general and efficacious call to salvation, although we are familiar with the theologies that have grown up around these terms. This, however, is not the place to discuss or evaluate such theologies. It suffices for our purpose to point to the biblical fact that God calls man to salvation.

The call to salvation, which is fundamental to every other call

of God, is first in emphasis and time, and first in experience. It is primary.

THE CALL TO DISCIPLESHIP

Christian discipleship is a biblical ideal to which every Christian is called. It is implied in the exemplary life of Christ and His call, "Follow me." It is implicit in the training program the Master pursued with His followers. It is explicit in the command of our Lord as expressed in the Great Commission and recorded in Matthew 28:18-20. "Make disciples" is certainly central in the commission, while going, baptizing, and teaching are the ways and methods for making disciples.

Christian discipleship is implied in the salvation of Christ and must, therefore, be clearly taught and emphatically preached as well as humbly and sincerely practiced. The concept of Christian discipleship was studied earlier.

THE CALL TO THE MINISTRY OF THE WORD

While the call to salvation is to all mankind through the communication of the gospel, and the call to discipleship is to all believers, the call to the ministry of the Word is selective, personal and specific. It must, therefore, of necessity be clearly distinguished from the call to discipleship, at least in the nature of the call, though not necessarily as far as time is concerned.

Here we come to a point of great confusion which we discover again and again in the minds of young people who honestly seek for God's will and call for their lives. Many of our present-day dedication or consecration services are of such a general nature that it becomes almost impossible for an honest Christian not to respond to the altar call. The writer experiences no difficulty here if the response is properly interpreted, either as a reaffirmation of previous commitments or as a basic decision to stop living for self and the world and to bring all of life under the lordship of Christ. This is a dedication to discipleship and does not necessarily involve a call to the ministry of the Word.

Therefore, this type of dedication must be distinguished from the dedication of life to the ministry of the Word in response to the call of God in whatever way the call may be coming. According to

church, he says: "But all these worketh that one and the selfsame Spirit, dividing to every man severally as he will" (1 Co 12:11). In the same chapter he says somewhat later, "And God hath set some in the church" (1 Co 12:28).

A passage which speaks rather convincingly to this truth is found in Hebrews 5:1-4. Here the writer establishes the divine qualifications of a priest, especially the high priest. Having emphasized the fact that the priest must be of men, that is, being possessed of true humanity for the purpose of true identification and compassion, he proceeds to establish the fact that the priestly office is by divine appointment and call rather than by human choice, no matter how much coveted. As Aaron did not choose this ministry nor was placed into this office by mere human election or appointment but was called of God, so no man taketh this honor, responsibility and ministry to himself. Thus the Aaronic example illustrates a general principle which upholds the sovereign call of God.

Well does Dr. William Barclay comment:

> The third essential of a priest is this — no man appoints himself to the priesthood; his appointment is of God. The priesthood is not an office which a man takes; it is a privilege and glory to which he is called. The ministry of God among men is neither a job nor a career; it is a vocation, a divine calling. A man ought to be able to look back and say, not, "I chose this work," but rather, "God chose me and gave me this work to do."[27]

Thus the Holy Spirit sovereignly exercises His authority in calling men to the ministry of the Word as He wills. Of course, whom He wills He also qualifies with the special gifts for such a ministry.

IT IS AN INDIVIDUAL OR PERSONAL CALL

That the call is individual or personal is richly illustrated in the Bible. We need only refer to such personalities as Moses, Aaron, Joshua, Samuel, David, Isaiah, Jeremiah, Jonah and Amos. The same principle of selectivity continues in the New Testament. We think of the twelve, Paul, Barnabas, Timothy. These men were conscious and persuaded of the fact that they had been called of God for the ministry of the Word, and they knew themselves responsible unto the Lord who had called them. Thus Paul tells us, "Let a man so account of us, as of the ministers of Christ, and stewards of the mysteries of God" (1 Co 4:1). He knew himself appointed and ordained of God as an apostle and a preacher and teacher of the Gentiles (1 Ti 1:12; 2:7; 2 Ti 1:11; Titus 1:3). It is the blessed privilege of a servant of the Lord to enjoy the glorious assurance in his mind that he is individually and personally called of the Lord to fill a specific place in the ministry of the church.

IT IS A UNIQUE CALL — A CALL TO THE MINISTRY OF THE WORD

We must emphasize here a principle which will not be appreciated by all. The writer would like to make it clear that he appreciates tremendously the wonderful response our times are witnessing among the so-called laity. This is of the Lord. We fully acknowledge the gracious hand of God in raising up strong spiritual leadership from among the so-called laymen. This is in perfect keeping with the sovereign and relevant operation of the Holy Spirit, and within the framework of the Bible. The Bible knows many great and godly laymen: Abraham, Joseph, Joshua, Gideon, Daniel, Nehemiah, etc.

It must be understood, however, that the Bible limits the personal, specific call to the ministry of the Word. We do not find in the New Testament that God calls a Christian to become a farmer, a businessman, a banker, a teacher, a technician or a politician in the same way as He calls a minister of the Word. Seemingly the Lord leaves the choice of our profession, occupation or position and the place of our labors to our common sense and our commitment to His providential guidance. Sanctified common sense, sound advice, careful evaluation of abilities, general usefulness and healthful Christian environment for the family are some important factors to help us in determining our life's vocation and place of residence and service.

This, however, is not so when it comes to the ministry of the Word. Here the call of God alone becomes the all-determining factor. In our day of general secularization and/or general equalization we must emphasize this important factor. The call to the ministry of the Word is unique.

While the Lord does raise up a leader or a special worker for a specific ministry and for a specific time and does release such a worker upon the completion of the task or mission, the call to the ministry of the Word according to the Scriptures is a call for lifetime. The place of the ministry may change; geographically we may be shifted.

The nature of the ministry, however, remains the same. A man, having been called of the Lord to the ministry of the Word, therefore, must carefully weigh his actions before he turns from this ministry to some other type of service or profession. It is not for us to judge, but often such a change is preceded by inner decay of the spiritual life and relationship to the Lord, though physical inabilities, too, compel many a man to transfer to another work.

IT IS A CALL TO A WORK

The ministry of the Word has several important divisions. Paul defines these ministries in a fivefold way in Ephesians 4:11 (ASV) when he says: "And he gave some to be *apostles;* and some, *prophets;* and some *evangelists;* and some, *pastors* and *teachers.*" In 1 Corinthians 12, he speaks of the various gifts of the Holy Spirit, gifts which have been bestowed sovereignly, yet for the specific purpose of mutual edification.

For our study we note only that no one person possesses all gifts. They have been sovereignly distributed and bestowed by the Holy Spirit to qualify a man for a special ministry in the church, the body of Christ. No one man can do every ministry equally well, and no one is called to do the whole ministry. This principle is in perfect keeping with the call of Paul. Here we read the words, "Separate me Barnabas and Saul for the work whereunto I have called them" (Ac 13:2). Here the life assignment of Paul is referred to.

Paul knew that he was called into a *work.* It was not a *field —* home field or foreign field, it was a *work.* Later he writes to the Corinthians that "every man's *work* shall be made manifest." Four times he uses the expression "man's work." It is significant that the word is in the singular and must not be confused with passages which speak of our works, such as 2 Corinthians 5:10, where Paul speaks of things done in the body. In 1 Corinthians 3:13-15, Paul speaks of our life work, our divine assignment for life, similar to the assignment he had received in Antioch, according to Acts 13:2.

Principally there are three ministries of the Word to be performed today:

1. *The ministry of shepherding the flock,* which embraces the various ministries in the local congregation. This is the service of the spiritual overseers and guides — the elders.

2. *The ministry of evangelism,* which definitely majors in the gospel-expansion and church-planting ministry at home and abroad. It principally refers to all pioneer work, whether on the home front or on the foreign field.

3. *The ministry of teaching.* Ephesians 4:11 does not strictly separate the teaching ministry from the pastoral work. The mentioning of the teacher in a specific and separate way in 1 Corinthians 12:28-29 justifies our distinction of the two ministries. The ministry of the teacher is one of consolidation, unification, edification, indoctrination and inspiration of the saints. Principally he is supplementing the ministry of the evangelist and complementing the ministry of the shepherds in the local church. He has a vital role to play in the total life and ministry of the church. It was the ministry of the itinerating teachers more than any other thing which unified the churches of the first several centuries and guided them in accomplishing the purposes of their Master.

Though we readily acknowledge the sovereignty of the Holy Spirit, who is relevant in His operations and ministry to the needs and demands of the time, it seems that in general the call to the ministry of the Word is with reference to one of the foregoing areas for which the Holy Spirit qualifies the individual in a special way. It seems more scriptural to think in terms of the above distinctions than drawing geographical lines and thinking in terms of home ministries and foreign ministries. The Bible does not make such geographical distinctions in connection with the call to the ministry of the Word. Certainly the apostles were not aware of the fact that they all would be led into "foreign missions" when the Lord called them and appointed them to the apostleship. The choice of the geographical area of service is a matter of individual leading, but not a matter of the call. The Bible does not distinguish between a call for the home field and a call for the foreign field.

It might be wise and prove beneficial to the cause of Christ if churches and mission boards would consider more carefully the above-mentioned biblical distinctions in the selection, appointments and assignments of missionaries. It could avoid the experience of many frustrations, disappointments and dissatisfactions, and result in greater efficiencies in the ministries at home and abroad. It remains a fact that the Lord gives to each one his work, his life assignment. This we must discover. To this we must give ourselves wholeheartedly. For this we can trust the Holy Spirit to qualify us. For this we must give an account someday before the judgment seat of Christ.

The same fact should also be carefully considered by graduates of various Christian institutions of higher learning. Too many are limiting the Lord in their appointments by setting geographical and cultural bounds. They want to be evangelists, Bible teachers, Bible institute and Bible college teachers, but it must be within a certain geographical and cultural area. They have never had a "call" to leave the homeland and go beyond certain geographical and cultural boundaries, so they say. This, indeed, is strange logic and peculiar interpretation of the Lord's hand upon us. While evangelists are needed to herald the gospel, the "called" and qualified evangelist waits within geographical and cultural specifications, not heeding the wide open doors and whitened harvest fields because they are within a different geographical and cultural area. While Bible institute, Bible college, and general Bible teachers are the crying need in numerous fields to train men for the ministry and to equip the church to fulfill her responsibility, the "called" and qualified Bible teacher waits within certain geographical and cultural limitations, not being able (or willing) to meet the tremendous need because it is not in his geographical and cultural specifications. What kind of logic or theology is this? Strange, indeed!

Practical Implications of the Call of God to the Ministry of the Word

The practical implications of the call of God to the ministry of the Word of God are far-reaching for the life of the individual believer. A positive response may transform a seemingly insignificant vessel into a vessel of glory and honor which may become a channel of immeasurable riches of God to untold multitudes of people. If negligence or disobedience leads to sidestepping the call of God, the life must be expected to be spiritually impoverished and dwarfed in spiritual stature. The consequences of either obedience or disobedience must be seriously considered and carefully weighed.

Our study here shall consider the preparation of the heart for the call of God, the realization of the call of God with special reference to the missionary, the persuasion of the call of God, the tests of the call of God, and the challenge of the call of God.

THE PREPARATION OF THE HEART FOR THE CALL OF GOD

The sovereignty of God does not exclude the responsiveness of man or preclude the careful and prayerful preparation of the heart of man for the experience of God. It remains man's responsibility to hear the call of God (compare the many statements in the gospels and the book of Revelation where we are challenged: "He that hath an ear, let him hear" Mt 11:15; Mk 4:9; 7:16; Rev 2:7, 11, 17, 29; 3:6, 13, 22).

We may compare the call of God to a telephone call. It means nothing to a deaf person at the receiver end, no matter how distinct, specific and individual the call from the other end may be. When the ear is closed, the mind preoccupied, and the will and purposes set, man is outside of hearing distance, and the call of God will never reach him. Many people never receive a call from the Lord, not because the Lord is not calling, but simply because they are not within calling distance. They are out of reach.

We must thus prepare our hearts for the call of God. For this we make several suggestions:

1. Make sure your body has become a living and sanctified sacrifice unto the Lord (Ro 12:1-2).

2. Make sure there is no conscious sin dulling your spiritual ear and spiritual sight (Eph 1:18; Col 1:9).

3. Make sure there are no preconceived personal plans and preferences (Ps 25:9).

4. Make sure you obey God daily and gladly in the little things of everyday life. Practice obedience to God and man (Lk 19:17; 1 Sa 15:22).

5. Make sure you are willing to go and to be used anywhere (Jn 7:17).

6. Form the habit of daily prayer, Bible study, and private meditations before the Lord (Josh 1:8; Ps 77:12; 119:15, 25, 45).

7. Form the habit of waiting patiently upon the Lord and expect Him to direct *every* step of your everyday life and doing (Pr 3:6; Ps 23:3).

8. Study carefully the Word of God relative to the purposes of

God for the Christian life and the Christian church. Get saturated with the Word of God (Ps 119:11, 104-5).

9. Study carefully the great spiritual needs of our day and prepare to meet them. Get a world vision and a world burden (Jn 4:35).

10. Spend much time in intercessory prayer for the cause and ministry of Christ at home and abroad (Mt 9:37-38).

11. Pray regularly and earnestly that God will make His will and call definite to you (Ps 25:4; 27:11; 143:8).

12. Rest assuredly in the promises of God and expect Him to meet you according to your need. He will make His will and calling sure (Ps 37:5, 7a; 32:8).

The clarity, depth and definiteness of the call of God will depend to a great extent upon the quality of the heart, the intensity of our fellowship with the Lord, and the degree of our willingness to obey the Master in His command and commission.

THE REALIZATION OF THE CALL OF GOD WITH
SPECIAL REFERENCE TO THE MISSIONARY

When we prepare our hearts in accordance with these great, yet simple, principles, God will not fail us, for the steps of a good man are ordered of the Lord. The question arises concerning how the Lord is extending His call to His servants. How am I made conscious of the call of God?

At this point great differences arise in the exposition and explanation of God's call. We should remember, however, that as no two conversions are exactly alike in their psychological experiences and expressions, so no two calls are exactly alike in their psychology.

In the main, God uses at least five approaches to the heart of man to make His call impressive and individual. To some God's call is issued:

1. *Through human instrumentality.* An example of this method of calling is found in the experience of Paul, the foremost apostle and missionary. Note carefully the following steps in the making of this great missionary:

In his conversion experience, Paul raises two questions: "Who art thou, Lord?" in which he addresses the Person of glory. The Lord answered, "I am Jesus, whom thou persecutest." This was a clear answer. In trembling and astonishment, Paul raises the second question: "Lord, what wilt thou have me to do?" It would have been easy for the Lord to directly inform His chosen vessel of His plans, purposes and calling. Instead, however, the Lord said, "Arise, and go into the city, and it shall be told thee what thou must do." In the city the Lord appeared to Ananias and revealed to him the call of Saul. And Saul humbly had to receive his call from human instrumentality. That he did so as from the Lord is clearly revealed in his statement in Acts 26:16-19, where he omits the human instrument completely.

Again, somewhat later we find Saul in Tarsus. A need arises in Antioch, and the Lord directs the attention of Barnabas to Saul. Barnabas, therefore, travels all the way from Antioch to Tarsus to extend the divine call to Saul. Thus Saul again had to receive the call through a human instrument. Why did not God speak to Saul in Tarsus and send him directly to Antioch? (Cf. Ac 11:25-26.)

Again, a group of five brethren are ministering to the Lord and fasting, and the Holy Spirit speaks. To whom? To the five brethren. This is clear. He does not say, "Barnabas and Saul, separate yourselves and present yourselves to the church." (Cf. Ac 13:1-3).

In all cases God uses human instrumentalities to make His call clear and sure.

God does so even in our days. He may use a brother or a sister, an elder, evangelist, teacher, missionary, or a mission board to issue His call to a "chosen vessel." While this method may humble us, yet it is divine and biblical.

We must warn, however, that not every suggestion, inquiry and invitation constitutes a call, and the individual must still make sure of the call in the presence of the Lord.

2. *God issues His call through reading of the Word of God and meditation upon it.* The Word of God reveals to us not only the history of God's actions but the will and purposes of God. In reading the Word we acquaint ourselves with His will and purposes.

As we meditate upon it, we are consciously and unconsciously being identified with the Word, just as the food we eat is being assimilated into our very life. Thus our minds and life become saturated and identified with the great purposes of God and shaped and molded in accordance with them. It is, therefore, nothing unusual that someone will know himself "called" to become a missionary and yet not be able to point to a definite experience or definite Scripture passage through which God extended the call to the person. The Word of God simply became a life-determining force in him. We dare to say that it is impossible to live in the Bible without developing a heart that beats warmly and fast for world evangelism. It is impossible to have the mind of Christ dominate our lives and not live for missions.

No one should be disturbed at not having experienced a special "call." In spite of this he may be destined for missions. The very fact that we "volunteer" for missions is an indication that we have imbibed the great and supreme purposes of God for our age. Unconsciously we are being prepared for it until we "volunteer" for it. As we volunteer, God makes this calling sure to us in our conscience, reason and consciousness as we wait before Him.

Someone has so fittingly characterized a missionary volunteer as

A Mind — through which Christ thinks.

A Heart — through which Christ loves.

A Voice — through which Christ speaks.

A Hand — through which Christ helps.

Let us never forget, however, that we are volunteers because Christ operates on our subconscious mind. As we wait patiently before Him and upon Him, He will make the call individual and sure, until we not only are willing to go, but until we *must* go.

3. *God extends His call through mission reports and mission studies.* Not a few missionaries have testified to the fact that as they listened to mission reports and the needs, possibilities and experiences of the mission field, God spoke to their hearts in a definite manner, convincing them that they must yield their lives to service in the foreign fields. As they further gathered information on and from the fields, God confirmed their initial impressions until these impressions matured into strong and motivating conviction. Only conscious dishonesty and volitional resistance will be able to keep them from going.

Perhaps the best illustration of this method is found in the life of the father of modern missions, William Carey. It is well known that Carey was a diligent student of the Word of God. He lived in the Scriptures. But it is also known that he was a keen student of world conditions, especially in relation to the spreading of the gospel story.

It has almost become proverbial in mission studies to speak of the cobbler and his mission map before him on the wall. On this self-constructed map he would add all the information he could find in books of geography, in newspapers, and especially in the reports of Dr. Cook's explorations in the South Pacific and of the East India Trading Company. The diligent accumulation of facts and figures became a burden too great to bear for the spiritual, sensitive, and scripturally nourished soul of Carey. Something had to be done. When no one was found to do the job, he volunteered to do it. Carey never hesitated through all his life and in the midst of most adverse circumstances to believe that God had used the method of reports and mission studies to issue this mission call in his own life.

Reports, facts, figures, maps and pictures are still a mighty force, and God uses these means to extend His call. No missionary, therefore, should weary of rehearsing "all that God had done with them, and how he had opened the door of faith unto the Gentiles" (Ac 14:27).

Mission conferences and systematic mission studies are a great need. They will prove a blessing wherever they are carried on in a sound manner.

4. *God extends His call also through crisis experiences.* This principle is vividly illustrated and verified in several Bible characters. We need only to mention Moses and his experience at Mount Horeb. The burning-bush experience could never be erased from his life; he knew God had met and commissioned him. All the circumstances, hardships and opposition of life could not obliterate the impression of the burning-bush experience.

The call of Isaiah is another illustration. Isaiah himself reports it to us. A careful study of the book will soon convince the reader that the two most impressive descriptions in Isaiah are found in chapters 6 and 53. The latter gives a detailed report of the Christ of God, the Lamb slain for our sins; the former is Isaiah's personal testimony of his call and commission. It was a real crisis experience for the prophet in an hour of outward complexities.

Numerous men and women of God had to be led into real crises in their lives before God could impress His call upon their consciousness and find a positive response. People who oppose altar calls for dedicating lives to mission services are opposing one of God's methods of making His call known to countless individuals. There is more in a crisis experience than an emotional upheaval; there may be the sound of the call of God for a life service. Not seldom God has to lead us into a crisis experience and throw us into chaos in order to upset our fixed patterns of thinking, behavior and complexes which are not in conformity with His will and purposes. Only after such a quake in our mentality, emotions and personality do we become capable of receiving new impressions and a divine call. Let no one despise crisis experiences; they are biblically well established and very often psychologically absolutely necessary. God utilizes them to impress His call upon our souls.

5. *Through sound, logical thinking.* We mention but one more approach which God uses to make His call impressive and clear. It is well illustrated in the following statements and testimonies:

Dr. Robert E. Speer once made the statement that the definite need on the field plus one's ability to supply that need constitute a "call" to the field. According to this position, the philosphy of the call is simple; opportunity plus ability equals responsibility. Responsibility in turn equals a call from God.[28]

C. T. Studd reasons: "If Jesus Christ be God and died for me, then no sacrifice can be too great for me to make for Him."[29]

Gilmour of Mongolia presents his way of reasoning: "Even on the low ground of common sense I seemed called to be a missionary. For is the kingdom not a great harvest field? Then I thought it only reasonable to seek the work where the work was most abundant and the workers were fewest."[30]

Keith Falconer of Arabia writes: "While vast continents still lie shrouded in midnight darkness, and hundreds of millions still suffer the horrors of heathenism and Islam, the burden of proof rests upon you to show that the circumstances in which God has placed you were meant by Him to keep you out of the foreign field."[31]

We frankly admit that we have no difficulty in accepting this as one of God's methods. Why should God speak less through reason than through crisis experiences or the other methods mentioned here? He may prepare us unconsciously for sound, biblical reasoning and lead us on by logical persuasion as well as by any other way. Though this is perhaps a less frequently employed method, it is no less divine.

God calls upon us: "Come now and let us reason together," and Paul writes: "Because we thus judge [or reason], that if one died for all, then were all dead: and that he died for all, that they which live should not henceforth live unto themselves, but unto him which died for them, and rose again" (2 Co 5:14-15). The little word "because" bases the preceding statement upon this part of the verse, namely, "For the love of Christ constraineth us." The implication, therefore, is that the constraining love of Christ is rooted in biblical thinking and reasoning as well as in biblical experience. God knows the psychological makeup of every individual, and He is sovereign and wise to adjust His approach to the individual to make His call individual and impressive.

THE PERSUASION OF THE CALL OF GOD

Though no two calls will be alike in their details and psychological impressions and expressions, I believe that every call which finds a positive response in the prepared heart will result in the following persuasions:

1. A deep conviction of the universal need of the gospel.

2. A deep conviction that God wills all people to hear the gospel, and that God is no respecter of persons.

3. The realization of our means to meet that need — the gospel of Jesus Christ.

4. A deep sense of personal inadequacy, inability and unworthiness.

5. The realization of our ability to meet that need (preparation) or our willingness to secure the ability (the willingness to prepare well).

6. A wholehearted and complete yielding to the task of meeting that need.

7. This is very often accompanied by an inner satisfaction, growing conviction, and peace and rest.

While perhaps not all missionaries will be able to analyze their own call into all of these components and some will find one element predominant in their own experience, while others will find another, I have based this analysis upon biographies and testimonies of many servants of God who have labored long, faithfully and successfully for their Master. Most of the missionaries have expressed an inner agreement with this analysis. Thus I believe it expresses in summary the nature of a matured call of God.

Let us not hurry until the call has matured. Too many are running, not necessarily without a call of God, but without a matured call of God. It is wise to observe that many obstacles are coming in the way of an outgoing missionary. They may be viewed as frustrations and make us unhappy and warp our personalities. They should be viewed as divine opportunities for saturation and maturation and thus enrich our lives. If Christ is really the Captain of our life, we will march on. He cannot be frustrated. Let us constantly make sure that He remains enthroned in our life, and our call will not only become inwardly sure but outwardly realized.

Well has Dr. Samuel Zwemer stated the main persuasions of the call of God as granted to a missionary: "The effectual call is 'The work of God's Spirit, whereby convincing us of the sin and misery of the non-Christian world, enlightening our minds in the knowledge of Christ's command and loving purpose to save mankind, He so renews our wills that we offer ourselves unreservedly for His service wherever His providence may send us.' "[32]

TESTS OF THE CALL OF GOD

While we do not believe that it honors God to ask for signs or constantly to "put out a fleece" to test God, there are, nevertheless, certain principles by which we may make our calling sure. These tests are well summarized by one writer:

1. Does it agree with God's general plan as set forth in His Word?

2. Can your circumstances be made to agree with what seems to be His leading?

3. Does the Holy Spirit bear continual witness that this is the will of God?

4. Are you still called when there is no challenge of adventure and no glamour of heroism? If called to an insignificant field, would you be willing to go? If you were the only one to stand, would you stand?

5. Are you willing to pay any price?

6. Are you merely "impressed" that you should go to a certain field, or is it a deep "conviction"?

These principles may be and should be freely used in testing the call of God for one's life. Since the tests of a missionary life are severe, we must honestly and seriously test our missionary calling.

Let us do diligence to prepare our hearts for the call of God and make sure that when the call reaches us, it will find a ready and joyous response.

Let us also make sure that we permit the call of God to mature in our lives, but not to grow stale and become ineffective. There is danger in premature action and there is danger in postpostponement.

> Wherever He may guide me,
>   No want shall turn me back;
> My Shepherd is beside me,
>   And nothing can I lack.
> His wisdom ever waketh;
>   His sight is never dim;
> He knows the way He taketh,
>   And I will walk with Him.
>   ANNA L. WARING

THE CHALLENGE OF THE CALL OF GOD TO THE MINISTRY OF THE WORD

The call of God bestows the highest honor upon man and becomes the greatest challenge to his life. No person, therefore, should think lightly of the call of God, for it deserves his most prayerful consideration and most diligent heed. The call of God should lead us to the deepest humiliation as well as to the most daring courage, until we can joyfully say with Paul, "I will most gladly spend and be spent for souls."

THE CALL OF GOD IS A CHALLENGE TO A LIFE OF SACRIFICE

It is an abiding principle of the kingdom of God that all spiritual ministries are based upon and associated with a life of sacrifice. Not even Christ was an exception to this divine principle. Indeed, He lived the life of the supreme sacrifice. Of Him we read that He laid aside the riches of eternity and became poor that He might enrich others (2 Co 8:9).

He divested Himself of the divine glory which was His inheritance from eternity (Jn 17:5, 24).

He emptied Himself of the form of God, which was His eternal abode of equality with the Father (Phil 2:5-8).

He sacrificed His human rights and honor when he stood before Caiaphas and in Pilate's hall and was spit upon and mocked and scoffed (Mt 26:67-68; 27:27-31; Mk 14:65; 15:16-20; Lk 22:63-65; Jn 18:22; 19:1-3).

He gave His life as a sacrifice for the sin of the world on Calvary's cross, the symbol of shame and crime. No one could take His life from Him; He gave it voluntarily (Jn 10:17-18).

Thus the principle of sacrifice pervades the life and ministry of Christ the Lord.

As the Master, so the servant is called to a life of sacrifices. This is clearly indicated in the words of the Master: "And it came to pass, that, as they went in the way, a certain man said unto him, Lord, I will follow thee whithersoever thou goest. And Jesus said unto him, Foxes have holes, and birds of the air have nests; but the Son of man hath not where to lay his head" (Lk 9:57-58).

"If any man come to me, and hate not his father, and mother, and wife, and children, and brethren, and sisters, yea, and his own life also, he cannot be my disciple. And whosoever doth not bear his cross, and come after me, cannot be my disciple . . . whosoever he be of you that forsaketh not all that he hath, he cannot be my disciple" (Lk 14:26-27, 33).

These statements are well borne out by the testimony of the apostle Paul when he said, "Yea, and if I be offered upon the sacrifice and service of your faith, I joy, and rejoice with you all" (Phil 2:17).

"I have learned, in whatsoever state I am, therewith to be content. I know both how to be abased, and I know how to abound: every where and in all things I am instructed both to be full and to be hungry, both to abound and to suffer need" (Phil 4:11-12).

The call of God is a challenge to a life of sacrifice. Loneliness, privations, and hardships that will deplete the physical strength and imperil bodily health are included in the call of God. Comforts and conveniences, homes and relationships must become secondary for the called of God. The Lord may require the sacrifice of health and life. Such is the challenge of the call of God.

THE CALL OF GOD IS A CHALLENGE TO A SERVICE
OF THE GREATEST NEED OF MANKIND

The needs of the world are many and tremendous. While God is not indifferent to any of the needs, He has ordained that His missionaries are to serve one particular need of the world, the spiritual need. This is the supreme need and, if we may term it that way, the need of all needs, the cause and root of all needs. The world is in a deplorable state economically, socially, politically and morally. These are, however, but the outgrowth and symptoms of the all-determining spiritual need of the world.

Man is first of all and primarily a spiritual being. It remains a fact that, by nature, man — the world over — is first of all a religious being. The cultural anthropologist will readily admit that man's economic, social and moral structure is religiously determined and interwoven with his religious beliefs. Only in the West has modern philosophy sought to split man in order to capture him for secularism and materialism. Only here religion is branded by some extremist as the "opium of the people." This deceit of all deceits is at present reaping its due reward in destruction and chaos.

The missionary who is called of God must keep his divine ordination clearly and constantly in mind. He is called to serve the spiritual need of mankind. His grave and constant danger is to be sidetracked and to labor in regard to the symptoms rather than on the cause of all illness.

As stated before, we do not deny the manifold needs of mankind, nor dare we look upon them in an indifferent manner. A missionary, however, must learn to commit all these needs to God and to remain conscious that he is called of God to meet one particular need of mankind, the deepest need in the soul of man, the spiritual need, which, if not met, will continue for all eternity and determine man's eternal destiny for woe or glory.

The gospel of Jesus Christ as recorded in the Bible is the only and sufficient remedy for this basic need. The missionary, therefore, must remain constant in the proclamation of the gospel of God. Only thus is he loyal and true to the call of God.

THE CALL OF GOD IS A CHALLENGE TO A SERVICE
WHICH PAYS THE GREATEST DIVIDENDS

While it is true that some of the pioneer fields have proven hard and difficult, and missionaries have labored long to see some people turn to Christ, it remains a fact that in most cases missionaries have seen in one generation a number of churches springing up and multitudes turning to the Lord.

Christ's admonition is as true today as it was in the days when He spoke the words: "The harvest truly is plenteous, but the labourers are few" (Mt 9:37). And again, "Say not ye, There are yet four months, and then cometh harvest? Behold, I say unto you, Lift up your eyes, and look on the fields; for they are white already to harvest" (Jn 4:35).

A ready and plenteous harvest is awaiting the laborer of God in most fields of the world. Reports and testimonies indicate that we are living in "days of reaping." The community movements in India are continuing to bring numerous people into the kingdom of God, while in Africa tremendous and transforming movements are increasing. Brazil manifests the fastest-growing Christian community in the world. Japan and Korea are reaching for the gospel, while Taiwan is yielding a rich harvest. In Indonesia, multitudes are turning to Christianity. Eager inquirers visit the servants of God almost everywhere in the non-Christian world. Harvesttime has come, but the laborers are few.

Truly, the call of God is a challenge to a service which pays rich dividends in immortal souls. Who, then, will heed the call of God and put wisdom into his life? Here is an opportunity to enrich ourselves for eternity.

THE CALL OF GOD IS A CHALLENGE TO THE DEEPEST
EXPERIENCES OF THE LORD IN OUR LIFE

I shall never forget the experience which was mine when I stood before a young, well-educated and highly intelligent missionary in the heart and desert of Australia and placed a foolish, though not honest, question before the man. The question was: "Why do you waste your precious life and time here in the desert among these lowest of all savages? Is there no more respectable job for you in

Australia?" Whereupon a tear and a look of glory appeared on the face of the young missionary as he emphatically said, "Had I two lives, this is where I would spend them, yes, had I a *thousand* lives, this is where I would invest them."

The glory of that face and the conviction of that voice have gone with me and have made the words of Christ more meaningful than ever before: "Lo, I am with you alway, even unto the end of the world." And again: "And they went forth, and preached every where, the Lord working with them."

It is my deepest conviction that the missionary of God is not only unique in his call and ministry; he is also unique in his experiences of the Lord. His life has the "thrills" as well as the "pills" of the Christian life and ministry. He experiences the companionship of the Lord in a unique way.

This is natural and just. The Lord asks no price for which He does not uphold a prize.

The distance from friends and relatives is balanced by the nearness of the Lord. The discomforts and inconveniences are outweighed by the comforts, peace, and joy the Lord provides. The moral and social evil to which he is constantly exposed is countered by the glory and presence of the Lord. The material and physical discomforts are overshadowed by spiritual enrichings. Thus the loss becomes gain. Our God is a just Master as well as a gracious one.

Here is the testimony of a man who ought to know. David Livingstone, whose heart lies buried in Africa, leaves the following words for us to ponder:

> For my part I have never ceased to rejoice that God has appointed me to such an office. People talk of the sacrifice I have made in spending so much of my life in Africa. Can that be called a sacrifice which is simply paid back as a small part of a great debt owing to God, which we can never repay? Is that a sacrifice which brings its own best reward in healthful activity, the consciousness of doing good, peace of mind, and the bright hope of a glorious destiny hereafter?
>
> Away with such a word, and such a view, and such a thought! It is emphatically NO sacrifice. Say, rather, that it is a privilege. Anxiety, sickness, suffering, or danger now and then, with a foregoing of the common conveniences and charities of life, may make

us pause and cause the spirit to waver and sink; but let this be only for a moment.

All of these are nothing when compared with the glory which will hereafter be revealed in and for us. I never made a sacrifice. Of this we ought not to talk, when we remember the great sacrifice made by Him who left His Father's throne on high to give Himself for us.[33]

To this David Brainerd adds, "I declare, now that I am dying, I would not have spent my life otherwise, for the whole world."[34]

Thus the call of God becomes the greatest challenge any man can ever face. Though it may call for a life of sacrifice, privations, and even sufferings, the Master is just in His rewards here and now, though He may withhold the major part of the reward for the time when we all shall stand before the judgment seat of Christ.

Blessed is the man who in faith and courage accepts the challenge of the Lord and thus discovers the heights of divine service, joy and contentment. We have yet to meet the missionary who regretted having responded to the call of God and having accepted the challenge of God.

BIBLICAL QUALIFICATIONS OF A MISSIONARY

A great deal of thought, studies and efforts have gone into the direction of the missionary enterprise and the preparation of the Christian missionary ever since the cause of Christian world missions was revived in the Christian communities during the last centuries. Never has the church or a missionary society been indifferent regarding the qualifications and preparations of men and women who were sent into the world for mission purposes. This became even more true after the Edinburgh Missionary Conference in 1910 with its resultant institutions and special courses to prepare missionaries more adequately.

Postwar developments and circumstances have forced us to rethink and soberly evaluate many of our patterns of ministries and dearly held programs for serving mankind. The demand and nature of our ministry are not in question. Our personnel preparation, patterns of organization, and methods of operation, however, need serious studies and evaluations. Are we relevant, effective and adequate in our service? Are we accomplishing the goal of God in and for our times?

These are piercing questions which demand honest, conscientious answers. More activity and expansion are not sufficient. Numerical advances and greater institutions are not necessarily an absolute proof of effectiveness and success. Christianity is first of all a matter of quality, not quantity. This demands a new look at the qualifications of the missionary.

The qualifications and preparation of a missionary are not easily measured, standardized or defined. In the final end, missionary work is person-to-person work and very much depends upon the natural resourcefulness, the personality, and the character of the Christian worker rather than upon mere academic training. Thus it must not be taken for granted that because an individual is a college and seminary graduate that he therefore qualifies for mission service, nor is it assured that such a graduate will do better in every case than *some* Bible institute graduate or individual trained on a lower level may do.

On the other hand, let it also be stated that we must free ourselves from the idea that because an individual is a fine, spiritual and studious person and has completed a Bible institute course, that such qualifications assure success. There is more to missionary preparation than can be defined on paper, though academic training of the right kind is of tremendous value, and degrees are important in many countries and for various positions.

In general, the preparation and qualifications of a missionary candidate are measured by several standards and labeled as:

1. spiritual qualifications
2. doctrinal qualifications
3. academic qualifications
4. physical qualifications
5. personality qualifications
6. social qualifications

Fine and comprehensive lists of qualifications have been prepared and are available by writing to almost any missionary society. It is well to study such requirements thoroughly and apply them carefully and honestly to oneself before making application to a mission society. The candidate should not have mental reservation, hoping that the society will make the necessary adjustments to accommodate him in his uniqueness or peculiarity which almost always is some kind of concealed eccentricity.

The qualification lists are not arbitrary collections of noble traits. They are necessities and demands of the work and cannot be disregarded. The heavy casualties, frustrations, separations and divisions often due to strong personal independence and the apparent inefficiencies on the mission fields have alerted many societies to greater care in the application of definite standards. Consultative conferences have been conducted to seek ways and means to remedy serious and costly experiences. Much has been learned and many improvements have been made.

The qualifications and preparation of the missionary today are determined by several factors:

1. the government of the country where the missionary is to labor
2. the conference or society the missionary is to represent in the work
3. the state of the church in the country where the missionary is to serve
4. the task which he is to accomplish and the position which he is to fill — educational, medical, church ministries, evangelism, technical service

All these factors enter in to determine the qualification of a missionary.

INDISPENSABLES IN MISSIONARY QUALIFICATIONS

In the final analysis, only the Holy Spirit is really able to qualify us for the commission of the Lord. The Word of God tells us, "Not by might, nor by power, but by my Spirit, saith the Lord." This solemn, yet encouraging, truth must always fill our consciousness. In order to be fruitful in the ministry of the Lord, we must learn to "walk in the Spirit."

The divine enduement and qualification, however, are not mechanical, for God neither sets aside our personality nor transgresses the laws of our mind. There is a human side as well as a divine side to our preparation. Our divine appointment becomes our challenge to qualify to the best of our ability for the divine assignment and commission.

There are certain absolutes and indispensables for every Christian worker who would be loyal to his Lord and his calling. These indispensables, which are universals for every servant of God, are spiritual rather than professional or academic.

In all Christian ministries Christ remains our supreme example. The "ideal Servant of Jehovah," He is our standard and pattern. We do well also to look at other personalities which the Bible upholds before us. From the Scriptures certain indispensables become evident:

The first indispensable. For any Christian worker the first indispensable is the satisfying consciousness that he has volitionally, honestly and wholeheartedy become a true disciple of Jesus Christ and that he is abiding in such discipleship (see the study on discipleship under the Great Commission according to Matthew). Unreserved commitment to Christ is fundamental.

The second indispensable. This is a deep and abiding consciousness of having been called by the Lord to the ministry of the Word or as a related "helper" (1 Co 12:28) in the ministry of the Word (as a doctor, nurse, teacher, technician, or social worker) and having been led to the place of the assignment and labor.

A third indispensable. This is the settled conviction that the Lord has committed unto us a message which is not only relevant and attractive, but which is absolute and final in present salvation and eternal destiny of man. This message is unique and sufficient and is based upon and derived from the Bible, God's revelation to mankind.

In like manner the candidate must be possessed by a deep confidence that the Lord will qualify him through the Holy Spirit for the assigned ministry by bestowing the necessary spiritual gifts and thus making it possible for him to render efficient and effective service and do justice to his calling (1 Co 12:1-11). Our attitude toward and knowledge of the spiritual gifts are most significant in our ministry.

It is also important to trust the Holy Spirit to give us love, wisdom, divine compulsion and divine authority to transmit the committed message to man, of whatever race or culture he may be. We are commissioned to "speak the truth in love" without fear or favor of man, neither adding nor subtracting from the Word. God is willing and able to enable us to communicate His message in an intelligible and attractive manner to man in his need of the Saviour.

Thus our confidence is not in ourselves; neither is our authority based upon cultural, academic or economic superiority. We rest in the conviction that our message is from God. It has no substitute, is unparalleled, must not be modified by subtraction or addition, and must be communicated in the power and wisdom and authority of the Holy Spirit who is able, willing and desirous to qualify us for the divinely entrusted task. We are not sent to join mankind in a common search for truth but are to make an authoritative (not proud or arrogant) declaration of divinely revealed truth.

A fourth indispensable. This is that attitude of mind which fully characterized Christ who emptied Himself, humbled Himself, made Himself of no reputation, and took upon Himself the form of a servant and became obedient unto death, even the death on the cross. "Though he was rich, yet for your sakes he became poor, that ye through his poverty might be rich." True *servanthood* was one of His basic indispensables.

A similar attitude characterized Paul who became "your servant for Christ's sake," and who was able to write:

> For though I be free from all men, yet have I made myself servant unto all, that I might gain the more. And unto the Jews I became as a Jew, that I might gain the Jews; to them that are under the law, as under the law, that I might gain them that are under the law; to them that are without law, as without law (being not without law to God, but under the law of Christ,) that I might gain them that are without law. To the weak I became as weak, that I might gain the weak: I am made all things to all men, that I might by all means save some. And this I do for the gospel's sake, that I might be partaker thereof with you (1 Co 9:19-23).

The missionary must be ready to be flexible, adaptable and sacrificial, to receive no credit but be willing to give credit, and even to be discredited, to be debased, to suffer and yet steadily and unwaveringly — without murmur and doubt — seek identification with other people in their experienced needs and demands in order to find points of contact and departure. He must seek ways and means to create within them a consciously felt spiritual need for the purpose of relating them to Christ who alone can meet their hearts' desire, forgive their sins, bestow eternal life, and give true and satisfying meaning to their lives. Only the mind of true servanthood can lead us to such relationships, identification and ministry.

A *fifth indispensable.* This indispensable relates the missionary's social attitude and relationship to his fellow laborers, be they fellow missionaries or nationals. Here the examples of Christ and Paul are most ideal and instructive. Neither of them was a "lone wolf" in the ministry. Christ had not merely a great following; He had most intimate friends, disciples and colaborers. His disciples were constantly with Him (Ac 1:21-22). They were His learners and His supporters who served with Him and prayed with and for Him and eventually became His apostles.

Paul had his colaborers too. He undoubtedly was conscious of his unique apostleship, his apostolic mission, authority and responsibility. Yet, his attitude toward his associates was most intimate and cordial. He knew them as

> fellow laborers (Phil 4:3; 1 Th 3:2; Phile 1, 24)
> fellow helpers (2 Co 8:23)
> fellow workers (Ro 16:3, 9, 21; Phil 2:25; Col 4:11)
> fellow soldiers (Phil 2:25; Phile 2)
> fellow slaves (Col 1:7; 4:7)
> fellow prisoners (Ro 16:7; Col 4:10; Phile 23).

They were his partners (2 Co 8:23), his companions (Phil 2:25), his helpers (Ro 16:3, 9), laborers together (1 Co 3:9). Freely he communed with them, traveled with them, and shared with them.

Paul speaks of his co-workers in noblest terms. It is well to note how the apostle characterized Timothy, Epaphras, Epaphroditus, Tychicus and others. There is not a word of criticism about them, though he painfully laments the fact that some had forsaken him and turned back to the world (2 Ti 4:10), while others suffered shipwreck in their faith (doctrine) (1 Ti 1:19-20; 2 Ti 2:17-18). Such wholesome attitudes are rare among the servants of God. They are the fruit of the Holy Spirit produced in a spiritually healthy personality and developed through a consistent life of meditation upon the Word of God and through obedience to the Holy Spirit. It is a divine art to live in healthy and uplifting relationships with fellow workers and fellowmen, especially in times and circumstances of pressures and tensions. Again, we must learn to trust the enabling grace of God.

A sixth indispensable. This indispensable is purity and depth of motivation. While sinful man can never reach beyond "human alloy" in his motivation, it is well for us honestly to recognize this fact and humbly confess it before the Lord. Let us not argue for absolute unselfishness in our motivation nor insist upon the absolute purity of our drives. We may be deceiving ourselves, for even the best of us lives in the flesh. Let us, however, sincerely seek not to live according to the flesh, humbly plead for daily cleansing of our motivation by the blood of the Lamb, and learn to live and labor in the Holy Spirit. It is well to evaluate honestly our motivation in the light of the motivation of Paul as presented in his own statements in his epistles.

A seventh indispensable. This is a high view of, and a deep loyalty to, the church of Jesus Christ. It is evident from the study of the New Testament that the church in her local setting and ideal position is central in the New Testament.

I have set forth the church in her relationship to the Lord, to the world, and to the missionary ministry in this world. The church's significance may thus be readily seen. No man can truly serve as a missionary in the New Testament sense of the word who is not in sympathy with the church of Jesus Christ. Neither can he truly identify himself with Christ, for Christ is supremely a Minister of the church. The missionary, too, is supremely a church-builder and a minister of the church. The right perspective of the church must be kept in mind.

Such are some of the indispensables of the Christian worker at home and abroad, in the churches and in missions. Thus, a missionary is a spiritually healthy personality developed through a consistent life of meditation upon the Word of God and through obedience to the Spirit of God; a matured personality who has learned to live in healthy relationships with fellow workers and fellowmen; a person with a message from God, based upon and derived from the Bible, God's revelation and message to mankind; and a person with the ability, love, divine compulsion and divine authority to transmit the message to mankind.

Hudson Taylor, the great man of God and missionary statesman, lists the following as the missionary's equipment:

1. A life yielded to God, controlled by His Spirit.

2. A restful trust in God for the supply of all needs.
3. A sympathetic spirit and willingness to take a lowly place.
4. Tact in dealing with men and adaptability toward circumstances.
5. Zeal in service and steadfastness in discouragements.
6. Love for communion with God and for the study of His Word.
7. Some experience and blessing in the Lord's work at home.
8. A healthy body and a vigorous mind.

The call of God is a most serious and sacred business and requires our best. Paul says, "So, as *much as in me is,* I am ready to preach the gospel" (Ro 1:15). Paraphrasing it, we would say, "I have mobilized and developed all the abilities within me and organized them for one purpose, namely, the preaching of the gospel of Jesus Christ."

This we must learn; this we must do to meet the challenge of the call of God.

8

The Dynamics of Missions

PENTECOST IS A UNIQUE EVENT in the history of mankind which is unparalleled in the history of religion. No other religion points to a cross (atonement), an empty tomb (triumph over death), and Pentecost (the invasion of divine and personal dynamic in time and space).

Pentecost, in one sense, is a once-for-all event in this dispensation. It is historical in that it took place at a specific place (Jerusalem), at a specific time (Jewish Pentecost), and upon a specific company of people (the disciples, or most probably the 120). In this sense it is a unique historical event only to be paralleled by a similar historical event when the Holy Spirit will be poured out upon Israel at the conversion of this people. Then Joel 2:28-32 will be fully realized in all its ramifications.

Pentecost, however, is not merely historical. It is a historical event with abiding, dynamic, existential consequences. The Holy Spirit did not merely come. He came authoritatively dispatched by the Father and the Son. He came to abide and to concretize the purpose of the triune God in this world. He came to actualize the salvation of God in Christ Jesus in the lives of men, families, tribes and people, to dynamize the lives of all who trust in Christ and who by faith appropriate the blessings of God in the gift of the Holy Spirit. He came to qualify those whom God calls out for His ministry by bestowing special gifts (charismata) upon them. These are abiding, existential consequences of Pentecost. The differences in the interpretation of the experience of these realities must not be permitted to subtract from or overshadow this blessed reality which must become existential by faith if man is to profit by it. Thus Pentecost is both historical and existential.

Pentecost is a crisis event of the Holy Spirit. No one will ever know the full implication of Pentecost for the Holy Spirit. What did it mean for the Holy Spirit to be sent into a hostile world as the Paraclete of the triune God? The Bible silently passes over this question.

It is evident from the pages of the Old Testament and the gospels that there never was a time when the Holy Spirit was not present in this world. We find Him operating in Genesis 1:2 and on from there in the universe and in the history of mankind. He was always the presence of God in this world. His omnipresence is well attested in the Old Testament (cf. Ps 139:1-12). He, indeed, is the God who is *here*.

Yet there was something new about His coming into the world on the day of Pentecost. He came as the divine Comforter, the Paraclete. Note that all references to the Holy Spirit by the designation are in the future tense (Jn 14:16, 26; 15:26; 16:7), just as the prophecies of Him in the Old Testament are cast into the future tense (Eze 11:19-20; 36:26-27; Joel 2:28-32). The Holy Spirit had been an outgoing Spirit from the beginning of creation (Gen 1:2). However, Pentecost was an unprecedented outgoing. The Holy Spirit has been present in a new and unequalled manner since Pentecost to perform the work of God. From a certain point of emphasis, this is the age of the Holy Spirit.

Because of this, Pentecost becomes the watershed of a new type of world missions. As the outgoing God, the Holy Spirit transforms the centripetalism of missions into a dynamic and urgent centrifugalism..

The "Come!" is replaced by a "Go!" and the inviting voice of the priest at the altar is superseded by the herald rushing from place to place to call a people unto God. The stationary and localized temple becomes a living and moving temple. The worship at a place and building becomes a worship in spirit and truth, bound neither by place nor building. Outgoing becomes the quality of the Christian gospel and of the Christian church, the temple of the Holy Spirit.

THE HOLY SPIRIT IN MISSIONS

The Holy Spirit is the divine Paraclete, a designation given Him by our Lord Jesus Christ (Jn 14:16, 26; 15:26; 16:7). It is His title and office designation. As Christ is known as Saviour, Redeemer, Advocate, etc., designating His official functions, so the Holy Spirit is called the Paraclete.

As Paraclete He is identified as the Spirit of truth (14:16; 15:26) and as the Holy Spirit (14:26). Thus we are not left in doubt who the Paraclete is. Twice we are informed that the Paraclete will be sent by the Father (14:16, 26), and twice we are assured that He will be sent by the Son (15:26, 16:7). We are also told that He will abide with us forever (14:16), that He will bring to the remembrance of the disciples "all things . . . whatsoever I [Christ] have said unto you" (14:26), that He shall testify of Christ (15:26), and that He will reprove and convict the world of sin, of righteousness and of judgment (16:7-8). Thus His ministry is in revelation-inspiration, instruction, witness-bearing and conviction. Most certainly this is not an exhaustive listing of the ministries of the Holy Spirit but rather a generalization of His major thrusts. Such thrusts are threefold: (1) the operation in relation to the production of the New Testament, (2) the operation in relation to the edification and inner building and preservation of the believers in the church, (3) the operation in relation to the world.

It is evident from the variations in translation that it is difficult to find an equivalent for the word *paraclete*. This is not because it is a mystifying word. Rather, it is so because it is such a "rich" word, a word so full of meaning and so variously used. No one word can truly transmit its meaning. Thus it is translated as comforter (KJV), someone to stand by the believer (Phillips), a helper (Moffatt, Williams), advocate (NEB), comforter, counselor, helper, intercessor, advocate, strengthener, standby (Amplified).

It is agreed that the literal transliteration of *paraclete* is "one who is called in"; some would reason, "one who is called in to help." However, what is the purpose of calling one in for help? What kind of help is needed?

William Barclay, after a presentation of considerable material, comes to the conclusion that *Paracletos* always means someone called in for help and to render a service.[1] In the Septuagint, he points out, it is often given the meaning of "comfort" and "moral support" which keeps a man on his feet and saves him from collapsing under the weight of pressure and tensions. He notes further that it is a Greek

court word used for calling in an advocate and counsel for the defense
of an accused person, and that it is the word for exhorting men to
noble deeds and high ideals, encouraging them in battle.

These are great thoughts derived from the study of the usage of
the word in general literature. No doubt they are all present in the
usage in our texts. However, they hardly express the full meaning
and depth of the words of Jesus as recorded by John.

J. Oswald Sanders also studies the usage and history of the word
and concludes: "The Latin word 'advocate' is a close equivalent of
the Greek *Paraclete*, and the figure throws much light on the work
of the Spirit. Both words mean 'to call to one's side for help,' especially against an accuser and judge. The ideal barrister of olden times
assumed a fourfold obligation. He was his client's representative,
pleaded his cause, defended his name, and guarded and administered
his property."[2]

Sanders takes perhaps too exclusively the legal aspect of the
word. However, he comes close to its major usage. It is evident that
a tremendous wealth of spiritual truth is expressed in that one word,
paraclete.

Having made the analysis, Sanders then raises the arresting question: "But on whose behalf is the Holy Spirit the barrister or advocate?" Then he responds with an answer which may be as startling
to the reader as it was surprising to me when I first read it:

> It may come as a surprise to some to learn that the Holy Spirit
> is not our Advocate, but Christ's. He himself said, *"Another Para-
> clete,"* implying that He was one *Paraclete*, and the Holy Spirit the
> other. "If any man sin," says John, "we have a *Paraclete* with the
> Father, Jesus Christ the righteous" (1 John 2:1). The Son is our
> Advocate with the Father in heaven, but the Spirit is the Advocate
> of the Son on earth. His office is to represent Christ, plead His
> cause, defend His name and guard the interests of His kingdom on
> earth, an office which He jealously and zealously fulfils. On the
> other hand, let it not be forgotten that the Spirit was given to be to
> us on earth, all that Christ would be, were He personally present.
> Christ has come in the person of His Spirit and is constantly at our
> side to strengthen and help.[3]

The words and interpretation of Sanders strike a sympathetic
chord in my mind. The concept that the gospel and the work of the

Lord have been "committed" to the church must be considered a relative fact. In the final end, it all rests in God. God the Father purposed and designed the plan of salvation; God the Son procured and assured the plan of salvation; God the Holy Spirit executes and administers the plan of salvation. Here is the source of its perfect design, the foundation of its perfect procurement, and the power of its perfect execution. Man, however, is God's moral, rational and responsible colaborer and collaborator. Man is more than just an instrument or tool. He is an agent who consciously, volitionally and voluntarily collaborates with God in the execution of the great drama of salvation upon this earth. Thus Paul thinks of himself as a bondslave. He is neither a slave nor a draftee. He is an ambassador, an apostle of Jesus Christ by the will of God. He speaks of himself as one "filling up the things lacking of the afflictions of Christ" (Col 1:24, free trans.), perhaps even as a co-worker with God (1 Co 3:9, exegesis here is not absolute). There may be more "investiture" in the words of Christ to Peter, " . . . and will give unto thee the keys of the kingdom of heaven" (Mt 16:19) than we are prepared to admit or to assume. The words of similar meaning spoken later to all disciples (Jn 20:23) and before this to the disciples and the church (Mt 18:16-19) may reach more deeply than we think.

The human involvement on the deepest level in the execution of the plan of salvation is no doubt real. It charges man with the most serious responsibilities and obligations. Man is under the mandate of God. However, the Holy Spirit is the divine Paraclete. In the final end and in the ultimate sense, the execution, administration and actualization of the divine plan of salvation rest with the authority, power and wisdom of the Holy Spirit. This is in perfect keeping with the total tenor of the Scriptures. It is clearly evident from the book of Acts and fully acknowledged by the apostles. They did not think of themselves as initiators, executors and administrators of world evangelism or world missions. Rather, they knew themselves to be temples of the Holy Spirit, a royal priesthood, the agents of the divine Paraclete who was residing in them to execute God's plan of salvation.

PENTECOST AND MISSIONS

Without entering upon a full interpretation of the meaning and significance of Pentecost, we can say that central to the event of Pentecost is the creation of a "body" or a "temple" for the Holy Spirit to actualize the plan of salvation.

A unique twofold mystic-realistic relationship characterizes the Holy Spirit. He is uniquely related to the written Word of God. Thus we are born again of the Spirit, and we are born again by the Word of God; we are sanctified by the Holy Spirit, and we are sanctified by the Word of God. No regeneration takes place apart from the Holy Spirit, and no regeneration is experienced apart from the Word of God. This must be held tenaciously and emphasized repeatedly in an age when mystic movements make themselves felt all over the world. The Holy Spirit is also peculiarly related to the believer. He regenerates, baptizes, indwells, seals, fills, enables and uses the believer to accomplish His purpose.

The believer individually and the church corporately become the temple of the Holy Spirit (1 Co 3:16; 2 Co 6:16; Eph 2:21-22). He resides upon the earth in the individual believer and in the church of Jesus Christ. The church thus is the habitation of God through the Spirit (Eph 2:22). This temple, which is also the body of Christ, is to serve specific purposes in the world through the Holy Spirit. "We are his [God's]workmanship, created in Christ Jesus unto good works, which God hath before ordained that we should walk in them" (Eph 2:10).

There was purpose in Pentecost. A new temple of living stones was being built; a new priesthood was being consecrated; a new creation came about; a new man was born to serve as an embodiment and as an agent for the Holy Spirit to actualize the divine plan of salvation for our age.

Through this new creation the Holy Spirit was to execute and accomplish the purposes of God. Though the ministries of the church áre manifold, no small portion of it must be devoted to world evangelism because the Holy Spirit is the Spirit of witness, restraint and conviction in the world.

The superintendency of the Holy Spirit in missions is evident from the book of Acts. Here it is also evident that the Holy Spirit was not only resident in but also President of the early church. When this happens there is a mighty all-out horizontal push in world evangelism.

From the book of Acts we note that the Holy Spirit is the Initiator, Motivator and Superintendent of world missions. All major steps of expansion were divinely initiated and divinely inspired. The Holy Spirit was the supreme Strategist. On the day of Pentecost He made the message universally understood by enabling the apostles to speak in the various languages present on that occasion in Jerusalem.

1. The Holy Spirit initiated the "leap across religious boundaries" and sent Philip to Samaria, Peter to Cornelius, the saints of Cyprus and Cyrene to Antioch, and Paul and Barnabas into the wide mission fields. The Holy Spirit clearly selected His unique messengers to carry forth the gospel of God. He confirmed the choice of the twelve on the day of Pentecost and in the days following that event, and He selected His "chosen vessel" for a specific ministry and gospel interpretation.

2. The Holy Spirit equipped His servants in an extraordinary way with great power and boldness to speak forth the message of God in season and out of season.

3. The Holy Spirit endued His servants to persevere in the midst of great obstacles, severe opposition, and brutal persecution. He sustained them in their martyrdom.

4. The Holy Spirit specifically guided His servants to the areas and people of special ministries while forbidding them to enter other fields.

5. The Holy Spirit graciously guided His servants in resolving grave tensions and problems.

6. The Holy Spirit mobilized the total body of the Lord Jesus Christ in the great task of evangelizing, inscribing into His church the principle of universal priesthood and the mutually sustaining body — life and service principles which can be neglected only at an awful cost to the world and grave peril to the church.

7. The Holy Spirit prescribed the major means by which the gospel must grow around the world and by which churches are born into the world as living witnesses to the Christ who died on Calvary's cross and triumphantly rose again. These means include the proclamation of the gospel, the energetic and dynamic witnessing of the saints to the meaning of the gospel in their personal lives, the prevailing prayers of the churches, the sacrifice of the saints and their will-

ingness to suffer for the gospel of Jesus Christ, and the expectation of divine interventions and powerful manifestations of God.

8. The Holy Spirit graciously guided in the formation of the churches and provided for the younger churches by inspiring the apostles to prepare an extensive and abiding literature for the guidance of the churches in their mission, the preservation of the message, the Christian way of life, and the apostolic principles and exemplary ways of ministries in accomplishing the purpose of God.

Thus the Holy Spirit as the divine Paraclete remained and does remain in charge of the divine plan of salvation. Here we find our rest in the midst of all confusion and bewilderment. He will not and He cannot fail in His mission. His fullness and pleasure can be enjoyed only in a joyous collaboration with and humble submission to His will and purpose. In His fullness we find the dynamic of world missions.

MISSIONARY DYNAMIC AND THE GOSPEL OF GOD

Earlier I referred to the mystic-realistic relationship which exists between the Holy Spirit and the Word of God. This we must firmly grasp. On the one hand, it will save us from a vague and subjective mysticism, and on the other hand, from a dry and lifeless orthodoxy which rests upon the letter without the life inherent in the Word.

Having considered the Holy Spirit, we naturally turn to the Word of God and particularly to the gospel of God as the power of God in missions.

Quietness of heart and discipline of mind are required to listen carefully to the Word of God and discern the voice of God. The gospel of God is not man's thought about God or man addressing God, it is God's gift to man in Christ Jesus, His only begotten Son. In it God addresses man in love and kindness. In it God offers to man his absolute and total restoration, heaven's eternal glory and life, and fellowship with Him for evermore.

We turn therefore to a study of the gospel of God as procured for us in Christ Jesus and revealed for us in the written Word of God.

THE GOSPEL OF GOD

The gospel of God constitutes the basic subject of New Testament revelation. It is God's final message to mankind.

The gospel as a divine commitment. The words *committed* and *commitment* loom high in Pauline vocabulary throughout his epistles. Paul knew himself to be committed to the Lord. He was conscious of being a bondslave of Jesus Christ. The apostle speaks of himself as a prisoner of Jesus Christ for the nations (Eph 3:1). This was true in a physical and in a purposive sense.

However, this is not his deepest usage of the word *commitment.* The apostle knew of a commitment made by God. He was conscious that the glorious gospel of the blessed God had been committed to his trust (1 Ti 1:11; Titus 1:3; 1 Th 2:4; cf. Ro 1:1-7; Gal 1:11-12; 2:7). Paul had been made a steward of the mystery of God (1 Co 4:1; 9:17). In this commitment lie the authority, greatness and urgency of his apostleship.

The content of the divine commitment is "good news" or "gospel." It is a message, not an institution, an organization — not even a dynamic movement. It is a message known as "good news." This we need to realize, and this we need to define more exactly and according to the Bible. What exactly is the gospel, the message committed unto us?

The gospel of God. While I cannot follow C. H. Dodd in his analysis of apostolic proclamation, we are indebted to him for an important principle of New Testament studies and preaching.[*] He established the fact that we can find in the New Testament a fundamental message, the kerygma, and a superstructure built upon this foundation, the Didache. To make the division as clear-cut as Dodd suggests seems impossible and inadvisable. However, the principle of duality in structure within a unity of function seems to be present in the New Testament. There is a foundational proclamation, a message which Paul terms uniquely "the gospel," the "gospel of God," and "my gospel." This is the good news of God for modern man, the message of evangelism which must be proclaimed among all nations for the purpose of evangelizing mankind. The basic elements of this committed message are outlined in several passages in the New Testament. Its principal characteristic is a "Person" rather than an idea, an impersonal ideal, a system of thought or a system of practices. The Christian proclamation centers in a Person — the Lord Jesus Christ. Thus the apostles preached Christ the Lord. In this proclamation, Christianity is unique. Hinduism preaches a fourfold *path* to salvation; Shintoism upholds the *way* of the gods; Buddhism announces the *way* of the elders with its *Eightfold Path;* Taoism makes known the *way* of heaven; Islam teaches the *Five Pillars* as the way of salvation. In contrast to the way, Christianity proclaims a Person. And in contrast to a way of duty or performances, the gospel invites people into a life of relationships. *Person-to-person relationship lies at the heart of Christianity.*

The gospel of Christ. In keeping with the above principle, Christ presents Himself rather than a system of thought in His message. The great "I am's" in the gospel of John are unequaled in the religions of the world. No founder of any religion has ever placed himself so completely into the center of His message and movement as Christ did. No man has ever said, "I am the light of the world . . . , I am the door . . . , I am the way, the truth, and the Life: no man cometh unto the Father, but by me . . . , I am the resurrection, and the life: he that believeth in me, though he were dead, yet shall he live." These are astounding — almost incredible — claims. Yet, the man Christ Jesus made them. He is absolutely Christocentric in His claims and presentation. No mortal has ever said, "I and my Father are one . . . , the Father is in me, and I in him . . . , he that hath seen me hath seen the Father . . ., all power [authority] has been given unto me in heaven and in earth . . . , the Father judgeth no man, but hath committed all judgment unto the Son: that all men should honour the Son, even as they honour the Father" (Jn 8:12; 10:9; 14:6; 11:25; 10:30, 38; 14:9; Mt 28:18; Jn 5:22-23).

This person-centricity is continued by the apostles. Thus Peter declares, "Neither is there salvation in any other: for there is none other *name* [not way] under heaven given among men, whereby we must be saved" (Ac 4:12). Paul, too, joins in and announces: "But of him [God] are ye in Christ Jesus, who of God is made unto us wisdom, and righteousness, and sanctification, and redemption (1 Co 1:30). Jesus is more than the sum total of all Greek philosophy and culture (wisdom), Roman law and jurisprudence (righteousness), Jewish religiosity and legalism (sanctification) and mystery salvation (redemption).

In Him "are hid all the treasures of wisdom and knowledge. . . . For in him dwelleth all the fulness [the *pleroma*] of the Godhead bodily." Therefore, in Him are ye perfect (Col 2:3, 9-10). Such is in part the Christocentricity of the New Testament in relation to salvation.

Rightly or wrongly, and we believe rightly, the writers of the New Testament put a Person, the Person known as Jesus Christ the Lord, into the center of all salvation. He is the hub and the heart of it. He procured it, He mediates it, He perfects it in us. Therefore He invites, "Come unto me, all ye that labour and are heavy laden, and I will give you rest" (Mt 11:28). The gospel according to the New Testament finds its source, content, meaning and glory in a Person, the Lord Jesus Christ. It also categorically declares that apart from Him there exists no salvation (Jn 3:36; 14:6; Ac 4:12; 1 Jn 5:11-12). Christ Himself is our life, our peace, our hope.

THE CHRIST WHO IS THE GOSPEL

The Person who stands at the center of the Christian gospel is beautifully portrayed in the gospel records and clearly defined and fully expounded in Acts and in the epistles. He is not merely existential. He is, above all, scriptural. He is word-mediated.

It is not my intention here to expound and defend biblical Christology as such. A *fourfold emphasis,* however, must be made to grasp the meaning and depth of the Christian gospel. Jesus Christ who is the center and heart of the Christian proclamation is presented to us in biblical revelation as *God.* He is none other than the eternal God, designated as the Son or the Son of God to indicate His official position within the Godhead and His metaphysical (not physical) relationship to the Father and to the Holy Spirit. The whole gospel of John and the major part of the Colossian epistle are devoted to the exposition and defense of Christ's eternal, unqualified and underived deity. Paul expresses his deity concept in designating Christ as Lord and in the Lord Jesus Christ. As God He is worshiped and honored by all believers of the Bible.

On the opposite pole is the doctrine of the incarnation of Christ which sets forth the fact that in Christ, God became true man. Throughout the New Testament His humanity is assumed and/or asserted. He is the Son of man, and the man Christ Jesus. The biblical doctrine of salvation demands both aspects, the deity and humanity in Christ Jesus. Only the God-man can save.

Thus deity and humanity are united in one Person. Humbly but firmly, we confess with Paul, "And without controversy great is the mystery of godliness: God was manifest in the flesh, and God was in Christ, reconciling the world unto himself" (1 Ti 3:16; 2 Co 5:19). While we cannot fathom the mystery, we believe it and we proclaim it.

However, the New Testament does not stop here. It adds to the mystery of divine incarnation the death-resurrection event. In fact, the incarnation was for the purpose of the death-resurrection event. Christ explicitly declares, "The Son of man came not to be ministered unto, but to minister, and to give his life a ransom for many" (Mk 10:45). And again, "Thus it is written, and thus it behooved Christ to suffer, and to rise from the dead the third day" (Lk 24:46).

Paul is the great exponent as well as the foremost herald of the gospel. Succinctly he declares, "Moreover, brethren, I declare unto you the gospel which I preached unto you, which also ye have received, and wherein ye stand; by which also ye are saved, if ye keep in memory what I preached unto you, unless ye have believed in vain. For I delivered unto you first of all that which I also received, how that Christ died for our sins according to the scriptures; and that he was buried, and that he rose again the third day according to the scriptures" (1 Co 15:1-4). Previous to this and in the same epistle he declares, "I determined not to know any thing among you, save Jesus Christ, and him crucified" (1 Co 2:2). Another significant summary is given in this epistle: "I have laid the foundation . . . other foundation can no man lay than that is laid, which is Jesus Christ" (1 Co 3:10-11).

A very similar and closely related message is conveyed in Romans 1:1-6 and Philippians 2:5-11. In both passages the incarnation and the cross-resurrection event are central.

The deity-humanity mystery and the cross-resurrection event are inseparably linked in the foundational message of the New Testament, the gospel of God and the gospel of our salvation.

REPENTANCE-FAITH AND THE GOSPEL OF GOD

This message is not presented only as a historic event, as glorious as that may be. Paul informs us that this took place "according to the scriptures," that is, in keeping with revelation which unfolds the loving and eternal purpose of God. Paul continues to inform us that the cross-resurrection event was for our sins. It was purposive, redemptive, substitutionary, adequate, final, perfect, and with eternal effects. Graciously and decisively God intervened on our behalf and dealt effectively and conclusively with sin in its guilt, filth and power complex. "Once for all" is written in bold letters over this event. Never again will the Lamb of God be slain because of sin or by the hands of sinners. We are sanctified through the offering of the body of Jesus Christ once for all. The gospel, therefore, includes the proclamation of God's gracious offer of forgiveness of sins made possible because Christ "was delivered for our offences, and was raised again for our justification" (Ro 4:25). The preaching of forgiveness of sins belong to the foundational Christian proclamation. This is in perfect accord with the words of Christ in His commission to the disciples, where he declares "that repentance and remission of sins should be preached in his name among all nations" (Lk 24:47). Similar are Paul's words when he writes, "In whom we have redemption through his blood, the forgiveness of sins, according to the riches of his grace" (Eph 1:7; cf. Col 1:14).

Forgiveness of sins, however, is organically related to repentance and faith or faith and repentance. We dare not neglect the preaching of repentance and faith. This is part of the gospel message. Repentance and faith are two tremendously important relational concepts. They relate man in his attitude to and separation from sin on the one hand, and appropriation of and commitment to Christ on the other. There is no need to debate whether repentance precedes faith or vice versa. In the New Testament this is a matter of emphasis in preaching rather than a chronology or even logic of theology.

As we turn back to Paul's classic passage on the gospel in 1 Corinthians 15:1-4, we need to note that Paul emphasizes both the subjective as well as the objective aspects. Thus he speaks of *receiving* the gospel in verses 1, 2 and 3, and of the objective aspect in verses 3 and 4. We need to preach both emphases.

It is of great importance to hold together in our proclamation the objective-subjective aspects of the gospel of our salvation. Here is another unique quality of the Christian message. Ethnic religions emphasize mainly the subjective aspects, while Islam and present-day Judaism depend principally upon the objective aspect of their religion.

But Christianity, rightly understood and correctly presented, holds together the objective-subjective aspects without fusing or confusing them, minimizing or neglecting either aspect. We must keep in mind that the emphasis of the objective to the neglect of the subjective will lead us into dead orthodoxy, while an overemphasis of the subjective will lead us into vague and indefinite mysticism. Such balance of emphasis is not synergism, it is evangelicalism and biblicism.

In his fine book, *Christianity Rightly So Called,* Samuel G. Craig devotes a lengthy chapter to this important aspect of Christianity.[5] It is a most illuminating discussion on a balance in the gospel proclamation. The preaching of divine, sovereign grace and human moral responsibility is kept in perfect balance throughout the Scriptures. This equilibrium must be retained if we are to be truly evangelical and effective.

THE GOSPEL OF GOD DEFINED AND DELINEATED

In the light of the above biblical facts, we are now ready to define and delineate the gospel in the following manner: The gospel concerns itself supremely with a Person, the Lord Jesus Christ, and man's relationship to Him.

This Person is presented to us in the deity-humanity mystery and in the cross-resurrection event. These are the four dimensions of the Person apart from which Christ ceases to be the Saviour of mankind. This is the objective aspect of the gospel.

In order to experience Jesus Christ as Saviour, man must be related to Him in a repentance-faith attitude, and he must appropriate the forgiveness of sins made possible by the sacrificial and substitutionary death and triumphant resurrection of Jesus Christ. Only as man becomes related to Christ by a living, personal faith does the potential Saviour become the actual Saviour. Only thus does man pass from spiritual death into life eternal, transferred from the kingdom of darkness into the kingdom of His dear Son. Only thus does he become a child of God and a member of the household of God. Without it man remains under the wrath of God, a stranger to the promises of God in Christ Jesus and an unreconciled enemy of God (Jn 1:12; 3:36; 5:24; Col 1:13; Eph 2:12, 19; 2 Co 5:20).

Thus we preach Christ Jesus the Lord, the God-man crucified and risen. And we proclaim the forgiveness of sins available to all mankind by repentance from sin and faith in Christ Jesus.

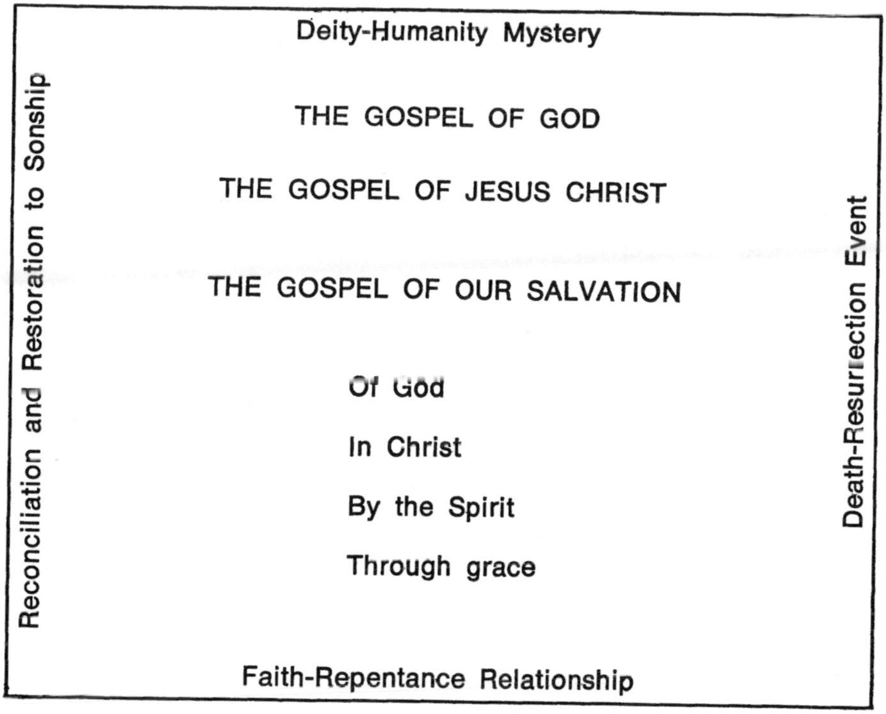

Fig. 6. The Gospel

This is the gospel, the "good news" of God to man. The gospel is also described in dynamic terms:

"The gospel is the power of God unto salvation" (Ro 1:16)

"The gospel of the grace of God" (Ac 20:24)

"The gospel of your salvation" (Eph 1:13)

"The gospel of peace" (Eph 6:15)

"The everlasting gospel" (Rev 14:6)

From our definition and delineation of the gospel emerge several facts which need to be underscored:

First, the gospel is divine in origin and content. It anchors in the God who is love. It originated in the heart of God. Indeed, the gospel is the love of God spilling over in fullness and glory for the benefit and salvation of mankind. Twice the Bible declares: "God is love" (1 Jn 4:8, 16). The height and depth of this declaration are difficult to fathom and impossible to define adequately, yet attempts must be made to do so. Thus Edgar Mullins writes,

Love may be defined as the self-imparting quality in the divine nature which leads God to seek the highest good and the most complete possession of His creatures. Love in its highest form is a relation between intelligent moral and free beings. God's love to man seeks to awaken a responsive love of man to God. In its final form, love between God and man will mean their complete and unrestrained self-giving to each other, and the complete possession of each by the other.[6]

The perfection of God's love is seen in the redeeming activity of Christ in a twofold way: (1) In His capacity for sacrifice. (Thus we are told: "For God so loved . . . that he *gave* . . . . God *commendeth* his love toward us . . . . Behold, what manner of love the Father hath *bestowed* upon us. . . ." Love cannot be separated from sacrifice.) (2) In the degree of love expressed by this sacrifice. He gave His only begotten Son.

This is love, indeed! This is love poured out! This is love bestowed! Wherever the gospel is proclaimed, the love of God is exalted. The gospel and the God who is love cannot be separated. The latter begets the former, and the former glorifies the latter.

As the gospel was begotten in the love of the Father, it bestows love and in turn begets love. Thus we love Him because He first loved us.

On the other hand, only as the gospel is proclaimed in love and motivated by genuine and sacrificial love can it really and fully unfold its divine character.

Second, the gospel is distinctive. The Bible does not know salvation apart from Jesus Christ the Lord, the deity-humanity mystery, and the cross-resurrection event. Jesus Christ is emphatically set forth as the solitary Saviour of mankind, without rival and equal in the sight of God and in the experience of man. The universal *Logos* salvation theory is an extrabiblical invention and convenience of man, a theological accommodation which is not revelational but rational. Good intentions are not necessarily also sound theological premises. The Bible knows no "alternative Saviour."

Neither does the Bible teach a *Kultur-Christentum* (Ritschl) which has dominated a great deal of Western ideology, and missiology. It motivated men in their strenuous efforts to "establish the kingdom of God" or "build the kingdom of Jesus Christ." Both liberals and evangelicals became enamored by this philosophy. Western civilization became practically equated with Christian culture and with the Christian gospel. It was taken for granted that as the gospel spread and rooted itself in the different parts of the globe, the world would become more and more Western (Christian). This philosophy expressed itself most fully in postmillennialism. The experiences of the past half century have thoroughly exploded and discredited this philosophy. Elements to it continue, however, even as does the "fallout" of an atomic explosion.

The "social gospel" philosophy must not be confused with *Kultur-Christentum*. While it is outwardly related by goals to this philosophy, it is of a different origin and has different roots.

This leads me to consider some most significant distinctions between the gospel and historic Christendom with its institutions and creeds, the gospel and its related cultural garment, and the gospel and Western mentality.

The Supracreedal Character of the Gospel. The gospel of Jesus Christ must not be confused with historic Christianity or Christendom as an ecclesiastical establishment. It must not be identified with the ancient ecumenical creeds, with more recent confessions of faith of various denominations, with systems of theology or with schools of Christian thought. All of these are the result of human deductions. Their formulations are relative. They are conditioned by occasions and immediate circumstances and are filled with accretions from the environment into which the gospel was originally planted and in which it has been growing. In each environment, human ambitions and speculations have been added. The accumulations of theological, philosophical and cultural factors have often beclouded the gospel and have often resulted in grave distortions of the divine message. Serious errors have crept in to dilute the gospel or to cover up its divine nature and purpose. Institutions have sought to institutionalize the gospel, to codify it in canon law, to capsule it in nicely formulated creeds, or to enshrine it in beautiful establishment. The supernatural nature of the gospel, however, has refused to be enshrined even in the most grandiose accouterments, be they in Jerusalem, Rome, London or anywhere else. As the power and wisdom of God, the gospel is too great and glorious to be codified, enshrined or neatly packaged. It has asserted its divine nature again and again by its great liberating power and broken through all humanly imposed limitations to live out its full divine character according to revelation as deposited in the Bible.

The Supracultural Character of the Gospel. The gospel is not a purely historical phenomenon. Though operating in history, it is not of history, as I have said earlier. Here I assert that the gospel is not an ethnic product. While it operates *in* culture, it is not *of* culture. It is in but also beyond culture. It makes and molds culture while at the same time judging culture. It is both *for* culture and *against* culture. It is the dynamic of culture and it is the most serious check on culture. The gospel is supracultural because it is supernatural in origin, nature, purpose, destiny and goal. Ecclesiastical and religious orders, as orders, are human institutions. They may be a robe in which the gospel clothes itself, but they do not belong to the nature of the gospel. Therefore, we are not interested in exporting ecclesiastical, theological or religious patterns and forms, be they Occidental or Oriental, Latin or African. We are commissioned to proclaim the gospel of our Lord Jesus Christ which transcends culture and regionalism. The judging, healing and enriching supracultural message with the power and wisdom of God will add a new dimension to any culture that recognizes Christ as Saviour and Lord.

Lest I should be misunderstood, let it also be said that wherever Christ enters a culture, it will not remain undisturbed. His presence is the divine transformation. He is the power of God. He is wisdom, righteousness, sanctification and redemption. Christ will leave no relationship and culture unaffected. While He will not endorse and sanctify all things, neither will He destroy all things. He makes all things *new*.

The late Dr. Kenneth Latourette has done the Christian people a great service by pointing out in his seven volumes on the *Expansion of Christianity* that the gospel has made a tremendous impact upon any society and culture which has embraced it, but nowhere has the gospel triumphed so completely that it did not experience the impact of the culture into which it came. There always has been this reciprocity to a lesser or greater degree. Because of this, we are compelled constantly to go back to the original sources of the gospel of Jesus Christ to understand the true nature and meaning of the gospel. The New Testament remains our unfailing authority and guide in all matters of doctrine and all principles for faith, life and ministries.

Marshall McLuhan well says: "When Christianity becomes environmental it loses that inner face necessary for that transforming power, that resonance that occurs between the little minority and the great big dark ground. When that bigger ground relationship loses its proportion, then the Church by becoming ground becomes a monster. When the bigger ground emerges you have a monster."[7]

The Gospel and Western Mentality. The Christian position, emphasis and insistence upon the uniqueness and soleness of the Christian gospel have been falsely attributed to Western mentality and religious imperialism. Such accusations, however, have resulted from unscientific and unhistorical perspective. Historically, this mentality roots in the Bible and originated with Palestinians. Christianity in its historical appearance is a non-Western religion, one of more than ten living world religions which spring from Asiatic soil. No one is more dogmatic on the uniqueness, finality, absoluteness, inclusiveness and exclusiveness of the Christian gospel than Jesus Christ Himself, along with the original apostles, especially Paul and the writer of the epistles to the Hebrews. Here Christ in all His bounty, beauty and fullness is presented as the unparalleled and peerless Lord, Saviour and High Priest.

We do not claim this gospel to be our invention, discovery or product. No credit whatever is due us because of the greatness and uniqueness of the gospel. It is not of Western origin and does not belong to us. It finds its origin and source in the God of all mankind. It is God's gift to all men. Thus it belongs to God and becomes the possession of all who in faith appropriate it as their own. No man can boast before God or pride himself in his position and spiritual possession. In all humility, however, we believe the gospel and joyfully and boldly proclaim it, calling upon all men to believe God and share in the salvation in Christ. We do not export religion. We are heralds of the gospel of Christ, believing that there is no salvation apart from Jesus Christ our Lord.

Third, the Gospel Is Relational. A further fact emerging from our definition of the gospel is the truth that *salvation procured in Christ Jesus becomes actual only in a living, personal repentance-faith relationship to Christ.* Only thus is man born anew and made a member of the household of God. Emphatically we are told that "as many as received Him to them gave He authority to become the children of God" (Jn 1:12). Similar statements could be multiplied greatly. The doctrine of faith is a prominent doctrine in the Bible. It cannot be disassociated from salvation.

The Bible knows of no salvation apart from Christ and of no salvation experience apart from a personal repentance-faith relationship to Him. The emphasis upon faith as the response of man to God in trust, commitment and appropriation is uniform throughout the Scriptures. Clearly the Bible declares, "But without faith it is impossible to please him: for he that cometh to God must believe that he is, and that he is a rewarder of them that diligently seek him" (Heb 11:6). Neither without Christ nor without faith can there be a salvation experience in the true biblical and spiritual sense. The salvation of God is bound up unalterably with a Person (Jesus Christ the God-man crucified and risen) and with a personal relationship to that Person (repentance-faith).

It adds up to a simple formula in dynamic relationships expressed in the negative: No Christ — no salvation; no repentance-faith — no salvation. Never does the Bible deviate from this order and principle.

THE GOSPEL OF GOD IN DISPUTE

"The Gospel in Dispute" (Perry) — such is the present-day state of affairs. The Christian position has been branded as religious imperialism and theological biogotry, and has been called by many other names. However, name-calling has never yet altered a fact or changed a truth. Christ claims absolute uniqueness in kind and quality. He is different and superior in degree and quantity. There is a qualitative difference too. The Christian gospel is unique, distinct, complete, perfect, adequate and final. It is the "non-mixer" (Hammer) on the one hand and the judge of all religions on the other hand. We are faced by "The Inevitable Choice" (Soper). "Jesus Compared" (Braden) compels me to make my choice.

Christ is the decisive dividing line. Whether the ethnic religions of the world contain truth and beauty is not the question. Impersonal truth by itself is rendered impotent by the sinfulness of man. Personality restoration, health and transformation are found only in person-to-person relationships. Man needs spiritual, social and moral healing.

He needs wholeness. Abstract truth cannot accomplish this. One sinner cannot restore another sinner, as one drowning man cannot rescue another drowning man. It is Christ, the Physician of God, the God-man who triumphed over death and brought life and immortality to light, who can save and make man whole. The question, therefore, is not one of truth and beauty in comparative religions. We ask whether Christ in the mystery of His deity-humanity and death-resurrection event is present. No religion, not even Christianity as religion apart from Christ, can forgive sins or bestow life. Religion cannot bring fulfillment to life, save man from his present guilt, filth and power of sin, or rescue him from the judgment and condemnation to come. Only Christ can do this. Christianity as a religion is not a competitor to other religions. Christ as Saviour, Lord and God is the rival of all other gods, whoever and wherever they may be. He is the solitary Saviour and Lord who inhabits a solitary throne in salvation and judgment.

In his beautiful little booklet on *The Uniqueness of Jesus Christ,* Max Warren presents:

1. The uniqueness of Jesus Christ as a revelation of the nature of God.

2. The uniqueness of Jesus Christ as a revelation of man as man is meant to be.

3. The uniqueness of Jesus Christ as a revelation of what man is, which is something very different from what he is meant to be.

4. The uniqueness of Jesus Christ as a revelation of God's trust in man.[8]

This is marvelous indeed. However, the presentation is incomplete and falls short of the fullness of biblical proclamation. We must add still more.

5. Jesus Christ as the unique one in lordship. He is the Lord of lords and the King of kings.

6. Jesus Christ as the unique one in saviorhood. He is the total Saviour, the Saviour of mankind and the individual in the totality of his being and in the totality of his relationships. He makes man *whole.*

7. Jesus Christ as the unique one in His enthronement. He is seated at the right hand of God, sharing the very throne with the Father (Rev 3:21).

The Word assures us that before Him "every knee shall bow, of things in heaven, and things in earth, and things under the earth" (Phil 2:10). In such an announcement the "good news of God" becomes "bad news" to all rival religions and gods, together with their devotees. It is incumbent upon us, therefore, to lift up Christ in order that all men everywhere might see Him now in His beauty, fullness, saving ability and graciousness. We must do this as much as is humanly possible, unencumbered by human tradition, cultural accretions and ecclesiasticism. The world needs to see Christ and not us in our institutionalism and culture.

THE GOSPEL OF GOD AND NON-CHRISTIAN RELIGIONS

The battle is on. For many it is all but over because they have submitted. The serious struggle and the strenuous search for a biblical and/or Christian answer to establish an adequate, just and satisfactory relationship between the gospel of God and the ethnic religions of mankind has been long. Men like Ram Mohun Roy, Sir Sarepalli Radhakrishnan, Mohandas Karamchand Gandhi, Masaharu Anesaki, Daisetz Teitaro Suzuki, Maulavi Saiyid Amir Ali, Mauliv Muhammed Ali — to name but a few — have fought bravely and logically to maintain their equality if not superiority to the Christian tradition. It cannot be said that these men are ignorant of Christianity, for they know its history, doctrines and claims. But they have entrenched themselves well in their own positions.

I cannot enter into a lengthy discussion of this most complicated and urgent subject, for this would require a volume in itself. Neither do I believe that this is the place to elaborate or debate the various answers and philosophies which have grown up around the subject and which at times have become quite belligerent. Some have sought to impose themselves upon missiology.

Some views which can be mentioned here are the "radical displacement" theory of many ultraconservatives; the "fulfillment" theory of J. N. Farquhar, H. H. Farmer and successors of liberalism (this view has also held captive some evangelicals); the "Discontinuity" theory of neoorthodoxy, expounded vigorously and most completely by Hendrik Kraemer and his school; the "Logos" philosophy of Justin Martyr, recently eloquently expounded by A. C. Bouquet and followers; the "*Heilsgeschichte* — universal history of religious consciousness approach" of Ernest Benz; the recent writings of E. C. Dewick, Edmund Perry, Stephen Neill; the ultranaturalistic "Reconception" theory of William Hocking and the related writings of Arnold Toynbee; the "Justice Concept" approach of Paul Tillich; the most recent "Dialogue" method which has captivated the imagination, mind and affection of countless philosopher-theologians but not, however, the ground-level missionaries. The latter are too close to the scene and too deeply involved in the reality struggle to embrace such views.

I find two radical weaknesses in the foregoing theories. First, they are basically philosophical rather than theological. They remind me of a Renaissance gospel more than a Reformation gospel in the struggle of the sixteenth-century life-and-death battle for Christian survival. They are man-to-man encounters rather than God-and-man encounter. While there are some noble exceptions, the general run is along that line. Second, they suffer from a nonbiblical, nonexegetical anemia. While this cannot be said of E. C. Dewick and Stephen Neill in their writings, no thoroughgoing exegesis characterizes any of these writings and debates, as the Jerusalem and Madras reports clearly indicate, and the almost countless writings in the debate verify. There is little of "What saith the Scriptures?" in their writings. Karl Hartenstein and a few others with him constitute noble exceptions.

In a biblical theology of missions we are supremely interested in the biblical attitude toward the nonrevelational or ethnic religions of the nations — religions other than those originating in and from the revelation of God as deposited in the Bible.

From the beginning let it be stated that there is room for differences of opinion and exposition of single passages. Charity, tolerance and Spirit-illumination must qualify us to find our bearing in these delicate matters. We must remain within the framework of the Bible. In no way dare we go beyond the Scriptures, but neither dare we fail to take note of their full scope of information. Honesty, openness and humility are needed to discover what God says about the religions of mankind, always keeping in mind that every man cherishes his religion as sacred.

I believe that the following list approximates a summary of biblical ideology, sentiments and verdict.

1. The Bible fully recognizes the existence of nonbiblical reli-

gions and considers them operating forces in the history of mankind. The reader need only consider the numerous references to idols, images and gods in the Old and New Testaments and their influence upon the people.

2. The Bible accepts the fact that man is an incurably and supremely religious being, a being created in the image of God. The Bible takes religion for granted and does not in specific terms explain its "origin." Religion appears on its first pages as fellowship between God and man in the Garden of Eden — God speaking to man, placing man under a mandate and expecting obedience. It was a religion in relationship, fellowship and collaboration, uniting God and man in his mind, purpose and work. At the gates of Eden we find religion in practice and ritual. The latter elements were added by the command of God because Abel offered his sacrifice by faith (Heb 11:4), and "faith cometh by hearing, and hearing by the word of God" (Ro 10:17).

From the gates of Eden, religion flows as a stream within the culture of man. Religion provides a basic motive, integrating force, direction and meaning (or lack of it) to life and history.

3. The Bible is silent about the origin of religion as an organized institution with its officialdom and practices. It is also silent about the "origin" of idols and idolatry. The numerous references to this extrabiblical practice (Young lists 127 references in total in his analytical concordance of the Bible) testify to its prevalence, distribution and variance in form and practice. It has become a tremendous and dangerous force within the total movement of mankind.

4. The Bible nowhere ascribes intrinsic spiritual values to any of the nonbiblical religions, values which it seeks to preserve or to assimilate in order to enrich or perfect itself. In the numerous references to idols and other systems of worship, there is not one positive statement presented. In fact, the names and characteristics ascribed to idols and images lead to the opposite conclusion.

Girdlestone in his Synonyms of the Old Testament informs us,

> Twelve different Hebrew words are represented by the English word "idol." Some of them point to the fact that an idol is a thing of naught; others are significant of the terror with which the worshiper of the false gods is inspired, or of the aversion with which the living and true God regards such objects; others again, refer to

the shape of the idol, to the material of which it is made, or to the position in which it is placed.⁹

Such descriptive words as iniquity, vanity, nothingness, terror, abomination, labor, grief, horror and the cause of trembling are used to characterize idols and idolatry. Not one complimentary word about the "aesthetic" or religious value of idols is found in the Bible. Neither is idol worship ever accepted as an indirect worship of the true God who is the being and living reality "behind" all idolatry.

The Bible knows nothing of such confusion. Indeed, Paul relates such worship to demons rather than to the living God (1 Co 10:19-21) and raises the serious question: "And what agreement hath the temple of God with idols?" (2 Co 6:16). In simple words, they have nothing in common, while in Revelation 9:20, idolatry is aligned with demon worship. Such charges and attitudes are difficult for the modern mentality, which is conditioned to compromise and tolerance, to accept. The sharp cutting edges of distinction between the two have been worn down.

5. The Bible most definitely commands the worship of God as the only true God (Ex 20:3-5). If it is argued that this command is given to Israel, then it must be likewise accepted that the whole moral structure of the Old Testament which is built upon the foundation of ethical monotheism is also applicable only to Israel. It should, therefore, not constitute a standard for conduct and/or judgment of the surrounding nations. Such, however, is not the attitude of the Old Testament prophets. Their thunderous voices ring out alike against Israel and the nations. They know of no double standard.

It is evident from the pages of the Bible that both the Old Testament and the New Testament consider all other types of worship as false, all other "gods" as rival gods, and all idolatry as sinful and harmful. They are an abomination to God and a terror and grief to mankind.

6. The Bible breathes the spirit of exclusiveness, intolerance, hostility and condemnation toward all forms of idolatry and worship of gods outside of Jehovah Elohim, the God and Father of our Lord Jesus Christ. The Bible does not sustain the philosophy of peaceful coexistence within the sphere of worship. The frequent destruction of idols and the uprooting of idolatry within Israel find God's approval, though the Bible does not enjoin physical warfare against

idolatry outside of Palestine. No physical violence against idolatry is enjoined upon the people of God in the Bible. However, the messages of the prophets and apostles uncompromisingly and condemningly ring out against this evil of all evils, the evil which seems to be the root and trunk from which all branches of evil feed. Because this is so, the final destiny of all idolaters shall be "in the lake which burneth with fire and brimstone" — the second death along with the cowardly, and unbelieving, and abominable, and murderers and sorcerers (Rev 21:8). In a similar manner Paul warns the believers at Corinth that the idolaters shall not inherit the kingdom of God (1 Co 6:9-10). The severity of the attitude of the Bible cannot be overemphasized.

7. The Bible condemns as "spiritual adultery" and godless apostasy all attempts of religious syncretism. Heavy judgments fell upon Israel for all attempts of religious synthesis and apostacy. The attitude of God is most dramatically manifested upon Mount Carmel when He physically and literally judged between syncretistic idolatry and worship of the true God.

8. The Bible considers the present religious status of mankind and the present form and practices of nonrevelational religions as the perversion and degeneration of an original revelation of God. Because of human sinfulness, the conscious, deliberate supression of truth, and the malicious intervention of Satan and God's judgment upon sin-loving man who loves darkness rather than light, the present situation has come about.

9. The Bible holds that the nonrevelational religions are part of that world system which is antagonistic to God, captivated by evil forces, and binding and blighting to man. No indication is found in the Bible that they are a preparation for Christ, that Christ is their fulfillment that Christianity is organically related to them and is to be built upon them. The Bible does not eliminate points of contact in the religious consciousness, institutions and expressions of man. The judging biblical attitude, however, is not against honest, sincere seekers after God and truth. Such there always have been, such there are at present, and such there will be. They form a separate chapter in the history of religion and salvation and must be dealt with separately. The Bible directs its attacks against the systems and system-builders.

The above thesis is well sustained by the theological interpretation of history by Paul and presented in Romans 1:18-25. It is a brief revelational and theological dictum of the historical record found in Genesis 1 — 11, covering the period of the racial revelation of God. It is remarkable how much of theology can be found in these eleven chapters. God indeed made Himself known to mankind, not only in creation but also in revelation. There is a continuity-discontinuity philosophy of revelation underlying biblical thinking. Originally God spoke to all men. But man, in the foolishness of his own heart, "changed the glory of the uncorruptible God into an image made like to corruptible man, and to birds, and fourfooted beasts, and creeping things." Yes, he "changed the truth of God into a lie, and worshipped and served the creature more than the Creator, who is blessed for ever."

Mankind began in monotheism. With his fall came degeneration which affected every area of life, including the religion of mankind. His one God became many gods; his one loyalty became many loyalties; his heart and mind became divided and pulled him in every direction. Man lost his God, his way, his direction, his meaning, his goal. Lostness became his condition and experience. In no other area did his lostness show up more fully than in his religious allegiances.

The evolutionary hypotheses in religion attempt to explain man's agelong climb from a vague awareness of some "otherness" to the height of ethical monotheism. Honestly, and for many years, I have searched for foundations for such hypotheses. The history of religions and anthropology offers no verifications. I am left with nothing but guesses, surmises and theories based upon shaky and unproven premises. To say the least, the theory is an importation of naturalistic accommodation. It is not founded upon verified facts or revelation.

We must guard against a simplistic interpretation of the outer phenomena and nomenclature of religion. I find no record in Genesis 1 — 11 that such was handed down from heaven to mankind "ready made." It seems more rational and scriptural to think that the outer practices, institutions and phenomena are a part of the total cultural development of mankind. Thus, from the very beginning there has been a distinction in the essential revelational message and the outer cultural garment of such a religion. This may not be so to the same degree with the religion of Israel which bears the stamp of revelation (direct and refined) in totality. However, there are *pneumena* and phenomena in all religious systems.

10. The Bible predicts the eventual and complete annihilation of all other systems of religious thought, the worship of other gods, and the ultimate and complete triumph of the worship and service of Jehovah Elohim, the Father of our Lord Jesus Christ. It looks to a time when He will be accepted and honored as the sole Lord of the universe.

Boldly the prophets forecast that "the earth shall be filled with the knowledge of the glory of the LORD, as the waters cover the sea" (Hab 2:14). Again, we are told that "He shall have dominion also from sea to sea, and from the river unto the ends of the earth" (Ps 72:8). All the nations shall constitute His inheritance, and the uttermost parts of the earth shall be His possession (Ps 2:8). Once again the prophet sees that "the LORD shall be king over all the earth: in that day shall there be one LORD, and his name one. And it shall come to pass, that every one that is left of all the nations . . . shall even go up [to Jerusalem] from year to year to worship the King, the LORD of hosts" (Zec 14:9, 16). A similar vision is seen by Isaiah in 60:1-9.

The clearest, fullest and most vivid presentation of the universal worship of the one true God is made by John in the book of Revelation. More than a chapter is devoted to the presentation. The nations are seen walking in the light of God and worshiping the true and living God because of the Lamb which is mentioned again and again (Rev 21:1 – 22:6).

Such a note of complete triumph and absolute victory is upheld by no other religion in the world. Indeed, here is the triumph of hope realized.

Thus, a Book which begins in absolute monotheism also ends in absolute monotheism. In the beginning God, and in the end God. He is the Alpha and Omega, the beginning and the ending. The risen Christ shall lead His cause in triumph until "he shall have delivered up the kingdom to God, even the Father; when he shall have put down all rule and all authority and power. And when all things shall be subdued unto him, then shall the Son also himself be subject unto him that put all things under him, that God may be *all in all*" (1 Co

15:24, 28). "For of him, and through him, and to him, are all things: to whom be glory for ever. Amen" (Ro 11:36).

11. The Bible insists on its own inclusiveness, exclusiveness, otherness and uniqueness, not only on its superiority and finality. The latter two terms are more appreciated in our present interreligious discussions because they allow for some relativity. One product may be superior to the other, yet of the same kind; it may be final, but this could be so in a series of developments. Thus to speak of Christianity in terms of superiority and finality still permits and admits the possibility of a certain organic relatedness. The Bible, however, will not admit to this, except that it relates Christianity historically, organically and revelationally to the Old Testament. Christianity claims to be the fulfillment of the latter.

The Bible makes no room for other religious systems as being related or as being legitimate substitutes or forerunners to Christianity. It simply does not relate itself to the extrabiblical religious systems, and it makes no room for them.

12. Thus the Bible claims its own incomparableness and rules out all "comparative religion" studies. It claims uniqueness of quality, totality of authority, finality in value judgments, exclusiveness of all foreign elements (syncretism), and inclusiveness of all revelation and truth. It does not argue in these matters. It confonts man with an inevitable choice. It makes life and death, heaven and hell, eternal life and eternal woe, eternal fellowship with God, and eternal separation from God depend squarely upon man's choice.

Such choice is not arbitrarily imposed; it is reasonably and intelligibly presented. God always deals with man as a moral, rational and responsible agent. Man makes his own destiny.

The Bible presents to man the most complete and comprehensive philosophical system as it relates to a rational world and life view. At the same time it gives meaning, direction and destiny to history.

The Bible is a safe guide to a sound and stable family life. Its precepts guide man to healthy personality development. It also fosters wholesome social, economic, class, racial, national and international relationships.

The Bible expounds a sound and consistent system of doctrine which is not irrational or detrimental to man's temporary and physical well-being.

The Bible offers to man what he needs most and that to which he aspires supremely, namely, forgiveness and deliverance from sin, new motivation, new and meaningful direction of life, peace, joy, power, assurance, security, and eternal life in the presence of, and fellowship with, God the Father of our Lord Jesus Christ. And all this He gives in free grace and abundance because of what God did for man in Christ Jesus and now makes real through the operation of the Holy Spirit.

Thus God calls upon us anew: "To whom then will ye liken me, or shall I be equal? saith the Holy One (Is 40:25)

THE GOSPEL OF GOD PROCLAMATION — AN EMERGENCY

Advisedly I have chosen the word *emergency* in regard to the proclamation of the gospel, rather than the word *urgency* because the latter is a relative term while the former implies crisis.

We are all acquainted with emergency situations. Emergency landings by aircraft are familiar announcements. An emergency means either a landing or a crash with all its horror and tragedy. Emergencies come upon us uninvited and challenge our strength and genius. They involve crises of life and death. When the siren breaks into the stillness of night, when flames burst from roof and windows, when firemen feverishly raise their ladders and race up into the smoke and flames, risking their own welfare and lives in order to rescue calling voices, we are aware that an emergency exists which taxes men to the utmost. Emergencies are crisis experiences.

No emergency, however, can compare with the emergency of gospel proclamation. Here we face a crisis not only of death and life but of spiritual and eternal welfare or eternal separation, destitution and death. Here, indeed, is an emergency. We need to think soberly, to realize, at least in part, the emergency into which the presence and possession of the gospel has placed us. It is an emergency of infinite significance involving the eternal bliss or misery of countless multitudes.

The emergency of gospel proclamation meets us on the pages of the Bible in several ways, two of which follow:

1. *The emergency arises out of plain statements of the Word.* Our Lord remains our pattern of life and ministry. His very presence

in the world bespeaks an emergency. The mystery of the incarnation is not something to mystify us. It was a divine *must* which the redemption of the world demanded, whatever those grounds for that demand may be. The cross is not a spectacle. It is a divine necessity and demand arising out of the very being of God. Meaningfully it illumines the character and the heart of God and demonstrates the cruelty and the awfulness of sin. A divine *must* is written over the cross.

So also were the toil and the tears. The prayers and the preaching of Christ are an essential part of the *must*. He Himself tells us, "I *must* work the works of him that sent me, while it is day: the night cometh, when no man can work" (Jn 9:4). At another occasion He remarks, "Say not ye, There are yet four months, and then cometh the harvest? Behold, I say unto you, Lift up your eyes, and look on the fields; for they are white already to harvest" (Jn 4:35). Similar words come to us elsewhere: "The harvest truly is plenteous, but the labourers are few; pray ye therefore the Lord of the harvest, that he will send forth labourers into his harvest (Mt 9:37-38).

Speaking to the point of urgency, F. D. Coggins remarks:

St. Mark makes a special point of the fact that the preaching ministry of Jesus began "after that John was put in prison" (1:14). We may detect a note of urgency here. The work must be carried on. No tyranny exercised by the State must be allowed to interfere with the proclamation of the message of God. If one is forced to drop the torch, another will pick it up.

This note of urgency is of frequent occurrence in the ministry of our Lord. It is represented by the use of the word "must" (for example Luke 2:49; Mark 8:31), where very often divine compulsion is implied. It is especially frequent in the Gospel according to St. John. "Normally," says Sir Edwyn Hoskyns, "in the fourth Gospel the verb *it is necessary* denotes a divine requirement (3:7, 14, 30; 4:20, 24; 9:4; 10:16; 12:34; 20:9) (*The Fourth Gospel*, p. 252).

We have it here in this classic first chapter of St. Mark. Jesus has been long in the council chamber of God (v. 35). He is sought and found by His friends, who tell Him of waiting crowds (vv. 36, 37). His reply is that He and they must push on to the next towns, "that I may preach there also; for to this end came I forth" (v. 38). There is an almost Johannine ring about that last phrase. Surely this is more than a geographical allusion. St. Luke (4:43) interprets it:

"for therefore was I sent." Indeed, we may well believe that these words give us an insight into our Lord's deep personal sense of mission. He was a man constrained by an urgent God-given vocation to preach.[10]

The imperative in the Great Commission reinforces this point and makes our emphasis most emphatic. The plain statements of the Word leave no choice to the obedient follower of Christ. There is a divine *must* which needs to lay hold of the Christian conscience in a new and deep way. In no uncertain terms the Lord tells us, "The gospel *must* first be published among all nations" (Mk 13:10). The evangelization of the world is confronting us and bidding us to "occupy till I come." The Christian lives in the *now* of evangelization and expectation.

This is well illustrated in the experiences of Paul, the foremost apostle to the nations. He admonishes the Corinthians, "We . . . beseech you also that ye receive not the grace of God in vain." God's own words are:

> In the hour of my favour I gave heed to you;
> On the day of deliverance I came to your aid.
> The hour of favour has *now* come; *now* I say, has
> the day of deliverance dawned (2 Co 6:1-2, NEB).

"Behold, *now* is the accepted time; behold, *now* is the day of salvation."

Now and *today* are emphatic words in the New Testament which speak of urgency, yes, even emergency. They demand action without delay. A study of Paul's life and epistles leads us to the conclusion that Paul lived at least in a threefold *now*. While these were, no doubt, in tension, they were not a contradiction in his mind. It was the *now* of world evangelization, the *now* of salvation, and the *now* of the anticipation of the return of the Lord. These theological tensions proved most creative in his life and were dynamic contributors to his missionary labors.

Whether it is the urgency of the commission, the coming night when no man can work, the great and plenteous harvest, the whitened harvest fields, the fleeting day of salvation, the imminent return of the Lord, the uncertainty of life, or the fast closing doors, there is a divine *must* involved, a must which creates an emergency from the divine point of view. Our insensitivity and hesitancy do not lessen the urgency of the case. We must *Run While the Sun Is Hot.* (W. H. Fuller). We must redeem the time for the days are evil (Eph 5:16). Delay may prove disastrous and fatal.

2. *The emergency arises out of the plight of the people.* There are blind or deceived dreamers who tell us again and again that the people are perfectly happy in their state and religion and that it is cruel and wrong to disturb and confuse them with another man's religion. Peculiarly, they do not advance such arguments against the importation of Coca Cola, Singer sewing machines, alcoholic beverages, tobacco and other evils of the Western or Eastern world.

The Bible does not thus represent the man outside of the gospel. He is not a perfectly happy creature. The lostness of man apart from Christ is much more keenly felt than it is possible to describe. Man is born with eternity in his soul. He is created for God and cannot find contentment and peace until he finds it in God. He has neither meaning nor destiny of life, neither peace nor hope. While he fears God, he yearns for Him and his heart cries out for Him. While he attempts to hide and escape from God, he seeks Him and longs for His presence, care and fellowship. He does not want God, yet he dreads to be without Him. He is man in *Widerspruch* (contradiction). The sense of loneliness, of being forsaken, of fear, guilt, dread, emptiness, lostness, insecurity and meaninglessness are all living realities in the heart and mind of the man apart from Christ.

Douglas Webster tells us, "There are two basic anxieties today: the search for security and the search for meaning."[11] Man considers himself not only in bondage of sin and superstition but also as being under the wrath of God and judgment to come. This is his natural existence. Who will ever measure the depth and meaning of Paul's words: "Remember then your former condition: . . . you were at that time separate from Christ, strangers to the community of Israel, outside God's covenants and the promise that goes with them. Your world was a world without hope and without God" (Eph 2:11-12, NEB). Apart from Christ, the world is empty of spiritual reality and value, for Christ is the sum total of all spiritual reality. He is life — abundant and eternal life. In Him are life and immortality. He is our peace, our joy, our hope. In Him are hid all the treasures of wisdom and knowledge. He is our wisdom, righteousness, sanctification and redemption. Apart from Him there are only disintegration, deterioration, destitution and death, eternal death.

The situation cannot be alleviated by offering man religion, plenty of religion. The world is filled with religion, but religion is impotent and cannot save man from his pathetic existence. It is the *no* to man in his sinful plight. Consciously or unconsciously, man cries out, "O wretched man that I am! Who shall deliver me from the body of this death?" The only answer provided is, "I thank God through Jesus Christ our Lord" (Ro 7:24-25).

It may be possible that here and there men succeed in doping themselves into religious numbness by an overdose of religious beliefs and practices. They mistake this numbness for peace and a foretaste of Nirvana. However, these would be the exception. With most people, religion is a wearisome search which never ends, never resulting in rest and peace with God. There is no such invitation in ethnic religions as we find on the lips of Christ who says, "Come unto me, all ye that labour and are heavy laden, and I will give you rest [*give* as a free and gracious gift]" (Mt 11:28). Consider the glorious message which sounded forth many hundreds of years before Christ uttered the invitation, "Ho, every one that thirsteth, come ye to the waters, and he that hath no money; come ye, buy, and eat; yea, come, buy wine and milk without money and without price" (Is 55:1). This is glorious "music" in the midst of religions' discordant works, merits and rewards.

The inadequacy of nonrevelational religions is an accepted fact in the Scriptures and is evident to Bible-believing and spiritually discerning people. It seems superfluous to argue the point. The facts of history and the testimonies of millons add their convincing language to the Bible and the Holy Spirit.

The spiritual plight of man creates an emergency which demands the speedy proclamation of the gospel among all nations and to every creature. Here is our call, our command, our rationale, our authority and our urgency. Together they constitute an overwhelming emergency.

THE GOSPEL OF GOD AND THE LOSTNESS OF MAN

The belief in life after death is so general and so deeply rooted in the nature of man that few question it as a fact. But the manner of existence after death differs greatly in interpretation. The Bible presupposes the survival of man after death, and it depicts the existence in very impressive imagery.] In terms of *quality,* it speaks of the existence after death as eternal life and eternal death; in terms of *place,* it presents to us heaven and hell — the city of God and the lake of fire; in terms of *relationship,* the Bible speaks of the presence of Christ on the one hand and being punished with everlasting destruction from the presence of the Lord on the other hand; in terms of *experience,* life after death is portrayed as entering into the joy and glory of the Lord and abiding under the wrath of God. Thus the Bible is clear and decisive in its presentation of the contrast which shall befall men.

It matters not whether the Bible uses figurative language, imagery or symbols to depict eternal verities. The fact remains that back of this imagery lies reality too deep to be comprehended by unaided human mind and too difficult to be portrayed in human language. Eternal reality always supersedes our capacities in language and imagery. Whatever our interpretation may be, we cannot get away from the certainty of several revelational facts:

1. *There will be a difference in the eternal state of man's existence.* Heaven with all its glory, joy and fullness of life in the presence of God will be the inheritance of some, while hell with all its horror and separation from God will be the plight of others.

This difference is well illustrated in the story of our Lord in Luke 16:19-31. Whether this portion is interpreted as an actual story or as a parable does not change the facts. The fact of a difference plus many other truths are clearly illustrated. Lazarus and the rich man are in different places, in different conditions. Both are conscious of their state with no prospects of change. One is experiencing blessings, the other pain.

The same principle of difference is again illustrated in Matthew 25:31-46. The judged are assigned to different places to exist under different conditions. Both groups are conscious of it, and neither group has any prospects of change.

Again the difference is dogmatically taught in Revelation 20:11-15 and 21:1 — 22:6. The unredeemed are committed to a place designated as a lake of fire, described as the second death. Death cannot mean extinction, or else there could be no "second death." There are no prospects of change and no hope of probation. The redeemed find their dwelling place in New Jerusalem upon the new earth (Rev 21:1-27) and in paradise (22:1-6). Here they are in the presence of the Lamb and the throne of God. Such is the plain teaching of the Word of God on the difference of man's eternal state.

After discussing the difference of the eternal state of man after death with a returned soldier from World War II, he justly denounced the brutality of war and concluded with a rare bitterness in his accusation against Hitler and what he called "his gang." This gave me an opportunity. Since he had previously vehemently denied all difference in the eternal state and strongly argued that all will enter heaven, my comment was, "You better change your mind about Hitler and 'his gang.' Since you insist that all go to the same place, what if the first man you meet in heaven is Hitler?"

"Oh!" he cried out. "That could never be!"

"But where will he be?"

"To hell with him," was the soldier's bitter reply.

"But there is no hell, according to your opinion."

"There must be one for *that* kind of people" was my friend's emphatic word.

Yes, there *must* be one. Even the darkened mind and dulled conscience of man demand a difference.

The Bible describes the final state of the lost under the figures of "eternal fire" (Mt 25:41, RSV); "outer darkness" (Mt 8:12); "torment" (Rev 14:10-11); "eternal punishment" (Mt 25:46, RSV); "wrath of God" (Ro 2:5; Jn 3:36); "second death" (Rev 21:8); and "eternal destruction . . . from the presence of the Lord" (2 Th 1:9, RSV). Such statements cannot be lightly dismissed, they speak of awful realities, whatever the exact nature of these realities may be. Man does well to heed the warnings of the Lord.

2. *The state after death is fixed and eternal.* The above references are sufficient to illustrate and establish the fact, although numerous other passages could be cited. However, it still is a fact that "if they hear not Moses and the prophets, neither will they be persuaded, though one rose from the dead" (Lk 16:31). People who will not be persuaded by the above passages will not be convinced, no matter how much of God's Word is being quoted. Their mind is made up that this just cannot be so. Their philosophical theology and metaphysics demand an answer which conforms to their reason rather than

revelation. Their arguments are elaborate. However, the Bible knows of no probation after death. Death marks the division and destiny; no return or change is promised or envisaged. This is a sobering and provocative fact.

To make "eternal" mean only "agelong" is not to read the complete Bible. There are many passages in which "eternal" simply means "endless." It cannot be limited.

The Bible knows neither the hope of annihilation nor the prospects of future restoration. These are extrabiblical theories to soothe the conscience and to accommodate reason. Revelation speaks otherwise.

3. *According to revelation, Christ is the only door into the presence of God, the only way into life, the only name in whom salvation is offered to mankind.* This I have established before.

This exclusiveness and inclusiveness in Christ seem incongruous to the modern mind which is taught to think in terms of relationships and comprehensiveness. Exclusiveness is branded as narrowness. It is termed religious or theological bigotry characterized by a primitive mentality and prescientific mind. Since we find it difficult to be classified as such, we are rather silent about a subject which seemed to be much alive in the teaching of Christ. We ignore the fact that the eternal lostness of man is at the center of the doctrine of atonement. Thus, "God so loved the world, that he gave his only begotten Son, that whosoever believeth in him should not perish, but have everlasting life" (Jn 3:16). A modern version of this verse could be: "God so loved the world that He inspired a certain Jew to teach that there was a good deal to be said for loving one another" (Coggan). However, the New Testament has eternally perishing mankind as its burden. Therefore, "the Son of man came not to be ministered unto, but to minister, and to give his life a ransom for many" — a ransom price to set many free (Mk 10:45). *Atonement* is a weighty subject and cannot be ignored. *Redemption* is focal in the New Testament. *Salvation* is a costly product of God in Christ. *Reconciliation* speaks of enmity as actuality. *Propitiation* confronts us with the reality of the just wrath of God.

These words speak of realities which cannot be dismissed lightly. They point to the serious plight of man whose sin made the act of God in Christ necessary. Perdition, eternal separation from the presence of God, and suffering in the "lake of fire" lie back of the gracious act of God in Christ.

God is "not willing that any should perish." He wills to "have all men to be saved, and to come unto the knowledge of the truth." This is glorious! However, we need to keep in mind that "there is one God, and one mediator between God and men, the man Christ Jesus; who gave himself a ransom for all, to be testified in due time." To that commission Paul was ordained a preacher and an apostle, a teacher of the nations in faith and truth (1 Ti 2:4-7).

The plight of man is serious both in time and in eternity. God has acted in Christ to establish a mediatorship between Himself and man. Through faith, men of every nation may now come by way of Christ and enter into vital relationship with God. This is salvation.

THE GOSPEL OF GOD AND NEOUNIVERSALISM

Neouniversalism is as mischievous, unbiblical and unchristian as the universalism of old, even though its premise is different. It is one of the most serious and pernicious enemies of the gospel of God and undercuts the nerve of missions more effectively than all other causes combined. The Bible knows of no universal salvation. In realistic terms and impressive symbolism it depicts the condition of lost souls enduring the eternal wrath and judgment of God which they have drawn upon themselves. Universal salvation sounds good to the natural man. It seems to be a logical deduction from the potential sufficiency and finality of the death of Christ and the richness of the grace of the Lord. However, in eternal and spiritual verities we dare not trust human judgment or logic. We must build upon revelation, for here is our authority and our sure foundation.

Extended treatises have been written on the gospel and on missions which either imply or express universalism of salvation as a hope or as a certainty. Somehow this heresy has crept in unawares and struck its roots deep into Christian thought. Today it is more a premise of theology than a theory to be debated. It is fast becoming an atmosphere which pervades the total life of the church.

Neouniversalism has been made a part of the God concept of modern theology. God, we are told, is working out His purpose not only within history but in the totality of history. The mission of God involves the totality of the cosmos and assures the complete and inclusive victory of God. Thus it is unthinkable that God's purpose should not ultimately and completely triumph in the total redemption of the cosmos. The salvation of all mankind is included in the *Missio Dei* ("the Mission of God") in and with the world. Grandiose indeed! Is it true? Who assures me of it?

"It" is involved in the Christ concept. Christ died to redeem all mankind. In Him total salvation was procured. The triumph and the glory of Christ thus seem to necessitate salvation of all men. Should He lose what He has redeemed? Would His victory be complete if total salvation would not be achieved? Could He ever be satisfied with less?

"It" is read into the election concept. God has elected to save man in Christ. Christ came and identified Himself with all mankind. Thus it logically follows that all men will be saved because all are in Christ. (Here is a serious confusion of Christ's identification with mankind for the procurement of salvation and the believers' identification with Christ for the appropriation of salvation).

"It" is found in the grace concept. Salvation being of grace and saving man from all sin, it is argued that it will eventually save man also from the sin of unbelief. Grace will triumph.

The serious problem with all of these premises is at least fourfold:

1. They limit themselves to a part of the revelation of God as given in the Scriptures. Thus they have an incomplete and a faulty view of the Bible as their foundation.

2. They base themselves upon logical deductions from partial truth rather than a proper and comprehensive study of the total truth of God, to the total neglect of many "tensions" and "polarities" in the Scriptures. Thus they seriously distort the true meaning of the God, Christ, election, and grace concepts as revealed in the Bible.

3. They are self-contradictory and self-destroying. In order to build a grandiose structure and system of thought, they destroy the equally grandiose fact of the moral grandeur and responsibility of man.

4. They are negating the subjective aspect of the objective-subjective principle of the gospel of God. The repentance-faith relationship of man to sin and the Saviour is ignored. Thus while magnifying the greatness of the act of God in Christ Jesus, it ignores

the repentance-faith principle and leaves man a neutral or nonpartici-
pating being in the whole matter of salvation. This will not stand
the scriptural test and verdict.

Therefore I reject this type of approach to the Bible and the
deduced doctrine of salvation. In fact, this theory destroys the
grandeur it seeks to enhance.

Man trusts his own imagination, logic and conclusions more than
he believes and obeys the Word of God. He builds his house upon
sand which will stand neither the rain of the judgment of God nor
the storm of the wrath of God.

Neouniversalism and the Evangelical Mentality. We must face
the fact that the doctrine of universal salvation is creating an atmosphere which makes missions difficult. It somehow affects the total
movement and dynamic of Christianity as it erodes the foundation,
saps the vitality, diverts the endeavors, and weakens the nerve of
missions. How deeply this cancer has eaten into even the evangelical
mentality is evident from a survey of thousands of young people, the
vast majority of whom considered themselves orthodox in their Christian convictions. Of those surveyed, most claimed to believe the Bible
to be true in its details. Yet only one-third firmly believed in the
lostness of men apart from their receiving the gospel of Jesus Christ
and personally relating to Him in faith and commitment. My own
studies in this matter confirm the accuracy of the above findings.

This is the peril of modern missions. This is why the gospel
proclamation does not seem relevant even to evangelical youth. This
is why social action seems much more urgent and relevant. Salvation
according to universalism has cut one of the main nerves of the missionary enterprise. It has modified the urgency of the imperative,
paralyzed the motive complex, and diverted the main energies of the
church into other channels. Missions and the salvation of people from
sin and eternal separation from God have ceased to stir the Christian
conscience and reinforce other biblical motives to primary and energetic action. Even the Christian church needs a *corrected concept
of God, a biblical concept* rather than a philosophical or sentimental
concept.

It remains a fact that a man's concept of God is his all-determining concept. Well does Robert E. Speer point out, "It is in the very
being and character of God that the deepest grounds of the missionary enterprise is found. We cannot think of God except in terms

which necessitate the missionary idea."[12] The clarity, depth and richness of the God concept in the consciousness of man and the church manifest themselves most fully in our concern and involvement for world evangelism, the primary *Missio Dei*.

Our basic question remains: What think ye of God? What think ye of Christ? What think ye of the lostness of man?

Dogmatically I assert that no man can hold seriously to the biblical concept of God, of Christ, the gospel of God, and the lostness of man and not experience crises in his mind and life. These tensions will create a state of emergency that will drive the honest and spiritually minded man to drastic action.

MISSIONARY DYNAMIC AND PRAYER

The Bible is a record of supernatural manifestations, interventions and activities. Many of these happenings are direct answers to prayers. "It is a noteworthy fact that there are 657 definite requests for prayer in the Bible, not including the Psalms, and 454 definitely recorded answers."[13] Prayer is a prominent subject in the Bible and a most significant exercise of faith by the saints and the church.

> Work backed up by prayer is too often the practice, if not the ideal, of the Church. If the world is to be won, that order must be reversed, and the Church learn to depend on prayer backed up by work. Christian work that thinks and plans and bustles and toils, but forgets to pray, is an almost pathetic spectacle. . . .
>
> It is important to realize that prayer . . . is something far more than a subjective spiritual exercise. . . . Prayer is a force which achieves objective results. It actually causes things to happen which otherwise would not happen. The Biblical theory of prayer is that it is a force at work.[14]

"Very effectual [dynamic] in its working is the prayer of a righteous man" (Ja 5:16, free trans.). This is a fact of tremendous significance. It is well documented in the Bible and richly demonstrated in history.

The book of Ezra leads us back many centuries and reports some marvelous experiences of Israel and Judah, the Old Testament people of God.

Because of sin and failure the people were given over in judgment to the nations of the world. Nebuchadnezzar had captured and destroyed Jerusalem and the temple. The wealth and prominent tribespeople had been taken to Babylon into captivity. Though the adjustments to Babylon had been difficult (Ps 137), the people eventually settled down and prospered.

In due time Babylon was subjugated and Medo-Persia became dominant. It is here that the story of Ezra begins.

Cyrus was king of Persia. In a vision the Lord spoke to him and ordered him to build the house of the Lord in Jerusalem. The attitude of Cyrus was commendable. He responded with a challenge to the people of Judah to return to their homeland and build the house of the Lord God of Israel. He also made financial arrangements and provided the means to have the work completed (Ezra 1:1-4, 7-8; 3:7; 6:4, 8).

At the same time the Spirit of the Lord moved upon the people of Judah in captivity and called forth an army of volunteers to return to Palestine and undertake the task as commanded (Ezra 1:5; 2:64-67). The hands of this volunteer army were strengthened by the goodwill and free gifts of the people who remained behind (Ezra 1:6; 2:68-70). Thus an open door, the good will of authorities, a volunteer army of builders, a supporting people, and the necessary means were provided for the cause of the Lord. Although the building of the temple did not proceed without difficulty, the work was eventually completed.

The action of Cyrus has been variously interpreted. It has been suggested that the king saw in Egypt his potential rival and that as a good politician he proceeded to build in Judah a friendly and supporting buffer state. It has also been mentioned that Cyrus introduced a more humane treatment of the people of captured states and thus he was returning the captives to their homeland.

It is not impossible that such motives were present in the mind of Cyrus. However, the sacred writer of the record looks behind the curtain of human feelings and thinking and sees the moving of the Holy Spirit and the action of God (Ezra 1:1, 5). God was present and He was at work. In keeping with Isaiah's prophecy, Cyrus became the Lord's servant (Is 44:28; 45:1).

According to Jeremiah's prediction, the time had come to rebuild the temple (Jer 25:12-13). Thus God moved into history and caused things to happen to fulfill His prophecy and purpose.

We could stop here and praise God for His faithfulness and we would not go amiss in it. God *is* faithful and he *does* stand by his promises. He *does* fulfill His prophecies. His plan and program are assured by Him, and His purposes are certain.

However, the biblical record does not view it thus. The mystery of the gracious movements of God in history here are led back one more step.

An elderly and godly man living in Babylon is well known to us. His name is Daniel. Although he is primarily a politician by profession and experience, he is above all a man of God and greatly beloved of the Lord. Time may have dimmed his eyes but not his vision. His concern for his people cannot be measured. His desire for their welfare is difficult to express. His faith in the prophets of God is absolute. His assurance of the faithfulness of God knows no wavering. His experience in answered prayer permits no doubting in God and His purpose, cause and people.

Upon the prayers of Daniel, the mighty and gracious hand of God was moved that stirred the spirit of Cyrus and moved the hearts of the people of the captivity. The mystery of history is unlocked in Daniel 9 – 10. Here this remarkable man records: "I Daniel understood by books the number of the years, whereof the word of the Lord came to Jeremiah the prophet, that he would accomplish seventy years in the desolations of Jerusalem. And I set my face unto the Lord God, to seek by prayer and supplications, with fasting, and sackcloth, and ashes: and I prayed unto the Lord my God." Then follows one of the most heart-stirring prayers of the Bible.

Similar is the experience in chapter 10.

The chronology of the chapters, dates and names is not too difficult to reconcile with the record of Ezra and history. The fact remains: Daniel prayed and, in response to his prayer, God invaded history and moved to accomplish His will and purpose.

Here is the key to many mighty and surprising movings of God in history. Someone prayed and God responded. It could really be that "if there should arise one utterly believing man, the history of the world would be changed."

However, it is a sad fact that unbelief too often clouds our vision and paralyzes us in the way to the highest and the greatest. This was not so in the life of our Lord. "When we think about prayer, we think, as a rule, instinctively of its limitations; the mind of Christ seemed always to be occupied with its possibilities."[16]

Prayer did occupy a very significant part in the life and teaching of our Lord. He is, indeed, *The Man of Prayer* (J. H. Strong). And we are exhorted to pray — persistently (Lk 18:1-8), in faith (Mt 21:21-22), in His name (Jn 14:14; 16:23), in sincerity (Mt 15:21-28), with fasting (Mk 9:29; Ac 13:2-3; 14:23), in specifics (Mt 20:32-33), according to His will (1 Jn 5:14), for laborers in the harvest (Mt 9:37-38), and unitedly (Mt 18:19).

PRAYER IN THE BOOK OF ACTS

The significance of prayer is well demonstrated in the book of Acts. While this book may well be entitled as the book of the Acts of the Holy Spirit, it is likewise the book of mighty prayer.

The dispensational setting of Pentecost dare not be minimized. The Old Testament calendar of God had foreshadowed it as an event and as to time. Thus, while Pentecost was not born *by* prayer, it was born *in* an attitude and practice of prayer. For ten days the disciples had faithfully "waited in Jerusalem" to be equipped for their world task. It is also noteworthy that Pentecost did not become a substitute for prayer. Pentecost intensified prayer. Thus, while from the divine side things happened according to the Holy Spirit, from the human side prayer played a major role. Of this the disciples were deeply conscious. Therefore, when their schedule became too crowded and threatened to interfere with their primary ministry, they called the multitude together and appointed deacons in order that they might give themselves to "prayer, and to the ministry of the word" (Ac 6:1-4).

Prayer not only emboldened the witnesses; it also gave them the stamina to suffer. It wrought miracles, and it also brought forth the first missionaries, as recorded in Acts 13:1-4. Prayer becomes the subterranean channel for the flow of spiritual dynamic throughout the pages of the book of Acts. The very fact that it is mentioned more than thirty times in this book is evidence of its theological and practical dominance in the mind and life of the early church.

PRAYER IN THE MINISTRY OF PAUL

The missionary significance and dynamic of prayer are best illustrated in Paul. "I bow my knees unto the Father of our Lord Jesus Christ" (Eph 3:14) is typical of Paul. "Next to the book of

Psalms there is no part of the Bible that contains such wealth of devotion, such depth of adoration, such height of thanksgiving and such width of intercession as Paul's epistles."[16]

Paul prayed for himself, for the brethren, and especially for the churches. No doubt it was Paul's prayer as well as his teaching that produced the quality Christians we read of in the New Testament. The comprehensiveness of his care for the churches can be seen by the petitions in his prayers. He prayed for love (1 Th 3:12-13), for sanctification (1 Th 5:23), for God's good pleasure (2 Th 1:11-12), for consolation (2 Th 2:16), for love and patience (2 Th 3:5), for corporate perfection (2 Co 13:7-9), for unity (Ro 15:5-6), for hope (Ro 15:13), for knowledge of God's will (Col 1:9-14), for full assurance of knowledge (Col 2:1-3), for the glory yet to come (Phil 1:15-21), for the triune indwelling (Eph 3:14-21), for perseverance to the end (Phil 1:9-11) (adapted from Zwemmer). Thus the great apostle labored in prayer for the churches under his care.

Paul, however, was also deeply conscious of his own needs and of his dependence upon the prayers of the saints. Thus he humbly and persistently asked for the prayers of the churches. "Brethren, pray for us" was his challenge and his plea. And from the various references and requests we can well formulate our missionary prayers. Some of the main references are as follows: Romans 15:30-32; 2 Corinthians 1:10-11; Ephesians 6:18-20; Philippians 1:19; Colossians 4:2-4; 1 Thessalonians 5:25; 2 Thessalonians 3:1-3; Philemon 22.

The requests are comprehensive. The churches are to pray for divine deliverance, for acceptance of Paul's service, for divine guidance, for boldness to speak the mystery of the gospel, for open doors to preach the gospel, for a free course of the word of the Lord. Somehow Paul never found it necessary to pray for finances. Neither did he appeal to the home churches for more missionaries. His toil and prayers produced a quality Christianity which provided both of these necessities for the expansion of the gospel and the growth of the churches.

PRAYER AND MODERN MISSIONS

Prayer has remained the lifeline of missions. Modern missions also can be traced to revival in prayer.

The Reformation gave back to the church the missionary message, but it did not give the church the missionary vision. Neither did it generate missionary dynamic. The latter two were born of Pietism. Philip Jakob Spener (1635-1705), August Herman Francke (1663-1727), Count Nicholaus Ludwig Zinzendorf (1700-1760) and the Moravian Brethren at Herrnhut became the true pioneers in modern missions. The movement was deeply rooted in prayer.

Herrnhut greatly influenced the great leaders of Methodism, and a marked revival of prayer for the non-Christian world resulted.

In 1723 Robert Millar, a Presbyterian minister of Scotland, published a pamphlet in which he urged prayer as the first known means for the conversion of the heathen world.

In 1744 a call was widely circulated to unite in prayer for the salvation of the non-Christian world. In 1746 a memorial was sent to Boston, inviting all Christians of North America to enter into a concert of prayer for a period of seven years.

In 1747 Jonathan Edwards of Northhampton responded by issuing a call to intercessory prayer on the part of all Christian believers for the spread of the gospel. Thirty-seven years later this stirring pamphlet was introduced into the churches of England by John Sutliffe in the Northhamptonshire Association, a gathering of Baptist ministers. Following the reading of the message, he moved that all Baptist churches and ministers set aside the first Monday of each month for united intercessory prayer for the non-Christian world. The motion was adopted and the Reverend John Ryland of Northhampton drew up a plan in which he challenged the churches to regular and earnest intercessory prayer for a world in darkness and sin.

The inevitable consequence of these prayer meetings was the organization of the Baptist missionary society known as "The Particular Baptist Missionary Society for Propagating the Gospel among the Heathen." It was founded in 1792 at Kettering, England.

In rapid succession, societies sprang up in Great Britain as well as on the Continent.

The story of Samuel J. Mills and his four loyal comrades and Williams College and the Haystack Prayer Meeting are foundational to American foreign missions. As the five students waited before the Lord in the shelter of the haystack, they discussed the spiritual darkness of the vast multitudes without Christ. They debated the possibility of realizing the Lord's command and its bearing in their own lives. Mills proposed that they devote themselves to sending the gospel to the non-Christian world. His immortal words, "We can do it if we will," have characterized much of American missions. Upon these words they knelt in prayer and then quietly went home. The hour was late and no one was aware that a crisis hour in the history of missions had come, an hour that would draw thousands of able-bodied American men and women into the service of world evangelization.

Prayer, indeed, is dynamic and works if exercised in the name of Christ and in the Holy Spirit.

Christian missions is a supernatural venture. Only supernatural resources can sustain it and make it dynamic. The contact with the Divine is imperative. Prayer is not optional; it is operational and decisive.

The history of missions abounds with evidences of divine intervention and gracious manifestation in behalf of the cause of missions. The history of the vast amount of prayers invested in the venture and the divine response to them will never be recounted on this side of eternity. Only in the blaze of divine light will we see the fullness of divine glory, faithfulness and manifestations. And to our great surprise, most of such manifestations will appear to be a direct response to some prayer. Someone prayed and God acted.

Here is the secret of divine dynamic. Here is the challenge to human helplessness. Here is the key that transforms human limitations into divine limitlessness. Here the church is on trial before God and the world. Here the church stands numbed in bankruptcy or filled with miracle and power. Prayer is the key that unlocks the divine resources of power and supply.

> Now I beseech you, brethren, for the Lord Jesus Christ's sake, and for the love of the Spirit, that ye strive together with me in your prayers to God for me;
> That I may be delivered from them that do not believe in Judaea; and that my service which I have for Jerusalem may be accepted of the saints;
> That I may come unto you with joy by the will of God, and may with you be refreshed.
> Now the God of peace be with you all. Amen (Ro 15:30-33).

Summary and Conclusion

By way of summary and conclusion I draw the attention of the reader again to the primacy and consistency of missions in the Bible. God is a God of missions. He wills missions. He commands missions. He demands missions. He made missions possible through His Son. He made missions actual in sending the Holy Spirit. Biblical Christianity and missions are organically interrelated.

Therefore Christian missions finds its authority, motive and purpose in the character of Christianity as revealed in the Bible with its concepts of God as Father, Christ as Saviour and Lord, the Holy Spirit as Advocate, and man as created in the image of God and for the fellowship and glory of God.

The Nature of Christianity

Christianity, according to the Bible, is not primarily a comprehensive philosophy, a higher way of life, a superior code of ethics, or a beautiful system of theology. It is all this and infinitely more. It is the worship of a Person. It is a walk with God. It is identification with Christ in life and purpose. Christianity objectively is the revelation of God in Christ as recorded in the Bible, and subjectively, the experience of Jesus Christ the Lord in His life, death and resurrection by faith through the gracious operation of the Holy Spirit. Upon that initial experience the Holy Spirit indwells the believer continuously to make Christ real in his soul, progressively transforming the personality into the image of the Saviour and identifying the believer with the purpose of God.

Christianity can never be disassociated from Christ as the eternal Son of God, the historic Son of Man, and the present glorified Lord, Mediator and High Priest at the right hand of the throne of God. Christ is the very essence of Christianity. Griffith Thomas is therefore correct when he speaks of Christianity as being Christ.

346

...RELIGION

...*leroma*), adequacy,
...ristianity from all relig...
...comparative-religion stud...
...the "incomparable religion" o...
...sal and sufficient Saviour and L...
...o believe. As such, Christ in His pe...
...and authoritative ground and efficient
...ns. He makes missions primary and im-

...ment for missions is not any word of Christ's.
...nd what He reveals and signifies. The words of
...te new duties. They revealed eternal duties, the
...lay back of all words in the nature of things and
...ife.

...ONS INHERENT IN THE NATURE OF CHRISTIANITY

...most important to grasp the fact that Christian missions
...ut of a proper interpretation of and relationship to biblical
...ianity rather than from certain precepts or commands recorded
...e Bible. In deep conviction we join Robert E. Speer who writes
...*Missionary Principles and Practice,*

> The last command of Christ is often set forth as alike the pri-
> mary and conclusive argument for missions. What was the last
> command of His lips must have been one of the dearest desires of
> His heart. But the work of missions is our duty, not chiefly because
> of the desire of His heart. He bade His Church to evangelize the
> world because He wanted it evangelized, and He wanted it evange-
> lized because He knew that it needed to be evangelized. Our duty
> in the matter is determined not primarily by His command, but by
> the facts and conditions of life which underlie it. Even if Jesus had
> not embodied the missionary duty of the Church in the "great com-
> mission," we should be under obligation to evangelize the world by
> reason of the essential character of Christianity and its mission to
> the world[1]

The final conclusion of Speer's rich experience and careful studies
of the subject is stated thus in *Christianity and the Nations:*

> It is in the very being and character of God that the deepest

...d of the missionary enterprise is to be foun...
...x of God except in terms which necessitate the m...

...he same position is well expressed by Phillips Br...
...ed by Speer in the same volume:

> It is the sincere and deep conviction of my soul whe...
> that if the Christian faith does not culminate and comple...
> the effort to make Christ known to all the world, that fait...
> to me a thoroughly unreal and insignificant thing, destitute...
> for the single life and incapable of being convincingly prove...
> true.[3]

Dr. James S. Stewart expresses himself in a similar ma...
Considering the various motives in missions, he concludes:

> There are, then, four words — Commission, Compassion, C...
> munity, Continuity — each of them representing at some period of t...
> Church's life a major element in missionary endeavor. But none...
> these, nor all of them taken together, can constitute the basic argu...
> ment. None of them touches the true profundity of this matter. In
> the last resort, the one reason for missions is *Christ*. He only is the
> motive. God's presence in Him is the only sufficient cause.
>
> The fact is, belief in missions and belief in Christ stand and fall
> together. To say "I believe that God so loved the world, that in
> Christ He gave everything He had, gave His very self," to use such
> words not lightly or conventionally but in spirit and in truth, means
> that the one who uses them binds himself irrevocably to make self-
> giving the controlling principle of life; and this is the very essence
> of missions. To put it otherwise, the concern for world evangeliza-
> tion is not something tacked on to a man's personal Christianity,
> which he may take or leave as he chooses; it is rooted indefeasibly in
> the character of the God who has come to us in Christ Jesus. Thus
> it can never be the province of a few enthusiasts, a sideline or a
> speciality of those who happen to have a bent that way. It is the
> distinctive mark of being a Christian. To accept Christ is to enlist
> under a missionary banner. It is quite impossible to be (in the
> Pauline phrase) "in Christ" and not participate in Christ's mission
> in the world. In fact, here is the surest test whether we have truly
> grasped what Christ was doing by His life and death and resurrec-
> tion, or whether we have failed even to begin to understand the
> Gospel that He brought. James Denney once heard a distinguished
> missionary say — "Some people do not believe in missions. They

have no right to believe in missions: they do not believe in Christ." That stringent comment is a salutary reminder that a missionary outlook is a direct inevitable deduction from a saving knowledge of Jesus. The sole ground of missionary endeavor is Christ.[4]

Missions is inherent in the very nature of Christianity and is a true product of our personal faith in proper relationship to a Spirit-enlightened understanding of biblical Christianity. Such a statement does not mean that missions need not be taught and nurtured in the Christian church or that it grows spontaneously or automatically. Nothing is spontaneous in Christianity. All must be cultivated and nurtured. But it does mean that when the whole counsel of God is taught, believed and obeyed, missions will cease to be considered a side work or something we may engage in or not. It will cease to be optional and "elective." It will not be merely *a* work of the church, beneficial and praiseworthy; it will be *the* work of the church, absolutely essential to the church to retain her Christian character and purpose. It will become primary and dominant in the purpose and activity of the church, with all powers geared toward accomplishing the task.

NEGLECT OF MISSIONS RESULTS IN SELF-IMPOVERISHMENT

The poverty and need of our present-day church is well expressed in the words of Dr. George Robson:

> At present the life of many congregations is sterilized by its self-centered character. The world-wide duty of the congregation is relegated to a secondary place and the congregation is proportionately non-efficient for the chief purpose of the church. What is needed is that all its endeavors should be so ordered as to sub-serve and culminate in world-wide service.[5]

Missions properly rooted in Christ and motivated by the Holy Spirit ceases to be a burdensome duty of the church. It becomes rather the outflow of the life of the church. It is lifted from a legalistic spirit of duty to the fruit of the Spirit generated from a life relationship to Christ.

> The spirit of Christianity is higher than legalism and it is of the spirit of legalism to press injunctions of courses of action where the underlying principles of action are unseen or unfelt. The men who

have done the work of God in the world are men in whom the Spirit of God was at work, and who would have done God's work even in the absence of expressed legislation as to the nature of the work God wanted done. So also in the Christian life we are called to possess, not primarily, the behavior of Christ, but His mind, from which the appropriate behavior will inevitably flow.[6]

A church that does not recognize the primacy of missions deprives herself of the most intimate relationship with her Lord, fails to identify herself with the primary purpose of God, robs her membership of the deepest experiences of the Holy Spirit, and denies the world the greatest blessings the Lord in grace has provided. She ceases to be truly Christian.

MISSIONS — AN EXPRESSION OF BIBLICAL IDEALISM

The above summary of the primacy of missions flowing from an inner life of the church is borne out by the life of Christ, the example of the apostles, and the experiences of the early church. Here missions is expressed in the fullness of biblical idealism. In its fullest and absolute sense it is the all-consuming purpose of God in the life, words, and work of Christ. It is the all-absorbing passion of the apostles of Jesus Christ, and it is the all-pervading concern and mission of the Holy Spirit, as it is so fully demonstrated in the book of Acts where the Holy Spirit was able to express Himself freely and His operation was unhindered.

The primacy of missions is written in large letters across the pages of the whole Bible. All the apostles gave themselves to missions, and only the sword could cut short their path to the uttermost part of the earth. Paul's deepest passion was "to preach the gospel, not where Christ was [already] named," and "to make all men see what is the fellowship of the mystery . . . warning every man, and teaching every man in all wisdom; that we may present every man perfect in Christ Jesus: whereunto I also labour, striving according to his working, which worketh in me mightily" (Ro 15:20; Eph 3:9; Col 1:28-29).

Thus Paul was consumed by a burning zeal for Christian universality which seemed strange to the Greek, arresting to the Roman, alarming to the Jew, and perplexing to some Christians. His highest praise goes to some churches whose "faith is spoken of throughout the whole world," and whose "faith to God-ward is spread abroad" (Ro 1:8; 1 Th 1:8).

All New Testament books grew out of the needs of mission churches. Beautifully the New Testament closes with the picture of complete and perfect triumph in missions. No church can divorce herself from missions and retain her true New Testament character and "apostolic succession" or relegate missions to a secondary place and retain her spiritual vitality.

In order to create strong and lasting motivation in missions, we are therefore faced with the tremendous task of clearly interpreting the essentials of Christianity, of securing sympathetic understanding of the counsel of God, of cultivating deep appreciation of Christ through personal experience of the reality of Christ, and of providing appropriate ways for a constant expression of such appreciation. This is, indeed, a great task, but it will be a work well worth our labors and prayers. Some may wonder what would happen if missions were accorded the primary place in our church program as taught in the Scriptures. In the words of Archibald McLean,

> I will tell you what will happen. . . . The power of Christ will be released in such measure as we have never seen it in our land before, and far and wide in our own land men will lay hold of our skirts and ask us to let them into our secret. What Christ is waiting for is the day when men and women — many or few, rich or poor, young or old — will hearken once more to His great command and will lay down their lives at His feet in absolute and unreserved obedience. When that is done, the church at home will enjoy a degree of prosperity she has never known.[7]

This is not wishful thinking. Present-day churches are witnesses to the fact that the Lord's blessings rest in a marvelous manner upon churches who make missions primary in their program. Wonderful growth has been experienced, debts have been liquidated, and spiritual refreshings have come down in an unprecedented manner. God is no man's debtor. The church that makes God's business her business will soon discover that God is in her midst to make her concerns His business. Indeed, they "went forth, and preached every where, the Lord working with them, and confirming the word with signs following" (Mk 16:20). Such may be our experience today. But we must "go forth."

Notes

Preface
1. Georg F. Vicedom, *The Mission of God* (St. Louis: Concordia, 1965), p. 4.

Introduction
1. Albrecht Ritschl, *Justification and Reconciliation* (New York: Scribner, 1900), p. 329.
2. John B. Champion, *The Living Atonement* (Philadelphia: Griffith & Rowland, 1910), pp. 149-50.
3. Douglas Webster, *Unchanging Mission — Biblical and Contemporary* (Philadelphia: Fortress, 1965), p. 1.
4. Georg F. Vicedom, *The Mission of God*, pp. 4-11.
5. W. O. Carver, *Missions in the Plan of the Ages* (Nashville: Broadman, 1951), p. 11.
6. Ibid., p. 12.
7. Harold Lindsell, *An Evangelical Theology of Missions* (Grand Rapids: Zondervan, n.d.).
8. Gerald H. Anderson, ed., *The Theology of the Christian Mission* (New York: McGraw-Hill, 1961), p. 13.

Chapter 1
1. Samuel Zwemer, *Into All the World* (Harrisburg, Pa.: Christian Pubns., 1943), pp. 43-44.
2. Wayland Hayd, *The Teaching of Jesus Concerning His Own Person* (New York: American Tract Soc., 1907).
3. See James Denny, *Jesus and the Gospel*, (New York: Armstrong, 1909), pp. 255-269.

Chapter 2
1. Robert E. Speer, *Christianity and the Nations*, (New York: Revell, 1910) pp. 17-18.
2. Edgar Young Mullins, *The Christian Religion in Its Doctrinal Expression* (Nashville: S. S. B. of the S. Bapt. Conv., 1917), p. 236.
3. Lesslie Newbigin, *The Finality of Christ*, p. 61.
4. D. R. Davies, *The Sin of Our Age* (New York: Macmillan, 1947), p. 33.

Chapter 3
1. Erich Sauer, *The Dawn of Redemption* (Grand Rapids: Eerdmans, 1955), pp. 56-57.
2. Rajah B. Manikam, *Christianity and the Asian Revolution* (New York: Friendship Press, 1954), p. 118.
3. James M. Stifler, *The Epistle to the Romans* (New York: Revell, 1897), p. 25.
4. Sauer, p. 94.
5. J. Philip Hyatt, *Prophetic Religion* (Nashville: Abingdon-Cokesbury, 1947), p. 149.
6. B. A. Copass, *A Manual of Old Testament Theology* (Fort Worth: Seminary Book Store, 1943), p. 13.
7. Elmer A. Leslie, *Old Testament Religion* (Cincinnati: Abingdon, 1936), p. 78.
8. Ibid.
9. Hyatt, p. 150.
10. Robert Martin-Achard, *A Light to the Nations* (London: Oliver & Boyd, 1962), p. 58.
11. Edward J. Young, *My Servants the Prophets* (Grand Rapids: Eerdmans, 1952), p. 205.
12. H. Wheeler Robinson, *The Cross in the Old Testament* (Philadelphia: Westminster, 1955), pp. 73-74.
13. H. A. Ironside, *Isaiah* (New York: Loizeaux, 1961), pp. 268-69.

352

Chapter 5

1. Edward Young, as quoted in *The Encyclopedia of Religious Quotations,* ed. Frank S. Mead (Westwood, N.J.: Revell, 1965), pp. 139-40.
2. W. A. Visser't Hooft, *Witness in Six Continents,* ed. Ronald K. Orchard (Edinburgh: Edinburgh House, 1964), p. 23.
3. Alexander R. Hay, *The New Testament Order for Church and Missionary* (Argentina: N. T. Missionary Union, 1947), pp. 33-34.
4. William Temple, "Let the Church Be the Church," message at Faith and Life Conference (Edinburgh, 1937).
5. Robert E. Speer, *Missionary Principles and Practices* (New York: Revell, 1902), pp. 34-35.
6. Karl Barth, "An Exegetical Study of Matthew 28:16-20" in *The Theology of the Christian Mission,* ed. Gerald Anderson (New York: McGraw-Hill, 1961).
7. Robert D. Culver, "What Is the Church's Commission," *Bibliotheca Sacra* (July 1968), pp. 239-53.
8. G. Campbell Morgan, *The Letters of Our Lord* (London: Pickering & Inglis, n.d.), p. 82.
9. Roland O. Leavell, *Evangelism, Christ's Imperative Commission* (Nashville: Broadman, 1951), p. 3.
10. Culver, p. 244.
11. Edvin Larson, *Christus als Vorbild* (Uppsala: Gleerup Lund, 1962), p. 44.
12. Ibid.
13. B. F. Westcott, *The Gospel According to St. John* (Grand Rapids: Eerdmans, 1951), p. 298.
14. Ibid.
15. Charles John Ellicott, *Bible Commentary* (London: Marshall, n.d.), 6:543.
16. Lyman Abbot, *Illustrated Commentary on John* (New York: Barnes, 1879), p. 208.
17. Ibid.

Chapter 6

1. Adolf Deissmann, *Paul, A Study in Social and Religious History* (New York: Harper Torchbooks, 1957), pp. 162-63.
2. Henry C. Thiessen, Lectures in Systematic Theology (Grand Rapids: Eerdmans, 1949), pp. 432-36.
3. Hugh Thomson Kerr, Source unknown.

Chapter 7

1. Marion R. Vincent, *Word Studies in the New Testament* (Grand Rapids: Eerdmans, 1957), 3:389.
2. B. F. Westcott, *St. Paul's Epistle to the Ephesians* (Grand Rapids: Eerdmans, 1951), p. 62.
3. Vincent, 2:41.
4. Westcott, *The Gospel According to St. John,* p. 298.
5. H. N. Ridderbos, *The Speeches of Peter in the Acts of the Apostles* (London: Tyndale, 1962), p. 18.
6. J. B. Lightfoot, *Epistle to the Galatians* (London: Macmillan, 1921), p. 97.
7. James Hastings, *Dictionary of the Apostolic Church* (New York: Scribner, 1926), 1:84.
8. J. C. Lambert, ed., *The International Standard Bible Encyclopedia* (Grand Rapids: Eerdmans, 1947), 1:203.
9. Adolph Harnack, *The Mission and Expansion of Christianity in the First Three Centuries* (New York: Harper Torchbooks, 1961), 1:327.
10. Ibid., pp. 327-31.
11. Ibid., p. 330.
12. W. J. Conybeare and J. S. Howson, *Life and Epistles of St. Paul* (Hartford, Conn.: Scranton, 1869), p. 442.
13. Vincent, 3:380.
14. Ibid., 4:322.
15. Westcott, *The Gospel According to St. John,* p. 62.
16. A. Plummer, *Dictionary of the Apostolic Church* (London: T. & T. Clark, 1926), 1:379.

17. W. E. Vine, *An Expository Dictionary of New Testament Words* (London: Oliphants, 1939), 2:44.
18. A. R. Fausett, *Bible Cyclopaedia, Critical and Expository* (Hartford: Scranton, 1902), p. 216.
19. Eusebius, *History Eccles III* (New York: Mason & Lane, 1839), p. 123.
20. Gerhard Kittel, *Theologisches Wörterbuch Zum Neuen Testament* (Stuttgart: Kohlhammer, 1949), 2:735.
21. See Harnack, pp. 331-36.
22. Ibid., pp. 341-42.
23. T. Watson Street, *On the Growing Edge of the Church* (Richmond: John Knox, 1946).
24. Stephen Neill, *Creative Tension* (London: Edinburgh House, 1959), p. 82fn.
25. Westcott, *The Gospel According to St. John*, p. 294.
26. Ibid., p 298.
27. William Barclay, *The Letter to the Hebrews* (Philadelphia: Westminster, 1957), p. 45.
28. Robert E. Speer, mission pamphlets.
29. C. T. Studd, mission pamphlets.
30. Gilmour, mission pamphlets.
31. Keith Falconer, mission pamphlets.
32. Samuel Zwemer, *Into All the World*, p. 202.
33. David Livingstone, mission pamphlets.
34. David Brainerd, mission pamphlets.

Chapter 8
1. William Barclay, *More New Testament Words* (New York: Harper, 1958), pp. 128-234.
2. J. Oswald Sanders, *The Holy Spirit of Promise* (London: Marshall, Morgan & Scott, 1954), p. 13.
3. Ibid.
4. C. H. Dodd, *The Apostolic Preaching and Its Development* (New York: Harper, 1949).
5. Samuel G. Craig, *Christianity Rightly So Called* (Philadelphia: Presbyterian & Reformed, 1946), pp. 137-66.
6. Edgar Mullins, *The Christian Religion in Its Doctrinal Expression*, p. 236.
7. Herbert Marshall McLuhan, as quoted by Janet Rohler, "McLuhan on Religion," *Christianity Today*, Feb. 13, 1970, p. 34.
8. Max Warren, *The Uniqueness of Jesus Christ* (London: Highway Press, 1969), p. 2.
9. R. B. Girdlestone, *Synonyms of the Old Testament* (Grand Rapids: Eerdmans, 1953), p. 303.
10. F. D. Coggins, *The Ministry of the Word* (London: Canterbury, 1945), pp. 62-63.
11. Douglas Webster, *Unchanging Mission – Biblical and Contemporary*, p. 26.
12. Robert E. Speer, *Missionary Principles and Practices*, pp. 34-35.
13. Edward S. Woods, *Modern Discipleship* (New York: Association Press, n.d.) p. 92.
14. Ibid., p. 89.
15. J. H. Oldham, Source unknown.
16. Samuel Zwemer, *Into All the World*, p. 164.

Summary and Conclusion
1. Speer, *Missionary Principles and Practices*, p. 9.
2. Speer, *Christianity and the Nations*, p. 8.
3. Phillips Brooks as quoted in ibid., p. 20.
4. James S. Stewart, *Thine Is the Kingdom* (Edinburgh: St. Andrew Press, 1956), pp. 14-15.
5. George Robson, as quoted by Archibald McLean in *The Primacy of the Missionary and Other Addresses* (St. Louis: Chr. Brd. of Pubns., 1921), p. 109.
6. Speer, *Missionary Principles and Practices*, p. 10.
7. McLean, pp. 30-31.

Bibliography

A WORD OF CAUTION

The books and articles listed here are not endorsed by the author. I am well aware that only some of these represent the biblical point of view. Several authors write from an evangelical position, evangelical however as defined by continentals. Not a few of the authors represent the neoorthodox school, while others are frankly liberal, some even radical. *The bibliography is not a guide for reading and absorption.* It is presented to the scholar who has learned to differentiate and to discriminate. As a whole, the listed books and articles are rather a "labyrinth" than a library. They are the best commentary on the present-day utter confusion, a confusion to the degree of bewilderment in missiology. This situation has come about because theologians and missiologists have left the secure foundations of the Bible.

With this introduction I present the list.

BOOKS

BIBLICAL STUDIES

Autrey, C. E. *Evangelism in the Acts.* Grand Rapids, Mich.: Zondervan, 1964.

Brown, Stanley. *Evangelism in the Early Church.* Grand Rapids, Mich.: Eerdmans, 1963.

Carver, William O. *Missions in the Plan of Ages.* Nashville, Tenn.: Broadman, 1951.

Chambers, Oswald. *So Send I You.* London: Marshall, Morgan & Scott, 1951.

Coleman, Robert E. *The Master Plan of Evangelism.* Westwood, N.J.: Revell, 1963.

Filson, F. V. *Three Crucial Decades.* Richmond, Va.: Knox, 1963.

Glover, Robert H. *The Bible Basis of Missions.* Chicago: Moody, 1964.

Goerner, H. C. *Thus It Is Written.* Nashville, Tenn.: Broadman, 1945.

Gordon, A. J. *The Holy Spirit in Missions.* Harrisburg, Pa.: Chr. Alliance Publ., n.d.

Graeber, J. D. *The Church Apostolic.* Scottdale, Pa.: Herald, 1960.

Horton, R. E. *The Bible a Missionary Book.* London: Oliphant, Anderson & Ferrier, n.d.

Hurst, D. S., and Jones, T. J. *The Church Begins.* Springfield, Mo.: Gospel Publ., 1959.

Lawrence, J. B. *The Holy Spirit in Missions.* Atlanta, Ga.: Home Mission Bd., 1947.

Love, Julian. *The Missionary Message of the Bible.* New York: Mac-millan, 1941.

Martin-Archard, Robert. *A Light to the Nations.* London: Oliver & Boyd, 1962.

Montgomery, Helen B. *The Bible and Missions.* West Medford, Mass.: Central Com. on United Study of For. Missions, 1920.

——. *Prayer and Missions.* West Medford, Mass.: Central Com. on United Study of For. Missions, 1924.

Morgan, G. Campbell. *The Missionary Manifesto.* Grand Rapids, Mich.: Baker, 1970.

Rowley, Harold H. *The Missionary Message of the Old Testament.* London: Carey, 1944.

Sanders, J. Oswald. *What of the Unevangelized?* London: OMF, 1966.

Stott, John R. W. *Our Guilty Silence.* Grand Rapids, Mich.: Eerdmans, 1967.

Walker, T. *The Acts of the Apostles.* Chicago: Moody, 1966.

——. *Missionary Ideals.* London: Church Missionary Soc., 1911.

Warren, Max. *The Uniqueness of Jesus Christ.* London: Highway Press, 1969.

Weiss, G. Christian. *God and the Nation.* Lincoln, Neb.: Back to Bible, 1966.

Wolff, Richard. *The Final Destiny of the Heathen.* Ridgefield Park, N.J.: Interdenom. For. Mission Assoc., 1961.

Zwemer, S. *Into All the World.* Harrisburg, Pa.: Christian Pub., 1943.

——. *Thinking Missions with Christ.* Grand Rapids, Mich.: Zondervan, 1935.

THEOLOGICAL STUDIES

Allen, Roland. *The Ministry of the Spirit.* London: World Dominion, 1960.

——. *Missionary Principles.* Grand Rapids, Mich.: Eerdmans, 1964.

Anderson, Gerald. *Christian Mission in Theological Perspective.* Nashville, Tenn.: Abingdon, 1967.

——. *The Theology of the Christian Mission.* New York: McGraw Hill, 1961.

Andersen, Wilhelm. *Toward a Theology of Missions.* London: SCM, 1955.

Autrey, C. E. *The Theology of Evangelism.* Nashville, Tenn.: Broadman, 1966.

Blauw, Johannes. *The Missionary Nature of the Church.* New York: McGraw Hill, 1962.

Boer, H. R. *Pentecost and Missions.* Grand Rapids, Mich.: Eerdmans, 1961.

Campbell, R. E. *The Church in Missions.* Maryknoll, N.Y.: Maryknoll, 1965.

Davison, Leslie. *Sender and Sent.* London: Epworth, 1969.

Dillistone, F. W. *Revelation and Evangelism.* London: Lutterworth, 1948.

Gensichen, H. W. *Living Missions.* Philadelphia: Fortress, 1966.

Hahn, Ferdinand. *Mission in the New Testament.* Naperville, Ill.: Allenson, 1963.

Horner, N. A. *Protestant Crosscurrents in Missions.* Nashville, Tenn.: Abingdon, 1968.

Liechtenhan, Rudolf. *Die Urchristliche Mission.* Zurich: Zwingli-Verlag, 1946.

Lindsell, Harold. *The Church's Worldwide Mission.* Waco, Texas: Word, 1966.

———. *An Evangelical Theology of Missions.* Grand Rapids, Mich.: Zondervan, 1970.

Newbigin, Lesslie. *A Faith for This One World.* London: SCM, 1961.

———. *The Finality of Christ.* Richmond, Va.: Knox, 1969.

———. *The Household of God.* New York: Friendship, 1953.

———. *One Body, One Gospel, One World.* London: Wm. Carling, 1958.

———. *Trinitarian Faith and Today's Mission.* Richmond, Va.: Knox, 1963.

Niles, Daniel T. *The Message and Its Messenger.* Nashville, Tenn.: Abingdon, 1966.

———. *Upon the Earth.* New York: McGraw Hill, 1966.

Orchard, R. K. *Missions in a Time of Testing.* Philadelphia: Westminster, 1964.

Ranson, C. W. *Renewal and Advance.* London: Edinburgh House, 1948.

Rooy, S. H. *Theology of Missions in the Puritan Tradition.* Grand Rapids, Mich.: Eerdmans, 1965.

Shepherd, Walter D. *Sent by the Sovereign.* Philadelphia: Presb. & Ref., 1968.

Soper, E. D. *The Philosophy of the Christian World Mission.* Nashville, Tenn.: Abingdon, 1943.

Speer, R. E. *Christianity and the Nations.* New York: Revell, 1910.

———. *The Church and Missions.* New York: Doran, 1926.

———. *The Finality of Jesus Christ.* New York: Revell, 1933.

Sundkler, Bengt. *The World of Missions.* Grand Rapids, Mich.: Eerdmans, 1965.

Tippett, A. R. *Verdict Theology in Missionary Theory.* Lincoln, Ill.: Lincoln Chr. Col., 1969.

Vicedom, Georg F. *The Mission of God.* St. Louis, Mo.: Concordia, 1965.

Visser't Hooft, W. A. *No Other Name.* Philadelphia: Westminster, 1963.

Webster, Douglas. *Not Ashamed.* London: Hodder & Stoughton, 1970.

————. *Unchanging Mission.* Philadelphia: Fortress, 1965.

————. *What in Evangelism.* London: Highway Press, 1964.

SUPPLEMENTARY STUDIES

Bright, John. *The Kingdom of God.* Nashville, Tenn.: Abingdon-Cokesbury, 1953.

Branscomb, H. *The Teaching of Jesus.* Nashville, Tenn.: Abingdon-Cokesbury, 1931.

Bruce, A. B. *The Training of the Twelve.* Edinburgh: T. & T. Clark, 1934.

Bruce, F. F. *The Spreading Flame.* Grand Rapids, Mich.: Eerdmans, 1964.

Curtis, Arthur H. *The Vision and Mission of Jesus.* Edinburgh: T. & T. Clark, 1954.

Denney, James. *Jesus and the Gospel.* New York: Armstrong, 1909.

Feine, Paul. *Theologie des Neuen Testamentes.* Leipzig: Hinrichs'sche, 1922.

Gaebelein, Arno C. *The Conflict of the Ages.* New York: "Our Hope," 1933.

————. *The Hope of the Ages.* New York: "Our Hope," 1938.

Green, Michael. *Evangelism in the Early Church.* Grand Rapids, Mich.: Eerdmans, 1970.

Harnack, Adolf. *The Mission and Expansion of Christianity.* New York: Harper, 1961.

Koenig, Eduard. *Theologie des Alten Testamentes.* Stuttgart: Chr. Belser A. G., 1923.

Kroeker, Jakob. *Das Lebendige Wort.* 17 vols. Giessen: Brunnen-Verlag, n.d.

Ladd, George E. *Crucial Questions About the Kingdom of God.* Grand Rapids, Mich.: Eerdmans, 1952.

Latourette, Kenneth Scott. *Christianity in a Revolutionary Age.* 5 vols. Grand Rapids, Mich.: Zondervan, 1969.

————. *A History of the Expansion of Christianity.* 7 vols. Grand Rapids, Mich.; Zondervan, 1970.

Leslie, Elmer A. *Old Testament Religion.* Cincinnati: Abingdon, 1936.

Meye, Robert P. *Jesus and the Twelve*. Grand Rapids, Mich.: Eerdmans, 1968.

Milligan, R. *Scheme of Redemption*. St. Louis: Chr. Brd. of Pub., n.d.

Moe, Olaf. *Paul the Apostle*. 2 vols. Minneapolis: Augsburg, 1950.

Ramsey, William M. *St. Paul the Traveller and the Roman Citizen*. Grand Rapids, Mich.: Baker, 1949.

Rowley, Harold H. *The Biblical Doctrine of Election*. London: Lutterworth, 1953.

Sauer, Erich. *The Dawn of Redemption*. Grand Rapids, Mich.: Eerdmans, 1955.

———. *From Eternity to Eternity*. Grand Rapids, Mich.: Eerdmans, 1954.

———. *The Triumph of the Crucified*. Grand Rapids, Mich.: Eerdmans, 1951.

Vos, Geerhardus. *The Self-Disclosure of Jesus*. Grand Rapids, Mich.: Eerdmans, 1954.

White, Reginald E. O. *Apostle Extraordinary*. Grand Rapids, Mich.: Eerdmans, 1962.

INTERNATIONAL MISSIONARY COUNCIL SERIES

The Christian Hope and the Task of the Church. New York: Harper, 1954.

Jerusalem Meeting – IMC, March 1928. 7 vols. New York: IMC, 1928.

The Madras Series – IMC. 7 vols. New York: IMC, 1939.

Missions Under the Cross. Ed. Norman Goodall. New York: IMC, 1953.

The New Delhi Report. New York: Association, 1961.

PERIODICALS

Church Growth Bulletin

Glasser, A. F. "Theology: With or Without the Bible." Vol. 3, no. 3.

Evangelical Missions Quarterly

Aune, David E. "Missions Divine 'Necessity.'" Vol. 3:75-83.

Chandapilla, P. T. "Training Leaders in India: How Jesus Trained the Twelve." Vol. 5:210-18.

Clowney, Edmund P. "Man's Fight with Lostness." Vol. 4:217-26.

Editorial Committee. "Missionary Faith." Vol. 1, no. 1, pp. 4-8.

Fenton, Horace L. J. "Where We Differ over the Message." Vol. 2:1-10.

Ford, Leighton. "Presence Versus Proclamation." Vol. 4:204-10.

Glasser, A. F. "What Has Been the Evangelical Stance New Delhi to Uppsala?" Vol. 5:129-50.

Hodges, Melvin L. "Spiritual Dynamics in El Salvador." Vol. 2:80-83.

King, L. Louis. "New Universalism: Its Exponents, Tenets, and Threats to Missions." Vol. 1, no. 4, pp. 2-12.

Lindsell, Harold. "Attack Syncretism with Dialogue." Vol. 3:203-8.

Maxwell, Leslie E. "He Also Gets a Penny." Vol. 2:11-13.
McGavran, Donald. "The Right and the Wrong of the Presence Idea."
    Vol. 6:98-109.
Montgomery, John. "Luther and Missions." Vol. 3:193-202.
Nichols, Bruce. "Toward an Asian Theology of Missions." Vol. 6:65-78.
Peters, George W. "Missionary Responsibility: Changeless and Relative."
    Vol. 1, no. 4, pp. 29-35.
Wagner, C. Peter. "The Evangelical Declaration of Bogata." Vol. 6:
    172-74.
————. "Latin America Congress on Evangelism." Vol. 6:162-71.
Yoder, Bill. "European Congress on Evangelism." Vol. 8:102-13.

International Review of Mission(s)
Ainger, Geoffrey J. "The Gospel of Freedom." Vol. 57 (Oct. 1968):
    417-23.
Allen, Derek W. "Christ's Teaching About Missions." Vol. 48 (April
    1959):157-67.
Allen, G. F. "Then and Now: A Study of the Young Church in the First
    Centuries and Today." Vol. 27 (Oct. 1938):652-61.
Allen, Roland. "Revelation of the Holy Spirit in the Acts of the Apostles."
    Vol. 7 (April 1918):160-67.
Andrews, C. F. "Hindu View of Christ." Vol. 28 (April 1939):259-64.
Azariah, V. S. "Caste Movement in South India." Vol. 21 (Oct. 1932):
    447-67.
Baillie, John. "World Missions of the Church: The Contemporary
    Scene." Vol. 41 (April 1952):161-69.
Barth, Markus. "What Is the Gospel?" Vol. 53 (Oct. 1964):441-48.
Baudert, S. "Zinzendorf's Thought on Missions Related to His Views of
    the World." Vol. 21 (July 1932):390-401.
Bevan, Edwyn. "Apostolic Gospel." Vol. 10 (July 1919):289-302.
Beyerhaus, Peter. "Three Selves Formula: Is It Built on Biblical Basis."
    Vol. 53 (Oct. 1964):393-407.
Blauw, Johannes. "Witness of Christians to Men of Other Faiths." Vol.
    52 (Oct. 1963):414-22.
Blow, Norman J. "Doctrine of the Church and Missions." Vol. 31 (Oct.
    1942):446-52.
Brough, J. S. "Eternal Source of Missions." Vol. 8 (Jan. 1919):7-17.
Cairns, David S. "Christian Message: A Comparison of Thought in 1910
    and in 1928." Vol. 18 (July 1929):321-31.
Cunliffe-Jones, H. "Meaning of the Church." Vol. 28 (July 1939):331-36.
De Silva, Lyn A. "Good News of Salvation to the Buddhist." Vol. 57
    (Oct. 1968):448-58.
Devanandan, Paul David. "Bangkok Conference of East Asia Leaders:
    An Impression." Vol. 39 (April 1950):146-52.

Dobbie, Robert. "Biblical Foundation of the Mission of the Church — I. Old Testament." Vol. 51 (April 1962):196-205.

———. "Biblical Foundation of the Mission of the Church — II. The New Testament." Vol. 51 (July 1962):281-90.

Ewan, A. L. "Motive of Missionary Service." Vol. 34 (July 1945):288-92.

Ferre, Nels F. S. "Fear, Duty and Love as Ultimate Motives for Christian Missions." Vol. 37 (Oct. 1948):393-402.

Frazer, Jean M. "One Church Renewed for Mission?" Vol. 56 (Oct. 1967):401-17.

Freytag, Walter. "Meaning and Purpose of the Christian Mission." Vol. 39 (April 1950):153-61.

———. "Missionary Thinking in Germany in Recent Years." Vol. 35 (Oct. 1946):391-97.

Frick, Heinrich. "Is a Conviction of the Superiority of His Message Essential to the Missionary?" Vol. 15 (Oct. 1926):625-46.

Fulton, Austin. "Missionary Nature of the Church: Reflections on the Christian Faith and Other Religions." Vol. 48 (Oct. 1959):389-97.

Glasick, Joseph. "The Mission of the Church in Today's World." Vol. 56 (July 1967):316-29.

Glover, T. R. "Missionary Motive." Vol. 3 (Jan. 1914):85-95.

Harkness, Georgia. "Theological Basis of the Missionary Message." Vol. 28 (Oct. 1939):518-26.

Hartenstein, Karl. "Theology of the Word and Missions." Vol. 20 (April 1931):210-27.

Hayward, Victor E. W. "Call to Witness — But What Kind of Witness?" Vol. 53 (April 1964):201-8.

———. "Call to Witness." Vol. 54 (April 1965):189-92.

Hebert, A. G. "Mission of the Church." Vol. 40 (Oct. 1951):385-92.

———. "Missionary Obligation." Vol. 39 (Oct. 1950):385-92.

Heim, Karl. "Christian Message in Relation to Non-Christian Religions, II. The Message of the New Testament to the Non-Christian World." Vol. 17 (Jan. 1928):133-44.

Hoeckendijk, Hans. "Evangelization of the World in This Generation." Vol. 59, (July 1970):23-31.

Hoekenduk, J. C. "Call to Evangelism." Vol. 39 (April 1950):162-75.

———. "Church in Missionary Thinking." Vol. 41 (July 1952):324-36.

Ilogu, Edmund. "Biblical Idea of Partnership and the Modern Missionary Task." Vol. 44 (Oct. 1955):404-7.

Jocz, Jakob. "Foreign Missions as a Theological Corrective." Vol. 35 (July 1946):256-62.

Knight, George A. F. "Our Truncated Faith." Vol. 33 (April 1944):167-73.

Kohnstramm, Ph. "Necessity for a New Philosophy and Its Bearing on Missionary Work." Vol. 19 (April 30):161-73
————. "Necessity for a New Philosophy and Its Bearing on Missionary Work, II." Vol. 19 (July 1930):321-32.
Kotto, Jean. "Church's Responsibility for the Missionaries It Receives." Vol. 53 (April 1964):153-61.
Kydd, A. S. "Missionary Situation and the Need of Revival." Vol. 23 (Oct. 1934):555-61.
Long, Charles. "Christian Vocation and the Missionary Call." Vol. 39 (Oct. 1950):409-17.
Mackay, John A. "Theology of the Laymen's Foreign Missions Inquiry." Vol. 22 (April 1933):174-88.
Mackichan, D. "Present-Day Phase of Missionary Theology." Vol. 3 (April 1914):243-54.
Mackintosh, H. R. "Secret of Vitality in the Pauline Churches." Vol. 5 (Oct. 1916):529-40.
MacLean, J. H. "Missionary Apologetics." Vol. 8 (July 1919):388-97.
MacNicol, Nicol. "Kingdom of God and the Missionary Enterprise." Vol. 35 (Oct. 1946):378-90.
Manson, William. "Biblical Doctrine of Missions." Vol. 42 (July 1953: 257-67.
————. "Mission and Eschatology." Vol. 42 (Oct. 1953):390-97.
Margull, Hans Jochen. "Teaching Mission." Vol. 56 (July 1927):180-84.
Mathews, Shailer. "Missions and the Social Gospel." Vol. 3 (July 1914): 432-46.
Micklem, Nathaniel. "Faith by Which the Church Lives." Vol. 27 (July 1938):321-32.
Moses, David G. "Christianity and the Non-Christian Religions." Vol. 43 (April 1954):146-54.
Moulton, J. Hope. "Word and the World." Vol. 2 (Jan. 1913):83-95.
Murray, J. S. "Mission and the Ministry of the Church." Vol. 52 (Jan. 1963):25-32.
Oldham, J. H. "Missionary and His Task, I. The Conditions and Demands of the Task." Vol. 3 (April 1914):284-96.
————. "Missionary and His Task, II. Problems of the Church in the Mission Field." Vol. 3 (July 1914):506-28.
————. "Missions and the Supernatural." Vol. 12 (Jan. 1923):59-71.
————. "Philosophical Interpretation of the Missionary Idea." Vol. 10 (Jan. 1921):63-76.
Opocensky, Milan. "The Message of Salvation for a Secular World." Vol. 57 (Oct. 1968):433-40.
Perry, Edward T. "Evangelism: A Type of Work or a Quality of Living?" Vol. 22 (Jan. 1933):63-68.

Potter, Philip. "From the Editor." Vol. 57 (Oct. 1968):393-98.

Rall, H. F. "Authority of Our Faith." Vol. 29 (Jan. 1940):130-39.

Richter, Julius. "Missionary Apologetic: Its Problems and Its Methods." Vol. 2 (Oct. 1913):520-41.

Ritson, John H. "Bible: An Unfettered Missionary." Vol. 11 (July 1922): 390-400.

Rouse, Ruth. "Missionary Motive." Vol. 25 (Oct. 1927):519-29.

Samartha, S. J. "The Quest for Salvation and the Dialogue Between Religions." Vol. 57 (Oct. 1968):424-32.

Schlunk, Martin. "Theology and Missions in Germany in Recent Years." Vol. 27 (July 1938):463-78.

Selilvane, G. M. "The Missionary and His Task at Edinburgh and To-day." Vol. 59 (July 1970):55-66.

Taylor, John V. "Report as Adopted by the Assembly — Renewal in Mission, Introduction to Section II." Vol. 58 (July 1969):148-52.

Truessel, E. "Missionary Vocation." Vol. 51 (April 1962):179-84.

Verghese, T. Paul. "Salvation." Vol. 57 (Oct. 1968):399-416.

Visser't Hooft, W. A. "Confessing Our Lord Jesus Christ as God and Savior." Vol. 57 (Oct. 1968):441-47.

Ward, Marcus. "Toward a Theology of Missions." Vol. 37 (July 1948): 249-55.

Warren, M. A. C. "Missionary Obligation of the Church in the Present Historical Situation." Vol. 39 (Oct. 1950):393-408.

Webster, Douglas. "P. T. Forsyth's Theology of Missions." Vol. 44 (April 1955):175-81.

Wright, G. Ernest. "Old Testament, a Bulwark of the Church Against Paganism." Vol. 40 (July 1951):265-76.

Yannoulatos, Anastasios. "Purpose and Motive of Mission." Vol. 54 (July 1965):281-97.

MISSIONARY RESEARCH LIBRARY BULLETINS

Jackson, Herbert C. "The Missionary Obligation of Theology." Vol. 15, no. 1.

Newbigin, J. E. Lesslie. "Bringing Our Missionary Methods Under the Word of God." Vol. 13, no. 11.

Scherer, James A. "The Service of Theology to World Missions." Vol. 14, no. 2.

Tillich, Paul. "Theology of Missions." Vol. 5, no. 10.

Selective Subject Index

Abraham, 58, 90-94, 99-103, 107, 109, 110-13, 152-53, 227, 274
Alexandria, 264
America, 27-28, 216
Antioch, 257, 275, 280
Apollos, 256, 262
Apostolic succession, 219-20
Asia, 88, 118, 145, 317

Babel, tower of, 92, 96
Babylon, 89, 107-8, 125-26, 339, 341
Baptist Society, 226, 344
Barclay, William, 233, 273, 301
Barnabas, 257, 273, 280, 305
Barth, Karl, 173
Brazil, 289
Britain, 216, 226, 344

Call of God, definition of, 285
Calvin, John, 148, 227
Carey, William, 226-27, 281-82
Centrifugalism, 21, 52, 174, 300
Centripetalism, 21, 52, 300
Chaldea, 92
China, 85, 118, 217
China Inland Mission, 227
Christianization, definition of, 12
Church, definition of, 202
Church Missionary Society, 226
Civilization, definition of, 12
Clement of Alexandria, 257
Clement of Rome, 257
Conybeare, W. D., 259
Cyprian, 220
Cyrus, 108, 125, 340-41

Davidic age, missions in, 114-18
Davies, D. R., 79
Decalogue, 97, 111
Depravity of man, 78-81
Diaspora, 257-58
Didache, 257, 263, 307
Dodd, C. H., 307

East India Trading Company, 282
Edinburgh Missionary Conference, 28, 291
Edwards, Jonathan, 227, 344
Egypt, 64, 102, 105, 107-8, 112, 340
England, 25, 344
Ephesus, 150, 237, 261
Eusebius, 260-61
Evangelization, definition of, 11, 210

Fatherhood of God concept, 42-43

God
    concept of, in O.T., 100-104, 107-8
    nature of, 57-60
    revelation of, by Christ, 42-43
Great Commission, 20, 39, 55, 132, 146, 161, 172-80, 198, 212-13, 220-21, 265-67, 268, 329

Haran, 92, 107
Harnack, Adolf, 257, 263
Haystack Prayer Meeting, 344
Heilsgeschichte, 10, 19, 24, 30, 37, 62, 76, 87, 93, 300
Holy Spirit in the world, 75-82
Hume, David, 107

Idolatry, 92, 125-27, 322-23
India, 85, 102, 118
Indonesia, 289
International Missionary Council, 10, 28
Irenaeus, 257
Ironside, H. R., 125
Isaiah, 24, 74, 105, 118, 121-27, 273, 282
Israel, 18, 23-24, 37, 42, 44, 49, 51-52, 58, 84-85, 93-127, 136, 139, 152-53, 167, 169, 173, 210, 218, 227, 299, 323-24, 331, 339

Japan, 289
Jerusalem, 21, 53, 115, 135, 139-40, 145, 177, 196, 235-36, 299, 305, 315, 321, 326, 339-40, 342
Jesus Christ
    fulfillment of O.T., 83
    fundamental purpose of, 45-47
    gospel portraits of, 36-39, 77
    universal mission of, 35-42, 47, 48-51
Jonah, 21, 108, 120, 169, 273
Justin Martyr, 320

Kingdom of God, 39-42
Knox, John, 227
Koinonia, definition of, 233
Kosmos, 38-39
Korea, 289

Limited atonement, 148
Livingstone, David, 290
London Missionary Society, 226

Luther, Martin, 215, 227
Millar, Robert, 344
Missio Dei, 9, 25, 337, 339
Missionary, definition of, 248-53, 261
Monolatry, 102-3
Monotheism, 88, 102-3, 106-7, 124-25, 152, 323, 325-26
Morgan, G. Campbell, 181
Mosaic age, missions in, 111-14

Neouniversalism, 336-38
Nineveh, 21, 108, 120, 169
Noachian covenant, 87

Origen of Alexandria, 257

Palestine, 107, 139, 145, 184, 252, 317, 323
Paraclete, definition of, 301-2
Patriarchal age, missions in, 110
Paul, 23, 30, 37-38, 41, 44, 53, 55, 60-61, 64, 70-77, 84, 92-93, 107, 111-13, 132-34, 137, 140, 143, 147-54, 163-68, 178, 181, 184, 186, 194, 201, 204, 212, 219, 221, 231-38, 245-47, 250-57, 261-63, 266, 272-73, 275, 279-80, 286-87, 295-98, 305-11, 324, 330, 331, 335, 342-43, 350
Pentecost, 21, 75-76, 134, 137, 139-40, 143-44, 175, 189, 196, 199, 203, 299-300, 303-5, 342
Persia, 118, 340
Peter, 36, 38, 53, 68, 137-46, 154, 179-80, 184, 251, 254-55
Philip, 53, 305
Phillips, J. B., 234
Pietism, 215-16, 221, 243
Plummer, A., 259
Polytheism, 88, 124, 129
Prophet phenomenon, 118
Prophetic age, missions in, 118-19
Protestant, 26, 46, 214
Protestantism, 26, 90, 98, 221
Protevangelium, 62, 71, 83, 85, 86, 90, 109

Reformation, 26, 214-15, 321
Religion
    of Israel, 87-110
    pre-Abrahamic, 94-96
Renaissance, 79, 92, 321
Ritschl, Albrecht, 12, 314

Rutherford, Samuel, 187

Salvation
    basic principles of, 64
    center of, 61-63, 65-66
    divine origin of, 64-65
    by faith, 70-71
    by grace, 67-70
    in Gen. 3:15, 85-86
    O.T. concept of, 105-6
    universality of, 71-75
Sanders, J. Oswald, 302
Schleiermacher, F. D. E., 66
Secularism, definition of, 12
Self-redemption, 95
Septuagint, 113, 200, 301
Sin
    history of, in Genesis, 94-96
    and suffering, 104-5
Socialization, definition of, 12
Son of man, 43-45
Speer, Robert E., 11, 55, 283, 347-48
Stephen, 140, 143, 144
Studd, C.T., 283
Sudan Interior Mission, 227
Sutcliffe, John, 344

Taiwan, 289
Tarsus, 163, 280
Taylor, Hudson, 217, 227, 297
Ten Commandments, 97, 111-12
Tertulian, 257
Theodoret, 260
Thiessen, H., 66, 209
Timothy, 204, 226, 255-56, 259, 261, 273, 296
Titus, 204, 226, 261
Transfiguration, 59

Universalism, definition of, 19
Universality, 19-25
    definition of, 20

Wellhausen, Julius, 106
Wesley, John, 227
Westcott, B. F., 194, 247, 252, 259, 268
Wheaton Congress, 28
Whitefield, George, 227
Wuest, K. S., 234

Zinzendorf, Nicholas, 344
Zwemer, Samuel, 35, 161, 285, 343

Scripture Index

OLD TESTAMENT

Genesis
1-2   15, 16, 81, 107
1-12   9, 22, 325, 103
1:2   74, 300
1:16, 28;
  2:8-9, 15   115-16
3   15, 16, 94
3:15   48, 62, 71, 86,
                     89, 109
6, 7   95
6:15   17
8:15 – 9:17   167
9:1, 8-9   87
9:8-17, 25-27   107, 109
11:1-9   89, 95
12:2   100
12:3   110
13:16; 15:5; 16:10;
  17:2, 4-6; 18:18   100
18:19   110
22:18   100
22:19   110
26:2-4   100, 110
28:13-15   100, 110
31:19, 32, 34;
  35:2, 4   92
49:10   110

Exodus
3:6-17; 4:5;
  6:2, 2-9   102
12:48   114
19:3-6   109, 111, 112
20:3-5   323

Numbers
9:14; 15:4   114

Deuteronomy
1:16; 10:18   114
14:1-2   42
29:11; 31:12   114
32:6   42

Joshua
1:8   278
24:2   90, 92

Judges
2:12   185

1 Samuel
15:22   278
25:27   185

2 Samuel
2:10   185
7:14   42

1 Kings
8:43   117

18:22   118
28:21   185

2 Kings
11:16   185

Ezra
1:1-4, 1-5, 5, 6, 7-8;
  2:64-67, 68-70;
  3:7; 6:4, 8   340

Psalms
2   42, 116, 326
8:3, 4   43
22:27   24
23:3   278
25   278-79
27:11; 32:8;
  37:5, 7   279
66; 67:1-7   116
72   116, 326
77:12   278
80:17   44
86:9-11; 98   116
103:13   42
117   116
119   278-79
137   340
139:1-12   300
143:8   279
145   116

Proverbs
3:6   278
3:12   42

Isaiah
1:18   270
2:1-4   123
10:5   108
11:3-4, 9, 9-10   24, 123
25:69   123
28:16   140
36-37   123
40-66   24, 112, 123
40:5, 18   126-27
40:25   126, 328
41:4   126
41:8-9   123
41:22   102, 125
42:1, 19   123
42:4, 6-7, 10   127
43:3-15   58, 102
43:10, 12, 13,
  21   112, 123-26
44:1-2, 7-20,
  21, 26   123-26
44:28 – 45:13   108, 340
45:4   123
45:21   125
45:22-23   126, 127, 270
46:1, 3-4, 5,
  9-13   125-27

48:3-5   125
48:12-13   127
48:20; 49:3, 5, 6   123
49:6, 26   127-28
50:10   123
51:2   92
51:4-5; 52:10,
  13 – 53:12   127
53   109
53:6   71
55-66   128
55:1-3, 6-7   270
56:7   49, 118
60-66   24
65:17   74
66:18-21, 21   128

Jeremiah
3:12   270
25:9   108
25:12-13   340
27:6; 42-51; 43:10;
  51:11, 20   108

Ezekiel
11:19-20   300
25-32; 38-39   108
36:26-27   300
37-48   24

Daniel
2:1-45; 7:1-28   108
7:13-14   44, 45
9-10   341
9:20-27; 11:1-45   108

Joel
2:20; 3:4, 6, 8-9   121
2:28-32   299, 300

Amos
1:3 – 2:3   107
5:8-9; 9:5-6, 7-15   122

Obadiah
1; 10:5-34;
  13:1 – 23:18   108

Micah
4:1-4   128

Habakkuk
2:4, 20   121
2:14   24, 121, 326

Zephaniah
1:2-3; 2:11;
  3:19-20   121

Zechariah
4:6   197
14:9, 16-19, 24   196, 326

Malachi
2:10   41

NEW TESTAMENT

Matthew
3:1-3   270
4:19, 21   185
5:13-16   49
5:24; 6:7, 32   51
6:10   49
8:5-13   48
8:22   185
9:6   45
9:9   185
9:37-38   223, 279,
                   289, 329
10:1-2   226, 251, 254
10:1-20   51, 168
10:38-39   186
11:15   278
11:28-30   270, 332
12:8, 32   45
13:15   18
13:36-43   45, 50
15:21-28   48, 51, 342
16:15-16   176
16:18   201
16:19   303
16:24-25   185-86
16:27; 17:9, 12, 22   45
18:16-19   51, 303
19:19   342
19:21   185
19:28   74
20:18   45
20:32-33; 21:21-22   342
21:28-32, 43   49-50
24:30   45
25:6   201
25:31-46   47, 333-34
26:24, 45, 64   45
26:67-68; 27:27-31   287
28:18-20   137, 176, 178,
            195, 251-52, 261,
                  266, 271, 309

Mark
1:2-3   270
1:14-15   39, 329
1:17, 20, 35, 36   185, 329
2:10, 28   45
2:14   185
3:13-19   168, 226,
                   251, 272
3:28-30   45
4:9   278
5:1-20   48
6:6-13   251
7:16   278
7:27   51
7:31-37   48

8:18-20 248
8:31 45, 329
8:34 185, 186
8:38; 9:9, 12, 31 45
9:29 342
10:42 51
10:45 37, 45, 46, 61, 67, 310, 335
11:17 49
13:10 37, 199, 330
13:26 45
14 43
14:9 50
14:21, 41, 52 45
14:65; 15:16-20 287
16:9-20 77, 101, 171, 176, 178, 190, 248, 251, 261

Luke
1:1 132
1:4 255
2:10-14, 25-32 48
2:49 329
3:3-6 48, 270
3:23-38 44
4:18-19 211
4:43 329
5:24 45
5:27 185
6:5 45
6:12-16 118
6:13, 9:1-6 251
9:22-24, 26, 44 45, 186
9:57-58 287
10:1-20 251
10:25-37; 29-37 50, 170
12:10 45
13:28-29 49
14:10-24 50
14:26-27, 33 186, 287
15:11-24 50
16:19-31 18, 333-34
18:1-8 342
18:22 185
19:10 45
19:13 266
19:17 278
21:27; 22:22, 69 45
22:63-65 287
24:25-27 9
24:36-49 9, 118, 170, 178, 248, 310-11

John
1:5 59
1:9 46, 50, 59, 77
1:10-11 52, 64
1:12 65, 312, 318
1:18 30, 42
1:29 20, 38, 48, 50, 71
1:43 185
2:13-27 49
3:3 84
3:7, 14, 30 329
3:8 59
3:14-19 20, 38, 47, 50, 270, 335
3:36 270, 309, 312, 333
4:1-42, 43-54 48
4:20 329
4:24 57, 58, 329
4:35 279, 289, 329
4:42 38, 50
5:12 65
5:22, 24-29 47
5:24 270, 312

6-8 250
6:33 38, 50
6:37 270
6:45 77, 80
7:17 278
7:37-39 195, 270
8:12 38, 50, 59, 308
9:4 329
9:5 38
10:9 308
10:11 46
10:16 329
10:17-18 61, 287
10:27 185
10:30, 38; 11:25 000
12:26 185
12:32 38, 77, 80
12:34 329
12:46 38
12:47 50
13:36 185
14:6, 9 308, 309
14:11 30
14:16, 26 300, 301
15:16 272
15:26 173, 177, 300, 301
16:7-8 77, 80, 195, 300, 301
16:8-15 38, 50, 173, 177
17:5 287
17:18 251, 268
17:21 50
17:24; 18:22; 19:1-3 287
20:9 329
20:19-23 168, 176, 178, 248, 251, 268, 303
21:19, 22 185

Acts
1:1 255
1:3 39
1:7-8 108, 176, 178, 248
1:17, 20-26 223, 254, 296
2:4, 17 144
2:14, 16, 22, 25, 34 139
2:23 136
2:32-39 135, 137, 139-41, 143, 180, 254, 270
2:44 141
3:13-26 109, 135, 137, 139, 141, 143, 254
4:4, 32 141
4:5 251
4:8 144
4:10 138, 143
4:10-11, 19 135, 140
4:12 135, 136, 137, 138, 251, 308, 309
4:28 136
4:31, 33 135, 143-44
5:29-32 135, 137, 141, 142-44, 254
6:1-4 144, 223, 242
6:5-10 140-41, 144, 226
7:2 143
7:38 200
7:52 135
7:55 144
8:1 21
8:12-13, 22, 37 141
8:17, 29, 39 144
9:15-16 168
9:17 144
9:31 53, 144
9:42 141
10:19 144

10:34-35 140
10:36 137
10:38 139
10:39 254
10:43 138, 141
11:4, 17-18, 21, 24 140-41
11:25-26 280
13:1 245, 257, 262, 280
13:1-2 144
13:2-3 272, 275, 342
13:4 160
13:49 235
14:4, 14 160
14:17 88
14:22 41
14:23 342
15:2, 4, 6, 23 254
15:13-20 140-41, 156
16:37 236
17:30 142, 270
17:31 47
18:24-28; 19:1 262
19:8 41
19:10, 20, 26 235
19:32, 39, 41 200
20:24 313
20:25 41
20:28 201
21:8 259, 260
21:20 53, 156
22:15 254
28:13-20 155, 168, 176, 178, 248, 254, 258, 266, 280
28:23, 31 41
28:27 18

Romans
1:1-7 149, 250, 254, 270, 307, 310
1:8 133, 351
1:13-17 133
1:14 113, 149
1:15 298
1:16 313
1:18-32 17, 77, 89, 92, 149, 325
1:18-3:20 18, 150
1:23 92
1:24, 26, 28 89, 107
2:5 334
3-5 152
3:10-12 84
3:21-5:21 149, 150
3:23 18, 84
3:25 60
3:29-30 152
4:25 311
5:6 17, 71
5:8 17
5:12 18, 84
5:12-21 72-73, 148-49
6:21 17, 18
7:24-25 332
8:7 18
8:17 150
8:19-21 72
8:28 270
8:29 70
8:32 65
9-11 56, 152
10:8-18 70, 133, 149, 269-70
11:13, 25 149, 154-56
11:33-36 56, 327
12:1-2 278

12:3-8 245, 272
12:18 41
14:9 181
15:15-19 150, 154-55, 272
15:15-24 233-35, 237
15:30-32 235, 334
16:3, 9, 21 296
16:24-27 149, 270
21:22 72

1 Corinthians
1-4 000
1:1 253
1:2 201, 270
1:9 270
1:17 258
1:30 308
2:1-2 147
3:9 195, 201, 196, 303
3:10-11 147, 220, 310
3:13-15 275
3:16 304
4:1 274, 307
4:6, 9 254, 256
4:16 133, 238
6:9-10 324
6:19-20 204
7:15 270
9:1-2 254
9:16-23 133, 166, 258-59
9:17 307
9:19-23 233, 295
9:22 154, 310
10:19-21 323
10:32 201
11:1 133, 185, 238
11:2, 22 201
12-14 219, 275
12:1-11 294
12:4-13, 31 225
12:8-11 245, 246, 262, 273
12:12 220
12:27 201
12:28-30 225, 245-46, 254, 262, 273, 276
14:33 204
15:1-4 183, 310
15:9 201
15:22 84
15:24 75, 326
15:28 41, 75, 326
15:58 133
16:12 262

2 Corinthians
1:1 253
1:10-11 343
3:18 184
4:4 17, 30
5:9-21 133
5:10 275
5:14-15 284
5:18 194
5:19 20, 71, 310
5:20 41, 312
6:1-2 330
6:16 304, 323
8:9 61, 286
8:23 221, 254, 256, 296
11:2 201
11:8 236
11:13 256
12:12 254
13:7-9 343
14:27 194

Galatians

1:1	254
1:11-12	307
1:15	270
1:19	253
2:8	254
3:8	110
3:26	150
5:13	270
6:10	170

Ephesians

1:3-21	55, 150-51
1:3 — 2:10	220
1:4	66
1:7	311
1:10	74
1:13	313
1:18	278
1:22-23	4, 7, 11, 41, 151, 201
2:1-22	17-18, 150-51
2:8, 9	67
2:10	304
2:11 — 3:12	150, 153
2:12	312
2:19	201
2:20	220
2:21-22	201, 304
3:1-12	133, 150-51, 154-55, 199, 203, 219, 272, 350
3:1-13, 14-21	150
3:11	26, 56, 66, 203, 210
3:14	151, 342
4:1-6, 9, 12, 16	150-51
4:11	245-46, 254, 259-60, 262, 272, 275-76
4:11-16	219
4:18	18
5:1	151, 185
5:16	331
5:20, 23	151
5:25-27	199
5:30	151, 201
6:10-20	150
6:15	313
6:18-20	235, 343
6:23	151

Philippians

1:5	233, 235, 236
1:9-11, 15-21, 19	343
2:1	233

2:5-17	61, 133, 165, 176, 287, 310, 320
2:22	221, 235, 254, 256, 296
3:10	195, 233
3:12	185
3:17	133, 185
4:3	296
4:10	133
4:11-12	287
4:14, 15	233, 235
4:18	236

Colossians

1:1	253
1:7	296
1:9-14	72, 278, 311-12, 343
1:15	30
1:18	41
1:20	74
1:23, 25	272
1:24	195, 219, 303
1:28-29	350
2:1-3	343
2:3, 9-10	308
4:2-4	235, 343
4:10, 11	296

1 Thessalonians

1:1	256
1:6	133, 185, 238
1:8	133, 351
2:4	307
2:6	256
2:12	270
3:2	296
3:12-13; 5:23, 25	343

2 Thessalonians

1:6, 8	270
1:8-12	75, 334, 343
1:8-19	21
2:14	270
2:16; 3:1-3, 5	343
3:6-7	133

1 Timothy

1:1	254
1:11	307
1:12	272, 274
1:19-20	296
2:1-7	17, 133, 148
2:7	155, 246, 261, 262, 274

3:2	262
3:5	201
3:15	201, 204, 219
3:16	310
5:17	262
6:12	270

2 Timothy

1:1	254
1:9	270
1:11	155, 246, 247, 262
2:2, 24	262
2:4-7	336
2:11	261
2:17-18	296
4:3	246
4:5	255, 259, 260
4:7-8	151
4:10	296

Titus

1:1	253
1:3	274, 307
1:5	204, 262
3:13	262

Philemon

1, 2, 23, 24	296
22	343

Hebrews

1:3	93
2:9	71
2:12	200
2:14	72
3:1	195, 250, 252
5:12	246, 262
7:27; 9:12, 26-28; 10:2, 10	73
11:4	322
11:6	70, 318
11:37-38	120
12:23; 13:20	201

James

2:1	137, 141, 143
3:1	246, 262
5:7-11	67
5:16	339

1 Peter

1:1	254
1:2, 22	142
1:3	143
1:8	144

1:18-19	138
1:20	66, 136

1 John

1:1-3	143
1:5	57, 58
1:7	138
1:9	80
2:1	302
2:2	20, 71, 138, 140, 148
2:3-4, 29	142
2:17	141
2:23	138
3:1	270
3:2	184
3:7	142
3:8	72, 138
3:23	138, 141
3:24	142, 144
4:4	193
4:8	57, 59, 313
4:9-10	136
4:13	144
4:14	136, 138, 140
4:16	57, 59, 313
5:2-4	142
5:11-12	37, 137-38, 309

Revelation

1:6	201
1:14	154
2:2	256
2:3	237
2:7, 11, 17, 29; 3:6	278
3:7	176
3:13	278
3:14-22	227, 270, 278, 319
5:8-10	154, 156, 201
9:20	323
13:8	66
14:6	313
14:10-11	334
19:20	75
20	15
20:10-15	18, 75, 333
21-22	15, 16, 74
21:1 — 22:6	326, 334
21:5	75
21:8	324, 334
21:9, 14, 22, 23	74
22:1-5	74, 333
22:17	270